WRITING AND DIGITAL MEDIA

STUDIES IN WRITING
Series Editor: **Gert Rijlaarsdam**

Recent titles in this series:

SHUM AND ZHANG
Teaching Writing in Chinese Speaking Areas

KOSTOULI
Writing in Context(s) — Textual Practices and Learning Processes in Sociocultural Settings

RIJLAARSDAM, VAN DEN BERGH AND COUZIJN
Effective Learning and Teaching of Writing

Related titles:

BROMME AND STAHL
Writing Hypertext and Learning: Conceptual and Empirical Approaches

DE CORTE, VERSHAFFEL, ENTWISTLE AND MERRIËNBOER
Powerful Learning Environments: Unravelling Basic Components and Dimensions

Related journals:

Learning and Instruction
Educational Research Review
Assessing Writing
Computers and Composition
Journal of Second Language Writing

WRITING AND DIGITAL MEDIA

EDITED BY

LUUK VAN WAES

University of Antwerp, Belgium

MARIËLLE LEIJTEN

University of Antwerp, Belgium

CHRISTINE M. NEUWIRTH

Carnegie Mellon University, Pittsburgh, USA

ELSEVIER

Amsterdam • Boston • Heidelberg • London • New York • Oxford
Paris • San Diego • San Francisco • Singapore • Sydney • Tokyo

Elsevier
The Boulevard, Langford Lane, Kidlington, Oxford OX5 1GB, UK
Radarweg 29, PO Box 211, 1000 AE Amsterdam, The Netherlands

First edition 2006

Notice
No responsibility is assumed by the publisher for any injury and/or damage to persons
or property *as* a matter of products liability, negligence or otherwise, or from any use
or operation of any methods, products, instructions or ideas contained in the material
herein. Because of rapid advances in the medical sciences, in particular, independent
verification of diagnoses and drug dosages should be made

British Library Cataloguing in Publication Data
A catalogue record for this book is available from the British Library

Library of Congress Cataloging-in-Publication Data
A catalog record for this book is available from the Library of Congress

ISBN-10: 0-08-044863-1
ISBN-13: 978-0-08-044863-3
ISSN: 1572-6304

For information on all Elsevier publications
visit our website at books.elsevier.com

Printed and bound in The Netherlands

06 07 08 09 10 10 9 8 7 6 5 4 3 2 1

All chapters in this book were independently peer reviewed prior to acceptance

Working together to grow
libraries in developing countries

www.elsevier.com | www.bookaid.org | www.sabre.org

ELSEVIER   BOOK AID
            International   Sabre Foundation

Contents

Section V: Social and Philosophical Aspects of Writing and Digital Media

Contributors

Bodil Andersson
Oribi AB, Paradisgatan 1, 223 50 Lund, Sweden, info@oribi.se

Naheel Baker
College of Applied Health, Nova Southeastern University, 3200 S University Dr., Ft. Lauderdale, FL 33328, USA, nbaker2@fau.edu

Teresa Cerratto Pargman
Department of Computer and Systems sciences, Royal Institute of Technology, Stockholm University, DSV, Forum 100, 164 40 Kista, Sweden, tessy@dsv.su.se

Lucile Chanquoy
Laboratoire de Psychologie Expérimentale et Quantitative EA 1189, Université de Nice-Sophia Antipolis, 24 avenue des Diables Bleus, 06457 Nice cedex 4, France, lucile.chanquoy@unice.fr

Ed H. Chi
Palo Alto Research Center, User Interface Research, 3333 Coyote Hill Road, Palo Alto, CA 94304, USA, echi@parc.com

Johan Dahl
Department of Linguistics, Centre for Language and Literature, Lund University, Box 201, 221 00 Lund, Sweden, Johan.Dahl@ling.lu.se

Marion Degenhardt
Zentrum für Weiterbildung und Hochschuldidaktik, University of Education Freiburg, Kunzenweg 21, 79117 Freiburg, Germany, degenhar@ph-freiburg.de

Matthias Finke
Computer Graphics Center (ZGDV), Fraunhoferstraße 5, D-64283 Darmstadt, Germany, matthias.finke@zgdv.de

Jean Noël Foulin
Laboratoire de psychologie EA 3662, Université de Bordeaux 2, 3 place de la Victoire, 33076 Bordeaux cedex, France, jean-noel.foulin@aquitaine.iufm.fr

Cheryl Geisler
Department of Language, Literature and Communication,
Rensselaer Polytechnic Institute, USA, geislc@rpi.edu

Ylva Hård af Segerstad
Department of Linguistics, Göteborg University, Box 200, SE-405 30 Göteborg, Sweden,
ylva@ling.gu.se

Sylvana Sofkova Hashemi
Department of Linguistics, Göteborg University, Box 200, SE-405 30 Göteborg, Sweden,
sylvana@ling.gu.se

Gail Hawisher
Center for Writing Studies, University of Illinois, 608 South Wright Street, Urbana, IL 61801,
USA, hawisher@uiuc.edu

Kenneth Holmqvist
Cognitive Science, Lund University, Kungshuset, 222 22 Lund, Sweden, Kenneth.
holmqvist@lucs.lu.se

Jana Holsanova
Cognitive Science, Lund University, Kungshuset, 222 22 Lund, Sweden, jana.holsanova@
lucs.lu.se

Suguru Ishizaki
Department of English, Carnegie Mellon, USA, suguru@cmu.edu

Melody Y. Ivory
The Information School, University of Washington, 330C Mary Gates Hall, Seattle, WA
98195-2840, USA, myivory@u.washington.edu

Victoria Johansson
Department of Linguistics, Centre for Language and Literature, Lund University, Box 201,
22100 Lund, Sweden, Victoria.johansson@ling.lu.se

Henrik Karlsson
Oribi AB, Paradisgatan 1, 223 50 Lund, Sweden info@oribi.se

Petter Karlström
Department of Computer and Systems Sciences, Royal Institute of Technology, Stockholm
University, DSV, Forum 100, 164 40 Kista, Sweden, petter@dsv.su.se

David Kaufer
Department of English, Carnegie Mellon, Pittsburgh, PA 15213, USA, kaufer@andrew.
cmu.edu

Mariëlle Leijten
Department of Management, University of Antwerp, Prinsstraat 13, 2000 Antwerp, Belgium, marielle.leijten@ua.ac.be

Eva Lindgren
Faculty of Teacher Education, Umeå University, SE-901 87 Umeå, Sweden, eva.lindgren@educ.umu.se

Charles MacArthur
School of Education, University of Delaware, 303 Willard Hall, Newark, DE 19716, USA, macarthu@udel.edu

Barry Mauer
Department of English, University of Central Florida, Texts and Technology PhD Program, Colbourn Hall, 301, Orlando, FL 32816, USA, bmauer@pegasus.cc.ucf.edu

Carol Moore
College of Applied Health, Nova Southeastern University, 3200 S University Dr., Ft. Lauderdale, FL 33328, USA

Christine M. Neuwirth
Department of English, Carnegie Mellon, Human–Computer Interaction Institute, Pittsburgh, PA 15213, USA, cmn@andrew.cmu.edu

Rivka Niesten
School of International, Cultural and Community Studies & School of Languages and Comparative Cultural Studies, Edith Cowan University & The University of Queensland, 2 Bradford St, Mt Lawley 6005, Australia & The University of Queensland, Queensland 4072, Australia, r.niesten@ecu.edu.au

Mike Palmquist
Department of English, Colorado State University, 1773 Campus Delivery, Department of English, Colorado State University, Fort Collins, CO 80523, USA, mike.palmquist@ColoState.edu

Daniel Perrin
Zurich University of Applied Sciences Winterthur ZHW, Institute of Applied Media Studies IAM, P.O. Box 805, Zur, Kesselschmiede 35, CH-8401 Winterthur, Switzerland, daniel.perrin@bluewin.ch

Thomas Quinlan
Educational Psychology, University of Washington, USA, tquinlan@ u.washington.edu

Robert Ramberg
Department of Computer and Systems Sciences, Royal Institute of Technology, Stockholm University, DSV, Forum 100, 164 40 Kista, Sweden, robban@dsv.su.se

Sarah Ransdell
College of Applied Health, Nova Southeastern University, 3200 S University Dr., Ft. Lauderdale, FL 33328, USA, ransdell@nsu.nova.edu

Henrry Rodriguez
Department of Numerical Analysis and Computer Science, Interaction and Presentation Laboratory (IPLab), Royal Institute of Technology, Stockholm, IPLab, NADA, KTH, 10044 Stockholm, Sweden, henrry@nada.kth.se

Stephan Schwan
Knowledge Media Research Center, Konrad- Adenauer-Straße 40, D-72072 Tübingen, Germany, s.schwan@iwm-kmrc.de

Gillian Sealy
College of Applied Health, Nova Southeastern University, 3200 S University Dr., Ft. Lauderdale, FL 33328, USA, gsealy@fau.edu

Cynthia L. Selfe
Department of English, The Ohio State University, 365 Denney Hall, 164 W. 17th Avenue, Columbus, OH 43210, USA, Selfe@osu.edu

Kerstin Severinson Eklundh
Department of Numerical Analysis and Computer Science, Interaction and Presentation Laboratory (IPLab), Royal Institute of Technology, Stockholm, IPLab, NADA, KTH, 10044 Stockholm, Sweden, kse@nada.kth.se

Elmar Stahl
Psychological Institute III, University of Münster, Fliednerstrasse 21, D-48149 Muenster, Germany, stahlel@psy.uni-muenster.de

Sven Strömqvist
Department of Linguistics, Centre for Language and Literature, Lund University, Box 201, 22100 Lund, Sweden, Sven.stromqvist@ling.lu.se

Kirk P.H. Sullivan
Department of Philosophy and Linguistics, Umeå University, SE-901 87 Umeå, Sweden, kirk.sullivan@ling.umu.se

Roland Sussex
School of Languages and Comparative Cultural Studies, The University of Queensland, Queensland 4072, Australia, sussex@uq.edu.au

Sylvia Tufvesson
Department of Linguistics, Centre for Language and Literature, Lund University, Box 201, 22100 Lund, Sweden

Per Henning Uppstad
National Center for Reading Education and Research, University of Stavanger, N-4036 Stavanger, Norway, per.h.uppstad@uis.no

Luuk Van Waes
Department of Management, University of Antwerp, Prinsstraat 13, 2000 Antwerp, Belgium, luuk.vanwaes@ua.ac.be

Pantelis Vlachos
Department of Statistics, Carnegie Mellon, USA, vlachos@stat.cmu.edu

Åse Kari Hansen Wagner
National Center for Reading Education and Research, University of Stavanger, N-4036 Stavanger, Norway, aase-kari.h.wagner@uis.no

Asa Wengelin
Department of Linguistics, Centre for Language and Literature, Lund University, Box 201, 22100 Lund, Sweden, asa.wengelin@ling.lu.se

Carmen Zahn
Knowledge Media Research Center, Konrad-Adenauer-Straße 40, D-72072 Tübingen, Germany, c.zahn@iwm-kmrc.de

Introduction

Christine M. Neuwirth, Luuk Van Waes and Mariëlle Leijten

In this book, we are concerned with the effects of digital media on the cognitive and social processes of writing on the one hand, and how the design of digital media supports writing and the study of writing, on the other. The researchers whose works are represented in this book were selected from among those who responded to a call for papers to bring together European, Australian and American research in writing and digital media in order to explore its cognitive, social and cultural implications from an international perspective. The aim is to expand communication among investigators from a range of disciplines and perspectives, all of whom are concerned with the fundamental processes of writing and learning to write.

In this introductory chapter, we frame the research and scholarship represented in this volume by tracing the major research areas in writing that inform and set the stage for writing and digital media research. We also outline some of the continuing issues and new developments. We close with an overview of the contents and organization of this volume.

1 Cognitive Processes in Writing

Research on the effects of digital media on writing processes is roughly 25 years old. In that period the concept of "writing and digital media" more or less evolved from a dichotomy to a tautology. Just as much writing research in the 1980s focused on understanding writing processes as opposed to analyzing writing products, many early studies in writing and digital media focused on tracing differences in composing with traditional pen and paper technologies vs. composing with word processors, for both experienced and inexperienced writers. (For reviews, see Bangert-Downs, 1993; Cochran-Smith, 1991; Goldberg, Russell, & Cook, 2003.) This research resulted in both a better understanding of how different mediums of production tend to shape writing processes (e.g., less upfront planning for writers using word processors), but also highlighted places in the dominant model of composing processes (the "Flower and Hayes" model) in which more elaboration was required (e.g., the role of the text produced so far). In the U.S., composition researchers moved away from studying writing processes from a cognitive perspective — indeed, many abandoned empirical studies altogether — and focused their attention on critical theory. This shift in focus resulted in much work on topics such as the acquisition of literacy by individuals marginalized because of race, age, gender, handicap or other differences in privilege and power, as well as studies of the literacy practices in actual workplaces. In psychology and education departments in the U.S. and psychology and applied linguistics departments in Europe, interest in cognitive processes of writing remained stronger, with researchers contributing insights into the nature of attention and working memory during writing, the role of automaticity in writing processes, along with changes in the model to account for beginning and developmental writing. Interestingly, the essays in this volume bring these divergent research strands together by reporting on work, for example, that studies the cognitive processes of learning-disabled students and the ways in which their specific difficulties can be facilitated by new digital media technologies, such as speech technologies. To some extent, cognitive processes of writing are now seen as a part of broader, socio-cultural processes of writing. Various research questions in the cognitive processes of writing remain unanswered, however, including how we should go about describing and understanding writing processes, how to work with the massive amounts of data that process-tracing studies produce, as well as thorny problems of relating cognitive (and social) processes to success or failure of written products.

2   Social Processes in Writing

Unlike cognitive processes in writing, social processes in writing have had no dominant theoretical framework, with researchers drawing on interactionist theories of the acquisition of linguistic competence (Hymes); activity theory and related theories, such as the "sociocultural perspective" (Bhaktin, Vygotsky); situated cognition and communities of practice (Brown, Collins & Duguid); and distributed cognition (Hutchins), among others. Although the theoretical frameworks vary, the resulting research expresses a set of common concerns. These concerns center largely on how social interaction, including activities such as collaborative writing and peer review, contribute to learning to write on how knowledge mediated through oral and written language is socially constructed, and on how social processes of writing such as writers interacting with each other and "subject matter experts," unfold in workplace settings. When the role of digital media is brought into play, we see work on the affordances of conversation through text rather than speech (and its drawbacks, such as more difficulty in reaching consensus), synchronous discussion in language classrooms, time and place independent communication, long-distance cross-cultural communication, student "publishing" via WWW and so forth. Many of the chapters in this volume explore these themes, either for first- or second-language acquisition. Analyzing interactions during collaborative writing, facilitated perhaps by digital analysis tools, is a wide-open research area, but key to understanding when these activities result in gains in writing quality and facilitate learning to write.

3   New Genres of Writing and New Literacies

Genre theory sees genres as communicative actions, that is, "solutations" — created by rhetors working in specific social and cultural milieus — to recurring needs or opportunities for communication (Miller, 1984). Digital media bring with them new or transformed genres. Indeed, digital media even bring into question the stability or fixity in the production and transmission of texts, a taken-for-granted feature of genres in print, but a feature that is missing in, for example, WWW sites in which contributors at multiple locations update material on a daily or even hourly basis. The lines between producers and receivers of texts have blurred. Video and animations are combined with written language in new ways. New genres have also formed around "conversations" in chat rooms. Digital media have been a fruitful site in which to test theories of genre emergence and evolution, explore automated classification of documents into genres and design systems in support of producing, using and assessing the effectiveness of new genres. The emergence of new genres, of course, creates many challenges to our concepts of literacy. Many new forms (hypermedia, WWW) make new demands on writers and writing pedagogies. The chapters in this book make contributions to various aspects of new genres, with design research and pedagogy predominating.

4   Overview of the Book

The previous sections provided framing of the chapters in this volume in terms of enduring issues in writing research, many of which cross-cut our arrangement of them. The chapters are arranged in five sections, each of which represents a segment of the theoretical, empirical and design work that constitutes the domain of writing and digital media.

4.1   Writing Modes and Writing Environments

The first section, Writing Modes and Writing Environments, contains three papers that draw upon fundamental theories and research from cognitive processes in writing to explore new modes and environments for writing, with a special focus on environments that support writing with speech technology. The authors note that this is a new medium that has continued to be developed and is, at least for some purposes, becoming a viable writing tool. Each paper takes up a different perspective by focusing on its potential and limitations for different groups of users (writers with learning disabilities, children and professional writers).

MacArthur's chapter provides an overview of the research on writing difficulties faced by students with learning disabilities and reviews the research on various socio-technical systems instruction coupled with technologies to help them. He concludes that technologies such as word processors, spell checkers and word prediction software can all help students when coupled with appropriate instruction, but that more research is needed to determine which software will be helpful to which students. He also concludes that the few studies on speech-recognition technology point to its being potentially the best support for students having difficulty with handwriting, spelling and fluency. A major theme in his discussion is the need to develop instructional methods that help students to take advantage of assistive tools.

This theme is taken up as well in Quinlan's chapter, which focuses more narrowly on the potential of speech technologies to assist children learning to write. He concludes that there is good evidence that speech technologies — despite the need to correct speech recognition errors — improve writing fluency for children with transcription-related fluencies. Speech recognition systems also typically contain speech synthesis capabilities, by which the developing text can be read aloud. Quinlan reviews the research on how children interact with "the text produced so far" and the potential of speech synthesis capabilities to assist in this process.

In the next chapter, Leijten and Van Waes report a case study of two professional writers, focusing in detail on the cognitive processes surrounding "the text produced so far." They examine the potential impact from three aspects: the visibility of the text, the moment of visual feedback and the correctness of the visual representation. Their case analyses highlight the importance of the "text produced so far" in the organization of writing process and documents the differences between writers who use this feedback while dictating.

4.2   *Writing and Communication*

In the second section, Writing and Communication, each chapter presents an empirical description of specific instances of writers communicating via new media for different purposes. These chapters substantially enrich our picture of the influences of new media on writing. Both Segerstad and Hashemi, and Niesten and Sussex are interested in examining new usage of language afforded by new media. Stahl et al. are interested in creating pedagogical situations that require communication in order to meet other goals, such as acquiring content knowledge or acquiring language skill.

Segerstad and Hashemi report on a project to investigate the writing by schoolchildren in a wide variety of settings (school and leisure) and by means of diverse channels of communication (e.g., manually, word processors, Web chat and text messaging via mobile phones). They take a detailed look at the lexical and structural differences in both school texts and texts created in the new media. They find that schoolchildren are clearly conscious of differences in language use in various situations, that their language use is adapted to new media (e.g., goals in the medium, level of synchronicity, method of text input, number of participants), and that new media encourages new, creative strategies for writing. They also examine the use of existing writing aids (spelling and grammar checking, word completion) and find them inadequate because of their focus on certain groups of writers (adults) and their disregard for the communicative situation or the medium (formal, informal).

Niesten and Sussex provide a theoretical framework — ludicity — for understanding language play and playfulness in Internet chat. They illustrate not only situations in which such play seems to be its own justification, but also situations in which it can be used to achieve social goals related to group membership. Whereas Segerstad and Hashemi focus on the ways in which schoolchildren, who may not have "mastered" formal written language, may unintentionally deviate from those conventions, and on the ways in which new media, although written, draw on conversational conventions, Niesten and Sussex focus on creative deviations (e.g., creating new words or using them in an unfamiliar or striking way). In addition to examining language forms, they illustrate lucid elements in semantics and pragmatics and relate them to the constraints of media and interactivity in new media.

They extend our understanding of computer-mediated communication by providing a framework that allows us to look at how participants exploit and play with the limits of the medium itself.

Stahl, Zahn, Schwan and Finke report on the design of collaborative hypervideo as a method to foster knowledge and literacy acquisition. They identify a wide variety of writing genres that the activity of hypervideo production requires (e.g., scripts, storyboards, non-linear chunks of text) as well as the social communication required in its production. They compare hypervideo-design to text writing, using a process-model-of-writing framework. They conclude with noting the potential of this research to advance our scientific understanding of the psychological mechanisms of collaborative text production.

In sum, the chapters in this section provide concrete examples of the properties of communication and social interaction, as well as examples of pedagogical opportunities afforded by new media.

4.3 Digital Tools for Writing Research

The third section, Digital Tools for Writing Research, contains reports of new digital tools for analyzing writing products and processes. These technologies are at the cutting edge of writing analysis tools. The authors of the first two papers report on tools for the analysis of Web sites. Chi's chapter reviews a half decade of his research at the Palo Alto Research Center that applies "information foraging" theory, in particular, information scent, to (1) predicting users' navigation in a Web site, (2) mining usage logs to understand the frequent goals of readers of a Web site and (3) building tools to augment user's experiences. These models have the potential to guide designers in building more effective web environments. Future research directions include integrating models of visual perception into the information scent model, to aid visual design decisions.

Ivory's chapter reviews the types of automated Web site evaluation tools from the perspective of Web content writers. She reports on a number of studies she and others conducted on what tools Web writers use and on an experiment that examined how usable Web analysis tools were for writers. She concludes that existing tools provide limited support and that more research is needed on how writers work in order to provide tools that support writers' work practices better than existing tools do.

The chapter by Kaufer, Geisler, Vlachos and Ishizaki describes an innovative system that automatically tags words and multiple-word patterns in documents with rhetorical categories, and provides a visualization component that allows users to see and explore these patterns in the documents. The chapter describes the design space of text coding and where the system is situated within the space, the development of the coding dictionary and its validation, and the application of the system to writing instruction, especially its application for curriculum designers and textbook authors in identifying rhetorical profiles of assignments, along with the legitimate language variations that lie within any given assignment. They conclude with plans for making the system directly usable for writing teachers and students.

Rodriquez and Severinson Eklundh demonstrate a more process-oriented perspective. They describe a tool that analyzes writers' patterns of behavior surrounding collaborative writing in a Web-based documentation sharing and annotation environment (Col·lecció), and provides visualizations of that behavior. The goals of the project are to explore ways in which writing researchers, and perhaps collaborators, can visualize important activities in collaborative writing. They identify several outstanding research issues, such as representing more activities of collaborative writers, understanding how more of the representation can be automated, and studying how collaborations might be affected by such visualization tools.

The chapter by Foulin and Chanquoy describes the use of a digital tablet to collect temporal data across pre-learning and post-learning spelling sessions in order to shed light on how spelling processes evolve with word spelling knowledge. The study shows that both spelling latency and transcription are sensitive measures of cognitive processes of spelling in children. The chapter outlines outstanding research issues concerning theoretical models of spelling that will help overcome current challenges in interpreting temporal data.

The final chapter in this section contains contributions from numerous researchers, all of whom are developing or using tools to record and analyze writing processes. Sullivan and Lindgren begin with an overview of the potential of digital tools not only to help form a more comprehensive theory of writing, but also to develop new approaches to the teaching of writing and language awareness, similar to the pedagogical uses of document analysis envisioned by Kaufer et al. Sullivan and Lindgren's introduction is followed by four chapters that describe research tools. Van Waes and Leijten describe Inputlog, which was developed to work primarily with Microsoft Word in a Windows environment to facilitate writing studies in which writers are able to use their usual word processor. The logging tool contains three modules: data collection, data analysis (text and pause analysis) and a play module that enable researchers to review a writing session. They conclude with plans for further development. Andersson et al. describe a tool to study the dynamic interplay between production and perception during writing, consisting of a text-logging tool, ScriptLog, combined with the eye tracking technology, along with an analysis tool to help researchers organize and analyze the data. They outline applications of the tool, such as studies of visual attention by more and less skilled writers and studies of how writers integrate text and pictures during the writing process. Perrin describes a methodology, called progression analysis, developed to study writers (i.e. journalists) in naturalistic studies, consisting of interviews and direct observations, computer logging of writing processes, and retrospective verbal protocols. Perrin illustrates the method with a detailed case study. Degenhardt describes the use of Camtasia, a commercially available audio screen recorder, in combination with Catmovie, a research tool to analyze the data. Degenhardt points to the advantages of using this kind of non-intrusive avi-recording and coding systems, such as students being able to use their normal writing tools, like a word processor, an HTML editor or a page layout program.

4.4   *Writing in Online Educational Environments*

The fourth section, Writing in Online Educational Environments, contains descriptions of environments intended to foster pedagogical goals, with each chapter describing the theory and research underlying the environment's design.

Karlström, Pargman and Ramberg contribute a chapter that reviews the history of computer-assisted language learning environments, with a focus on the use of language technologies, developed in computational linguistics. They argue for an approach that uses language technologies as resources and opportunities to help learners explore language, rather than as technologies that deliver knowledge about language to students.

Palmquist's chapter provides a comprehensive review of writing environments since the 1980s and argues for a tighter integration of instruction and feedback tools with such environments. As a case study for such an environment, he describes Colorado State University's Web-based system, outlining its features, current uses and research underway, and reporting its reception by users and its effects.

Uppstad and Wagner argue for studies that link writing processes and products, while acknowledging the methodological difficulties of doing so. They describe a study in which they used ScriptLog (see Andersson et al., this volume) and SpaceStory, an environment consisting of eight pictures telling the story of a space adventure. They report a pilot study in which they relate pause time in writing to lexical diversity in the texts three children produced, and discuss the study in relationship to skills in writing.

4.5   Social and Philosophical Aspects of Writing and New Media

The last section, Social and Philosophical Aspects of Writing and New Media, contains two chapters that look at issues in digital divide as well as a chapter that reflects on digital impermanence. Here the emphasis is on larger societal implications of writing and digital media.

Ransdell, Baker, Sealy and Moore examine the digital divide, arguing that a neglected aspect of the digital divide is bilingualism and the underrepresentation of languages other than English among Internet sources. They illustrate this argument with data from children in the South Florida region of the United States.

Selfe and Hawisher, with Lashore and Song, contribute a chapter that reviews the research on the global digital divide and traces the acquisition of digital literacy by Lashore (Nigeria) and Song (China). The goal of the chapter is to provide first-hand accounts of the acquisition of digital literacy — success stories — of two students who faced the digital divide and "won," and to document the conditions that can both contribute to and detract from people's successful encounters with literacy.

Mauer — in a symbolic last chapter — reflects on the phenomenon of data loss in the age of digital media and how it affects individuals, institutions and societies. As our society transfers its archives from print to digital media, an unintended consequence results; we lose a great amount of data. This essay aims to generate more discussion about the issues related to data loss. The effects of data loss can be profound; without access to vital data, our access to history may be severely diminished. Data loss threatens to undermine individual lives and major institutions. Mauer identifies the National Archives and Records Administration (NARA) in Washington, DC as a site of data loss at a national level, and suggests mourning as a means of coping with data loss. To facilitate the mourning of data loss at a national level, the author proposes a monument to lost data.

Taken together, the chapters in these five sections represent a broad sample of scholarly work in writing and digital media. They demonstrate the relevance of theories of cognitive and social processes in writing to the study of digital media, the value of empirical analyses of specific instances of digital writing, and the effects of particular technologies on the performance of writers. They give us a picture of new tools that will potentially aid researchers seeking to deepen our understanding of both the processes and products of writing, new environments that may improve our pedagogies, and greater awareness of the larger societal challenges posed by digital media. Together they suggest the promising work that is emerging in this area and the mutual benefit that can result from better integration of ongoing work across disciplines and continents.

Acknowledgments

It took the input of many people to prepare this book. We would particularly like to thank all the authors for their contribution to *Writing and Digital Media* and their patience in the review process. Without them this book would not have been possible. We would also like to thank all the referees for carefully reading and commenting on earlier versions of the chapters. Their hard work and expertise were essential in maintaining the quality standards of the series, *Studies in Writing*. We also owe many thanks to Prof. Dr. Gert Rijlaarsdam, the series editor, who gave us the opportunity to edit this book and supported us enthusiastically throughout the preparation stages of this publication. Finally, we wish to thank Bruce Roberts, Joanna Scott and the production team of Macmillan India Ltd. (Elsevier) for their initiative to continue the book series and, of course, also for their professional guidance in the publication process.

The preparation of this book was partly funded by the University of Antwerp (Belgium).

Section I:

Writing Modes and Writing Environments

Chapter 1

Assistive Technology for Writing: Tools for Struggling Writers

Charles MacArthur

Individuals with learning disabilities (LD) and others who find writing challenging often struggle with basic transcription processes, including handwriting or typing, spelling, capitalization, and punctuation. Problems with transcription affect motivation and interfere with students' ability to attend to higher order processes such as planning and evaluation. Computer tools, including word processing, spelling and grammar checkers, speech synthesis, word prediction, and speech recognition software, offer support to writers, but they also have limitations. This chapter analyzes the growing body of research on the benefits and limitations of these tools with students with LD and other struggling writers. In addition to research on specific types of assistive technology, the chapter discusses general issues such as the inevitable tradeoff of burdens when adopting new writing tools and the need for instructional methods designed to take advantage of the power of particular writing tools.

1 Introduction

Mark, a fourth-grade student with dyslexia, struggles with both reading and writing. In his classroom, students write back and forth with the teacher in dialogue journals. The teacher has difficulty reading Mark's entries because of his severe spelling problem, and Mark has difficulty reading her responses. Word prediction software with speech synthesis helps him to participate independently in this class activity without direct teacher support.

Marcia, a high school student with a learning disability who is probably college bound, reads with good comprehension, though slowly, but struggles to meet school demands for writing reports and essays. The combination of a planning strategy and speech recognition software enables her to write longer and better quality papers.

Writing and Digital Media
Copyright © 2006 by Elsevier Ltd.
All rights of reproduction in any form reserved
ISBN: 0-08-044863-1

MacArthur, C. (2005). Assistive technology for writing: Tools for struggling writers. In L. Van Waes, M. Leijten & C. Neuwirth (Vol. Eds.) & G. Rijlaarsdam (Series Ed.), Studies in Writing: Vol. 17. Writing and Digital Media (pp. 11–20). Oxford: Elsevier.

These two examples, both actual cases from my research, illustrate the potential of computers to support writing and writing instruction for students with learning disabilities (LD) and other struggling writers. For these students, the basic transcription processes of getting language on paper — particularly, handwriting, spelling, and overall fluency — create significant barriers to effective writing. Problems with transcription affect motivation and interfere with students' ability to attend to higher order processes such as planning and evaluation. Computer tools, including word processing, spelling and grammar checkers, speech synthesis, word prediction, and speech recognition software, have considerable potential to reduce these barriers. However, there are also significant limitations to this potential. This chapter reviews the research on the benefits and limitations of computer tools to support transcription. Most of the research has been conducted with students with LD, though it is probably applicable to other struggling writers. The term *assistive technology* is used here to refer to technology that supports individuals in overcoming barriers due to a disability.

As prelude to the review, I would like to comment on three general issues that affect interpretation of any findings regarding the use of assistive technology to support struggling writers. First, it is important to keep in mind issues of motivation, burden on working memory, and training in the use of the tool (MacArthur, 2000). All transcription tools remove one burden but impose some additional burden on working memory or require additional training. For example, word processing removes concerns with handwriting, but requires typing, which may slow text production and take attention away from the content of writing, unless the student has developed fluent typing skills. Whether a new tool will increase or decrease the overall cognitive burden depends on the skills of an individual student and the quality of training. Furthermore, the value of accurate text in a given social context and the motivation and cognitive ability of a student determine how much burden is acceptable. For example, an elementary school student whose teacher encourages students to write first drafts without concern for spelling, may not benefit from software that increases spelling accuracy but slows the writing process. On the other hand, a college student with LD who is expected to produce accurate work may need to expend the extra effort to produce correct text. Thus, findings must be interpreted with an eye on context and individual characteristics, and both benefits and limitations should be analyzed.

Second, technology by itself is unlikely to produce major improvements in students' writing. Good instruction takes advantage of the capabilities of the technology to improve students' abilities to plan, revise, and write fluently. While there is a place for direct comparisons of technologies (e.g., handwriting vs. word processing), research investigating combinations of technology and instruction is also important. Thus, it is important to consider the specific writing tasks and related instruction used in research in interpreting the findings.

The third point hardly needs to be mentioned in a book such as this. Technology and the familiarity of students with technology change rapidly. The design details of computer tools can make a significant difference, as Haas (1996) has shown in her studies comparing older 40-line monitors with larger, higher-resolution monitors for word processing. Researchers can deal with the rapid change, first, by designing studies to investigate basic capabilities of technology and, second, by attending carefully to how the details of the technology affect users. Even so, the rapid development of technology creates an inherent limitation for research on technology and writing.

The chapter is organized as follows. First, as background, the chapter provides a brief overview of research on the writing problems of students with LD including correlational studies and dictation studies supporting the claim that transcription difficulties contribute to the poor quality of their writing. Second, studies of word processing are discussed including studies of the overall impact of word processing on written products and studies of the combination of revising instruction and word processing. The remaining sections focus on specific assistive technology tools that can support accurate transcription. The third section discusses research on the benefits and limitations of spell checker and on instructional methods to help students use them more effectively. Fourth, the chapter considers whether speech synthesis can assist in editing by reading text back to students. Fifth, several studies demonstrating the benefits and limitations of word prediction with students with severe spelling deficits are analyzed. Word prediction software predicts what word the user intends to write based on initial letters and syntax and presents a list of words for the user to select; thus, it can support spelling in ways different from spell checker. Finally, the chapter reviews research on dictation using speech recognition software, including research on its use to compensate for poor transcription skills on writing tests.

2 Writing of Students with Learning Disabilities

Students with LD have difficulty with both the composing processes of planning and revising and with the transcription processes of getting language onto paper (for a review, see Troia, 2006). First, they have less knowledge of the characteristics of good writing and the requirements of various genres (Englert, Raphael, Anderson, Gregg, & Anthony, 1989). Second, they engage in relatively little planning, and have few strategies for generating or organizing content (Graham, Harris, MacArthur, & Schwartz, 1991). Third, their revising is limited primarily to correction of errors and minor changes in wording that do not affect meaning; often, they introduce new errors in the process of recopying a paper to fix previous errors (MacArthur, Graham, & Schwartz, 1991). Finally, they have difficulty with the transcription processes required to get their sentences into print — spelling, handwriting, capitalization, and punctuation (Graham, Berninger, Abbott, Abbott, & Whitaker, 1997). As a result of these difficulties, their written products, in comparison to those of their normally achieving peers, contain more errors of spelling, handwriting, and other mechanics and typically are shorter, less coherent and organized, and lower in overall quality (Graham et al., 1991).

Transcription problems are important both in their own right and because of their impact on the overall writing process. They are important in their own right because errors distract readers from the message that a writer is trying to communicate and, in extreme cases, render the message incomprehensible. On writing tests, errors influence judgments about overall quality of writing.

Perhaps more important, transcription problems interfere with the overall composing process and affect both overall quantity and quality of writing. Evidence from correlational studies demonstrates that proficiency with transcription affects the quality of writing at least through elementary school. For example, in a study involving 600 students in grades 1–6, Graham et al. (1997) found that handwriting fluency and spelling explained a sizable proportion of the variance in length of composition (41–66% across the grades) and in quality (25–42%). In addition, studies using interference with reaction time to study attention processes (Olive & Kellogg, 2002) show that handwriting demands interfere with composing for children but not adults.

Another way to investigate the impact of transcription is to compare dictation and handwriting. For primary grade children, dictated compositions are longer and higher in quality than handwritten papers (King & Rentel, 1981). However, for upper elementary, middle school, and college students, dictated compositions may be longer than handwritten ones, but are generally not higher in overall quality (Hidi & Hildyard, 1983; MacArthur & Cavalier, 2004; Reece & Cummings, 1996; Scardamalia, Bereiter, & Goelman, 1982). In contrast, for middle and high school students with LD and other poor writers, dictated compositions are both substantially longer and qualitatively superior to compositions written via handwriting or word processing (Graham, 1990; MacArthur & Graham, 1987; Reece & Cummings, 2004). Differences between dictation and handwriting for children but not adults have also been found using contrived writing tasks (Bourdin & Fayol, 1994).

Computer tools that support transcription may directly support writers with LD as compensatory tools, as when they help writers avoid and correct their errors. They may also enhance instruction and the development of transcription skills by freeing writers to focus on higher level composing concerns, by motivating practice, and by providing models of correct form.

3 Word Processing

Word processors are flexible writing tools that can support struggling writers with many aspects of writing, especially transcription and revision. The ability to produce an attractive final publication with the errors corrected can be highly motivating for students who struggle with spelling and handwriting. Word processing makes it easier to separate composing and transcription concerns by focusing on planning and ideas in a first draft, secure in the knowledge that errors can be fixed later without tedious recopying.

Although it facilitates transcription, word processing also introduces the new burden of typing. Unless students have received typing instruction, the attention required by typing and the slower rate of production may negatively affect the length and quality of writing (Graham, 1990). One study comparing handwriting and word processing on test essays (Russell, 1999) found that the effect of word processing depended on typing skill; it had a positive effect on quality for high school students with above average typing speed (20+ wpm) but a negative effect for students with below average typing.

Word processing appears to be especially beneficial for struggling writers. A meta-analysis (Bangert-Drowns, 1993) found that use of word processing in writing instruction programs produced a positive though small impact on the quality of students' writing. However, this small effect is better viewed as a combination of a moderate effect size ($d = 0.49$) for nine studies of 'basic' writers and a non-significant effect size ($d = 0.06$) for 11 other studies. One study that focused specifically on students with LD (MacArthur, Graham, Schwartz, & Shafer, 1995) evaluated the effectiveness of a model of writing instruction that integrated word processing and instruction in planning and revising strategies. Students in

12 experimental classes made greater gains in the quality of their narrative and informative writing than students in 10 control classes who received a process approach to writing without computers or strategy instruction. This study did not isolate the effects of word processing. Rather, it demonstrated the effectiveness of writing instruction that included word processing and strategies designed to take advantage of word processing capabilities.

The effects of word processing have also been studied in short-term experiments comparing word processing and handwriting as means of producing text. Vacc (1987) found that middle school students with mild disabilities wrote more slowly, made more revisions (mostly mechanics), and produced shorter texts with word processing; no differences in quality were found. MacArthur and Graham (1987) found that middle school students with LD wrote more slowly with a word processor and made more revisions during the first draft but fewer revisions between drafts; no differences were found on the final papers in length, syntactic complexity, vocabulary, errors, or overall quality. Limited typing skill may have influenced the results of these two studies. However, another study (MacArthur et al., 1995) used students who had participated in a full year curriculum with regular instruction and practice in typing and word processing; no differences were found between handwritten and word-processed compositions in overall quality, length, or spelling, capitalization, and punctuation errors. Note the similarity in results in the two studies despite the improvements in technology and the greater experience of students in the later study.

The limited evidence with students with LD indicates that word processing by itself may affect rate of composing (depending on typing skill) and the amount and timing of revision, but that it has little impact on written products. However, word processing in combination with instruction designed to take advantage of its capabilities may have positive effects on the quality of writing. Word processing may facilitate instruction about writing processes and enhance motivation in ways that improve students' writing achievement over time.

One particular area in which word processing may facilitate instruction is revising. Skilled revision involves identification of problems, diagnosis, and either revision or wholesale rewriting to fix the problems (Flower, Hayes, Carey, Schriver, & Stratman, 1986). Word processing does not directly help students learn how to evaluate their writing, diagnose problems, or fix those problems. However, word processing does reduce the physical burdens of revising and provide a clear copy of the revised text and, thus, may increase motivation for learning about revision. Three related studies investigated whether a combination of word processing and instruction in revising strategies would increase the amount and quality of revision and improve the overall quality of writing by students with LD. The first study evaluated a solo revising strategy (Graham & MacArthur, 1988). The other two studies investigated peer-revising strategies with instruction provided by research assistants (Stoddard & MacArthur, 1993) and by teachers in classrooms (MacArthur, Schwartz, & Graham, 1991). Research has demonstrated the value of peer response in improving revision (Rijlaarsdam, Couzijn, & Van den Bergh, 2004). In all studies, students wrote all drafts and made revisions on a word processor without a spell checker. In all three studies, instruction had positive effects on the number and quality of revisions, improvement from first to final draft, and quality of the final draft. In the classroom study (MacArthur et al., 1991), the control condition included word processing and peer response groups but not instruction in specific revising strategies, thus, supporting a conclusion that specially designed instruction is needed to help students take advantage of the power of word processing to improve revision.

4 Spell Checkers

Not surprisingly, spell checker are helpful to students with spelling problems. In a study of young adolescent students (ages 11–14) with LD who had moderate to severe spelling problems, students corrected 37% of the spelling errors in their compositions with a spell checker, compared to 9% unaided (MacArthur, Graham, Haynes, & De La Paz, 1996). College students with LD (McNaughton, Hughes, & Clark, 1997) used a spell checker somewhat more effectively, correcting 60% of their errors using a spell checker compared to 11% with handwriting.

The interesting question about spell checker is not whether they can help students to correct their errors, but what the limitations are and how those limitations might be reduced. The most serious limitation is that they fail to detect spelling errors that are other words, including homonyms and other real words (e.g., *sad* for *said*). In the MacArthur et al. (1996) study, 37% of students' misspellings were not detected for this reason. A second serious limitation is that the correct spelling may not appear in the list of suggestions, especially when words are severely misspelled (e.g., *fernitcer* for *furniture*). In the same study, the spell checker failed to suggest the correct spelling for 42% of identified errors. Other limitations of spell checker, which accounted for smaller numbers of uncorrected errors, include the possibilities that students may not recognize the correct spelling in the list of suggestions and that proper names may be falsely identified as errors.

Students can learn strategies to use spell checker more effectively. McNaughton, Hughes, and Ofiesh (1997) taught high school students with LD to (a) generate additional suggestions when the intended word was not in the list of suggestions (e.g., try a phonetic spelling) and (b) proofread a hard copy looking for errors the spell checker missed. The strategies helped the students to identify and correct substantially more of their errors.

The design of spell checker software can also make a difference. For students with LD, it is important that the spell checker include phonetic rules in generating suggestions. Smaller, or adjustable-size, dictionaries can reduce the number of errors that are not detected by flagging uncommon words. Some spell checker also flag homonyms, asking the user to consider whether the correct word was used. Finally, the addition of speech synthesis can help some students to select the correct word from the list of suggestions. However, no experimental evidence supports the effectiveness of these design features.

5 Speech Synthesis

Most research on speech synthesis for students with LD has studied its use as a support for reading (for a review, see MacArthur, Ferretti, Okolo, & Cavalier, 2001). However, it might also help students in revising. By listening to their text, students might be able to use their oral language skills to identify and correct errors they would miss by reading. Very limited evidence is available on this possibility. In one study (Borgh & Dickson,

1992), elementary school students wrote on a special word processor that prompted them to check for errors; half of the students used speech synthesis along with the prompts. No differences were found in overall amount of revision or on the length and quality of papers. Raskind and Higgins (1995) asked college students to detect errors in their papers under three conditions — speech synthesis, human reader, and no assistance. Students detected more errors in the speech synthesis condition, but the differences were not large in absolute terms (35% vs. 25% detection), and data on actual correction of errors were not reported. For additional discussion, see Quinlan (this volume).

6 Word Prediction

Students with severe spelling problems may have difficulty using spell checker successfully. The spell checker may not be able to help with badly misspelled words, or the students may not be able to read their own writing after finishing. Word prediction software offers another option for spelling support. Word prediction was originally developed for individuals with physical disabilities to reduce the number of keystrokes needed. It works by predicting what word the user intends to type based on the first letter(s). For example, if I have typed, *Pears are my f*, the program might offer a list of predictions including *friend*, *favorite*, and *first*. If I continue by adding an *a* to the *f*, the program would update the list, eliminating words that do not start with *fa* and adding new words. I could then insert the word in the text by typing the number of the word or clicking on it. Most word prediction systems also provide speech synthesis to help students read the list of words. Depending on the sophistication of the program, predictions will be based on syntax and recently used words as well as spelling.

Newell et al. (1992) reported case studies of 17 students using word prediction. Most of the students had physical disabilities, primarily cerebral palsy, though students with visual and hearing impairments, developmental delay, language disorders, and LD were also included. Of the six students who had mild to moderate language and LD, five showed improvements in accuracy of spelling, quantity of writing, and motivation.

MacArthur (1998, 1999) conducted three related studies of word prediction with 9- and 10-year old students with severe spelling problems, using single-subject designs that support causal conclusions about the effects of treatment on individual students. In the first study (MacArthur, 1998), five students wrote dialogue journals with their teacher, using a word processor in the baseline condition and word prediction with speech synthesis in the treatment condition. The word prediction program began with a vocabulary of 300 common words to which were added all words used by the teacher and student in their dialogue. In this study, the software was well adapted to the writing task. The speech synthesis made it possible for the student to read the teacher's entry fluently. The vocabulary was relatively small and targeted on the words used in the dialogue. The treatment had a substantial effect on the legibility and spelling of writing for four of the five students. During baseline, the writing of these four students ranged from 55 to 85% legible words (i.e., readable in isolation) and 42 to 75% correctly spelled words. All four increased their percentage of both legible and correctly spelled words into the range 90–100%.

The other two studies (MacArthur, 1999) used word prediction software with a larger vocabulary and a more sophisticated prediction algorithm that used information on syntax and frequency of use by individual users. Effects of word prediction were limited to an improvement in spelling for one of three students. More detailed analysis of process data showed that students had difficulty using word prediction to find the correct word. In order to accommodate a large dictionary, the program used a fairly complex interface to predict words. For example, the word list changed as each new letter was typed, making it necessary to monitor the list continuously. Students also had difficulty when they did not type the initial letters correctly. The writing task and the software were not well matched because the journal-writing task did not demand the large vocabulary that made the program difficult to use. In a follow-up study with the same students, the writing task was changed to a controlled task demanding a larger vocabulary. Students wrote from dictation using selections from graded reading passages at their instructional reading level. Under these conditions, word prediction clearly improved legibility and spelling for two of the three students. Error rates were still high, but were substantially better with word prediction than with word processing or handwriting.

A more recent study (Handley-More, Deitz, Billingsley, & Coggins, 2003), which also used a single-subject design with students with LD and severe spelling problems, found similar effects; two of three students made substantial improvements in legibility and spelling. Thus, the available research supports the use of word prediction software with students with severe spelling problems. The studies also revealed that design issues, such as the size of the vocabulary, its match to the writing task, and the complexity of the interface, make a difference in the impact. Further research is needed to replicate and extend the findings to other groups and to investigate the potential impact on vocabulary use.

7 Speech Recognition

Dictation using speech recognition software represents potentially the most complete solution for students who have difficulty with handwriting, spelling, and overall fluency. As summarized above, the dictated compositions of students with LD are substantially longer and qualitatively superior to compositions written via handwriting or word processing (Graham, 1990; MacArthur & Graham, 1987; Reece & Cummings, 1996). However, despite dramatic improvements in the quality of speech recognition software in recent years, it still has important limitations in comparison to dictation to a person. First, accuracy is limited, even after training the system to understand an individual voice. Second, users must articulate carefully, must dictate punctuation and formatting, and must avoid extraneous vocalizations. Third, users must learn to recognize and correct new types of mistakes; in place of the spelling errors in handwritten or word-processed texts, users need to search for incorrect words in texts dictated using speech recognition. All of these limitations represent new cognitive burdens in place of the old burdens of handwriting and spelling.

On the other hand, speech recognition has an important advantage over normal dictation to a tape recorder in that the writer has access to the text already written (Reece & Cummings, 1996). Leijten and Van Waes (this volume) address this issue thoroughly.

A few studies of speech recognition with students with LD are available. Higgins and Raskind (1995) studied the effects of speech recognition with college students with LD. Students wrote essays under three conditions: speech recognition, dictation to a human who transcribed via handwriting, and unassisted (i.e., handwriting or word processing without a spell checker at the student's choice). Quality ratings were significantly higher in the speech recognition than the unassisted condition. Quinlan (2004) selected middle school students who had significantly lower written language than oral language scores and compared them to students without such a discrepancy. All students composed four brief narratives using handwriting and speech recognition. Students with writing problems, but not the average writers, wrote longer papers using speech recognition. However, the poor writers' dictated papers were not rated higher in quality than handwritten papers.

MacArthur and Cavalier (2004) investigated the feasibility and validity of speech recognition software and dictation to a scribe as accommodations for tests involving extended writing. By law, students with disabilities are entitled to accommodations, or modified test procedures, to remove barriers due to their disabilities, as long as the accommodations do not change the construct measured by the test. The study compared the effects of speech recognition, dictation to a person who typed on a visible screen, and handwriting on the writing of high school students with and without LD. In a repeated measures design, all students received training in speech recognition and then wrote essays in all three conditions. The students with LD made fewer total errors with speech recognition than handwriting. Students with LD produced higher quality essays using speech recognition than handwriting, and even better essays when dictating to a person. No statistically significant differences of condition were found for students without LD. The differential impact on students with and without disabilities was interpreted as support for the validity of the accommodation. See Quinlan (this volume) for a more complete discussion of research on speech recognition and developing writers.

8 Concluding Comments

Although the research on assistive technology for writing is not extensive, it does provide evidence that computer tools can offer significant support to writers who struggle with the basic mechanics of writing. Word processing, in combination with instruction designed to take advantage of its capabilities, can help students learn to revise and improve their writing overall. Spell checker clearly help students with spelling problems, and their limitations can be at least partially overcome with special instruction. Word prediction appears to be of value for students with severe spelling problems. Speech recognition has, perhaps, the widest applicability as it addresses concerns with handwriting, spelling, and fluency.

However, each of the tools has limitations and imposes new cognitive burdens on users. Word processing requires typing. Word prediction requires careful attention to word choices and slows the writing process. Speech recognition requires training, careful articulation, and new editing skills. Consequently, the tools will be useful for some struggling writers and not others. The implication for research is that more work is needed to determine which users are likely to benefit from particular tools. The immediate practical implication is that individual assessment of skills and trials with various computer applications are needed to match students and tools. A related practical concern is the use of these technology tools in schools and other environments. Students and teachers need training and support, and some of the tools pose practical problems for use in school settings (e.g., dictating in classrooms).

Except for word processing, which has been studied in combination with instruction, these applications have been investigated as compensatory tools, which support production of text but are not designed to improve the user's skills. However, Raskind and Higgins (1999) argued that regular use of technological tools might have transfer effects on skills. They presented preliminary evidence that regular use of speech recognition improved the reading skills of high school students with LD. Further research is needed to investigate transfer effects for tools such as spell checker, word prediction, and speech recognition. It is likely that obtaining transfer effects will require the development of instructional methods that use the capabilities of the tools with the goal of increasing students' independent skills.

Fifteen years ago, most word processors used in schools did not have integrated spell checker or high-quality screens; high-quality speech synthesis required special hardware; word prediction was available only in specialized augmentative communication devices; and speech recognition required users to dictate isolated words. The rapid changes in technology present significant problems to schools and researchers. Schools have difficulty updating their technology and training their staff. Researchers are challenged to design research that will have meaning beyond the current status of the technology. Research and development is needed to understand the benefits and limitations of these tools with various students and to develop and evaluate models for use of the tools in classroom situations.

Chapter 2

Young Writers and Digital Scribes

Thomas Quinlan

Speech recognition technology (SR) gives new viability to dictating, and in so doing may offer benefits to young, struggling writers. To become skillful writers, children must develop fluent text production (i.e., transcription). Composing via pen and paper requires the close coordination of handwriting and spelling, which can overwhelm the capacities of some young writers. Alternative writing tools can provide children with writing difficulties another means for attaining fluency. Relative to handwriting, SR enables less-fluent writers to produce longer texts with fewer surface errors. This chapter examines how SR can serve to accommodate children's writing difficulties.

1 Introduction

Dictating a text is as old as writing itself. Throughout history, poets, prophets, saints, and statesmen have employed the services of professional scribes. While most people today serve as their own scribe, convenience and necessity remain compelling reasons for dictating. Speech recognition technology (SR) gives new viability to dictating, and in so doing promises freedom from the burdens of handwriting and typing. SR systems based on computer programs such as Dragon Naturally Speaking (2004) and IBM's Via Voice (2004) will take dictation, and even read-aloud the developing text. While the underlying technology of SR continues to develop, current versions deliver sufficient accuracy to make SR a viable writing tool. While developed primarily for commercial uses, SR also has educational applications for young, struggling writers.

2 Transcription and Children's Writing Fluency

A close look at the processes of writing can help explain why many children have difficulties learning to write. Writing requires a variety of problem-solving and is among the

Quinlan, T. (2005). Young writers and digital scribes. In L. Van Waes, M. Leijten & C. Neuwirth (Vol. Eds.) & G. Rijlaarsdam (Series Ed.), Studies in Writing: Vol. 17. Writing and Digital Media (pp. 21–29). Oxford: Elsevier.

most complex cognitive behaviors required of children. Ideas must be translated into words, which are strung into sentences, represented orthographically, then inscribed letter by letter. Accordingly, writing involves the coordination of multiple processes (Hayes & Flower, 1980; Kellogg, 1996). Writing processes are thought to draw upon a common, limited capacity system, in which information is temporarily stored and processed, i.e., working memory (McCutchen, 1996). In solving a variety of problems, processing demands can often exceed processing capacity. Cognitive overload poses an ongoing threat to writers of all levels, because writers as they develop tend to grapple with increasingly sophisticated problems. Experienced writers often set sophisticated goals, which requires them to grapple with thorny problems, i.e., knowledge transforming (Bereiter & Scardamalia, 1987). Conceptual- and linguistic-intensive problems involved in planning, revising, and translating, have been shown to draw heavily upon cognitive resources (Piolat, Roussey, Olive, & Farioli, 1996). Thus, skilled writing can be cognitively demanding. Children's writing is also demanding, but for a different reason. Children may struggle with production problems — getting words on the page (i.e., transcription). "Transcription" has been defined as the transformation of mental language representations into text (Berninger & Swanson, 1994). For children, transcription typically encompasses the processes responsible for spelling and handwriting.

Composing via pen and paper can overwhelm the cognitive resources of young writers. In handwriting, words are transcribed letter by letter, which requires a tight coordination between handwriting and spelling. Bourdin and Fayol (2000) found that inefficient handwritten transcription can interfere with word storage, which could disrupt the translation of ideas into words (i.e., formulating). When transcription becomes automatized, other writing processes can function more efficiently (Bourdin & Fayol, 1994). For these reasons, fluent handwriting/spelling has been considered a prerequisite for writing development (Kellogg, 2001; McCutchen, 1996).

Handwriting fluency predicts writing skill for younger but not older children (Berninger & Swanson, 1994), suggesting that handwriting processes become increasingly automatized with age and experience. For many children, however, handwriting processes can remain inefficient in spite of practice. Graham and Weintraub (1996) estimate that approximately 20% of all school children struggle with handwriting. Producing text via handwriting has shown to be particularly difficult for those with learning disabilities (LD), both for children (Graham, 1990) and adults (Gerber et al., 1990). In addition, weak spelling skills may tend to compound handwriting problems. Thus, producing text can be problematic for those with weak spelling skills, such as children with LD (Moran, 1981; Poteet, 1979).

Although "transcription" refers to particular skills of the writer, these skills are evoked through interaction with a particular writing tool. For example, writing with a pencil or pen involves a particular array of processes, including recall of orthographic representations, parsing into graphemes, recall of graphemic forms, and execution of graphomotor function. In contrast, alternative writing tools may impose fewer demands upon the writer, and so provide alternative routes to automatized transcription. For example, typing appears to involve less-complex graphomotor function than handwriting, and so may be less demanding. SR differs from keyboard-based word processors in method of input, i.e., dictation versus typing. During dictation, transcription entails the processes responsible for speech articulation, which should be highly automatized in most children, including those with LD. Thus, dictation should be a very fluent mode of composing.

3 Dictating

In his studies of skilled adult writers, Gould (1980) found that dictated texts were not significantly better or worse in quality than handwritten texts. He concluded that "Good authors were good authors and poor authors were poor authors, regardless of method" (Gould, 1980, p. 20). However, this cross-modal parity apparently does not hold for all children. Children generally compose longer texts via dictation (Graham, 1990; Hidi & Hildyard, 1983; McCutchen, 1987; Reece & Cumming, 1996; Scardamalia, Bereiter, & Goleman, 1982). While typically developing children tend to produce higher quality texts via handwriting (Scardamalia et al., 1982), children with LD do better with dictation (Graham, 1990; Graham & Harris, 1989). Thus, for children with writing difficulties the general fluency advantages of dictation enable them to produce better quality text.

In traditional dictation, it is the scribe or typist who actually produces the text. In SR dictation, the SR system translates the spoken utterance into text. Thus, SR presents the writer with a visible display of the developing text. If the developing text "is a very important part of the task environment," as Hayes and Flower (1980) assert, then its absence could potentially hobble a writer. Results from a few studies that simulated SR, by employing a hidden typist, suggest that the developing text may indeed play a vital role in speech-based composing. In a study by Reece and Cumming (1996), children (ages 11–12) composed texts by (1) hand, (2) traditional dictation, and (3) simulated SR. In the simulated SR condition, children dictated to a hidden typist, but they could view their text during composing. The texts produced via simulated SR were superior in quality to both dictated and handwritten texts, for both typically developing and poor writers. The authors concluded that simulated SR was an "optimal" mode of composing.

3.1 Children Dictating and the Developing Text

The results of Reece and Cumming's study (1996) raised a question; How might seeing — and presumably reading — the developing text influence dictating? Scott Beers and I (Beers & Quinlan, 2000) investigated this question by employing a variation on the "hidden typist" methodology. In the simulated SR condition, the visibility of the developing text was controlled. To view their own texts, children were required to push a mouse button, which activated a monitor display for 20 s. In the first experiment, older (ages 13–14) and younger (ages 10–11) children without LD composed three short argumentative essays in response to a writing prompt (e.g., Should the voting age be lowered to 16?). Essays were composed via handwriting, traditional dictation, and simulated SR. Writing modes and prompts were counterbalanced across participants. In the 2 (group) $\times$ 2 (mode) analysis, we found that eighth grade children composed essays that were longer and more coherent, relative to fifth grade children. Also, eighth grade children activated the developing text significantly more often than their younger peers. For children in both grades, simulated SR texts were longer than handwritten texts, but shorter than dictated texts. Children paused more often during the simulated SR condition, relative to traditional dictation. And, for eighth graders, handwritten and simulated SR texts were more coherent than traditional dictation texts; whereas coherency of fifth graders' texts did not differ across modes.

These results reveal an interesting phenomena: Children were most fluent while dictating, but the presence of the developing text served to moderate this fluency. As one possible explanation, reading their own texts caused children to choose their words more carefully. However, only for older children did seeing the developing text lead to better quality writing, as measured by text coherence. It would appear that older children interact with their own texts in a particularly fruitful way. Given these two productive effects, dictating fluency and reading-during-writing, we might expect older children to more fully benefit from using SR.

If younger, relatively inexperienced writers use the developing text less effectively than older writers, what might we expect from children with weaker reading skills? We replicated the first experiment with a group of children with LD, ages 10–13 (n = 29). The results showed that these children with LD often activated the developing text, at a rate comparable to the children without LD. Also, a similar pattern for text length was observed, with simulated SR texts being longer than handwritten texts, but shorter than dictated texts. In an assessment of holistic quality, we found that simulated SR texts did not differ from traditionally dictated texts, but that both were significantly superior to handwritten texts.

The results of this second experiment suggest important points about the composing of children with LD. Here again, we observed that dictating (in either traditional or simulated SR modes) helped make children more fluent. Because handwriting is particularly problematic for these children, improved fluency provided a huge benefit by improving both text length and text quality. Children with LD often consulted the developing text, which altered the course of composing; however, the presence of the developing text did not lead to improved text quality. Like the younger children in the first experiment, these children with LD seemed unable to use the developing text to their advantage, such that simulated SR seemingly offered no particular advantage over traditional dictation.

3.2 Real (i.e., Non-Simulated) Speech Recognition Technology

Few studies have investigated children composing with actual, non-simulated SR. To convert speech to text, SR compares audible signals of a spoken phrase to a resident template (Horsman, 1983). To improve the accuracy of the speech-to-text conversion, recent versions of SR also include syntactic and lexical information in the comparison. Current SR systems accept continuous speech input, have large vocabularies, and require relatively little training.

Higgins and Raskind (1995) examined undergraduate students composing via (1) handwriting, (2) dictating to a scribe, and (3) SR. In the scribe condition, participants could view their text as it was handwritten by the scribe. The results showed that participants composed significantly higher quality essays in the SR condition, relative to the handwriting condition. In a similarly designed study, MacArthur and Cavalier (2004) examined children with and without LD composing across the same three modes, i.e., handwriting, dictating to a scribe, and SR. For children with LD, texts composed in the scribe condition were judged superior in quality to SR texts, which were rated superior to handwritten texts. Such a result suggests that children with LD found dictating to a scribe even easier than dictating to SR. For the non-LD children, text quality did not differ across conditions. These results, although somewhat mixed, suggest that dictating with SR benefits children with writing difficulties (i.e., children with LD) more than typically developing writers.

3.2.1 Speech recognition technology and children with writing difficulties   Helping children overcome writing difficulties can mean finding the right combination of writing tool and writing strategy. Accordingly, I (Quinlan, 2004) investigated children composing with SR in combination with advance planning. In this study, two groups of children (ages 11–14), fluent and less-fluent writers (n = 41) composed a series of four narratives, two via handwriting and two using SR, with and without advance planning. Children were shown a picture prompt and asked to compose a story about it. Children were allotted 10 minutes for composing, of which they could use some or all.

In the SR condition, children used systems based upon Dell Optiplex 400 PCs (with 128 MB of RAM and a Pentium IV processor, running at 1.7 GHz), with Parrot (VXI Corp.) headset microphones, running Dragon Naturally Speaking Professional, version 5 (2002). These SR systems represented the state of the art of generally available components at the time of data collection, in the winter of 2002.

In order to use the SR systems effectively, children received three hours of direct instruction and guided practice. First, I demonstrated SR dictating technique by composing a paragraph, during which I modeled proper microphone placement, dictating technique, and verbal commands. In particular, children were shown how to use verbal commands to correct recognition errors, e.g., "Correct that" and "Scratch that." Next, before using the SR systems, I led the children through some speech exercises designed to improve enunciation. Then, children were guided through the process of creating their own voice files, which are integral to using SR. Finally, children practiced using SR by composing stories on such topics as "my favorite vacation" and "an ultimate adventure."

While learning to use SR, children also received instruction on how to plan their stories using a research-validated planning strategy (Graham & Harris, 1989; Sawyer, Graham, & Harris, 1992). Children with LD tend to dictate better quality texts when they plan them first (De La Paz & Graham, 1997). Planning instruction began by my explaining that good stories tell: Who did what, where it happened, when it happened, and how (i.e., the "Five Ws"). I asked children to repeat the mnemonic (i.e., "who, what, where, when, and how") and to provide examples of how each might be used in a story. Children were then given a graphic organizer, which integrated the five "Ws" into story grammar elements. Children were asked to use the graphic organizers to plan their practice stories. Before starting the experimental writing tasks, children were required to demonstrate the ability to use SR, which consisted of dictating a paragraph with minimal recognition errors (<20%).

The results indicated that less-fluent writers benefited from SR. In the handwriting condition, fluent writers' narratives were judged qualitatively superior to narratives of less-fluent writers, in terms of length, quality, and surface errors. Also, fluent writers spent more time composing than did less-fluent writers. Interestingly, narratives composed via SR did not differ significantly across groups. For less-fluent writers, SR narratives had significantly more words and fewer errors than handwritten narratives. Although SR did not significantly improve quality, a strong relationship between quality and text length suggests that longer texts tended to be of better quality.

Composing with SR also helped less-fluent writers to produce more-readable text. The handwritten narratives of less-fluent writers showed a greater percentage of misspelled words, relative to those of their more fluent peers. However, composing with SR caused a significant reduction of misspellings for less-fluent writers. Since writing by hand requires the coordination of spelling and handwriting, weak spelling skills may have contributed to children's relative dysfluency. When using SR, spelling knowledge is not essential to the dictation of whole words and phrases, but is integral to the detection and correction of SR errors. Children's dictating skill varied widely, with some children evoking many more recognition errors than other children. Children generally corrected recognition-errors frequently, but the amount of error correcting did not differ significantly across groups. For less-fluent writers, SR provided a means for producing cleaner texts, with fewer errors.

In the narratives of less-fluent writers, the effects of SR are apparent to the reader. The narratives below (see Figure 1) exemplify the average performance of less-fluent writers, in terms of length, quality, and surface errors. The same less-fluent writer, with the aid of advance planning, composed both of the following narratives:

(a) *Jimy he cold fly. The next day he tried to fly he jumped in the air he floted and fell, then he tried agin, and he went really hi in the air then he went over the bildings and hills. He went over everything! No body code see him any whare.*

(b) *One day while Bobby was playing baseball outside, the sun was shining and he thought he god! God was coming towards him walking on clouds and waving, at him. He was shocked at first but he realized he was not in trouble, he was only been visited. He was awful bright and in white. He was awful nice even as large as he was. Soon he had to go, when he did leave I was disappointed.*

Figure 1: Two narratives produced by a less-fluent writer, via (a) handwriting and (b) speech recognition technology.

In comparing these two narratives, the reader will notice that the SR text is longer, with more substantive detail. For example, the SR narrative describes the emotions of the protagonist, which include being "shocked," then "disappointed." By noting these internal states, the writer builds narrative complexity by showing how events affect the character. In contrast, the handwritten narrative seems almost telegraphic, conveying only the basic elements of the story, with few details. Surface errors represent another salient disparity. In spite of its relative brevity, the handwritten narrative has numerous spelling errors, which most readers would find intrusive; in contrast, the SR narrative is more readable, having fewer surface errors. Generally, the SR narrative is longer and more readable than the handwritten narrative.

The results of this study vividly illustrates how children's writing difficulties can sometimes be a function of the writing tool. Less-fluent children in the present study presented with between 4 and 8 years of formal handwriting experience; yet, with minimal practice, SR enabled them to compose more fluently and accurately. Further, these benefits were realized in spite of the distraction of frequently correcting SR errors. This improved fluency underscores how pen and paper can be incredibly problematic for some children. Increased fluency offers numerous benefits to struggling writers, such as the ability to complete written assignments more successfully, and thereby to participate more fully in classroom writing activities. Further, the reduction of spelling errors, along with typesetting, can lead to improved readability, making it easier for writers to review their own texts. By improving fluency, SR affords an avenue for children to move beyond a preoccupation with transcription, to focus on what they want to say and how they want to say it.

Some will argue that educators should focus on remediating writing difficulties, rather than accommodating them. True, intensive handwriting instruction has shown to improve the handwriting fluency of struggling writers (Berninger et al., 1997). Also, composing with SR could take time away from the practice of handwriting, causing handwriting skills to atrophy. To the extent that handwriting remains the norm in many schools, fostering handwriting makes sense. However, the proliferation of PCs in the schools is steadily eroding this hegemony, with typing skills becoming as important handwriting skills. In the context of computer interfaces, typing becomes simply another mode of input. As a mode of input, handwriting should be viewed as a means, not a goal in itself. Writing educators are most concerned with helping children to develop the ability to: (1) organize and express ideas, (2) employ a genre- and audience-appropriate voice, and (3) construct mellifluous sentences using apt words. If a child has struggled with handwriting for many years, he or she runs the risk of not ever achieving these important writing skills. A fluent mode of composing, like SR, gives children a means for producing texts, and so a means for developing writing skills.

4 Speech Synthesis

At this point, evidence suggests that SR can improve writing fluency for children with transcription-related difficulties. In addition, some evidence suggests that SR might support children's writing in another way. SR systems often include speech synthesis (SS), by which the developing text can be read aloud. To convert text to speech, SS performs a grapheme-to-phoneme conversion, which gives a computer the capability of reading text aloud (Dutoit, 1997). As a writing tool, SS can provide children with an alternative means for reviewing their own texts.

Writers may read their own texts for a variety of reasons. Obviously, reading is necessary for editing and revising. Writers may also reread in order to plan, using the developing text to guide the generation of content (Kaufer, Hayes, & Flower, 1986). Some children may be hindered from doing much reading-during-writing. In contending with the demands of basic planning and transcription, children may be preoccupied with getting words on the page. Reading-during-writing would tend to compound those demands, especially if it cued additional planning or revising. Bereiter and Scardamalia (1987) observed how younger, less-experienced writers often avoided unnecessary complications, adopting a "knowledge-telling" approach. In contrast, skilled writers often set sophisticated goals, which required them to solve complex problems, an approach they called "knowledge transforming." In knowledge transforming, problem-solving involves a dynamic interaction between the text and the writer, which surely depends upon reading. The ability to adopt a knowledge-transforming approach likely depends upon highly fluent reading skills, which many children, especially those with LD, do not have. If SS could provide these children with a more fluent means of interacting with the developing text, it could enable them to adopt a more sophisticated approach to writing.

Do writers actually reread the developing text? Gould (1980) found that business executives were capable of composing business letters of comparable quality, with or without the developing text visible during composing. However, this feat does not reveal how writers typically interact with their texts. Breetvelt, Van den Bergh, and Rijlaarsdam (1996) observed that, for skilled writers (i.e., lawyers), reading became a significant predictor of text quality after 10 min of composing, with the relationship increasing in strength, reaching a maximum at 30 min. Further, writing models indicate that reading is integral to skilled writing (Hayes, 1996; Hayes & Flower, 1980; Kellogg, 1996).

4.1 Children's Reading-During-Writing

Because we know little about how children read-during-writing, it is difficult to assess the potential effects of SS, as a means for reviewing the developing text. In the dictation studies reviewed above (Beers & Quinlan, 2000), the presence of the developing text mattered most for older children, and raised the possibility that more experienced writers may reread the developing text for the purposes of planning or for formulating. In a subsequent study (Beers & Quinlan, 2006), we investigated (1) how children interacted with the developing text and (2) whether differences in writing tasks influenced reading-during-writing. We asked girls and boys (10–14 years of age) to compose a narrative and an essay. Children dictated their compositions to a typist, while a designated monitor allowed them to view the developing text. During composing, we recorded the location and duration of children's eye fixations on the designated monitor, using the Erica eyetracking system (Eye Response Technologies). Before composing each text, we conducted a short calibration procedure. Children were allotted 10 min for composing.

During analysis, we viewed a play-back of the writing session on the ERICA system, in which children's eye fixations were displayed as a red "x" moving around the text. Fixations were coded manually as (1) reading, (2) monitoring, or (3) off-text. "Monitoring" was operationalized as fixations occurring within two words (approximately 10–15 characters) of the point of inscription. Fixations were coded as "reading" if they: (1) involved one or more forward fixations, and (2) occurred more than two words above the point of inscription, in the developing text.

The results showed that boys and girls differed markedly in their approaches to reading the developing text. Overall, all children spent the vast percentage of time watching/reading at the point of inscription (i.e., monitoring). Boys engaged in more monitoring than girls. Relative to boys, girls spent a greater percentage of time reading-during-writing. Girls also spent more overall time composing and produced qualitatively superior texts. In the U.S., girls consistently and significantly outscore boys in national assessments of writing and reading skills (e.g., National Council of Education, 2002). A follow-up analysis indicated that, for boys, *t*-units composed immediately after reading were significantly longer than *t*-units composed without reading. This evidence suggests that children may read in order to coordinate the formulation of the sentences, with girls being more able or willing to employ this strategy.

What do these results suggest about children's using SS to read their own texts? Research has shown that SS can help support children's editing. In MacArthur's (1998) study of five children with LD (ages 9–10), SS with word prediction improved the legibility and spelling accuracy of the children's journal entries. In Lewis' (1998) study of children with LD, who composed with various combinations of writing technologies (which included spelling and grammar checkers), SS with word prediction led to the largest decrease in spelling errors from pre- to post-test. However, these study designs make it impossible to tease apart the effects of SS and word prediction.

A study by Borgh and Dickson (1992) focused exclusively on the effects of SS on children's writing. Two groups of children without LD, 24 younger (ages 7 and 8) and 24 older (ages 10 and 11), composed a series of four stories on a word processor equipped with SS. When the writer typed terminal punctuation, such as a period or exclamation mark, the word processor would read-back the just-completed sentence. The writer could then opt to revise or edit this sentence, have the whole text read back, or continue composing. Participants composed four stories, two in regular word processing mode and two in the SS mode. The authors found that children rarely opted to hear a read-back of the entire text. This SS tool, with automatic sentence read-back, significantly increased sentence-level editing, but did not increase story-level editing or story quality.

Whether SS provides the type of reading support children need most, remains to be seen. While SS may help children detect spelling errors, children should tend to make fewer misspellings when composing with SR. To have a strong positive impact on the quality of children's writing, SS must support children's efforts to read their own texts globally. Revising studies indicate that effective revising involves adopting a global reading strategy (McCutchen, Francis, & Kerr, 1997; Wallace, Hayes, Hatch, & Miller, 1996). Future studies should examine ways in which SS might help children to selectively read-back their own texts, in order to facilitate global revising.

5 Conclusion

In order to become skillful writers, children must develop fluency with at least one writing tool. Ideally, a child might become fluent in both handwriting and typing, the two most commonly available writing tools. However, some children have an on-going struggle with the graphomotor and spelling demands of writing. For these children, SR can offer an alternative route to fluency. The accuracy of current-generation SR systems — much improved over earlier systems — makes them viable as writing tools. A given child's success with SR likely depends upon adequate training, which should include instruction in dictating techniques and error correction. Granted, composing with SR might lead to a further weakening of a child's handwriting skills, via lack of practice. However, the benefits derived from improved writing fluency should more than offset this possible negative effect, both in the short term, with the ability to successfully complete school assignments, and in the long term, as composing practice facilitates the development of writing skills.

Chapter 3

Repair Strategies in Writing with Speech Recognition: The Effect of Experience with Classical Dictating

Mariëlle Leijten and Luuk Van Waes

This chapter describes the repair strategies of writers who have started using speech recognition systems for writing business texts. The writers differed in their previous writing experience. They either had classical dictating experience, or they were used to writing their texts with a word processor. The study confirms the potential hybrid character of speech recognition as a writing mode. One of the main differences between classical dictating and dictating with speech recognition is that the writer gets the dictated text displayed on the screen almost immediately, making it directly accessible in a word processor. As previous research has shown, the interaction with 'the text produced so far' is a crucial aspect in the organization of the writing process. The case study presented here also lends support to this idea. The extent to which the developing text influences the writing process may depend upon the extent to which writers make use of it while dictating. The writers' interaction with the text produced so far is also influenced by errors that occur in the representation of the dictated text, e.g., due to (technical) misrecognition by the software. In the case study described in this chapter, we observed that the interaction with the imperfect text on the screen can either lead to a highly recursive writing process in which every error is repaired almost immediately, or it can also lead to a less recursive writing process in which repairs are made at the end of a section or a first draft. Speech recognition seems to create a writing environment that is open for different writing styles.

1 Introduction

'See what you say' was one of the slogans that was used to promote speech recognition software for dictating purposes in the early years of this technology. Indeed, the fact that

Leijten, M., & Van Waes, L. (2005). *Repair strategies in writing with speech recognition: The effect of experience with classical dictating. In L. Van Waes, M. Leijten & C. Neuwirth (Vol. Eds.) & G. Rijlaarsdam (Series Ed.), Studies in Writing: Vol. 17. Writing and Digital Media* (pp. 31–46). Oxford: Elsevier.

the technology enabled writers to quickly produce a visual representation of the spoken text, combined benefits of dictating machines and word processors. The software released in the mid-1980s did not quite fulfil this promise. However, 20 years later, speech recognition systems have improved dramatically (especially versions adapted for specific professions like law and medicine have a very acceptable speech to text conversion level, delivering up to 99% accuracy, after the programme has been carefully trained). As is the case with other digital media, speech recognition software is still improving. Consequently, it should be kept in mind that studying the use of this software and its implications for the writing process research will be further influenced by this evolution. However, even in this stage of the technical developments, the new writing mode enables us to gain insight into aspects of the writing process that are difficult to isolate in other writing modes.

The use of speech recognition in writing is extensively described by MacArthur and Quinlan (in this volume). They also give an overall review of the growing body of research on writing and speech technology, with special attention to studies on writers with learning disabilities.

In the present study, we would like to present a case study in which two writers were observed during their first weeks in using speech technology for their day-to-day writing tasks. Both writers were lawyers: one was experienced in classical dictating (using a dictaphone); the other had no dictating experience at all. The focus of this study is on the way the writers interact with the dictated text that appears on their computer screen when dictating to the computer. More specifically, we observed the interaction with the 'imperfect' text produced so far. Due to (technical) misrecognition of the spoken text — especially in the adaptation phase — the text on screen is not always a perfect representation of what has been dictated. This imperfect text produced so far might cause an extra cognitive load and might also distract the writers during the planning of new text.

1.1   Speech Recognition and Writing

Looking back in time, dictation and writing seem to have a 'cyclic relation' with each other. That is certainly a conclusion one can draw when reading Honeycutt's (2004) analysis of dictation as a composing method in Western history. In his description of the long history of dictation, he clearly shows "how dictation's shifting role as a form of literacy has been influenced by the dual mediation of technological tools and existing cultural practices" (Honeycutt, 2004, p. 294). By travelling through the history, he shows that slight changes in the material conditions of reading and writing radically changed the relationship between author and text. The introduction of speech recognition as a writing tool for dictation practices might change this relationship once again. In contrast to more recent dictation practices in which there was a distinct gap between composition and written production, this new technological implementation brings together the oral and the written representation of the text. This characteristic of the new writing context created by voice recognition is the central starting point of this chapter. For a more detailed description of speech recognition and text-to-speech, we would like to refer to Quinlan (this volume).

1.2   *The Text Produced So Far and Writing Media*

Since speech recognition brings together the oral and the written representation of text, we would like to describe speech recognition as a hybrid writing mode. It combines characteristics of both classical dictating and keyboard-based word processing. Especially the new characteristics of the 'text produced so far' play a crucial role in writing with speech recognition. We think speech recognition has three particular points of interest related to the interaction with the text produced so far: visibility of the text produced so far, moment of visual feedback, and the correctness of the visual representation. Classical dictating does not create any immediate visualization of the text produced so far. Related to this, previous studies show that classical dictating is characterized by a high degree of linearity in the text production (Schilperoord, 1996). Writers dictate sentences or phrases one after the other and only few revisions are made. Revising almost exclusively takes place mentally before the text is dictated to the recorder. Keyboard-based word processing on the other hand is characterized by immediate visual feedback of the text produced so far. Therefore, the computer writing process is typically characterized by a high degree of non-linearity (Severinson Eklundh, 1994; Van Waes & Schellens, 2003). Most computer writers consider a paragraph, or even a sentence, as a unit that is planned, formulated, reviewed and revised in short recursive episodes (Van den Bergh & Rijlaarsdam, 1996). The constant feedback on the screen offers them the opportunity to revise a lot, without losing the overview of the final text (Haas, 1989; Honeycutt, 2003). In word processing, tools like cutting and pasting also facilitate revising.

In contrast to the traditional dictating mode, writers using speech technology get immediate written feedback on the computer screen. This previously mentioned technical characteristic creates the possibility to review the text in all stages of the writing process either by speech or by keyboard, opening the gates to non-linearity. However, this written feedback, other than in keyboard-based word processing and typed output of classical dictating, can contain misrecognitions that are of a different kind than ordinary typing errors.

As the writing model in Figure 1 shows, the text produced so far is an important component of the task environment in monitoring the writing process and it is closely related to the composing medium.

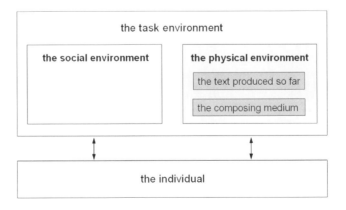

Figure 1: Synthesis of the writing model of Hayes (1996, p. 4).

The evaluation of the text produced so far is a very complex task, both in keyboard-based word processing and in classical dictating. Studies by Wood, Willoughby, Specht, and Porter (2002) and Haas (1996) have shown the importance of the physical availability and the 'sense' of the text produced so far. In their opinion, computer technologies might not sufficiently support the memory and organizational demands that writers need. These cognitive demands to keep the '<u>sense</u>' of the text, however, differ for each writer. Consequently, we assume that writers with different previous experience in the use of writing modes may require different ways to facilitate their writing process.

In our research project, we observed 20 professional writers who worked with speech technology as a writing device for the first time. This group was divided into two groups: a group with previous classical dictating experience and one without previous classical dictating experience. The participants were all observed when writing in their own professional context. In previous articles (Leijten, 2005; Leijten & Van Waes, 2005b), we described two case studies that focussed on the adaptation, learning, and writing processes of these initial speech recognition users. We tried to answer the question whether the writers' previous writing experiences (keyboard-based word processing versus classical dictating) would influence their adaptation to writing with speech recognition. The very detailed analyses of the case studies showed that the writer with previous classical dictating experience adhered more explicitly to the habits developed in the traditional dictating writing mode, whereas the writer without previous dictating experience stuck more to a fragmented writing process typical for a writer using a word processor. Speech recognition seems to create a writing environment that is open for different writing styles. Both writers explicitly use the speech mode as an input device, but hold to their previous writing profile throughout the adaptation process and hardly seem to deviate from the style that they reported in a questionnaire on writing profiles (Jacobs, Opdenacker, & Van Waes, 2005). In other words, the speech recognition mode itself does not seem to trigger writers to adapt a specific writing style, as opposed to what happens when writers have to adapt to write their texts in either the dictating or the word processor mode.

An additional quantitative study (Leijten & Van Waes, 2005b) that focussed on the use of writing modes (speech versus keyboard & mouse) showed that writers with previous dictating experience make less use of the speech mode than writers without previous dictating experience. Especially in the second half of the writing process, the use of speech input decreases for the experienced group. We could not find an explanation for these results solely based on these studies. Why do experienced dictators not use speech as much, although they already have experience in this way of writing? Is the text produced so far on the screen — and especially the misrecognitions — too distractive for them compared to their previous writing experience? Instead of a (correct) mental representation of the text produced so far, the writers are now faced with a (imperfect) visualized text on the screen. Therefore, a possible explanation for the lower percentage of speech input for experienced dictators could be that, based on their experience, they prefer to correct the errors in their text in the keyboard & mouse mode. For classical dictators, the speech mode might be primarily associated with the production of new text, and the keyboard & mouse mode with the revision of the first draft. This would seem a possible explanation since we see that also the number of switches or shifts from 'speech input' to 'non-speech input' drops considerably in the second half of the writing process for the experienced dictators.

To support this reasoning, we describe a case study in this chapter in which we explore the writing strategies related to repairs, and describe the relation between the use of writing modes and the repair behaviour.

In the preceding section, we have situated the present study in the broader context of previous and related research. In Section 2, we present the research questions. In the next section, we shortly describe the research project this study is based on and present the categorization model we developed to analyse the 'repair behaviour'[1] of the writers. In the repair analysis, we study the way in which the participants deal with technical problems and revisions while writing. In Section 4, we give a detailed analysis of the case study in which the writing process of a participant with previous (classical) dictating experience is compared with a participant who did not have this experience. The participants are both lawyers with comparable working and computer experience. The characteristics of their writing process are described from the different perspectives presented in the categorization model. Conclusions are drawn in Section 5, followed by a discussion of the broader perspective of the research project and related to further research.

2   Research Questions

As a sequel to the previous studies on the influence of speech recognition on writing processes, we would like to focus this study on the repair strategy of initial speech recognition users. We would like to explain why experienced dictators make less use of the speech mode than non-dictators. Because the participants in the study were either familiar with word processing and classical dictating or only with word processing, we were able to take up this dissimilarity in their initial writing experience. The main research question of this study is: What is the effect of errors in 'the text produced so far' on the reviewing strategy of novice speech recognition users? Subquestions are: How are repairs distributed over the writing process? What is the effect of repairs on the monitoring of writing modes? When do writers (prefer to) repair an error during the writing process? To answer these questions, we have developed a categorization model that has enabled us to describe the specific characteristics of the errors that could occur in speech recognition-based writing.

3   Description of the Case Study

In this section, we describe the categorization model we developed to reveal the repair strategies of the writers involved in the study. First, we give a description of the participants and the writing tasks that they were involved in. Then, we explain the design and procedure of the research study (for a full description see Leijten & Van Waes, 2005b).

---

[1] We have adapted the notion of 'repair' from research in the field of conversation analysis. Among other things, it is used to refer to corrections of misunderstanding and mishearing in natural speech (Schegloff, Jefferson, & Sacks, 1977).

3.1   Participants and Writing Tasks

The two participants in this case study, Frederik and Steven, were selected from the larger group of participants that took part in the research project described above. Because the focus in this study is on the difference in writing experience, we selected, on the one hand, a lawyer who did not have any previous dictating experience, and on the other a lawyer with the same amount of working experience and the same learning style[2] (Kolb, 1984), but with significant experience in classical dictating. The different tasks the participants conducted were job-related and were part of their normal writing activities, e.g., letters, e-mails or reports. During the observation sessions, we collected both product and process data. The product data gave us information about the length of the texts (e.g., number of words, mean words per sentence), and the duration of the observation. The process data provided us with information about the gradual development of the writing process.

3.2   Design and Procedure

Because the participants were novice users of speech recognition software, they first watched an introductory video — provided by the software company — about the use of the speech technology programme.

The participants were asked to use the speech recognition system during their day-to-day work for about at least 3 hours a week. They could decide for themselves how to use the software and were not restricted to using speech input only. In total, we observed the participants five times, after 1, 3, 6, 9 and 12 hours, while writing in their own environment. In the hours in between, the participants worked for themselves with the speech recognition software.

We collected the writing process data with an online screen camera (Camtasia™) and a sound recorder (Quickrecord™). The online screen camera did not interfere with the writing process of the writers. Apart from a small icon in the tray bar, the recorder was not visible when it recorded all the writer's actions. Because of the combination of the different input modes (keyboard, mouse and speech) we could not use existing key logging programmes.[3]

3.3   Categorization Model: Repairs

To describe the repair process data, we developed a categorization model (Appendix) that takes the complexity of the hybrid writing mode into account and makes the enormous amount of process data accessible for further research.

---

[2] According to Kolb's taxonomy, both Frederik and Steven are accommodators. They scored high on active experimentation and concrete experience. Kolb's model states that people with an accommodative orientation tend to solve problems in a trial-and-error manner.

[3] At this moment we are developing a logging tool that can log speech input (more information on www.inputlog.net).

The model is based on earlier taxonomies for the analysis of writing processes (Severinson Eklundh, 1994; Faigley & Witte, 1981; Hayes & Flower 1980; Karat, Halverson, Horn & Karat, 1999; Lindgren, Sullivan, Lindgren, & Miller, 2006; Van Waes, 1991), and is complemented with new categories that were observed while analysing several recorded sessions in detail. Activities related to the problem-solving process of the participants using speech recognition are the most important additions to the existing taxonomies. This category is referred to as 'repair' behaviour. We use the term 'repair' to refer to the recursive actions writers perform when dealing with technical problems (caused by using keyboard & mouse and speech input) and revisions that occur during the writing processes (for a more detailed description of the model, see Leijten & Van Waes, 2005b).

4 Case Study

The participants, Frederik and Steven, were observed while writing different types of business texts during their day-to-day work. Therefore, their observation sessions differed somewhat in length. For this study, we eliminated the data of the first observation session (after 1 hour), because of the exploratory character. The mean time of the observations in the case study is 21'59" (Frederik: mean = 19'01", Steven: mean = 24'57"). During the observed writing sessions, Frederik produced an average of 19 words/min and Steven 13 words/min.[4] Because of the variable length of the observation sessions, the texts also differed in length. Their texts were between 267 and 449 words per session (Frederik: mean = 355 words; Steven: mean = 330 words).

4.1 General

In this case study, we coded 575 repairs[4] in the four observation sessions in which the participants either solved a technical problem in their text or made a revision (Frederik: mean = 76.25 per session and Steven: mean = 67.50 per session). A technical problem can be labelled as a misrecognition when dictated text is misrecognized and words appears differently than was intended. When a command is misrecognized and the computer performs another action, the technical problem is called a command misrecognition. For example, instead of executing the command 'end of the sentence' correctly, 'end of the sentence' appears on the screen.

In Table 1, the number of repairs per minute is presented. The table shows that Frederik executes 4.02 repairs/min on average, while Steven carries out about 2.70 repairs/min.

Of all repairs, technical problems represent 70% and revisions about 30%. In absolute numbers, only a few revisions were made in every writing session (min. 10–max. 34). Perhaps this is due to the large number of technical problems the writers encountered. As a result, these errors could have distracted the writers.

Table 2 shows that Frederik has to deal with different types of technical problems than Steven. Whereas Steven has a lot of command misrecognitions to repair (44.4%), Frederik

---

[4] Some numbers might differ from previous studies because the categorization model in this article is more elaborated than in Leijten and Van Waes (2005b).

Table 1: Mean number of repairs, problems and revisions per minute.

	Frederik (+D)		Steven (−D)	
	Mean	**SD**	**Mean**	**SD**
Repairs per minute	4.02	0.28	2.70	0.60
Technical problems per minute	2.89	0.72	2.04	0.70
Revisions per minute	1.13	0.60	0.66	0.14

Table 2: Type of technical problems in percentages.

	Frederik (+D)	Steven (−D)
Technical problems	$n=221$	$n=205$
Misrecognitions	62.4%	51.3%
Command misrecognitions	12.7	44.4
Dictated text as command	5.4	0
Other	19.5	4.4

has a lot of 'other' technical problems. Frederik had to deal with many unaccountable errors caused by the software. This might be (partly) explained by the fact that Frederik — in contrast with Steven — does not actually 'train' the software by repeating words that are misrecognized. Frederik prefers to correct errors as they appear and not to prevent them from happening again, whereas Steven anticipates certain errors and adapts his writing behaviour to the speech technology.

More than 60% of the repairs (technical problems and revisions) are situated at the sentence level, which is quite a high percentage of higher-level repairs. Previous analyses of the reviewing behaviour showed that in general writers who write on a computer are more concerned with lower-level aspects of the texts (Van Waes & Schellens, 2003). Frederik treats both types of repair similarly. He solves about 75% of the technical problems and the revisions within the section, and 25% outside the section. Steven seems to adapt his strategy to the type of repair. He solves 93.1% of his technical problems within the section. For revisions, this percentage is 63.6. Also the goal of the revisions differs for both participants. Frederik mostly revises to make formal changes and to correct typing errors (64.3%), whereas Steven's revisions are for 69.7% content based.

4.2   Distribution of the Repairs over the Writing Process

If we take a look at the distribution of the repairs over the writing process, we notice that Frederik carries out more repairs in the second half of the writing process than in the first half, 67% versus 33%. Steven, on the other hand, performs 56% of his repairs in the first half and 44% in the second half of the writing process. If we divide the writing processes of Frederik and Steven in five intervals (see Figure 2), a more clearly defined pattern emerges. Frederik's writing process is characterized by some repairs in the beginning, but he performs

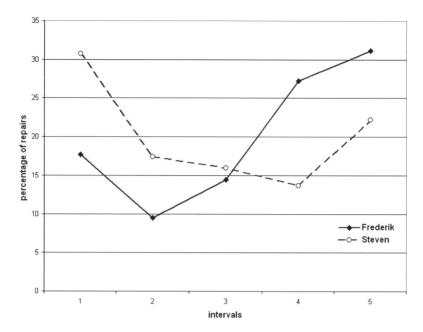

Figure 2: Percentage of repairs per interval (5).

most of his repairs at the end of his writing sessions. Steven, on the other hand, begins his writing session with a large amount of repairs. We can explain this difference by referring to Steven's strategy to dictate also personal names, addresses, postcodes and numbers (cf. supra). This causes a lot of speech recognition problems, which he prefers to repair with speech immediately, in order to be able to use them later on again. In the middle of his writing process, some repairs occur, but reaching the end, the amount of repairs increases again, mostly because of his intensive revising of his text in the final stage of the writing session.

This pattern is affirmed by the number of attempts to repair an error. Frederik solved 88% of his repairs in the first attempt compared to Steven's 66%. In 26% of the repairs, Steven is willing to try two to three times. Frederik will try two to three times in only 10% of his repairs. The repair strategy of Frederik is more static than Steven's. The example in Figure 3 illustrates Frederik's repair behaviour. In this fragment, he is confronted with a misrecognition. To repair it, he switches from speech recognition to keyboard & mouse — using shortcuts.

As mentioned above, we analysed the repairs on two different levels: the level of the error and the level of the error correction. These levels differ only in 2.30% of the repairs of Frederik. Steven on the other hand more frequently tried to repair errors on a different level than the actual problem occurred. In 11.48% of the repairs the levels differ. To illustrate this strategy we have transcribed a short fragment in which Steven solves an error that occurred at word level (Figure 4). However, instead of only deleting the word 'a' he prefers to dictate the whole text segment again.

The distribution of technical problems and revisions over the two halves are almost the same for both writers. In the first half of the writing process, repairs consist of 80% technical problems, and in the second half this amount drops to 70%. Similar to the reviewing

0.10.10	Now she has agreed in a contract with buyer with her buyer	that before the 20th of September
	Now she has agreed in a contract |wit buyer |[35] with her buyer	that before |a 20th septemvir |[36]
	✎	|[35] ✎ctrl + ←←← ctrl + ⊠⊠ ctrl+ →→ ✎

Figure 3: Short transcription of repair behaviour Frederik (+D).

0.02.47	You state that my client has to get these before the end of the month	before the end of the month
	You state that my client has to get these | a before the end of the month |[10]	before the end of the month
	✎	<undo |[10]>

Figure 4: Short transcription of repair behaviour Steven (−D).

behaviour in writing with a word processor, both writers revise twice as much in the second half of the writing process as in the first half.

4.3   Effect of Repairs on Modus Monitoring

Speech recognition enables writers to produce and to revise their text with speech input. Consequently, writers that switch between the subprocesses of formulating and revising can either choose to stick to the same writing mode or to switch between writing modes. In our previous analyses we noticed quite a lot of mode switches. From a cognitive perspective, and based on the observation that in the adaptation phase writers often experienced problems in navigating their text with speech, we hypothesized that these mode switches might frequently co-occur with the writer's decision to execute a revision or other repair.

In contrast to what we expected, our analyses of the case study analysis show that both Frederik and Steven do not switch writing modes in about 75–80% of the repairs. However, their overall writing profile is quite different. If we analyse the most preferred writing mode before a repair, we see a contrastive picture. Frederik uses keyboard & mouse before a repair in 73.4% of the cases as opposed to Steven who uses speech in 75% of the instances. In other words, Frederik holds on to using keyboard & mouse, while Steven prefers to continue to write with speech. The occurrence of errors in the text produced so far hardly seems to influence this behaviour.

If we refine the analysis and take a closer look at the first and second half of their writing processes, we see an even more different pattern for Frederik and Steven (Table 3). In general, Frederik has to deal with more repairs in the second half than in the first half, but he also switches more from speech to keyboard or mouse in the first half. Steven on the other hand, shows a more constant pattern.

If we add to this the distribution of the writing mode and the mode switches within both halves, we see quite an inconstant pattern for Frederik. In the first half of the writing process, the writing modes of speech versus keyboard & mouse are used almost equally before a repair, but in the second half Frederik prefers to write and make repairs with keyboard & mouse. That is the reason why he almost does not have to switch in the second half; his main writing mode is already keyboard & mouse. However, in the first half he switches about 35% from speech to another writing mode.

Table 3: The percentage of writing modes and switches per half of the writing sessions.

	Frederik (+D)		Steven (−D)	
	1st half (*n* =101)	**2nd half** (*n* =204)	**1st half** (*n* =151)	**2nd half** (*n* =119)
Writing mode used before repair				
Speech	49.5	15.2	84.8	63.0
Keyboard & mouse	50.5	84.8	15.2	37.0
Type of writing mode switch				
No switch	60.4	81.4	78.1	82.4
From speech to keyboard or mouse	34.7	12.3	14.6	16.8
Other	4.9	6.4	7.3	0.8

Steven's mode behaviour is quite constant in the first and second half of his writing process. Although the percentage of speech before a repair drops from 85% to 63%, Steven prefers speech in the first and in the second half of the writing process. He leaves the speech-writing mode to make a repair only in 15% of the total amount of switches in the writing process. In other words, he prefers to produce and repair his text with speech recognition.

4.4   Immediate or Delayed Repair of Errors

When writing with speech recognition, writers have two options to repair an error. Their first option is to repair it immediately, and they can try to write a 'first time final draft'. The second option writers have is to dictate a first draft without paying much attention to technical problems or revisions, delaying the repair of errors to the final writing phase. Frederik's and Stevens writing processes can be characterized by a combination of both options (see Table 4).

If we take a look at the moment and direction of the repairs (immediate versus not immediate and backward versus forward, cf. supra), we notice that about 83% of Steven's repairs are solved immediately, and that Frederik solves only 43% of his repairs immediately. Furthermore, we see that about 86% of Steven's repairs are backward movements in the text as opposed to 53% for Frederik. In other words, Frederik basically opts to repair and revise his text after a section has been completed, or even waits until the first draft of the text is completed. This organization of the writing process corresponds to research findings that report a more linear development of the writing process of dictators in contrast to a more recursive development of the non-dictators' writing processes.

In general, Frederik saves 43% of his repairs for the second draft, whereas Steven solves his problems in 87% of the time in the first draft. Both participants deal differently with technical problems and revisions. Table 5 shows that Frederik solves most of his technical problems in the first draft (65.6%), but postpones revisions to the second draft (64.3%). Steven on the other hand, prefers both to solve technical problems and to revise in the first draft.

Table 4: Moment and direction of repair.

	Frederik (+D) %	Steven (−D) %
Moment of repair		
Immediate	43.0	83.3
Not immediate	57.0	16.7
Direction of repair		
Backwards	52.5	86.3
Forwards	47.5	13.7

A further analysis of the repair behaviour shows that Frederik only solves 35% of the misrecognitions immediately. This is in contrast with Steven, who solves 79% of the misrecognitions immediately at the point of utterance. The percentage of command misrecognitions solved immediately is even higher for Steven, 98%. He does not seem to tolerate this kind of large error. Frederik solves 57% of the command misrecognitions straight away, and seems not to notice the others in the text produced so far at this stage in the writing process. In Table 6, we refine the type of errors into the categories: size, technicality and location of error.

Both participants differ in the amount and type of errors they solve immediately. However, both writers do solve nonexistent words as a result from typing errors immediately. They both do not tolerate this kind of larger error in their text. Frederik almost solves all the keyboard & mouse errors in his text, but is more tolerant of the other categories. Steven is not that tolerant, and prefers to immediately solve almost all larger errors, typical speech recognition errors and errors that are located at the point of utterance.

5   Conclusions and Discussion

In this chapter, we have described the repair strategies of two writers with different dictating experience. The study confirms the potential hybrid character of speech recognition as a writing mode, since it combines characteristics of both classical dictating and keyboard-based word processing. One of the main differences between classical dictating and dictating with speech recognition is that the writer gets feedback on the screen almost immediately. The case analysis presented here also lends support to the idea that the interaction with 'the text produced so far' is an important aspect of the task environment in the organization of the writing process (cf. also Hayes' model). It certainly influences the writing process, but also the extent to which writers use this feedback while dictating differs.

Both participants explicitly use the speech mode as an input device, but also seem to hold to their previous writing profile. Frederik maintained the writing habits he developed by using traditional dictating devices, while Steven holds to his word processing writing style and relies more heavily on the visual feedback of his dictation that appears as typed text on the screen. In other words, the speech recognition mode itself does not seem to trigger writers to adapt a specific writing style, as opposed to what happens when writers have

Table 5: Percentage of technical problems and revision per draft (1st and 2nd).

	Frederik (+D) %	Steven (–D) %
Technical problem		
1st draft	65.6	89.2
2nd draft	34.4	10.8
Revisions		
1st draft	35.7	80.3
2nd draft	64.3	19.7

Table 6: Percentage of errors immediately repaired.

	Frederik (+D) %	Steven (–D) %
Size of error		
Small error (≤2 characters)	47.72	67.24
Large error (>2 characters)	47.03	95.51
Technicality of error		
Typical speech recognition error	40.48	89.63
Keyboard & mouse error	96.15	60.00
Location of error in sentence		
End	64.10	94.15
Beginning and middle	17.78	39.43

to adapt to write their texts in either the dictating or the word processor mode (Schilperoord, 1996; Van Waes & Schellens, 2003).

One of the main differences in the writing process of both writers seems to be related to the mode monitoring in combination with the switching behaviour. Although the amount of switches is comparable for both writers, the strategies to control the writing mode seem to be different. On the one hand, we can conclude that there is no direct effect of repairs on the monitoring of writing modes, because repairs do not directly lead to mode switches, viz. Frederik and Steven do not switch writing modes in about 75–80% of the repairs. On the other , we can conclude that both participants differ in the way they repair their texts. In sum, Steven mainly repairs errors immediately (and backwards) as opposed to Frederik who often postpones the repair of errors, resulting in more grouped (and mostly forwards) repairs. They have developed other strategies. Frederik regularly *ignores* errors that appear in the text produced so far and *postpones* repairing errors to a later stage. Steven some-times *anticipates* on errors and switches writing modes to avoid errors. For example, instead of trying to dictate personal names they switch - before he has to dictate them — to keyboard & mouse and type the name with keyboard & mouse.

So, both participants differ in the way they prefer to repair errors. They also differ in the amount and type of errors they solve immediately. Frederik prefers to solve almost all the keyboard & mouse errors in his text, possibly because he does not have to switch writing modes to solve these repairs. He seems more tolerant of the speech recognition errors and often postpones the correction of those errors. Overall, Steven is not that tolerant and prefers to immediately solve almost all larger errors, typical speech recognition errors and errors that are located at the point of utterance. However, both writers do solve almost all nonexistent words immediately. They seem not to tolerate these kinds of errors in their text.

Is it strange that a writer who prefers a first time final draft, like Steven, does leave some errors in the text unnoticed? Are those errors not solved intentionally or are they overlooked? A possible explanation could be that smaller errors and errors in the beginning of the sentence are easier to miss. Earlier research has already shown that rereading of the text produced so far with the intention to further generate and formulate text, is characterized by a high degree of conceptuality. Writers in those instances do not really evaluate the correctness of their text, but only observe the 'gestalt' of what has been written as a trigger to further text production. So, on the one hand the interaction with the text on the screen can lead to a highly recursive writing process in which every error is repaired almost immediately, but on the other it can also lead to a less recursive writing process in which repairs are made at the end of a section or a text and left unnoticed at the point of utterance.

In an experimental follow-up study, we would like to further explore the repair behaviour of the participants and more specifically the interaction with a (imperfect) 'text produced so far'. We would like to identify different characteristics of the (imperfect) 'text produced so far', and select material from our corpus as input data. In a controlled experiment we would like to present this material to participants in a writing task, in order to be able to better describe the interaction with the 'text produced so far', and evaluate the cognitive load caused by imperfect representations.

Notes

This doctoral research is supervised by Prof. Dr. Mr. P. van den Hoven (University of Utrecht, The Netherlands), Dr. D. Janssen (University of Utrecht, The Netherlands) and Prof. Dr. L. Van Waes (University of Antwerp, Belgium).

This study is part of a 'New Research Project' on the influence of speech recognition on the writing process (Research grant of the University of Antwerp 2000–2002 and 2002–2004).

Acknowledgements

We would like to thank all the people who participated in this study, and especially Frederik and Steven, for their willingness to learn to work with speech recognition and let us observe them while doing so. We are also grateful to Lernout and Hauspie (ScanSoft, now Nuance) who gave us a free license to work with VoiceXpress Legal™ during the course of this study.

Appendix: Categorization Model for the Repair Analysis

REPAIRS

Type of repair	1. Technical problems	2. Revisions
Writing mode before repair	1. Keyboard 2. Mouse	3. Speech
Writing mode during repair	1. Keyboard 2. Mouse 3. Speech 4. Keyboard & mouse	5. Combination speech & keyboard or mouse 6. Training module
Absolute time	Absolute time of start correction in writing process	
Halves	Position of the correction in writing process by dividing session into two equal halves	
Level of correction	1. Character 2. Word 3. Sentence segment	4. Sentence 5. Section 6. Punctuation
Remoteness of correction	1. Within sentence 2. Within section	3. Outside section
Writing phase	1. First draft	2. Second draft
Direction of correction	1. Backward (before point of inscription) 2. Forward (after point of inscription)	

TECHNICAL PROBLEMS

Type of technical (taxonomy partly based on Karat et al., 1999)	1. Single misrecognition 2. Multiple misrecognition 3. Command misrecognition (symbol/punctuation)	4. Command mis-recognition (function keys) 5. Dictation as command 6. No recognition 7. Other
Intention & outcome	1. Word 2. Symbol 3. Function key	4. Navigation 5. No input/output
Cause of technical problem	1. User 2. Speech recognizer	3. Environment 4. No explanation
Number of attempts	Absolute number of attempts to solve problem	
Success rate	1. Successful	2. Not successful
Location of the error in the sentence (mathematical)	1. Beginning 2. Middle	3. End
Occurrence of error	1. In speech recognition 2. In keyboard & mouse mode	3. In both writing modes

Appendix: (*Continued*)

Existence of output error	1. Occurrence in SR	2. Occurrence in SR & K&M
Error size	1. Small ($\leq$2 characters different)	2. Large ($>$2 characters different)

REVISIONS

Type of revision	1. Addition 2. Deletion 3. Substitution	4. Reordering 5. Permutation
Goal of revision	1. Form 2. Meaning	3. Typing errors

Section II:

Writing and Communication

Chapter 4

Learning to Write in the Information Age: A Case Study of Schoolchildren's Writing in Sweden

Ylva Hård af Segerstad and Sylvana Sofkova Hashemi

A great deal of our communication is done by means of writing. Today, in addition to pen and paper, we use computers, the Internet and devices such as mobile phones. Current technology helps us to produce texts easily and rapidly and literacy rates have never been so high. How do children and adolescents use writing today? How do information and communication technologies influence writing in other domains? Is the use of writing in the new media a 'threat' to the standard written language? How can writing aids be adapted to better support the writing process? These questions are central to the three-year project Learning to Write in the Information Society which we report on here. The project investigates language written by schoolchildren in different writing settings and the effects of computers and other channels of communication, e.g., web chat and text messaging via mobile phones. For this project, we gather formal as well as informal texts, written both by hand and by computer. We also carry out writing experiments with e-mail, SMS and web chat. Texts in computer-mediated communication share several features with texts written by children, displaying reductions that are not found in traditional writing and imitations of spoken language.

1 Introduction

The role of written language has clearly changed in the past few decades due to the emergence of new information and communication channels (e.g., Herring, 2001). A great deal of our communication is done by means of writing, which in addition to traditional pen and paper, is mediated by the computer, the Internet and devices such as mobile phones.

Hård Af Segerstad, Y. & Sofkova Hashemi, S. (2005). Learning to write in the information age: A case study of schoolchildren's writing in Sweden. In L. Van Waes, M. Leijten & C. Neuwirth (Vol. Eds.) & G. Rijlaarsdam (Series Ed.), Studies in Writing: Vol. 17. Writing and Digital Media (pp. 49–63). Oxford: Elsevier.

Word processing and sending messages via e-mail are among the most common activities on computers for both adults and children. Other popular channels of communication that enable written interaction are web chat and instant messaging on the Internet, as well as short message service (SMS or text messaging) via mobile phones.

Computers influence our writing in many ways and are well suited for all three stages of the writing process: planning, writing and revision. Texts are produced easily and rapidly with current technology and widely distributed. Writing is no longer the sole domain of writing professionals like journalists, novelists and scientists. People write more in general these days, both adults and children. In general, writing on a computer enhances both the motivation to write, revise or completely change a text (e.g., Daiute, 1985; Jedeskog, 1993; Pontecorvo, 1997).

Although writing is increasingly mediated by *information and communication technologies* (ICTs), such as word processors, chat and mobile phones, we know little about how children actually use this technology, how their writing is performed in different settings and whether there is any influence from their writing during leisure time on their writing at school. Previous studies have focused on children's use of new communication tools or their writing acquisition as such (e.g., Suoranta & Lehtimaki, 2004; Liberg, 1990; Pontecorvo, 1997).

The research presented in this chapter describes a project called *Learning to Write in the Information Society*, initiated in 2003 at the Department of Linguistics at Göteborg University, Sweden. The project is sponsored by *Vetenskapsrådet* (The Swedish Research Council). The project focuses on the following questions: *How do children and adolescents use writing today? How do ICTs influence the writing in other domains? Is the use of writing in the new media a 'threat' to the standard written language? How can writing aids be adapted to better support the writing process?* The project aims to investigate written language by schoolchildren in different writing settings and the effects of the use of computers and other channels of communication, such as web chat and text messaging via mobile phones.

We collect texts written by schoolchildren at intermediate and senior levels (aged from 10 to 15), both texts written in school (for example, free narratives and reports) and texts written during leisure time (for example, SMS and web diaries). We are able to study the whole writing process by observations in the classroom. This includes studying, how they interact with different writing aids, such as spelling-, grammar- and style checkers. We interview them about their writing habits and experiences of writing.

In the following, we will give a short description of the studies that form the background of the present project. It is followed by a section in which we discuss writing activities, undertaken at school as well as during these children's leisure time. We will also give an initial analysis of the data, which have been collected, and then briefly describe the writing programs and writing aids that the pupils utilize with the purpose of demonstrating how these could be modified to give better support to children and adolescents and their writing needs. We will conclude with a discussion on the consequences of written language in change and a short section on future work within the frames of the project.

Boldface and underlining in the examples indicate features, such as spelling errors and reductions.

2   The Idea Behind the Project

The findings from our doctoral dissertations form the basis of the present project. This work involved analyses of texts written by children aged 9–13 years (Sofkova Hashemi, 2003) and use of written language by teenagers and young adults in computer-mediated communication (Hård af Segerstad, 2002). The analyses of the texts from such different situations showed interesting similarities. Texts written by children very often display reductions on various levels compared to traditional writing. They are also often speech-like in character, which is a prominent feature in texts in computer-mediated communication. Generally, the texts in the two studies were found to diverge in several ways from standard writing. However, the reasons why they did are different. Children at the beginning of the process of learning to write have not yet realized that they have to pay attention to different factors in spoken and written communication. Adult SMS communicators (i.e., people who are no longer in the writing acquisition stage), for instance, reduce their messages with the aim of saving time, effort and space (each message only allowing for 160 characters). We found it interesting to investigate further, which strategies schoolchildren use when they write using the new types of communications media, and how these channels of communication affect their writing acquisition as well as their use of writing in more formal situations, such as writing at school.

The above-mentioned studies (Hård af Segerstad, 2002; Sofkova Hashemi, 2003) that preceded the present project, also made it clear that writing aids, such as spelling and grammar checkers in word processors and 'auto text' (or predictive text input or 'intelligent dictionary', see for instance www.nokia.com) software used to ease text production in mobile phones, did not adequately support the needs of writers in the situations in which they were used. Writing tools in word processors follow normative written language grammar, and use rules that are based on texts by adult writers, developed to help adults with their writing difficulties. Thus, the tools are not sufficiently targeted to support children in their writing process. From a pedagogical point of view, the tools do not help children in their writing acquisition or allow them to practice writing.

Writing tools in mobile phones are based on a limited corpus of linguistic material, which is adapted to a different type of written communication that has quite different conditions than communication via SMS messages (e.g., MacKenzie & Soukoreff, 2002; Gutowitz, 2003). Better adapted and thus more effective writing aids would have to consider the situations in which communication takes place as well as corpora based on the kind of language that is used by different populations in the various media. Further analyses would have to focus on how schoolchildren use these writing aids and how tools can be improved to support children's writing acquisition and writing needs.

3   Writing in School

In the initial phase of the project, we established contact with the intermediate and senior levels (160 children aged between 10 and 15) of three randomly chosen primary schools in the Gothenburg area. Teachers, parents and children all agreed to participate in the study.

We started by gathering texts written in school, observing the writing activities, interviewing the pupils about their writing habits and encouraging them to share texts written in their leisure time. We describe in the following section the on-going writing activities at the three schools and present an initial analysis of the school texts written by the pupils involved in the project.

3.1   Writing Activities at the Schools

From the interviews with the pupils and our observations in the schools, it is clear that the amount of text production is relatively large at all three schools. The types of text material are similar in all the schools. The material consists of assignments that often integrate several subjects, from book reviews, reports on geography and society, historical essays, art studies, etc. The pupils report on their 'research work' in booklets or on 'wall charts'. In addition to factual reports, the booklets include short narratives, poems, drawings and pictures. Another type of text comprises narratives and themed assignments, often connected to some activity the pupils have experienced (e.g., a visit to a museum), thoughts about the future or the past (e.g., 'Letter from the future', 'School memories'), or texts on a given topic. The pupils practice reading comprehension, parts of speech and sentence analysis in their reading books. Handwriting and dictation were scheduled once a week at one of the schools, while the other two schools only offered handwriting training occasionally.

We chose to gather the narratives for the project rather than the factual reports for the reason that research assignments can be presented as bulleted lists and they often include more or less successful paraphrases of different texts from schoolbooks or the Internet. Currently our collection consists of about 400 narratives with themes, such as fairy tales, ghost stories, 'letters from the future' and texts based on headings of different kinds.

The majority of the texts were written by hand. From the initial analysis of the interview material, it seems that many children claim that they prefer to write by hand. They mention that this is because they consider it to be faster, more personal and because it gives them time to think. Others voice more or less the opposite opinion, maintaining that writing on a computer is faster and is more aesthetically pleasing. Furthermore, many of those also point out that writing on a computer saves them the effort of forming letters and aching wrists. In situations where the pupils know that others will read or in some way evaluate their written texts, they consider spelling and layout especially important.

Our observations at the schools reveal that the working procedures of text creating, access and placement of the computers influence the outcome of the writing. The teacher's directions often require the pupil to draw a mind map, write a list of words as notes or even a whole draft by hand before beginning the actual writing. At the intermediate level, we found that there are fewer computers per pupil (approximately 2 per 20 pupils) than at higher levels (approximately 10 per 20 pupils). We also found that the computers at the intermediate level were of inferior quality compared to those at the senior level. According to the pupils, it seems that on the senior level there are enough computers that are considered to be of reasonable quality. However, it seems that gaining access to these computers is sometimes difficult, it may involve looking for a computer in a classroom where a lesson is going on. When this is the case, pupils will often choose to write by hand or take their work home and use their own computer.

Writing on a computer in school often involves making a fair copy from a handwritten draft. Writing directly on a computer almost never occurs in school. School computers are used mostly as typewriters or for searching the Internet, which involves downloading pictures and, to some extent, searching for facts. Only one school used different pedagogical programs e.g., for language and mathematics instruction. This school also scheduled computer lessons and had an IT teacher. At the other schools, this responsibility was taken care of by the form teacher, with varying results. Chat, games and unlimited Internet access were permitted in one of the schools. Schoolwork always took priority, however. At the other schools access was limited or explicitly prohibited and pupils who were discovered chatting or surfing on some prohibited site on the Internet (e.g., *Lunarstorm*) had their access permission revoked.

3.2 School Texts

The pupils were at different stages in writing acquisition. At the intermediate level, most of them had passed the stage of learning to form letters and words. They learn how to segment words, form clauses and express themselves in many different contexts and for different purposes. They improve their grammatical, discursive and strategic competence to convey their thoughts or the content of the message to the reader (cf. Lundberg, 1989; Liberg, 1990; Pontecorvo, 1997; Håkansson, 1998). Our previous studies (Sofkova Hashemi, 2003) show that some of the problems children who are learning to write encounter concern spelling, word segmentation, the use of capitals and punctuation. Furthermore, their writing clearly reflects the language they know best — the spoken language (cf. Teleman, 1991; Sofkova Hashemi, 2003). Their texts are clearly influenced by spoken language and often include different spoken forms (e.g., *våran* 'our', *den dära* 'that there'), reductions on various levels typical for spoken language (e.g., *rasa* instead of *rasade* 'fell', i.e., the tense ending on verbs is dropped), direct speech, onomatopoetics and dialectal expressions. Grammatical violations are also quite frequent (about nine times more frequent than in texts written by adults, cf. Sofkova Hashemi, 2003). Among the most usual errors are -ed tense dropping (as shown above), omitted or added words in clauses, agreement in noun phrases, verb form after auxiliary verbs, choice of words, etc. (cf. Sofkova Hashemi, 2003). Written language is generally standardized with less (dialectal) variation compared with spoken language. Learning a written language means not only acquiring its more or less explicit norms and rules, but also learning to deal with the overall writing system (cf. Teleman, 1991).

Initial analyses of the collected texts from the schools show occurrences of spelling errors and split words, as in example (1), where a consonant is missing in *ville* 'wanted' and the compound *färgglada* 'colourful' is misspelled in the first part (*g* is misplaced by *j*) and split into two words.

(1) *Vikingarna **vile** ha **färj glada** kläder* (girl, 4th year)
   The Vikings **wanted** to have **colour-ful** clothes.

The influence of spoken language is also obvious and is characterized for example, by the use of different spoken variants, as the dialectal *vart* instead of *varit* 'been' in (2) below. A quite common phenomenon concerns the realization of the personal pronouns *de* 'they' and *dem* 'them', also seen in (2). The text in the example shows a grammatical violation in the number agreement between the plural pronoun *många* 'many' and the singular noun *land* 'country':

(2) *Vi tittade på hur många land vikingarna hade vart, i och*
b.l.a. hette frankrike ("frankeriket.") **Dem** *hade också* **vart** *i Asien,*
Afrika, Amerika, och Europa (boy, 4th year)
We looked at how **many country[sg]** the Vikings had **been** to and among other things
France was called ("franken-empire"). **Them** had also **been** to Asia, Africa, America
and Europe.

Clauses are often joined together without conjunctions, as in example (3). This sample
also contains four misspellings, where the first one by reducing the final 't' in *det* 'it' creates a new form *de* 'they'. The three others all lack consonants (*kulle* 'hill', *stack* 'drove',
pinne 'stick').

(3) *Sen la dom jord över så* **de** *blev en* **kule** *sen* **stak** *dom ner en* **pine**. (girl, 4th year)
Then they put earth over so **they** became a **hill** then they **drove** a **stick** into the ground.

Speech-like reductions occur, such as omission of tense endings on verbs, as in example (4).

(4) *Jag satt och läste en bok som* **handla** *om två män som var*
vilsna ute på havet och dom var i en ganska lik situation som vi
var i nu. (boy, 7th year)
I was sitting and reading a book that **be[spoken past]** about two men that were lost out
at sea and they were in a rather similar situation to the one we were in now.

In (5) we see an example of an incorrect form of the verb in an infinitive phrase. Here
the infinitive forms (*gå* 'go', *ta* 'take', *sätta* 'put') are the correct forms rather than the
present tense used. The underlined words mark misspellings, first the word *frysen* 'the
freezer' written with double *s*, then two words are written together *den i* 'it into' and,
finally, a compound word is split into three parts *mikrovågsugnen* 'the microwave oven'.

(5) *Det har blivit en vana av studerande barn* **att går** *till* <u>*fryssen*</u> *och* **tar** *ut en fryst pizza*
och **sätter** <u>*deni*</u> <u>*mikro vågs ungnen*</u>. (boy, 6th year)
It has become a habit of studying children **to goes** to <u>the freezer</u> and **takes** out a frozen
pizza and **puts** <u>it-into</u> <u>the micro-wave-oven</u>.

We find other relatively common inconsistencies in spelling and grammar, as in (6). In
this sample, the writer uses the form *är* 'is/are' and the non-standard spoken variant *e*
'is/are' in the same text. This text also gives a good example of adjoined sentences.

(6) *Jag har varit här i Mallorca och jag glömde säga att jag äger ett hotell Grand hotell*
det **är** *därför jag köpte huset här. Jag har två barn som* **e** *7 och 10 år dom* **e** *intresserade av tennis.* (boy, 8th year)
I have been here in Mallorca and I forgot to say that I own a hotel Grand hotel this is
the reason I bought the house here. I have two children that **are** 7 and 10 years old they
are interested in tennis.

4   Writing during Leisure Time

Our data collection also contains various kinds of texts created during leisure time, mainly web diaries and self-presentations, SMS messages, a few chat sessions and e-mail messages. We describe below the writing activities typical of the pupils' leisure time and present our initial analyses of the text material from web diaries and SMS messages.

4.1   Writing Activities During Leisure Time

The interviews that we conducted with the pupils reveal that all of them have access to computers at home and that most of them also have Internet access, which is not at all uncommon in contemporary Sweden. Many of them chat every day during their leisure time, either using *MSN Messenger* or community web sites, which they are members of. In these communities, it is common to have a text-based presentation of oneself (sometimes also with photos or drawings), which is updated from time to time. The members chat with friends and other people who are logged in, and many of them also write their own diaries if that is an option. Many of the older pupils are members of *lunarstorm.se*, while others are members of sites, such as *helgon.net*. Young girls talk about horses on *stallet.se* ('the stable.se'), entertain themselves with witchcraft à la Harry Potter at *hogwarts.nu*, or visit *kamrat.nu*. Younger boys prefer to play games, both on-line (e.g., *runescape.com*) and locally on their computers. Some of them are also members of *hogwarts.nu*.

On-line chatting using instant messenger tools, such as *MSN Messenger* completely dominates writing activities during leisure time. Many pupils, mostly found in the older age group, also write and send SMS messages to their friends. However, as this service is not free of charge, it is not as widespread as chatting on-line which does not cost anything. E-mail was found only to be used occasionally and seems to fulfil quite different goals, such as transferring files with texts for school assignments between the school and the home or to send files containing sounds and graphics.

Some pupils write diaries by hand at home and also their own narratives, both by hand and on a computer. A few pupils said that they create their own magazines or comics at home and a few also write letters in the traditional sense. The pupils at all three schools have homework more or less every day, but specific writing assignments do not seem to be common. However, many pupils take their school assignments home, either because they do not have enough time to finish them in class or because they prefer to write in peace and quiet in their home environment. Those who choose to write at home using a computer very often type directly without the use of handwritten drafts.

4.2   Web Diaries and SMS

Out of the texts that the pupils created during their leisure time, we were able to examine texts written in various environments, mainly web diaries and self-presentations, SMS messages and a few chat sessions and e-mail messages.

Our previous analyses of texts from e-mail, web chat, instant messaging (short messages between people who are on-line, transmitted instantly) and SMS show that new technology puts demands on the user who has to adapt his or her writing and language according to the specific conditions of the situation. These communicative situations differ in several ways from one another, for example, in terms of the goal of communication, level of synchronicity, method of text input and number of participants involved. An SMS message, for instance, is limited in the number of characters it may contain and is rather cumbersome and time-consuming to type on the keypad of the mobile phone. Added to this is the fact that there is only a tiny screen on which to read the text. Language use in the different modes of computer-mediated communication reveals several strategies used in order to save time, effort and space, as well as to compensate for information that might be missing in written media (Hård af Segerstad, 2002).

Computer-mediated written language often has speech-like characteristics, and usually implicitly refers to persons, things and actions that are immediate and obvious to the interlocutors. Language use is often reduced compared to standard writing, and words and phrases are frequently abbreviated. The so-called *smileys* or *emoticons* are used in imitation of facial expressions and convey attitudes and frames of mind. Both underscore and capitalizations are used in imitation of tone of voice and for expressing emphasis. Asterisks framing words or expressions typically convey activities, attitudes or frames of mind. Information that can be easily understood without explicit reference is often left out, as in the case of omission of subject pronoun, auxiliary verbs and prepositions. Reduction or omission, of verb endings and the occurrence of invectives and dialectal expressions give messages the character of spontaneous spoken language (see Hård af Segerstad, 2002).

A preliminary analysis of texts gathered from web diaries shows that spelling is not considered very important, which is exemplified in (7) below. Example (7) also highlights how capitals are used to express emphasis. Use of sentence-initial capital is often neglected, as shown in (8) and (9). Abbreviations on both word and phrase level are frequent, exemplified in (8) in which *kul* ('fun') is abbreviated as *ql*, and in (9) in which *i alla fall* ('anyway') is abbreviated as *iaf*.

(7) *JJJJJJJJJJJJJJJJJJAAAAAAAAAAAAAAAAAAA **severige van** över **negeria** haha vi vinner säkert fotbolls-VM haha vi är mäktiga heja **sverig*** (boy, 8th year)
     YYYYYYYYYEEEEEEEEEEEESSSSSSSS **seweden wonn** against **negeria** haha we will surely win the soccer-world cup haha we are powerful go **swedn**

(8) *nu ska jag ringa emma.... jätte **ql**!!!* (girl, 6th year)
     now I will call emma.... great **fun**!!!

(9) *en jädra bra dag är det **iaf**. hittills.* (girl, 8th year)
     a bloody good day it is **anyway**. so far.

English words and expressions are common in the web diaries, as shown in examples (10) and (11).

(10) *det snööaar på **the mountain of darkness**. uääch..trååk..ont i huvet..* (girl, 8th year)
      it is snooowing on **the mountain of darkness**. ouch..boooring..pain in the head..

(11) **The point** *är att jag kan inte ha en pojkvän* ... (girl, 8th year)
   The point is that I'm unable to have a boyfriend ...

We also find smileys and asterisks conveying frames of mind of various kinds. An example of a crying smiley is shown in (12). Asterisks in example (13) mark sighing and a rather tired state of mind. In (13), we find further examples of spoken language influence, where the pupil chooses to abbreviate *är det* 'is it' to *e d* and to render *inte* 'not' in the dialectal form *itte*.

(12) *jag mår jättedåligt. :'(muääääh*... (girl, 8th year)
   I'm feeling really bad :'(uaaaa...

(13) *nästa vecka **e d** ju Karaoke kväll ***suck*** men ska **itte** sjunga ska sköta maskinen*
   puhh (girl, year 8)
   next week **it is** Karaoke night *sigh* but will **not** sing will take care of the machine
   whew

Language use in the web diaries is often influenced by spoken language, containing dialectal expressions, speech-imitating spelling and reductions of various kinds, as shown in example (14) below. It shows several of the phenomena already mentioned; capitals used for emphasis, speech-imitating spelling and reductions on word level, a whole string of dialectal expressions (*GÖÖÖT* 'goood', *serru* 'you see') and invectives (*fan* 'damn'), abbreviated words (*e d* -> *är det* 'is it', *d e* -> *det är* 'it is'), omission of sentence initial capital, omission of sentence final full stop, splitting of compounded nouns (*jul lov* -> *jullov* 'Christmas holidays'). At the end of the entry we find a creative neologism (*bästpussen*), meaning 'super great', or the like — the meaning is somewhat difficult to figure out).

(14) *GÖÖÖT!! serru e d jul lov fan va gött d e asså*
   aja de e bara bästpussen! (girl, 8th year)
   GOOOD!! you see is it Christmas holidays damn how cool it is man well it is just super great!

We have also analysed SMS messages sent by the pupils. These are often much shorter than the entries in the web diaries, mostly for the simple reason that an SMS is limited in the number of characters per message. The messages are also different in the sense that they are used for social interactions, such as asking how someone is doing, what they are up to and what their plans are, as well as expressing all manner of salutations. These messages show lexical and structural features similar to those that we found in the web diary entries. Messages that consist of multiple sentences are often strung together without full stops and capital letters to mark sentence boundaries. Smileys and English words are also used, as we see in (15).

(15) *Gott nytt år **babies** ;) (alla **girls**, kan inte skicka till alla*
   för mina fingrar dör här i vetlanda) puss puss (girl, 8th year)
   Happy new year **babies** ;) (all [you] **girls**, can't send to everybody
   cause my fingers are dying here in vetlanda) kiss kiss

Spoken language influence is evident in different types of word level reductions, as the three examples below illustrate. In (16), we also encounter proper names rendered in lower case only (*mona* and *alice*). Dialectal expressions, such as the particle *la* corresponding to the standard *väl* 'well' used in (18) with a cohortative meaning are also common, as well as the non-standard abbreviations *lr* for *eller* ('or').

(16) *Hej **va gö** du då? **Ja e me** mona och alice.* (girl, 6th year)
      Hi **what** you **doin**? **I am with** mona and alice.

(17) *Tack **dt** samma **cs** på **onsda** kjam ankan* (girl, 8th year)
      Thanks **the** same to you **see** you on **wednesday** huggies the duck

(18) Du kan **la** slå en pling om du **e** hemmsa **lr** nåt? (girl, 8th year)
      Why don't you call me if you **are** home **or** something?

The strategies exemplified above are some of those occurring in the initial analyses of web diary entries and SMS messages that we have gathered so far. Written language here is used in unconventional ways conveying the spontaneous, informal and speech-like nature of the situation, as well as revealing the relation between the participants. Many of the strategies seem to have been developed in order to save time, effort and space. Much of what at first sight looks like sheer linguistic joy of exploration and experimentation may also be ways to overcome matters that might be experienced as cumbersome in text-based communication, and at the same time also to express the writer's personality and command of the various media.

Our interviews revealed that most pupils strongly feel that they write very differently in school situations compared to how they write during their leisure time. They do not, however, see this as a problem, but claim that they are able to change styles with ease. They are often able to give quite concrete examples of the differences in their writing. For example, they mention heavy use of slang expressions, smileys, as well as abbreviations on word, phrase and sentence level. Spelling and things such as the use of sentence-initial capital and standard punctuation are considered to be of less importance in informal texts. What is important is that the receiver can understand the content of a message, and the pupils claim that most of the time it is evident from the context. There are pupils, though, who do not change styles, but claim that they always write 'as usual'. In general, the pupils in our study are clearly conscious of the differences in language use in various situations, which goes against the sometimes voiced fear that they do not have this ability or such insights.

5   Writing Programs and Writing Aids

Some of the subgoals of our project are to investigate how children and adolescents use writing aids in different writing situations and how writing aids influence the writing process. Do they give enough support or could the technologies be developed to support the written production of pupils even more? The writing aids that are available to the pupils in this project are, above all, linguistic editing tools in word processors and prediction software in mobile phones.

5.1   Linguistic Tools

In the section on writing activities in school, we noted that the pupils often start their writing in school by creating a mind map, a list of words or a first version of the text by hand.

They write a fair copy of the handwritten draft either by hand or on the computer, depending on their preferences, the teacher's instructions, or general computer access. When the pupil writes on the computer, the *Microsoft Word* editor and its tools are used without exception, both at school and at home. At all three schools, Word is set so that the pupil gets support during the actual writing, i.e., spelling and grammatical violations are highlighted by colours in the text while the pupil writes.

Our interviews show that the majority of the pupils consider themselves to be good at spelling, but express positive views about spelling and grammar checking tools as support for their writing. Many state that they correct the errors that the computer highlights directly in the obvious cases. Otherwise, they use the right button on the mouse and choose among the alternatives that are displayed. They mention that the computer often marks correct words as incorrect, but this mostly concerns proper names and words they have made up themselves. In cases when they are really uncertain about what is wrong with the text that is selected, or if the computer does not give any alternatives, they usually ask the teacher or another pupil. Others quit the selection in hopes of getting the correct answer from the teacher later on.

How are linguistic tools used in reality? Spell checkers are standard nowadays in most word processors, but they often do not manage to give alternatives to the errors of schoolchildren, partly because their spelling mistakes are too far from the target word, they are phonologically based or coincide with an already existing word. This often requires that a context of more than a single word be analysed and that other methods than those commonly used to construct spelling tools be used. Furthermore, the suggestions for correction are often too many and sometimes not even close to the word. The fact that spell checkers are based on completely different types of errors and texts is clear from the example in Figure 1 that illustrates the response to a common type of error in the schoolchildren's texts. The correct suggestion only occurs as the fourth alternative, despite the fact that the original word *hennes* 'hers' differs only in the exchange of a vowel. It is especially noteworthy that the second (*händes* 'happened' in passive voice) and the third (*häpnes* probably 'the amazed') alternatives given are not even existing words in Swedish.

Figure 1: Example of Microsoft Word's spelling correction of a common type of error.

One gets similar results when using the grammar checker. Computer-based grammar checking for Swedish is fairly recent and has primarily focused on the needs of adult writers (Sågvall Hein, 1999; Arppe, 2000; Birn, 2000; Knutsson, 2001; Domeij, 2003; Sofkova Hashemi, 2003). Our previous research shows that grammar checkers do not sufficiently support schoolchildren in their writing development, due to the fact that their errors display a different distribution than in adults (schoolchildren's errors are largely influenced by spoken language). Many types of writing problems are not taken into account and the comments on the errors found are often difficult for pupils to comprehend. Grammar checkers cover on average 58% of the errors in newspaper texts or student compositions, while the coverage in texts written by schoolchildren is around 12% (see Sofkova Hashemi, 2003). In addition, as mentioned above, the writing tools do not help the children in their writing acquisition or allow for practice.

5.2   *Auto Text in Mobile Phones*

In SMS communication many pupils make use of 'auto text' software (predictive text input or 'intelligent dictionary' functions). Most modern mobile phones include software that makes text input easier and faster by decreasing the number of times required to press the button to write words, e.g., 'T9' and 'eZiText' (www.t9.com or www.zicorp.com). The program, or writing tool, is based on word frequency data from a word list that in turn is based on a collection of linguistic material (MacKenzie & Soukoreff, 2002). Sequences of button selections are translated to the most frequent word corresponding to a word with exactly the same sequence of letters in the linguistic material. The advantage of the auto text tool is that it requires fewer button selections in order to input a text in the phone in comparison to the older 'multipress' technology.

The pupils that use the auto text function in their phones feel that writing gets easier. They are, however, not happy with the tool's frequent incorrect guesses, which makes it too laborious to change and go back to multipress. Many of them store old messages and their own words in the memory of their phone, e.g., slang, proper names, abbreviations and made-up expressions.

As noted above, the problem with the auto text tool is partly due to its being based on a limited corpus of linguistic material, which is adapted to a different type of written communication that has quite different conditions than communication via SMS messages. As we have seen, language use in SMS messages displays many speech-like features and new types of abbreviations. These speech-like features and abbreviations have no support in the writing tool that is part of today's mobile phones. Our observations and other studies (cf. Gutowitz, 2003; Kasesniemi, 2003) show also that many users state that the problem when the writing aid suggests incorrect words becomes too tiresome and time-consuming, and they would rather manage without it. A better adapted and more effective writing tool would need to consider the situations in which communication takes place as well as corpora based on the kind of language that is used in text messages via mobile phones and spoken language.

In Figure 2, we show a picture of a mobile phone displaying the auto text tool suggestion for the intended word *ses* 'see' in the phrase *Vi ses!* 'we see each other' (i.e., 'See

Figure 2: Example of auto text tool suggestion for a common phrase in SMS communication.

you!'), that is quite common in SMS communication. The first suggestion that the writing tool gives is the word *per* and it is not even the proper name *Per* but more like in expressions *per capita*, that makes it even more evident what type of texts this tool is based on.

6   Consequences of Changes in Written Language

There is a complex network of interacting factors that influence language use. For instance, we vary our language use, based on whether the communication is spoken or written, with whom we communicate and what our goal is. A job application is designed quite differently than an SMS message to one's best friend. Other well-known factors that influence communication and language use include age, gender, level of education, social background, and the like (cf. Herring, 2001). It is evident that language use varies and does not look the same all the time and in all situations.

The speech-like deviations from the norms and rules prescribed in standard writing that are found in the texts written by pupils, such as speech-like grammatical structures and spelling mistakes, occur mostly due to the fact that the writers are in the process of acquiring written language and that they are not used to expressing themselves in writing. They apply the knowledge and experience that they have acquired so far about the language surrounding them in their home environment, in school and in their leisure time. Entries in web diaries and SMS messages written by one and the same pupil are naturally influenced by that, but it is also evident that they consciously use an informal and speech-like tone of voice and adapt their writing according to the conditions of the situation in order to save time, effort and space. The speech-like qualities in these types of texts probably come from the specific production conditions of the different media. Minding one's spelling and using upper and lower case and punctuation are not of great importance in most computer-mediated communication situations. From the interviews, we understand that the pupils find it more important that the content of the message is comprehensible to the receiver.

The school children's language use is found to be adapted to new media, and also to encourage new, creative strategies for writing. The increase in use of written language through many different types of computer-mediated communication might also leave traces in texts produced in other circumstances and for other purposes. One might speculate whether this particular type of language use, e.g., new kinds of abbreviations, will be conventionalized enough to be accepted in written texts for other purposes outside computer-mediated communication or even in spoken language. As in all language change, it depends on whether a sufficient number of users will find this type of written expression effective enough to replace existing usage. As long as schoolchildren are taught and are given a chance to practice writing according to the standard norms, and are made conscious of stylistic differences, they will have a firm basis to move on from. They will then be equipped to adapt their own written language to suit the conditions of their communication. Concurrently with the change in language use, norms for standard writing will also eventually change.

Results from the initial analyses of children's texts in our project cannot be said to support the sometimes voiced fear that the standard norms of writing are threatened by the pupils' massive use of writing in other media (cf. Kasesniemi, 2003). The tendencies towards spoken language characteristics and other deviations from standard writing that are found might be influenced by heavy communication in ICTs, it might also be influenced by the children's unfamiliarity with the writing system. It is too early to say with any certainty what the actual causes are. The initial analyses of school texts do not reveal any great frequencies of the new types of abbreviations that are common in web diaries and SMS. Nor do we find any texts containing smileys or asterisks, for instance, used in the same manner as in computer-mediated communication.

Another observation that we made is that, given the present state in the development of writing tools, neither writing acquisition nor the new uses that writing is put to are supported by writing aids of sufficient quality. The existing writing aids are inadequate because of their focus on certain groups of writers and their disregard for the communicative situation or the medium. Language use varies, but the writing aids found in word processors or mobile phones are still based on standard writing and adult writers' texts for more or less formal purposes. Writing aids adapted to a certain type of writers, based on a certain type of texts for specific purposes, will only work effectively under those particular conditions. When they are used for text production under other conditions, they are not capable of giving good enough support, simply because they are not adapted to meet the conditions of other situations.

7   Future Work

The future work in the project involves deeper and more thorough quantitative and qualitative analyses of the collected material, both the texts produced in school and the texts written in the new media, as well as a survey of the interview material. Comparative studies will consider modality (e.g., handwritten vs. computer-written), age and writing situation (i.e., school vs. leisure production). We will look at the lexical and structural differences in both school texts and texts created in the new media.

In a more controlled writing task, the pupils will use the writing tool *ScriptLog* (this volume), originally developed at the Department of Linguistics at Göteborg University. This tool keeps a record of all events on the keyboard (i.e., the pressing of alphabetical and numerical keys, cursor keys, the delete key, space bar etc., and mouse clicks), the screen position of these events and their temporal distribution (the time that elapses from one keyboard event to the next) and, in addition to presenting the end product, it can give information about the whole incremental development of the text. In particular, this tool can be used to study editing patterns in the writing process that can give valuable insights into how pupils work with their texts.

Another future step to take is to analyse the influence of writing tools on writing by studying pupils in interaction with spelling and grammar checkers in word processor and the mobile phone auto text. The results of this study should reveal how writing aids influence children's writing, and what the specific needs and requirements for writing aids are for this particular writing population. Moreover, the study should shed light on how writing aids can be improved to enhance writing development and instruction in school and to make them more suitable to the writing situation in which they are applied. More information about the project can be found at *www.ling.gu.se/~sylvana/SkrivaIT*.

Chapter 5

Ludicity and Negotiated Meaning in Internet Chat

Rivka Niesten and Roland Sussex

The language used in Internet chat constitutes a large body of language data-in-use, and one which is notorious for its asystematic, irregular, creative and unstable characteristics. There have been some studies of the formal irregularities of Internet chat language, and of its exercise of humour in different modes. There has, however, been less work on language play and playfulness in Internet chat — ludicity in the sense advocated by Crystal (1998) and Sussex (2004). The exercise of creative playfulness with language involves not only the forms of language, but also speech acts, aspects of interactive language use and competitive interaction in the chat environment. Such language play can be its own justification, or it can be directed to the social manipulation of group membership in chatline communities. Ludicity offers a framework for the investigation of patterned behaviour in Internet chat.

1 Introduction: Conversation and Internet Chat

Negotiation of meaning in face-to-face conversations belongs to the area of conversation analysis, an outgrowth of the traditions of ethnomethodology (Goffman, 1981; Sacks, 1992; Schegloff, 1972). Contemporary conversation analysis (Ten Have, 1999) has made major progress in areas like turn taking, theme development and tracking, adjacency pairs, openings and closings, and speech acts. This research depends on a coherent, synchronous interactive environment with acceptably low levels of noise — in the communication theory sense of factors potentially interfering with interactive efficacy. Synchronous environments can be either face-to-face or remote, and either audio or video, for instance via telephone or radio, or audio or video teleconferences. But in either case they involve interactions in real time, with appropriate linearity of contributions and content. In other words, even where speakers interrupt each other, or where there may be more than one speaker

Niesten, R., & Sussex, R. (2005). Ludicity and negotiated meaning in Internet chat. In L. Van Waes, M. Leijten & C. Neuwirth (Vol. Eds.) & G. Rijlaarsdam (Series Ed.), Studies in Writing: Vol. 17. Writing and Digital Media (pp. 65–75). Oxford: Elsevier.

contributing simultaneously to the conversation, the coherence of the interactions is sufficient to sustain continued contributions. If not, the contributions tend to fall away, and the conversation peters out, or changes course or topic.

This relatively orderly organization takes on a different perspective in Internet chat ("IC").[1] Conventional wisdom has it that IC is a poorer medium. While this is inevitably true to some extent in the absence of face-to-face contact, IC has a number of ways of working with, exploiting and compensating for the factors which, we argue, are closely associated with ludicity. The differences between face-to-face and IC communication can be described on a number of dimensions:

- IC is a written, typed medium, limited by the speed of typists, networks and servers.
- IC is only weakly synchronous (Hutchby, 2001). IC contributions are usually sent to the server for distribution to the other chat members only when the writer presses the RETURN key to dispatch what is usually a line of text, though in some systems like Hotline the limit may be as much as 2049 characters.
- IC is not live, either physically, or in audio or video terms. Participants therefore miss most of the non-verbal content of the contributions, which some researchers have claimed are between 65% and 90% of the total information (Mehrabian & Ferris, 1967; Mehrabian & Wiener, 1967). In spite of the use of emoticons (smileys) and such devices, which are specific to and characteristic of IC, the overall interactivity of IC is less rich than that of real-time conversation. Conventions of interaction, relevance (Grice, 1975; Sperber & Wilson, 1995) and turn taking which are broadly followed in face-to-face and real-time interactions are not as relevant in IC, but important compensatory practices do exist.
- IC contributions are displayed in order of receipt by the server. This means that multiple participants may display their contributions in parallel, in chronological order of receipt at the server, but not in chronological order of transmission by the contributors.
- This means that threads can overlap, and multiple threads can be running at the same time, or that a new thread may be launched before a currently running thread is brought to a proper conclusion.

All these factors show that the negotiation of meaning in IC is a rather different activity from what happens in synchronous face-to-face interactions. They also help to differentiate IC from Instant Messaging, a (usually) one-to-one real-time interactive version of email; and SMS, again a usually one-to-one interactive conversation, but limited by slower input rates from the cell-/mobile-phone keyboard, and by slower response times. This makes it only weakly synchronous, though advances in bandwidth are making this genre converge to some extent with IC.

Attempts at the analysis of IC texts have tended to focus on the ways in which IC deviates from face-to-face practice in synchronous conversations: for instance, in discussions of topic persistence and decay, and multiple topic overlap (Herring, 1999; O'Neill & Martin, 2003; Riffel, 2003). We also find treatments of multiple concurrent participants,

---

[1]"IRC" or "Internet Relay Chat" is strictly speaking the name of the software developed by Jarkko Oikarinen in 1988. These terms are sometimes used in a generic way to refer to quasi-synchronous Internet chat interactions. We separate the two by using "IC" as the generic term. The data in this paper comes from a corpus collected from the Hotline IC environment (Niesten, 2005).

obscurity, confusion and ill-formedness, especially in orthography, morphology, lexis, grammar and pragmatics; and studies of social variation in IC (Paolillo, 2001). The dominating themes have been either the special features of IC expressiveness, like emoticons and the use of orthographic devices like punctuation; or the irregularity, ill-formedness and chaotic nature of much raw IC text.

The success and communicative attraction of IC show how well IC has succeeded in spite of its technologically limiting parameters. In order to achieve this success, IC must have a functionally sufficient formal regularity in order for coherent meaning to be negotiated: it would make no sense to try to communicate in a medium where minimal requirements of recognizable and recognized practice did not exist. One cannot communicate without shared structure.

The problem, however, is to find a rationale for this shared structure. The structure itself is not stable: indeed, much of IC is concerned with the rolling re-definition of the structure, by trying out and exploring new and different ways of exploiting the keyboard for expressiveness in the negotiation of meaning. Simply relating IC features to standard language features by some metric of deviation, whether qualitative or quantitative, will take us some way towards a greater understanding of IC, as in the polylogue model (Kerbrat-Orecchioni, 2004). But it does not provide a rationale to unite the interactive features of IC under a communicative framework. In this paper we lay the bases for a more elaborated analysis of IC interactivity (Niesten, 2005). The wider intellectual context of this study includes the notion of groundedness in conversation (Clarke & Brennan, 1991) and the ways in which participants in conversations negotiate a shared set of information, roles and goals. But the data discussed here interpret information, goals and roles in a way which is strongly influenced by the nature of the IC medium itself. In one sense it involves a shifting of emphasis from the informational to the phatic (Malinowski, 1923), since a large proportion of the interchanges are to do with the establishment and maintenance of social interactivity; and when communication purposes are intended, they may not be correctly received without a knowledge of the codes which are typical of different flavours of IC. In this process, what is particularly distinctive about our data is its emphasis on competition and, even more clearly, on ludicity.

2　Ludicity

In this paper we present ludicity, a development of the notion of "playfulness", as a framework for the exploration of IC interactions. Ludicity has been described by Crystal (1998) as a key feature of healthy social interactivity. Ludicity can involve creativeness, in the sense of creating new words or using them in an unfamiliar and striking way (Sussex, 2004); in a somewhat different sense, it can be concerned with dramatic performance (Danet, Ruedenberg-Wright, & Tamari-Rosenbaum, 1997). Alternatively, enjoyment in word-play can be its own end, or it may have a social or other purpose.

Playfulness is uncontroversially a necessary part of an overall framework for speech acts in social space. What is distinctive about ludicity is its focus on language form (orthography, grammar and lexis), which in IC can take on not only an interactive but also a competitive character which is driven by language forms, and where the focus is partly on the interchange of content, and partly on an interactive and spontaneous challenge to create and use language forms in an innovative way. Successful participants can create new non-standard norms (e.g. aberrant spellings) which are taken up by other participants, and which may persist for several interchanges until they are overtaken by other more successful modifications, or may actually become normative for the practice of the specific group of IC participants. Ludicity, then, emerges as a variety of motivated, often competitive playfulness with potentially persisting consequences. It thus brings together, and also goes beyond, several themes which have previously been discussed in the framework of playfulness and IC (Bechar-Israeli, 1995; Danet et al., 1997; Crystal, 2001), including irony (Hancock, 2004), playfulness in the context of feminist linguistic theory (Krolokke, 2003), as well as the broader context of joking and everyday talk (Norrick, 1993). The whole question of IC talk in the wider context of Computer-Mediated Discourse has been addressed by Herring (2001), who provides an umbrella context for the present analysis.

3   Method

In this paper we use data from Hotline (in full: Hotline Community of Practice), an IC environment with advanced interactive features (Brown, 1999). In such negotiated interactive chat environments there are two kinds of channel: public, which is accessible to all on-line; and private, where communications can be directed privately to a particular individual. In this paper we deal only with public postings. The data were collected between April 2001 and March 2002, when Hotline Communications went permanently off-line.

Hotline (http://en.wikipedia.org/wiki/Hotline_Communications) was chosen for this study because in its day it was at the forefront of peer-to-peer networking. It strongly reflected the ethos of hackers (Levy, 1984) and the heady early days of the Web and the Internet, with its combination of vision and raffish behaviour, and its population of technologists, artists and a group of collaborators remarkable for their heterogeneous origins and aims. Its community was characterized by an accumulation of regular participants, and the formation of intra-group practices and conventions which defined the community. It showed hierarchical organization, with a small group of system administrators ("reds") controlling the other levels of participants, as well as clearly identifiable groups of regular users and newcomers ("newbies"). In order to be an advanced user of Hotline it was necessary to adjust to the new conventions, and participants coming from other Internet Chat communities such as Internet Relay Chat (IRC) needed to re-acculturate to the new environment and conventions. Hotline was a particularly strongly integrated, focussed and in some cases intense example of cyber community. The properties of language interaction, creativity, competition and ludicity were regularly demonstrated in clear, and often heightened or exaggerated, form. Hotline is not a typical, or even mainstream, example of IC. Its early members were programmers and hackers, and they set a style and interactive pattern, which heightens the regular features of IC. These properties made it particularly suitable for the present study.

The public chat aspect of Hotline meant that it could be easily logged and did not require ethical clearance. The captured logs span a year and amount to nearly a million words of running text. These logs were collected at random times and the length of capture time was also random. At the time of the study, the Hotline website indicated that there were three million persons with copies of the programme and a further 200,000 additional downloads per month. Even though the programme allowed users to create their own communities, the central Hotline server had the potential to attract a widely based sample of IC users over a year of collecting data. This spectrum covered newbies to advanced users, both genders, a range of ages, locations and speech patterns.

This study is ethnomethodological and qualitative–interpretive, and it makes only secondary use of basic descriptive statistics. Key concepts and theories emerge from indexing the lexicon, grepping for key words, concordancing and commentaries from informants. Examples in this paper provide instantiation of key findings. While most of the data in this paper derives from the full dataset, statistics for tokenization are based on a pilot study of 27 pages of text. The larger study by Niesten (2005) involves understanding the narrative text to show how individuals create an "online self", how they interact in on-line play, and how they become part of the community from newbie to advanced community member.

4 Results

In the sense in which we use it in the present paper, and drawing on Crystal (1998) and Cherny (1999), language play and language games include language forms (Section 4.1), semantics and pragmatics (Section 4.2), illocution (Section 4.3) and perlocution (Section 4.4).

4.1 Language Forms

Language forms are the most studied area of IC. Playfulness can involve any of the levels of language: orthography, phonology, morphology, syntax or lexis. Playfulness involves the use of unexpected or non-standard forms. Puns, for instance, which are common in IC, offer an alternative interpretation through a chance coincidence of form (homophone, homograph, homonym). As text, IC is spontaneous, irregular, quirky, often formally incomplete or ill-formed, and only sketchily edited. It carries many properties of spoken or quasi-spoken language in often ad hoc and unstable written forms. The Hotline data provide a rich variety of examples:

- quasi-phonetic spelling: *thanx, sux*
- plurals or three person singulars in -z: *beginnerz, hugz*
- colloquial usage: *gonna, hafta, oughta*
- playful changes of vowels: *nekid, gewd*
- reduplication of letters or punctuation marks for emphasis: *loooooooooooong, byeeee, eeevillllll: AAAH!!!!!!!* (Jacobson, 1999; Lea & Spears, 1992)
- by convention, capitals imply shouting: "*NOW AM YELLIN! AH NEED HELP!*"
- abbreviations and acronyms (only 0.065% of the tokens), of which there are several hundred, now established in hacker use for more than two decades: *lol* ("laughing out loud", and many others)
- conventional re-spellings, for instance playing on puns: *Windoze* (doze), *Nutscrape* (Netscape)
- morphological and word-forming creativity, especially with lexis well known in the computing domain: geek forms *geekdom* and *geekdomicity*. Lag (the time it takes for an entered message to be read by others) forms *lagfreeness* and *lagometer*.

- emoticons like :-) (only 0.09% of the tokens), designed to compensate for the emotional and related cues present in face-to-face interaction (Chenault, 1998; Dabiri & Helten, 1998; Flaherty, Pearce, & Rubin, 1998; Hinner, 2000; Jacobson, 1999; Jaffe, Lee, Huang, & Oshagan, 1995; Orth, 2000; Stevenson, 2000; Storrer, 2001)
- high frequency of ellipsis and of incomplete grammatical structures or words.

4.2 Semantics and Pragmatics

The Grice (1975) maxims offer four principles for the orderly management of conversation (quantity, quality, relevance and manner). All four are regularly flouted in IC. Among the more obvious features of IC ludicity are the deliberate misreading of speech acts, and the deliberate manipulation of thematic (thread) sequence in non-standard ways, which violate the relevance and manner maxims in particular. In IC we often find instances of deflecting a thread, interrupting it deliberately, or subverting it in various ways (Cherny, 1999). Threads tend to decay, or to have to compete with parallel simultaneous threads, with discontinuous contributions (Example 5).

Ludic motivations intersect with three principal kinds of speech acts in IC. The linguistically most conventional involves system messages, most often when participants join the group, change their names, or are removed from the group through the action of one of the "reds" (system administrators). Here the language format is set by the system. Interventions from the reds belong here too, usually in standard or near-standard English, and warning offending participants about their behaviour and the consequences (Example 7).

Somewhat less conventional in linguistic form are what we may call "stage directions", comments about what is happening outside the chat sequence. They constitute 4.14% of the text's tokens (Hinner, 2000; Orth, 2000; Stevenson, 2000). They are also variously called "actions", "poses", "emotes", "metatokens", "3rd person", and "internal message" representing "kinesic signals", and are usually marked by an asterisk or angle brackets outside the main text. In "stage directions" the overall tenor is less excited and outrageous than the chat itself. Stage directions often deal with building and managing imaginary worlds ("MOOs": Cherny, 1999; Turkle, 1995). Participants usually refer to themselves in the third person, as do children at play, commenting on their participation in the game from the position of a more external observer:

(1)   *** nawty sweetzy (w/o evil) bathes in champagne
      *** HL Help TechC jumps in tha'bath too..
      *** HLOrbitR backstrokes thru the beverages
      *** super redneck cracks open a can of bud
      *** Laura Palmer bathes in donkey's milk
      *** HLOrbitR watches milky Laura
      *** nawty sweetzy (w/o evil) pulls everyone into the champagne for a champagne breakfast super redneck: not without my budweiser
      *** nawty sweetzy (w/o evil) feeds mierlot orb reguritated blah HL Help TechC: ewwwwwwwwwwwww..
      *** HL Help TechC gets outta'the tub to "tinkle"

4.3 Illocution

IC involves conversation, so it involves participation and, in varying ways, collaboration. It is interactive. It also tends to be incremental — Crystal refers to "ping-pong punning" (1998, Chapter 1). It is often competitive in the wilful display of inventiveness, creativity, surprise and challenge. The most witty, outrageous or successfully insulting contribution — the latter especially in flaming channels — wins by the approbation of the participants, and through shaming the rest into silence or impotent fury. The overall tone is high spirited, with elements of showing off, display and egotism, self-preening and putting-down of others.

Ludic behaviour in IC is often without an ulterior communicative goal: high-spirited playfulness principally for its own enjoyment, where negotiation is a matter of shared and competitive wit (Section 3). But any item, usually a word, sometimes a phrase, in a contribution is a potential target for ludic exploitation: an expressed or implied challenge "Can you understand what I am saying, and can you go one better?" It is then up to the contributors to rise to the challenge and to extract the maximum from the emerging thread until it runs out of material or is overtaken by, or subsumed in, a new thread. This collaborative–competitive exploitation can be interpreted as a complicit strategy whose result (and perhaps motivation and goal) is to overcome the limitations of the medium itself. Meanings so negotiated are the process and the result of ludic interplay.

The bulk of IC talk, however, consists of a wide range of interaction and conversation interplay. It shows only a limited use of the first person. A number of the interactions fit into the conventional Question/Answer or adjacency pair frameworks, and we pay little further attention to them here, except insofar as they demonstrate aspects of wit. But for the rest, the conventional Austin-type illocutionary acts do not comfortably cover the kinds of speech acts involved in many of these interactions, so we present some refinements of Austin's categories as working hypotheses designed to elucidate the negotiation of meaning in IC talk. Much of this is concerned with wit and inventiveness.

The first refinement of Austin involves displays. These resemble Austin's constatives or statements, except that some or all of the content depends on either language form or the display of inventiveness. This may constitute text, as with the *teef* trope in Example (7). Or it may involve ASCII art, which exploits the keyboard for graphic purposes. The lower end of these are smileys or emoticons; at the upper end are creations of considerable ingenuity. Wilkins (1991), Danet, Wachenhauser, Cividalli, Bechar-Israeli, & Rosenbaum-Tamari (1995) and Stevenson (2000) comment on paralinguistic signals in ASCII art like:

(2)   <red>----------<----------<------@
      (red rose) (Danet, 2001); or

(3) | – | E / – \ \ / `/ |):   _ _
      | – | E / – \ \ / `/ |):   (Y)
      | – | E / – \ \ / `/ |):   = = =
      | – | E / – \ \ / ` / |):
      | – | E / – \ \ / ` / |):   ⌁_⌁
      eggplant: nice one D |
      M'Ack*: good One Heavy
      M'Ack*: that looks like a Upside down PEAR!

where even the user's name *Heavy* is graphically re-rendered. A display can stand on its own, or it can be interpreted as an invitation to word-play. This can take the form of incremental participation, as in the following system-level sequence of name changes, which combines the set formula *is now known as* with ludic name-making:

(4)   <<< Leeloo Ekbat De Sebat is now known as Scarlet Diva >>>
      <<< Bruce is now known as Scarlet Pimpernel >>>
      <<< It is now known as SCARLET KALI >>>
      <<< Papageno is now known as Scarlet Papageno >>>
      <<< Scarlet Papageno is now known as Scarlet Gigolo >>>
      <<< Mauro is now known as Scarlets Balls >>>

Here everyone adds "scarlet" to their names; then Papageno changes the focus of play to the head noun and becomes "Scarlet Gigolo".

This incremental word gaming is central to Hotline IC. Sometimes the interchange is collaborative, a to-and-fro exploration of a theme in a more or less directionless way, a good-humoured sharing of sallies of wit, something like Crystal's "ping-pong punning":

(5)	1	A	*** MacMan pours Orb a strong cuppa coffee
	2	B	<<< LoneWolf is now known as M@ >>>
	3	B	Mauro: Bye superfool
	4	A	*** HLOrbitR downs it in one
	5	C	HLOrbitR: heya Mauro :)
	6		Mauro: Orb .... Love at first sight :)
	7		HLOrbitR: hah
	8		Mauro: heh
	9		HLOrbitR: ;)
	10		MacMan: Mauro loves your furry teef, Orby.
	11		HLOrbitR: ya gotta love em dontcha
	12		Mauro: Mac, tell me, what "teef" mean ?
	13		C64 Rules!: toofies
	14		HLOrbitR: lol
	15		MacMan: teeth, Mauro
	16		HLOrbitR: freshly de-furred
	17		C64 Rules!: de-greened
	18		super redneck: Can I have the fur off the teeth?
	19		HLOrbitR: that too
	20		*** HLOrbitR collects fur up offa the floor
	21		*** MacMan like the Psychedelic Warlords, disappears in smoke
	22		Mauro: haaa, so orb should have furry teeths???? :))
	23		*** HLOrbitR mails it wrapped up with a big pink bow
	24	D	MacMan: •• poof ••
	25		HLOrbitR: cya MM
	26	C	HLOrbitR: nah they've been de-furred Mauro
	27		HLOrbitR: brushed

28	E	invito: someone can help me about find a
		cracker for macromedia products for mac
29		<<< jay looking for M@ is now known as jay >>>
30		C64 Rules!: ritz?
31		Mauro: hehe, better so Orb :)
32		C64 Rules!: saltine cracker?
33		super redneck: lol

This example shows the interplay of concurrent themes: the "coffee" stage direction A theme recurs in line 4, and the "tooth" C theme returns in line 26. There is good-humoured teasing of Mauro, presumably an Italian participant, over the *teef... toofies...teeth* trope, with wilful development of the fur into something that can be swept up and mailed. And there are puns over *cracker*, either an illegal password to "crack" and use commercial software or a biscuit/cracker.

Playfulness can be either incremental or competitive, where different contributors try to get the last word, or at least outdo the previous contributors. This kind of "sparring" involves returning a sally with interest, but without serious intent to wound. However, competition can escalate to provocation, which is the standard tenor of flaming channels. The reds on Hotline do not let the tone reach this point, and intervene to warn or exclude transgressors (Example 7). These rules are known by in-group users, and newbies have to learn them quickly or suffer exclusion. The rules embody a shared set of agreed constraints on the limits of chat — agreed by the in-group, and on their behalf imposed by the reds on the rest.

4.4   *Perlocution, Groups and Group Solidarity*

Austin's (1962) "perlocution" involves the effects of illocutions on the hearer(s). IC contributions often evoke laughter, smiling, groans and chuckles (Baym, 1995; Morkes, Kernal, & Nass, 1998; for visual components, see Danet, 2001). IC extends from burlesque and the display of the vulgar to the high aesthetics of intellectual wit. Sometimes, however, ludicity has a more social function in terms of groups and the management of their membership and dynamics (Section 4). This function of ludicity can be less benign. It links in with linguistic, cultural and other strategies to protect and insulate the members of in-groups from intruders and aspiring members from outside. In such cases negotiated meaning exploits ludic interplay for ulterior purposes like exclusion from participation, and uses knowledge or information to control social space. The entry key depends on wit and ludic skill.

Within the overall "IC culture" of the IC community as a whole, each chat community has its own culture and group structure (Reid, 1991). Inter- and intra-group differences are played out in language, ludicity and power. The chat environment tends to break into three distinct groups: an "in-group", an "out-group" and an "inter-group". The "in-group" comprises knowledgeable and accepted group members who are skilled in texting techniques and who have built up or shared a history and a culture of negotiated meanings and codes with fellow participants. New users ("newbies") make up the out-group. The inter-group is made up of those who are attempting to be admitted into the in-group. In-group people meet as friends and take on a series of roles, which may or may not match their off-line physical identities (Turkle, 1995). Their status is based on in-group solidarity, shared tropes and role-play. They may publicly ridicule and deride new-bies, exploiting their in-group solidarity; privately, however, they may also assist newbies. The inter-group attempts to distance itself from the out-group and attempt to merge their code with the in-group. Differentiation between the groups shows a typical asymmetrical power situation. The experts possess not only the secret code, but also the legitimation to vary that code, and to impose language practices and norms on those out-side the inner circle. Gaining inner membership requires aspirants to share a framework of socio-cultural knowledge, which is acquired by exposure to group norms, and by experimentation with language and tropes to acquire in-group speak by a process of hit-and-miss and occasional feedback or ridicule from the in-group members. To take a sim-ple example: a word which has been misspelled may be the beginning of adopting a new non-standard word into the conversation which only those involved in the interaction and their friends can know. This new word is then incorporated into the community lexicon and is used both as a source of play, and as a marker of the limits between the "in-group" and the others.

(6)   Murray: I watched 2 RM videos
        DM 86 98 00: prOn?
        Murray: no, lol
        |<itt3n: likes p®0n
        DM 86 98 00: with videos?
        *** TheArtist likes prOn too
        *** |<itt3n likes p®0n
        *** Irish has nuttin' against prOn but prefers to make his own
        TheArtist: heh

Or there is the creative use of diminutives and nicknames ("nicks"). Newbies may hesitate to use these forms for fear of intruding, but in-group diminutives are used between people who are well known to each other. HLOrbitR is commonly called *orb, orbit* or *orbitr*, but her friends call her *orby, SupaOrbit.* Qpalzm is commonly known as *qp* but his friends call him *kiwi* (as he is from New Zealand).

   Newbies seeking acceptance may be welcomed and helpfully advised, especially if they show a responsible attitude towards reading the system documentation and asking respectfully for guidance. Unwitting transgressions may evoke a formal warning:

(7)   Jean Reno [HL: Please, we do not allow unnamed users on this server. Change your
        name in options (left-most icon on the toolbar). You will be kicked in 1 minute if
        you don't comply.

But the accumulated ludic practices of the in-group can be turned against them. They can be ridiculed for trying IRC routines on Hotline IC or for trying to find someone else to communicate with in French and other languages. Experienced users may taunt them with a showoff display of arcane (and actually fictitious) knowledge about "leech ratings" (in theory, the ability to acquire information without reciprocating), spoofing (pretending to be someone else) and spamming (sending unwanted material) without incurring the expected ire of the reds.

Or newbies may be confronted with multilingual code-switching:

(8)   Lysenko: si, poi diventiamo piovre tentacolari come la dea Kali...
        (Italian: yes, then we'll become poor octpuses like the Goddess Kali)
        KALI l'incant: ahahaha più braccia sono un vantaggio ahahaah
        (Italian: ahahaha ... more arms are an advantage ahahaah)
        Snow Princess: Kolja!!! PRIVET!!!
        (Russian: Kolja! Welcome!)
        Lysenko: speak english, please, snow princess
        Lysenko: here we speak only english

Newbies of any language group may find ready acceptance, or they may be deliberately misled through the use of secret codes undocumented in the standard manual. Users can be gulled into entering specific sequences of characters, can unwittingly kick themselves off the session, or can find that their nickname has been changed to "Bacon", and anything they type appears on the screen as "pork"; with the only escape being to log out. This kind of playfulness is sharper, more confrontational, more divisive and more calculated to wound. The newbie who survives this initiation will be respected as a robust member of the in-group community, and will be licensed to torment other newbies in good time.

5   Conclusion

From the point of view of ludicity, a central result of the present paper is that the nature of the ludic sparring in our Hotline corpus is crucially determined by, and is a reaction to, the interactive text medium: one negotiates meaning in a particular medium by exploiting and playing with the limits of the medium itself — potentially an extension of McLuhan's (1964) dicta on the medium being the message.

   Ludicity, then, provides a framework in which we can relate formal, semantic and pragmatic aspects of language to the special set of constraints of media and interactivity provided in on-line chat. Meaning is negotiated not merely in terms of conventional conversation analysis, but rather as interactive sequences of ludic interventions, structured along a gradient from display for its own high-spirited enjoyment, through collaborative theme-exploration and competitive sparring, to the more aggressive routines used for group protection and the testing of newbies. Ludicity is expressed as an in-group code, unstable, developing, but still subject to certain regularities in speech acts, especially when we supplement the Austin set with categories like display and ludic competition. These belong with our evolving understanding of the overall culture of computer-mediated communication (Churchill & Bly, 2000) and its discourses, as well as the rapidly widening technical and social use of SMS and Instant Messaging, all of which promise to raise even further the profile, and the complexity, of ludic IT-based communication.

Acknowledgement

We are grateful to Richard Baldauf, Chris Neuwirth, Peter White and an anonymous reviewer for valuable criticism of an earlier draft of this paper. Remaining infelicities are our responsibility.

Chapter 6

Knowledge Acquisition by Designing Hypervideos: Different Roles of Writing during Courses of "New" Media Production

Elmar Stahl, Carmen Zahn, Stephan Schwan and Matthias Finke

This chapter reflects on different roles of writing in the context of learning by hyper-video design. Hypervideo is defined as a specific kind of hypermedia that combines non-linear information structures and dynamic audio–visual information presentations. In hypervideos, users watch video information and are able to access additional information like texts, pictures or further videos by clicking on links within the video. We used collaborative hypervideo design as a method to foster knowledge and literacy acquisition in a series of university courses. Designing hypervideos requires a great variety of writing processes like creating scripts and storyboards to produce the video information, producing non-linear chunks of text for the additional information and exchanging e-mails between the authors. Therefore, theoretical models and empirical results of research on writing builds a helpful heuristic to organize these courses of designing new media.

1 Introduction

Nowadays, in the age of computer technology, literacy cannot be reduced to the ability to read and write ordinary texts. Instead, due to the advent of computer-based types of information transmission and exchange, the concept of literacy has to be substantially enriched (Messaris, 1994). An advanced literacy concept then encompasses the ability to understand different kinds of symbol systems (numeric, pictorial and verbal) as well as their combinations used in different kinds of representations like texts, pictures, animations or moving images, and to be able to work with diverse types of media like text books, videos or hypermedia (a detailed discussion about the influence of new media on writing is given in

Stahl, E., Zahn, C., Schwan, S., & Finke, M. (2005). Knowledge acquisition by designing hypervideos: Different roles of writing during courses of 'new' media production. In L. Van Waes, M. Leijten & C. Neuwirth (Vol. Eds.) & G. Rijlaarsdam (Series Ed.), Studies in Writing: Vol. 17. Writing and Digital Media (pp. 77–88). Oxford: Elsevier.

the chapter of Hashemi in this volume). With the growing use of digital information systems, advanced literacy concepts also include "digital" skills, like the ability to deal with non-linear information structures and to interact with technological systems (see also the chapter of Hawisher & Selfe in this volume). Additionally, with the availability of cheap and easy to use digital cameras, video production software or HTML-editors, many people do not only strengthen their skills of understanding "multi-media" — information, but also acquire the ability to produce different types of multimedia on their own. Correspondingly, today's concepts of literacy may further be enhanced by including self-regulated multimedia production skills, too.

The acquisition of advanced literacy skills can be combined with deep knowledge acquisition and understanding in formal educational contexts: Commonly this is accomplished by project works sometimes also labelled as *learning by design* (e.g., Reimann & Zumbach, 2001), where students collaboratively develop a multimedia product on a given topic over an extended period of time. From the constructivist perspective of situated cognition it is assumed that an active and constructive process of solving such a complex task should increase students' literacy, result in a deeper understanding of the topic that is presented within their product and having positive side effects, like the acquisition of more general cognitive, meta-cognitive and social skills (Carver, Lehrer, Connell, & Erickson, 1992; Liu, 2003).

In this chapter we focus on such *design activities* involving multimedia products by giving the example of designing the so-called "hypervideos" that integrate audio–visual information of videos with text-based information (see Section 2). As our starting point, we will compare complex hypervideo-design tasks to text writing, because from our perspective, a beneficial overlap between the affordances of writing a text and designing a hypervideo exists.

Firstly, on a concrete level, designing hypervideos encompasses a great variety of writing processes. For example, in professional film production, a film is planned in a recursive circle of different writing processes starting with short summaries of the main idea, progressing to screen-plays and ending with storyboards that explain the contents of each short setting in a very concrete way. Further on, designing hypervideos includes producing non-linear chunks of text, formulating commentaries in accordance with static or dynamic pictorial material as well as e-mail or chat communication. In other words, although its *results* typically consist of a complex array of (audio–) visual materials, *the process* of authoring hypervideo depends largely on written material and text-based social communication.

Secondly, on an abstract level the author of a text and of a (hyper-) video have the same goal: They produce a coherent medium that allows the audience to understand the presented information easily. In both cases, the special affordances of a particular rhetorical space (provided by the anticipated audience, the media, the genre, etc.) have to be considered carefully. Frederiksen, Donin-Frederiksen, and Bracewell (1986) developed a model of the reciprocal transfer between mental and textual structures during writing. They assumed that an author of a text has to develop a conceptual frame structure of the content, representing the global meaning, then to generate propositions, to transfer the propositions into sentences and then into a coherent text. This model allows us to claim that the general task in writing — to build a mental model about the contents and to transfer them into an external representation — is the same as in multimedia production. The difference is that the generated propositions are transferred to texts in writing; and in hypervideo production a part of them is further transferred into video. Nevertheless, some of the main issues during the planning activities (how to transfer individual knowledge into a meaningful information structure?) are comparable.

This chapter presents a didactical perspective on the beneficial overlap between the affordances of writing a text and designing a hypervideo. We use writing as a method to gain deeper understanding of the topic in our project on hypervideo design. On the other hand, producing hypervideos is a task to foster the writing skills and thus to teach writing. Our experiences are based on four university courses in which students collaboratively designed hypervideos. In the following sections, the concept of hypervideo with its specific characteristics will be addressed, and the relevance of common models of writing processes with regard to collaborative projects of designing a hypervideo will be considered. Then, an outline of the university seminars will be given. Here, special emphasis will be put on the diverse writing processes, which took place during the projects.

2 The Concept of Hypervideos

Hypervideo is defined as a specific kind of hypermedia that combines non-linear information structuring and dynamic audio–visual information presentations (videos presenting realistic images or animations). In hypervideos, video information can be linked with different kinds of static visual information (texts, pictures, tables, graphs). Users always start by viewing a video sequence and then may mouse-click on selected visual objects within the video images to access additional information units (Finke, 2000). The main difference between video in traditional hypermedia and hypervideos lies in the importance attributed to the video presentation. In hypermedia, videos are often illustrative and optional. In hypervideos, video sequences form the "backbone of the system" (Zahn, Schwan, & Barquero, 2002). Thus, videos and the additional information elements are interwoven in ways that videos can be viewed interactively and navigated in a non-linear order.

These medium specific characteristics have important implications for educational contexts where learners interact with hypervideo components during knowledge building (Zahn, 2003): The first implication is that filmic codes constitute the primary means of symbolic expression. Therefore, dynamic visual information can be used to show dynamic contents both explicitly and realistically to others. Additional audio information may further support the presentation of dynamic contents by enabling dual coding and dual cognitive processing (Paivio, 1986). And more generally spoken, video, as dynamic and figurative information can represent a powerful means of efficiently communicating knowledge. Video can situate abstract contents, enhance the motivational power of a presentation and the authenticity of a learning experience.

The second implication of the hypervideo-specific characteristics with regard to educational contexts is that the filmic presentation (unlike traditional TV or video) is not a continuous stream of audiovisual information but may be integrated with abstract symbol systems and then be arranged according to various structural patterns. These possible information structures range from films with multimedia footnotes to networks of short

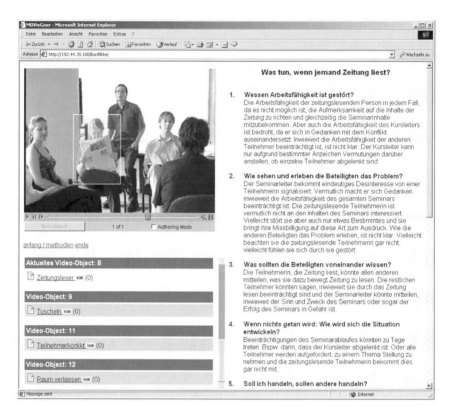

Figure 1: An example of a screen from a hypervideo designed in our courses. The user always starts with watching a video (upper left side). In the video, sensitive regions (temporal–spatial links) appear — shown here as a transparent rectangle. Users can mouse-click on these links and then the video stops and additional information like a text is shown on the right side. On the lower left side, all available links are shown in a navigation bar. If a user clicks on a link, the video jumps to the chosen sequence in the video and the associated additional information is shown as well.

videoclips. Each of these possible structures may be applied to the tasks of designing multimedia products depending on specific educational sub-goals.

In our projects, we started out with using hypervideo structures based on a "film with footnotes" metaphor (see Figure 1). These projects will be described in more detail below. Beforehand, we will reflect on the writing processes involved in hypervideo production.

3   Writing Hypervideo

According to the unique attributes of hypervideos, their design includes several writing processes, which seem essential to support the deep processing of a given topic. As was noted in our introduction, these writing processes include creating scripts and storyboards for video sequences, writing commentaries for the audio track and producing non-linear chunks of text.

3.1 Designing Video Nodes

If a hypervideo is designed from scratch, scripts and storyboards for the videos have to be written, which describe the scenarios and the spoken texts. In larger film projects, this writing process consists of different steps: It starts with the presentation of the *main idea* of the film, written down in one or two sentences. Then the *treatment* is developed, outlining the idea and the moods that the main scenes of the film should communicate in a short abstract of one or two pages. In the next step, a *scenario/expose* is written, dissecting the film into discrete scenes. Then a *book* is written, describing the scenes of the film in detail. Afterwards, the *screen-play* is written, which means that the texts are supplemented with sketches of how the scenes should look like. In the last step, *storyboards* are created that present the scenes of the film in temporal order in the form of comic strips presenting camera perspectives that are accompanied by written descriptions of the scenes and the dialogues (see Figure 2). In sum, this so-called preproduction phase of a film is mainly a writing process. The main challenge is to transfer meaning into audio–visual information. Students have to learn how to describe a story, the actions, situations and actors within their texts. The storyboards must be detailed enough to transfer this written information into the language of film.

ca. 22sec		Nah	Sprechblase Prüfungsliteratur (*Link zu Prüfungsamt*)	Ersti sinkt langsam in sich zusammen - sein Gesichtsausdruck wechselt von fröhlich zu verzweifelt. Diplomand redet weiter (im Hintergrund)	D: „... Ach, wenn ich an die Berge von Prüfungsliteratur zurückdenke ... Am Anfang dachte ich noch, es würde irgendwann besser und weniger... aber irgendwie wurde es doch immer mehr...."
30sec		Halbnah		Ersti zusammengesunken, Diplomand sieht den Ersti an und stockt. Versucht verlegen abzuwiegeln (redet schnell)	E: „Ohje!" (seufz) D: „Oh. – Ähm, ich wollte Dich jetzt nicht ... Also – du bist jetzt so geknickt... Ach, weiß du, es ist alles gar nicht so schlimm. Geht total schnell um – die paar Semester. Und so viel Arbeit ist es dann eigentlich auch wieder nicht."
1sec		Nah		Gesicht des Ersti – immer noch verzweifelt - zusammengesunken	D: „Du machst das schon..."
7 sec		Halbnah	(Witz: Sprechblase „Termin" – Link zu Zeitmanagementtraining o.ä.)	Diplomand sieht nervös auf die Uhr und seht hastig auf	D: „Ach, schon so spät... – ich muss jetzt auch leider... Ja tut mir leid. Muss jetzt echt los. Hab noch nen wichtigen Termin..."
3sec		Halbtotale		Diplomand entfernt sich von der Bank, Ersti hebt kurz zum Abschied die Hand	E: „Tschüss!"
6sec		Nah		Ersti – etwas verlorener Gesichtsausdruck - zweifelnd	E: „Ich mach das schon..."

Figure 2: An example of a page of a storyboard from one of our courses.

3.2 Writing Spoken Commentaries for the Audio Track

Further on, linear texts corresponding with the video images have to be written for the audio commentary. These texts may be either redundant or complementary, or else they may even include meta-information to understand the video. Redundant commentaries describe verbally what is also seen in the video image (e.g., a video presents a girl entering a room with the commentary saying "Here you see Laura entering a room"). Complementary commentaries give additional information to the contents shown in the videos (e.g., a video presents a therapeutic scenario about feedback rules and an audio track gives more general information about these feedback rules). Commentaries including meta-information to understand the video might consist of questions or hints that help to analyse and understand the information in the video more deeply (e.g., the video shows a complex scenario about classroom management and the spoken text asks "Where in the video shot would you search for potential classroom conflicts?") The great challenge in writing these different kinds of audio tracks is to match the information in the texts with the information presented in the video nodes and avoid large gaps between the two. Design principles for audiovisual information presentation can help to produce such coherence and contiguity (see e.g., Mayer & Moreno, 2002).

3.3 Writing Non-Linear Content

All written information to be presented has to be segmented into nodes of information. An important issue is to decide which information should be presented as a video node or as a text node. For the text nodes some general principals of node design within hypermedia have to be considered. Nodes present information in a fragmented form (Whalley, 1993). Therefore, a widespread recommendation is to design nodes following a "just enough" principle (e.g., Gerdes, 1997). Each node should only contain the necessary amount of information. Details or examples should be presented in separate nodes, which can be read whenever required. Each node should also be written in a way that can be called "cohesive closeness" (e.g., Gerdes, 1997). It means that the main information in each node must be comprehensible without reading further nodes. Further on the video and text nodes have to be linked to each other in a meaningful way. The links have two important and closely related functions: Firstly, they enable the user to navigate within the hypertext. A user has to rely on links if she wants to get to the desired text passage (Dillon, 1996). Therefore the selection of offered links has a great influence on the recipient's navigation (Wright, 1993). Secondly, links represent the semantic relations between the node contents. The recipients have to interpret the links on this semantic level. Therefore problems of comprehension could arise, if recipients have inappropriate expectations about its purpose (Gray, 1995). Consequently, linking nodes is a sensitive task that should result in a deeper processing of the information content (as was suggested in previous works, Stahl, 2001; Zahn, et al., 2002). Further information about navigation in hypermedia and how to construct hypertext information systems can be found in the chapter of Chi in this volume.

4 Models of Writing Hypervideo

As described above, designing hypervideos as an instructional strategy is highly related to research on writing in a dual sense: Collaboratively designing hypervideo includes writing processes on different levels, especially if the design is done from scratch. Additionally, the process of designing a hypervideo can be compared with the process of authoring a text (the same argument was made by Dillon, 2002 for the design of any hypermedia), because students have to construct an artefact that demands to match the content to be presented with the constraints given by the specific media and genre.

Hence, we consider it reasonable to adapt existing models of writing as a framework to define the demands and possibilities of hypermedia/hypervideo design projects and to organize courses of hypervideo design. In accordance with such existing models of writing, designing hypervideos is defined as *a cognitive process of complex problem solving with the goal to create a coherent combination of videos, texts and pictures for a specific audience*. Therefore, the processes of planning, translating and reviewing that are presented in the classical Hayes–Flower writing model (e.g., Hayes & Flower, 1980, 1986) can be used as a heuristic to structure the process of designing hypervideos as well. *Planning* incorporates cognitive activities like generating ideas and goals about the contents, the design of the hypervideo as a whole and about its various information units (video and text nodes). *Translating* includes the development of the material. For the design of hypervideos, this is a highly complex task: Students have to shoot and edit the videos, write corresponding texts, find an appropriate design and structure the video and text nodes to form a coherent structure. In the *revision* process, incoherence and problems of comprehension are diagnosed and the nodes and the overall structure will be revised. Hayes and Flower (1986) differentiate between two strategies to do so: In the "rewrite strategy" a whole paragraph/text is written anew without any diagnosis of the specific problems. In the "revise strategy" specific problems are diagnosed in detail and then specific changes are made. For video nodes, such revisions can be very demanding and therefore "rewriting" seems not as efficient as the "revise strategy". In sum, the three processes postulated by the Hayes–Flower model provide a useful over-all framework to understand the demands and possibilities of learning by designing hypervideos.

Hayes (1996) presented an extended version of this model including several individual and environmental factors assumed to affect the writing process.

Individual factors incorporate motivational and affective states of the person who is writing, their working memory, long-term memory and prior knowledge. For example, in order to write a text or to design a hypervideo, a student author needs appropriate task schemas to understand the goal of the task and the processes to accomplish it. Further on, knowledge about the genre is needed: Newspapers, books, articles, etc. follow conventions of style and layout (Dillon, 2002) and knowledge about texts and genres is important for text comprehension (e.g., Hayes, 1996; Kintsch & Yarbrough, 1982) and text production (e.g., Kellogg, 1994; Torrance, 1996). Concerning the design of new media, such as "hypervideo", students sometimes do not have any appropriate cognitive schemas available, instead relying on more familiar media formats.

Environmental factors incorporate social factors given by the anticipated audience and the collaborators in the design process. For example, in order to write a text in collaboration with others, students have to *share and negotiate* their content knowledge, as well as task schemas, task goals and task relevant strategies. This adds to the educational value, but also to the complexity of the task and models of collaborative writing (Lowry, Curtis, & Lowry, 2004) need to be considered carefully when hypervideo design courses are structured. Additionally, different modes of collaborative writing (as proposed by Lowry et al., in their taxonomy) apply to different phases of the hypervideo-design process, as will become obvious in our course descriptions below.

However, in educational contexts, where knowledge acquisition is an important goal of designing hypervideos, it seems particularly necessary to encourage reflection on the contents while students design hypervideo structures. Potential problems that might arise in such projects include that either too much attention is paid to the design of hypervideo while the contents are only included with "copy and paste" (see also Bereiter, 2002), or that students present the contents in a way that is inappropriate for the format of hypervideo. A consequence of both cases is that students may either develop only a superficial comprehension of the subject matter presented by their products or acquire superficial media-related knowledge and skills and become frustrated with the outcome of their joint design efforts. Therefore it seems necessary to find an appropriate balance to encourage conscious reflection on the contents on the one hand and reflection about the hypervideo design on the other. This assumption is made in analogy to ideas from research on writing traditional text and on collaborative writing in knowledge building communities: In their "knowledge-transforming model", Bereiter and Scardamalia (1987) claimed that writing promotes knowledge acquisition *only* when authors formulate their text within a continuous interaction between their content-related knowledge on the topic addressed in the text and their rhetorical knowledge on the design of the text and its structure (see Bereiter, 2002; Bereiter & Scardamalia, 1987). In this process, both aspects have to be considered carefully and in relation to each other: How to present the contents in a comprehensible way, i.e., what are the constraints arising from the contents? And how to do this for a specific audience, in a specific medium and in a specific genre, i.e., what are the constraints from these rhetorical factors?

Similarly, in her "expert-group" model, Scardamalia (2002) considers collaborative learning in knowledge building communities as dependent on the presence of collective cognitive responsibility that support the continual improvement of ideas and the (critical) reflection of information content within a learning community.

Stahl and Bromme (2005) used the "knowledge-transforming model" as a heuristic to examine conditions and processes of learning by constructing hypertexts and to develop a course design for hypertext writing. They argued that constructing hypertexts places special constraints on the design of the documents through the features of hypertext, and that it is necessary to consider these constraints carefully to initiate a learning process (e.g., Bromme & Stahl, 2002, 2005; Stahl, 2001; Stahl & Bromme, 2005). The constraints that might initiate knowledge transforming processes are given by the nodes, the links and the multilinear structure of hypertexts: As Stahl and Bromme (2005) described in detail, the processes of writing nodes, selecting appropriate links and planning the overall structure and flexible ways of reading might result in a deeper knowledge about the concepts within a subject matter, their semantic relations, a deeper comprehension of semantic structures within the subject matter and to a more flexible use of this new knowledge.

These considerations also apply to hypervideo design. Additionally, in designing hypervideos it is important for the collaborating students to consider and discuss which symbol system is appropriate for which kind of information. Which information should be presented as dynamic information in the videos and which are better suited to be presented as static information in the additional text nodes? The necessary group decisions determine the processes of creating nodes, setting links and designing an overall structure. They might contribute to more detailed mental models about the main concepts and to appropriate situational models of the whole topic (in the sense of Kintsch, 1998; Kintsch & Van Dijk, 1978), which should help students to understand the topic more deeply and to use it more flexibly in transfer situations.

5 Experiences with Students Designing Hypervideos in Advanced University Courses

Our experiences with students collaboratively designing hypervideos derive from three successive seminars conducted at the University of Muenster between 2003 and 2005 and one at the University of Linz that was run in 2003. The seminars were offered as courses on e-learning with the goal to teach students how to produce old and new media. The main issue of the seminars was to examine if it is possible to complete such a complex task during a regular seminar. The hypervideo design task had two purposes: Firstly, students should gain practical knowledge in designing hypervideos. This should contribute to their literacy of designing learning environments. Secondly, the design process should foster a deeper understanding of the topic to be processed.

After a series of theoretical introductions about the role of different kinds of media in learning scenarios, students had to design hypervideos about topics like "techniques of presentation and moderation" or "conflict management". These topics are considered an ideal subject matter to be presented in combinations of videos and annotated texts.

Within each seminar, students worked in collaboration with each other in order to design hypervideos for an anticipated audience. The design of a hypervideo required coordinated activities of our students since the writing processes were carried out as a collaborative endeavour, as already mentioned. Also, the brainstorming, outlining, drafting and the necessity of organizing and managing the group communication added a further level of writing tasks.

According to Posner and Baecker (1993), the whole process of collaborative writing can be decomposed according to four axes, namely the individual roles of the participants (e.g., writer, consultant, reviewer), their activities (ranging from brainstorming over planning and writing to editing and reviewing), the methods of document control (e.g., centralized, independent or shared) and the concrete writing strategies (e.g., single writer, separate writers or joint writing). Collaborative writing also can take different forms (e.g., sequential *vs.* parallel, see Lowry et al., 2004). Collaboration was supported by partly prestructuring the design process for the students, which included several modes of collaborative writing: The seminars always started with an extended literature inquiry. The students skimmed about 20 books about the chosen topic and selected relevant contents. They summarized them in short abstracts, which were written collaboratively in modes of parallel writing (Lowry et al., 2004). Afterwards, main topics for the films were selected. In the second phase of the seminar, students had an introduction in the medium of film and film language given by a professional film technician and then the storyboards were planned and written. This collaborative writing occurred in the mode of reactive writing (Lowry et al., 2004). After the planning phase, the videos were filmed and cut (for cutting we again had a professional film technician who supported the students), and additional text nodes were written (again in the mode of parallel writing). At the end of the seminar the different video and text nodes were integrated and linked in the hypervideo and revisions of the material took place.

The courses represented a mixture of face-to-face and distributed collaboration. Distributed collaboration and discussion was supported by e-mail and a simple computer supported writing system. The system certainly did not include features like those suggested by Cerratto Pargman (2003) or by Rodriguez and Severinson Eklundh in this volume. However, our students could compensate for this sub-optimal situation within their weekly sessions where they collaborated face-to-face.

The final products of the courses were hypervideos including between 8 and 14 videos with an average of five to six additional information nodes per video. As could be concluded from interviews with the students (we extensively discussed about the seminar, the possibilities of hypervideos and their products on a round table with all the students, the lecturer, his tutor and the programmer of the hypervideo software for about half a day), their products and questionnaires/reports that they completed, the students had gained substantial experiences with the design of a learning environment and they understood more about the topic presented within their hypervideo. They enjoyed their task and rated the seminars very positively. On the other hand, the project was time consuming and therefore students had to be motivated to work outside the regular seminar time. Further on, students had no experience with this medium and had inconsistent task (or goal) schemas at their disposal, as became evident in the diversity of their hypervideo products especially in the first seminars: Some student groups produced hypervideos that were comparable to instructional films, presenting all information in the videos in a linear order with only irrelevant additional information units; while others developed hypervideos in which the video part was nearly irrelevant, and instead all of the important information was given in the additional information texts. Therefore we propose to enhance consistency and appropriateness of the students' task schemas by structuring the task of designing the hypervideos into subtasks. The instructional plan of Stahl and Bromme (2005) for organizing courses of writing hypertexts could be used as a guideline for our courses in hypervideo design as well.

A highly problematic aspect especially of the first seminars was that they were organized as a sequence of separated processes (selecting material — writing storyboards — filming — writing text nodes — integrating the nodes in the system). The students had no possibility to see how their material looked like in the hypervideo-software until the end of the seminar. It was hard for the students to imagine how their product might look like. This hindered planning processes and further on, no real revision processes took place. In the following seminars, the feedback of the students had resulted in upgrades within the software: Some helpful new features were integrated into the hypervideo system that allow a much easier handling of the software and facilitate the authoring process. We also changed the course design to enable our students to do all steps of the authoring process within the hypervideo software itself. In the second seminar in Muenster we used a "concept map video" that structured the phases of hypervideo-design described above (for technical reasons this was not possible during the third seminar in Muenster). This made it possible for the students to work with the hypervideo-software from the beginning of the seminar. All materials they developed during the processes of planning and translating was linked to the adequate location within the "concept map video". This "integrative process" enabled students to get familiar to the software from the beginning. Therefore it was easier to monitor and structure the authoring process of the video and text nodes. The other students were able to comment and discuss about all material that was integrated in the concept map videos. This facilitated to integrate revision processes in the early steps of the design process. In this "integrative process" the drafts of the material were successively exchanged with further versions, until the end product was ready.

Concerning the *collaborative* aspects of hypervideo design several observations emerged. Firstly, in line with findings from other studies (Noël & Robert, 2004), the various small teams of students, which made up the whole project, showed a great diversity in their organization. Whereas in some groups, strict roles and corresponding activities were defined, other groups showed tendencies towards a more shared approach, where everybody in the group took part in the different activities of planning, writing and editing. In some groups, each team member worked more or less independently on his writing part, whereas in others, every piece of text was planned and discussed in the group. Secondly, the teams used various writing tools, both traditional and computer-based, in a flexible manner. For example, besides taking notes during team discussions in a paper-and-pencil manner, some groups started to use a text processor in conjunction with a document repository during their group discussion, thereby creating a kind of computer-based shared memory. Between the face-to-face meetings of the group, these notes were then further elaborated or rewritten in an asynchronous manner. Therefore, the computer-based document repository acted as a kind of focal point, around which all other group activities, whether face-to-face or online, individual or collaborative, were organized.

6   Conclusion and Future Prospects

To summarize our experiences, we can conclude that our task of designing hypervideo within a university course was a successful endeavour in several respects. Firstly, it was possible to implement the task of designing hypervideos from scratch in a regular university course. Secondly, we have some indirect evidence that students acquired media-related knowledge and literacy skills with regard to designing learning environments, dealing with audio–visual information and also with the required writing tasks. For example, the students' discussions about their products progressively became more professional during the seminar: Our students progressively used technical terms in appropriate ways and with a shared understanding of their meaning (e.g., for film language like "establishing shot", "over the shoulder shot"). This became obvious from their discussions among each other and the way they analysed each other's storyboards, videos and additional information as well as from the discussions with our "external" partners like the film technicians and our software engineer. Secondly, students judged hypervideo production as having fostered their active knowledge acquisition about the topic to be presented. In comparison to our standard seminar in which students are usually only reading and discussing on articles given to them by their lecturer, students in these seminars took more time to search for and to discuss relevant literature on their own. Nevertheless, we have no objective empirical evidence yet showing that the students acquired significantly more content knowledge in these seminars than in other courses. Thirdly, we could use the experiences and students' feedback to further elaborate on our course design and improve the authoring software. We assume that this should facilitate the students' understanding of the design process of learning environments as well as their comprehension of the contents they are "writing" about. This progress can be seen by comparison of the products that were designed over the years. The hypervideos of the latest seminars are of higher quality than the first ones.

Nevertheless, a lot of open questions still remain. We know now that it is possible to realize hypervideo design tasks and integrate them into regular university courses, and that the models and results in writing research give an inspiring framework to organize and structure such courses. We do not know yet exactly which cognitive processes are involved in hypervideo design in detail and have little evidence about those cognitive processes that foster knowledge acquisition. Thus, concerning future perspectives, controlled experiments need to be conducted to investigate selected aspects of collaborative hypervideo design in a laboratory learning setting.

Further on, the modes of writing within a hypervideo design are only partly encompassed by traditional models of text production. In particular, three attributes of writing in the context of multimedia production deserve a closer look: Its collaborative nature and dependence of collaborative writing on computer-based writing tools (see Cerratto Pargman, 2003; detailed reflections about (collaborative) digital writing environments are also presented in the chapter of Palmquist in this volume) as well as its necessity to accord with non-textual, audio–visual material. Therefore, hypervideo production in the context of a learning by design approach does not only exemplify a great diversity of possible situations under which writing takes place, but may also be examined in detail to advance our scientific understanding of the psychological mechanisms of (collaborative) text production. Especially since technology is developing fast in this area of audio–visual multimedia, software becomes much easier to handle and therefore we can now investigate such issues in a way that was not possible some years before.

Section III:

Digital Tools for Writing Research

Chapter 7

Web Analysis Tools Based on InfoScent™: How Cognitive Modelling Explain Reader Navigational Decisions

Ed H. Chi

Cognitive behavioural theories of how people make navigational decisions can greatly inform writers of Web content. We have been working for the past five years on modelling user actions on the Web. Our work has shown that a great deal of information about user actions can be recovered from the informational cues processed by the user during navigation. We call these informational cues by the name of "Information Scent" or "InfoScent™." By carefully analysing the way Information Scent interacts with users, we can gain deep understandings of how to construct hypertext information environments. We have also built tools that enhance the reading experience by interactively summarizing the most relevant passages for skimming, and highlight links the user might want to explore further. In this chapter, we describe this Information Scent theory and the implications for website writer/designers and readers/browsers.

1 Introduction

The Web has emerged as a global information environment. Given this, researchers are interested in understanding how to make it as useful as it can be. However, despite its success, we have little amount of theory about how to build large hypertext media websites. Most current design practices for websites are based on empirical observations and intuitions derived from the experiences of Web designers. What is really needed is a practical model of how users utilize and navigate information in hypertext environments. The hope is that from the model we would be able to analyse information environments and inform designers how to build effective web environments.

Chi, E.H. (2005). Web analysis tools based on InfoScent™: How cognitive modelling explain reader navigational decisions. In L. Van Waes, M. Leijten & C. Neuwirth (Vol. Eds.) & G. Rijlaarsdam (Series Ed.), Studies in Writing: Vol. 17. Writing and Digital Media (pp. 91–104). Oxford: Elsevier.

This chapter describes our experience of building a cognitive model of user behaviour for the Web. In our model, how a reader navigates through a digital hypermedia collection like a website is guided by their evaluation of the relevancy of each piece of information.

Information Scent (or *InfoScent*™) is the user's perception of the value and cost of accessing a piece of information. Users have some information goal — some specific information they are seeking or they are trying to obtain. The content of web pages is usually presented to the user by some snippets of text or graphic called *browsing cues*. Foragers use these browsing cues to access the *distal content*: the page at the other end of the link. Information Scent is the imperfect, subjective perception of the value, cost of information sources obtained from browsing cues. People formulate these perceptions from the informational cues that writers embed in the hypertext. For example, if a reader of a website is looking for "snowboard tune up kits," various concepts such as "wax," "iron," and "vice clamps," would trigger actions, while "hiking" or "rubber gloves" would not.

The understanding of how users utilize Information Scent to formulate navigational decisions is therefore essential to the scientific understanding of how readers deal with hypertext information.

In this chapter, we will summarize the research that has been conducted on Information Scent. This research can be used by both writers and readers of websites.

First, for designers and writers of websites, InfoScent™ is used to conduct Web analysis of two types: (1) the use of InfoScent™ to predict how users with specific information goals might surf a given website and (2) the use of InfoScent™ to mine usage logs to understand the common goals of readers of a website. We summarize our past work in these two types of Web analysis. The goal here is to use Information Scent to evaluate website designs both during and after development of the site.

Second, for readers and browsers of websites, we show how Information Scent can be utilized to construct new kinds of reading tools. One reading tool interactively highlights passages that the user might be interested in reading. Another reading tool helps users choose hyperlinks to explore further.

2 Information Scent Model

Various Web writers and designers have advocated particular ways to create usable hypertext media. Much advice of this type has focused on "rules of thumb" or design "guidelines." These advice can be useful but are formulated without an informed scientific understanding of how people actually use and navigate within hypertext environments. What is needed is a way to generalize these guidelines into a working cognitive model that could explain reader's navigational decisions, and predict their movements in hypertext space. The domain of understanding and modelling human behaviour is at the foundation of psychology.

Indeed, Herb Simon, a noted psychologist, economist, and professor at Carnegie Mellon University proposed in 1957 the idea of "Bounded Rationality" for human decision-making (Simon, 1957). He claimed that humans face much uncertainty about the future and the cost in acquiring information in the present. Thus, he put forth the idea that this uncertainty limits the extent to which humans can make fully rational decisions. That is, they have only "bounded rationality."

These ideas directly led to many ideas we have proposed for modelling users on the Web. So, while users do optimize their behaviour for consuming the most relevant information, they can only optimize to a certain extent because they often only have incomplete information goals and many uncertainty about the quality and source of information.

Indeed, our Information Scent model came directly from the field of cognitive psychology in a theory called Information Foraging (Pirolli & Card, 1999). Information Foraging seeks to explain human behaviour during information seeking. What we discovered was that the optimal foraging theory used in the study of ecology could be used to explain human's information seeking behaviour. Just as bees and birds must decide what flower patches to explore to optimize energy gain from the food sources, human users must decide what websites and what page links to choose to explore for optimize information gain.

Our work in Information Scent models on the Web is an application of Information Foraging Theory. These models help us understand how particular environmental conditions affect the navigational decisions of Web surfers moving from web page to web page, deciding among a myriad of hyperlink choices. The way Web surfers optimize their navigational choice is based on "bounded rationality." They can only guess at the value and the cost of accessing a piece of information beyond a hyperlink. Information Scent is the amount of value and cost of a piece of information conveyed by the cues that surround that hyperlink.

Figure 1 pictorially explains the idea that the snippets around a hyperlink gives off proximal cues that enable users to make inferences about the value and cost of accessing content on a distal page. For example, proximal cues might be anchor words or images around a hyperlink such as "buying a *gift certificate.*" Upon clicking on the hyperlink underlined in the phrase, the user is transported to a distal page that allows the user to purchase a gift certificate.

There have been other efforts to apply cognitive models to engineering websites. Ivory describes in a separate chapter of this book various commercial and research tools for assessing the usability of web pages. The chapter describes the variety of tools that are available and their characteristics. Information Scent is one of the major approaches to evaluate user navigational decisions.

Other works are also notable. In particular, Blackmon, Polson, Kitajima, & Lewis (2002) suggested ways to extend Cognitive Walkthroughs to predict navigational choices by applying Latent Semantic Analysis (LSA). Their approach is also based on an

snippet   content

(proximal cues)   link   (distal page)

Figure 1: Users forage for information by surfing along links. Snippets provide proximal cues to access distal content. Proximal cues could be specific words that trigger action, for example.

Information Scent model. In their work, Cognitive Walkthroughs are enhanced to predict user navigational decisions by measuring Information Scent using LSA.

Kaur and Hornof (2005) also build on the Information Scent model to actually compare various techniques to measure Information Scent to predict user behaviour, including LSA and Point Mutual Information (PMI) techniques.

3 Implication of Information Scent Model

Information Scent was first applied to the Web by Chi, Pirolli, and Pitkow (2000) and later expanded by Chi, Pirolli, Chen, and Pitkow (2001) and Heer and Chi (2002). The development of this model has several important implications:

(1) First, a scientific understanding of human behaviour in web surfing is fundamental to understanding how users read on the Web. A great deal of literature on Web usability is now available, with most based on empirical design principles and "rules of thumb" (Krug, 2000; Nielsen, 2001; Spool, Scanlon, Schroeder, Snyder, & DeAngelo, 1999). Certainly, experience with building websites can inform us a great deal about what works and what does not work. This is analogous to learning to build a log cabin through trial and error. However, eventually we need to build large and complicated buildings and structures that require engineering principles to calculate the loads on the beams and optimal shapes, informing us about what is possible and what is not possible. The same knowledge is required in creating website architecture and design. We use the Information Scent model to actually make predictions about the usability of these websites.

(2) Previous analysis of web surfing activities is based on statistical analysis and modelling of Web usage traffic, typically through Web log analysis, in-lab/remote-instrumented browser log analysis. We are interested in using the Information Scent model to predict surfing paths without any usage data. This moves us forward from first-order descriptive statistics to predictive statistics. A new capability, for example, would be making predictions about the usability of a website even before it is launched live in front of real users. The development of a predictive model could greatly accelerate our ability to understand alternative designs. A predictive model in web surfing represents a new step towards Web analytics.

(3) Given a predictive model of how surfers are likely to navigate, we can use it to enhance current practices of how users read and consume information on the Web. For example, if we know the information goal of the user, and can predict where they are likely to go, we can direct their attention to hyperlinks that are more relevant to them. We can also highlight passages that they are more likely to want to read. By dynamically changing the information environment to reflect what they might be interested in, we are effectively warping the information environment so that they can consume information with greater efficiency.

4 Bloodhound Project: A Preditive Model of Web Surfing

Here we will describe briefly the way Information Scent is used to automate the discovery of Web usability issues.

According to usability experts, the top user issue for websites is difficulties in navigation. We have been developing automated usability tools for several years, and here we describe a prototype service called InfoScent™ Bloodhound Simulator, a push-button navigation analysis system (Chi et al., 2003).

Our assumption is that, for the purposes of our analyses, users have some information goal, and their surfing patterns through the site are guided by information scent. The link with the highest amount of information cue (or *scent*) is the link with the highest probability of being followed.

The analysis method is based on computational models of *Spreading Activation* (Anderson, 1990) used in the study of relevancy in human memory. Spreading activation works with a weighted graph of associations between chunks of information. Starting from an initial chunk of information ("source"), activation spreads from one chunk to another chunk through association links that specifies the probabilistic strength between the two chunks. Activation flows from one chuck to another chunk much like water flowing through a system of pipes with varying widths. Spreading activation predicts that highly activated chunks of information are highly relevant to the source chuck. This process is highly similar to Bayesian Inference of a probabilistic network, or a Markov-chain process.

Conceptually, the simulation models an arbitrary number of users traversing the links and content of a website. The users have information goals that are represented by strings of content words such as "Xerox scanning products." For each simulated user, at each page visit, the model assesses the information scent associated with linked pages. The information scent is computed by comparing the users' information goals against the pages' contents. Figure 2 shows one depiction of this process.

The essential idea is to compute the probability of ending up at a particular node in the graph. Given that each edge specifies the probability of transition through that pair of nodes, we can compute the conditional probability of ending up anywhere in the entire graph. Applying this to the simulation of users moving through the Web, we use the nodes in this graph to represent each page. We compute the transition probability of moving from one page to another page based on the strength of the Information Scent. We then use spreading activation to simulate users moving through the website with these transition probabilities.

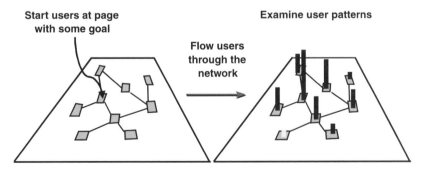

Figure 2: Spreading activation.

A data flow model of the algorithm is presented in Figure 3. First, the website is crawled, enabling us to extract its content and the linkage structure. By comparing the user information goal to the content and the information cues that exist on each page, we calculate the transition probability of moving from one page to another page based on that information goal. This transitional probability is the Information Scent that is collected into the Scent Matrix. Each entry *[i,j]* in the Scent Matrix specifies the probability a user with that information goal will move from page *i* to another page *j*. The spreading activation algorithm is then used to simulate users flowing through this network. The result of this simulation is then analysed to create a set of predicted user paths and a set of metrics for the usability of the website.

The key to the algorithm is the computation of the amount of the Information Scent for each link on each page. The information scent value for a link used by the simulation is computed from the amount of information cues as represented by a text snippet or icon for that link.

Bloodhound, given a transient user information goal, automatically analyses the information cues on a website to produce a usability report. We presented a user study involving 244 subjects over 1385 user sessions that shows how Bloodhound user profiles correlates with real users surfing for information on four websites (Chi et al., 2003). The idea is that, by using a simulation of user surfing behaviour, we can reduce the need for

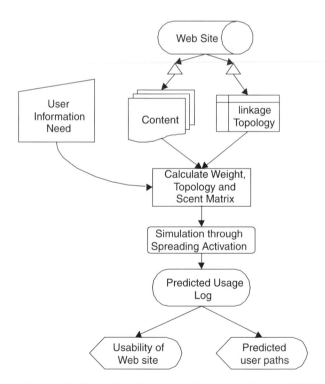

Figure 3: Flow chart of the Web User Flow by Information Scent (WUFIS) algorithm.

human labour during usability testing, thus dramatically lowering testing costs, and ulti-mately improving user experience. The Bloodhound Project is unique in that we apply a concrete Human-Computer Interaction (HCI) theory directly to a real-world problem.

5 LumberJack Project: Understanding Web User Goals

The beauty of the Information Scent model is that it can be used for both predicting user behaviour as well as used to understand user behaviour. In the LumberJack project, we seek to understand how InfoScent™ can be used to understand what the users must be interested in, given that we have logs that state their choices in the links and pages they chose to read.

Web Usage Mining enables new understanding of user goals on the Web. This under-standing has broad applications, and traditional mining techniques such as association rules have been used in business applications. We have developed an automated method to directly infer the major groupings of user traffic on a website (Heer & Chi, 2002; Chi, Rosien, & Heer, 2002). We do this by combining Information Scent model with multiple data features of user sessions in a clustering analysis.

We describe a method for inferring the information goal of a user based on the user's traversal path through a hypertext collection. A user typically forages for information by making traversal decisions based on the user's task. For example, at any point in a traversal through the website, the user has expressed her interest in various pieces of information by the decision to traverse certain links. A well-travelled path may indicate a group of users who have very similar information goals and are guided by the scent of the environment. This user's traversal history is a list of documents that approximates the information goal. Therefore, given a path, we would like to know the information goal expressed by that path. Given a traversal path through a hypertext collection, what can we say about the information goal expressed by that traversal path?

In order to compute the information goal of a traversal path, we make the following observation. The input to the model should be a list of documents and the order in which they were visited. The output is weighted keyword vector that describes the information goal. Notice that this is the direct reverse of the simulation given by the predictive model formulated in the section above. The input to the model above is a weighted vector of key-words that describes the information goals, and the output is a list of documents that are visited by the simulated users. Therefore, intuitively, we need to reverse the flow of the above model to obtain a list of user goal keywords. Without going into much further detail, the inferring algorithm can be accomplished by doing many of the same analyses for the predictive algorithm above. Figure 4 describes the data flow of this algorithm.

We further developed this work into a prototype service for clustering user profiles called LumberJack, a push-button analysis system that is both more automated and accu-rate than past systems. This service enables us to understand how user goals are clustered in the usage of a website. We have performed an extensive, systematic evaluation of the proposed approach, and have discovered that certain clustering schemes can achieve cate-gorization accuracies as high as 99% (Heer & Chi, 2002).

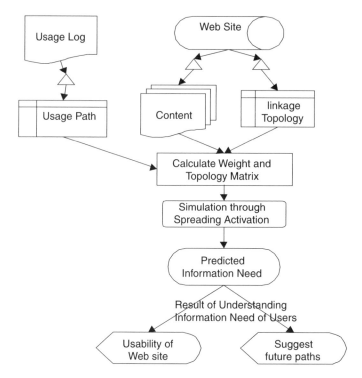

Figure 4: Flow chart for the Inferring User Goal by Information Scent (IUNIS) algorithm.

6 ScentTrails Project: Directing User Attention to Relevant Hyperlinks

In our work with the two algorithms above, we discovered that the Information Scent model can also be used to construct end-user applications for more efficient browsing of websites. One example project in this area is ScentTrails (Olston & Chi, 2003). Our work is motivated by the observation that two predominant yet imperfect interface modes currently exist for locating information on the Web: searching and browsing. While they exhibit complementary advantages, neither paradigm alone is adequate for complex information goals that lend themselves partially to browsing and partially to searching.

Keyword searching allows users to identify pages containing specific information quickly; each search is tailored to a user's particular information goal, when formulated as a list of keywords. In contrast, browsing is advantageous when appropriate search keywords are impossible to determine. For example,

- The user's information goal may not be fully formed at the outset and the user may not be certain of what she is looking for until the available options are presented during browsing.
- Even if the full information goal is known at the outset, the exact terminology used on the web pages may not be known, and therefore searching often will not yield the correct result.

- Certain information goals, such as ones that involve semantic predicates like "price < $200," cannot be expressed using existing general-purpose keyword search technology.
- Finally, browsing is appropriate when a great deal of information and context are obtained along the browsing path, not just at the final page.

Searching and browsing offer complementary advantages. However, neither modality is well equipped to handle rich or complex information goals consisting of multiple criteria; some criteria lend themselves well to searching and others are better suited to browsing. Regrettably, it is difficult to reap the benefits of both searching and browsing simultaneously by simply switching between the two modalities.

To integrate browsing and searching smoothly into a single interface, we introduce a novel approach called ScentTrails. Based on the concept of information scent, ScentTrails highlights hyperlinks to indicate paths to search results. In ScentTrails, the user enters keywords representing the portion of his or her information goal that is initially known and amenable to search. ScentTrails then annotates the hyperlinks of web pages with search cues. These search cues are indications that a link leads to content that matches the search query.

This annotation is done by visually highlighting links to complement the browsing cues already embedded in each page. The degree to which links are highlighted is determined by an Information Scent algorithm. An example is shown in Figure 5. A portion of the Xerox.com website was modified by our ScentTrails proxy, which increased the font size of certain links to display search cues for the partial information goal "remote diagnostic technology." Links in a large font lead to product descriptions containing that phrase. Search cues may appear in different gradations (for instance, high, medium, low) depending on degree of relevance and distance in number of hops; search cue gradations are computed using an Information Scent algorithm operating over page content and link topology.

By considering both the search and browsing cues together, the user is able to make informed navigational decisions and efficiently locate content matching complex information goals that lend themselves partially to searching and partially to browsing. This interface enables users to interpolate smoothly between searching and browsing to locate content matching complex information goals effectively. In a user study, ScentTrails enabled subjects to find information more quickly than by either searching or browsing alone (Olston & Chi, 2003).

7 ScentHighlighting: Directing User Attention to Relevant Passages

Another readers' tool we created using the Information Scent model is ScentHighlighting, which is a way to direct users' attention to the most relevant passages according to their information goal. Indeed, reading researchers have noticed a change in everyday reading activities. Readers are increasingly skimming instead of reading in depth. Skimming also occur in re-reading activities, where the goal is to recall specific facts surrounding a topic. Bookmarks and highlighters were invented precisely to achieve this goal. This fundamental shift in reading is what motivated many researchers to examine the possibilities for enhancing modern-day reading activities (Nunberg, 1996; Golovchinsky, Marshall, &

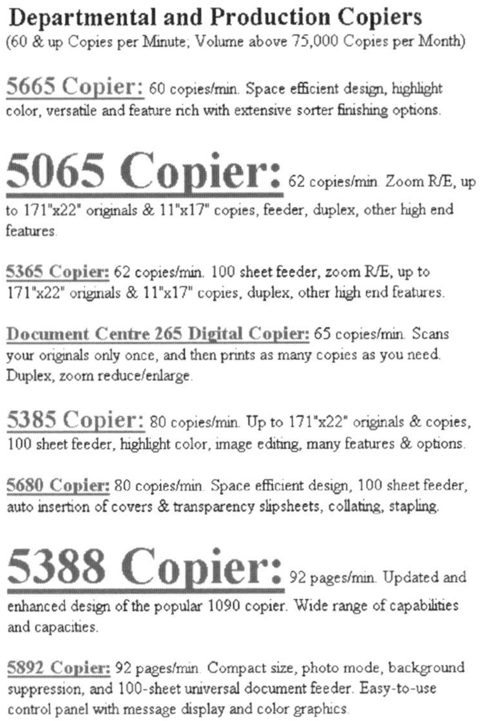

Departmental and Production Copiers
(60 & up Copies per Minute; Volume above 75,000 Copies per Month)

<u>5665 Copier:</u> 60 copies/min. Space efficient design, highlight color, versatile and feature rich with extensive sorter finishing options.

5065 Copier: 62 copies/min. Zoom R/E, up
to 171"x22" originals & 11"x17" copies, feeder, duplex, other high end features.

<u>5365 Copier:</u> 62 copies/min. 100 sheet feeder, zoom R/E, up to 171"x22" originals & 11"x17" copies, duplex, other high end features.

<u>Document Centre 265 Digital Copier:</u> 65 copies/min. Scans your originals only once, and then prints as many copies as you need. Duplex, zoom reduce/enlarge.

<u>5385 Copier:</u> 80 copies/min. Up to 171"x22" originals & copies, 100 sheet feeder, highlight color, image editing, many features & options.

<u>5680 Copier:</u> 80 copies/min. Space efficient design, 100 sheet feeder, auto insertion of covers & transparency slipsheets, collating, stapling.

5388 Copier: 92 pages/min. Updated and
enhanced design of the popular 1090 copier. Wide range of capabilities and capacities.

<u>5892 Copier:</u> 92 pages/min. Compact size, photo mode, background suppression, and 100-sheet universal document feeder. Easy-to-use control panel with message display and color graphics.

Figure 5: The ScentTrails technique highlights hyperlinks that would lead to pages that satisfies the information goal of "remote diagnostic technology."

Schilit, 1999). For all these skimming activities, readers need effective ways to direct their attention towards the most relevant passages within text.

For the purpose of skimming, we are exploring ways to automatically highlight potentially relevant sentences and passages in electronic text using conceptual modelling (Chi et al., 2005). The SuperBook project probably conducted one of the earliest studies on the effectiveness of query term highlighting (Egan et al., 1989). In an evaluation study, they found increased user performance when the target information was actually highlighted and decreased user performance otherwise. Many systems designed for browsing and reading after SuperBook used dynamic query term highlighting, including search engines such as Google and Yahoo showing of cached pages.

Here we extend the dynamic highlighting technique to actually highlight conceptual related keywords and sentences. We are interested in ways in which the user attention can be warped by the structure of the information environment, so that user can become more productive. The key to the idea, therefore, is to intelligently extract summary sentences that are relevant to the topic profile. Using topic keywords, we propose to direct reader's attention by automatically highlighting relevant text. We have enhanced skimming activity by conceptually highlighting sentences within electronic text that relate to a topic profile.

The topic profile can be specified on-the-fly by the user, or can be generated from the user's reading and browsing history.

Figure 6 shows an example of the sentence and keyword highlights made by our system with the user profile interest of "Marburg" virus for a portion of a book page. As shown in the figure, related keywords are highlighted, and the most relevant sentences are highlighted in yellow.

We highlight sentences by first computing related conceptual keywords. A sentence is highlighted if it contains conceptual keywords that are highly relevant to the topics. We do this by computing what conceptual keywords are related to each other via word co-occurrence and spreading activation. Spreading activation, as described previously, is a cognitive model developed in psychology to simulate how memory chunks and conceptual items are retrieved in our brain. Word co-occurrence, on the other hand, has been used in statistical language processing (Schuetze & Manning, 1999), and is constructed by understanding how often conceptual keywords occur near each other in the text. Therefore, this model is suitable for our purpose of identifying related conceptual keywords and sentences.

We have implemented ScentHighlights in an electronic book (eBook) system called 3Book (Card, Hong, Mackinlay, & Chi, 2004). Here we illustrate how ScentHighlights can help readers locate relevant passages. We first type in the keywords into the search box (Figure 7A). Searching forward from the beginning of the book produces the result shown in Figure 7B.

Zooming up to the relevant passages that were highlighted on the left page showed that the author of the passage had worked on creating an anthrax weapon (Figure 8A). Zooming up to the relevant sections that are highlighted on the right side of the page gave us exactly the information we were seeking (Figure 8B). Searching forward or turning to each new page will continue to produce highlights that are only relevant to the search keywords entered.

We see that the anthrax symptoms are nasal stuffiness, twinges of pain in joints, fatigue, and a dry persistent cough. Because of the ScentHighlights technique, the relevant passages all have been highlighted. The conceptual keywords that caused the sentences to be highlighted are also highlighted in grey, distinguished from exact keyword matches in pastel-like colours. The spreading activation process had produced highlights that were

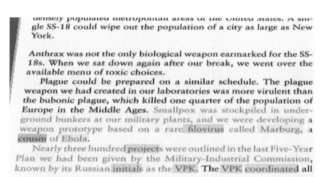

Figure 6: Example sentence and keyword highlights made by ScentHighlights.

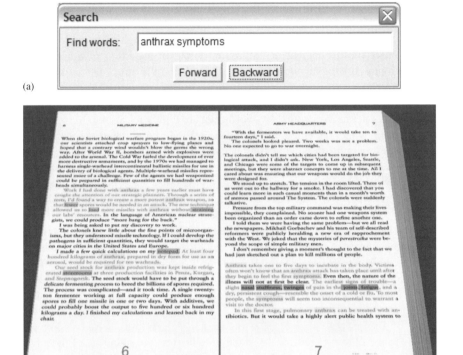

Figure 7: Keyword search box (a); highlightings obtained for "anthrax symptoms" (b).

extremely relevant to the task at hand. A user study on ScentHighlighting is part of an ongoing research at Palo Alto Research Centre (PARC) to study productive reading.

8 Limitations and Future Work

There are some severe limitations of the current model. While the Bloodhound and LumberJack systems can be used to measure, predict, and understand user behaviour, they are not yet able to directly suggest design changes. Tools based on guideline validation are quite suitable for suggesting design changes, and in this way, guideline checkers are somewhat more practical than our predictive models currently. However, since guidelines are not to be followed blindly, it is unclear that the suggested design changes are really any better than designers' own intuitions.

One potential extension to this current work is that Information Scent theories have not yet fully been extended to the problems of understanding the visual perception of proximal cues. Therefore, visual design decisions such as link or advertisement placement is not yet included in the model. Some initial integration of visual perceptual models into

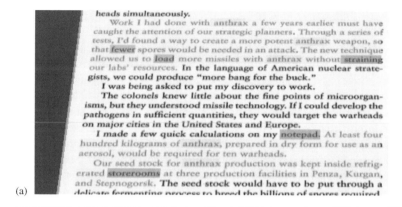

heads simultaneously.

Work I had done with anthrax a few years earlier must have caught the attention of our strategic planners. Through a series of tests, I'd found a way to create a more potent anthrax weapon, so that fewer spores would be needed in an attack. The new technique allowed us to load more missiles with anthrax without straining our labs' resources. In the language of American nuclear strategists, we could produce "more bang for the buck."

I was being asked to put my discovery to work.

The colonels knew little about the fine points of microorganisms, but they understood missile technology. If I could develop the pathogens in sufficient quantities, they would target the warheads on major cities in the United States and Europe.

I made a few quick calculations on my notepad. At least four hundred kilograms of anthrax, prepared in dry form for use as an aerosol, would be required for ten warheads.

Our seed stock for anthrax production was kept inside refrigerated storerooms at three production facilities in Penza, Kurgan, and Stepnogorsk. The seed stock would have to be put through a delicate fermenting process to breed the billions of spores required

(a)

Anthrax takes one to five days to incubate in the body. Victims often won't know that an anthrax attack has taken place until after they begin to feel the first symptoms. Even then, the nature of the illness will not at first be clear. The earliest signs of trouble—a slight nasal stuffiness, twinges of pain in the joints, fatigue, and a dry, persistent cough—resemble the onset of a cold or flu. To most people, the symptoms will seem too inconsequential to warrant a visit to the doctor.

In this first stage, pulmonary anthrax can be treated with antibiotics. But it would take a highly alert public health system to

(b)

Figure 8: Zoomed detail of the highlights of left page (a); zoomed detail of the highlights of right page (b).

Information Foraging theory has been conducted by Pirolli, Card, and Wege (2001), but more work is needed to understand how visual perception models can be integrated with Information Scent models.

As mentioned in Ivory's chapter in this book, there are various efforts in building automatic evaluation tools for website design, but there has been a lack of studies of developers using these tools and their effectiveness. This is a clear area for future work.

More importantly, our hope is that the Information Scent model bridges the gap between theory and practice and will serve as a unifying theory that future evaluations and frameworks can be build upon. Future extensions and development of the model will undoubtedly add to its power and mitigate its current limitations.

9 Conclusion

Reading is a unique and essential human activity that furthers the mind and soul of our collective knowledge and history (Fischer, 2003). Therefore, Human-Information Interaction must directly study and make sense of the reading activity (Sellen & Harper, 2001). Reading as an activity is governed by the complexity of the information environment in which it occurs. The over-abundance of information affects the material selected for reading, as well as the depth in which it is studied. The amount of available time and resource to understand written text is shrinking in our ever-busying life. These changes in our environment have directly affected the way we interact with written text (Sellen & Harper, 2001). Increasingly, reading is occurring online in blogs and on the Web, and less so on paper.

We have examined and utilized theory from cognitive psychology to help Web surfers to optimize their information gain from reading on the Web. Information Scent, as a model derived from Information Foraging theory, has proven to be a powerful model for predicting Web user surfing behaviours as well as inferring user information goals from their log traces.

We also examined ways in which information scent can be used to create new and novel reading interfaces. Indeed, as readers increasingly adapt to new ways of obtaining information, digital technology will have to keep up with their varied information goals and strategies for obtaining the most relevant pieces of information. Indeed, as Bush said, "The difficulty seems to be, not so much that we publish unduly in view of the extent and variety of present-day interests, but rather that publication has been extended far beyond our present ability to make real use of the record" (Bush, 1945).

Acknowledgements

The work described here are the results of collaboration with Peter Pirolli, Jeff Heer, Chris Olston, Lichan Hong, Julie Heiser, Michelle Gumbrecht, Jim Pitkow, Kim Chen, Stu Card, the UIR research group, and the Bloodhound Project Team in the ASD/Y-Axis development group at PARC. I would also like to thank the reviewers for suggestions that improved this paper. This research was supported in part by an Office of Naval Research grant No. N00014-96-C-0097 to Peter Pirolli and Stuart Card. The user study portion of this research has been funded in part by contract #MDA904-03-C-0404 to Stuart K. Card and Peter Pirolli under the ARDA NIMD program.

Chapter 8

Automated Web Site Evaluation Tools: Implications for Writers

Melody Y. Ivory

The Web plays an important role in our society — enabling broad access to information and services. Nonetheless, the usability and accessibility of web page contents are still pressing problems. Content writing guidelines exist, but writers need tools to help them to conform to guidelines that are often vague, voluminous, contradictory, or difficult to apply. Automated web site evaluation tools are one potential solution to this problem. There are over 50 commercial and research tools for assessing many web page aspects, including issues that are relevant to writers. This chapter discusses the space of automated evaluation tools, in particular their advantages, limitations, and implications for writers. It summarizes web professionals' use of the tools in practice and empirical studies on the tools' efficacy. In general, the tools were not developed with content writers in mind. This chapter describes research needed to improve the tools so that they can benefit writers.

1 Introduction

Content plays an important role in web sites, as well as in the World Wide Web. From its inception, Berners-Lee intended the Web to be a vehicle for sharing ASCII text, which included links to other text (i.e., hypertext) (Berners-Lee & Fischetti, 1999). The current Web has evolved radically from its first instantiation: Web sites can have complex navigation mechanisms, functionality, and graphical designs. Despite the complex and graphical nature of sites, ASCII text or content is still their most important asset. For instance, an analysis of ratings assigned to a large sample of sites revealed that judges' and users' assessments of content, rather than graphics, were more correlated with overall site ratings (Sinha, Hearst, & Ivory, 2001).

Ever since the Web became available to a broad user population, users have experienced numerous usability and accessibility problems. Consequently, a plethora of design

Ivory, M.Y. (2005). Automated Web Site Evaluation Tools: Implications for writers. In L. Van Waes, M. Leijten & C. Neuwirth (Vol. Eds.) & G. Rijlaarsdam (Series Ed.), Studies in Writing: Vol. 17. Writing and Digital Media (pp. 105–114). Oxford: Elsevier.

guidance (e.g., guidelines, articles, texts, and other resources) exists to support web professionals in producing effective sites. Despite the importance of content, early design guidance focused mostly on graphic design and the mechanics of HTML coding, accessibility in particular (e.g., Levine, 1996; Lynch & Horton, 1999; W3C, 1999). In more recent design guidance, there is a shift in focus to content. For instance, Nielsen's empirical studies on web writing provide guidance for writers (Nielsen, 1997), and texts focus exclusively on writing content for the Web (e.g., McGovern, Norton, & O'Dowd, 2002; Price & Price, 2002).

Despite the abundance of design guidance, conforming to it is a historical problem (Lowgren & Nordqvist, 1992; Souza & Bevan, 1990) that plagues content writers as well. Prescriptive guidelines are often voluminous, vague, conflicting, or divorced from the context in which sites are being developed, thus making such guidance difficult to apply. To mitigate this problem, researchers and vendors developed tools to assess whether or not a design conforms to specific guidelines. These tools are a potentially useful addition to the web site development process.

In this chapter, we discuss automated web site evaluation tools and their implications for content writers. Section 2 summarizes the characteristics of automated evaluation tools. Section 3 discusses web professionals' use of the tools and presents findings from empirical studies. Current tools provide limited support for content evaluation and are somewhat inadequate overall; Section 4 describes research and functionality needed to better support writers.

2   Automated Evaluation of Web Sites

There are over 50 commercial and research tools for automated evaluation of web sites (see Ivory, 2003). The tools automate evaluation in two important ways:

- *Analysis.* Software automatically identifies potential problems.
- *Critique.* Software performs analysis and suggests improvements.

All the tools that we describe in this chapter support analysis and a subset support critique. We discuss the anatomy of an automated evaluation tool and then summarize five predominate types of tools. Throughout our discussion, we focus on the application of these tools to web content.

Figure 1 depicts the anatomy of automated evaluation tools. The top part of the figure shows that a web site design is influenced by the intended users, their tasks, and the assumptions made about the technology that they will use to access the site. Tools also make assumptions about web site users (e.g., computer or Internet experience, reading level, and other abilities), their tasks (e.g., browsing or searching for information), and the technology that they use (e.g., web browsers, Internet connections, and assistive technology). For example, the tool may assume that users are sighted, browsing for information, and accessing the site via a computer with a 56.6 K modem and a 15-inch monitor. As another example, the tool may assume that users are blind, browsing for information, and accessing the site via a computer with a 56.6 K modem and screen reader. It is important to note that these assumptions may not match the factors that influenced the design of the

Web Site Design

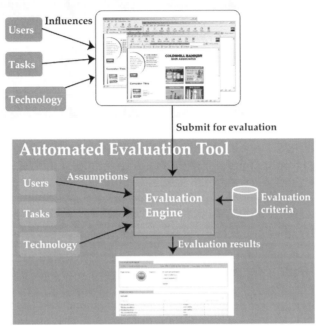

Figure 1: Anatomy of an automated web site evaluation tool.

site. All tools have criteria (e.g., server response time or guidelines), which they use to evaluate a site. They typically present evaluation results in a graphical or textual report.

Based on our studies (summarized in Section 3), we identified seven factors for beneficial tools. We also added a factor to reflect our interest in content evaluation.

- *Empirical validation.* The tool is based on adequate empirical validation (e.g., usability tests to verify the effectiveness of produced sites).
- *Time of application.* The tool is applicable during all design and implementation stages.
- *Content consideration.* The tool considers web page content in its assessments.
- *Context consideration.* The tool enables the writer to customize the site's evaluation, based on its context (i.e., intended users, tasks, technology, etc.).
- *Site effectiveness.* The tool produces successful sites (i.e., effective, efficient, and satisfactory).
- *Adaptability.* The tool accommodates changes, such as new guidelines, legislation, or implementation technology.
- *Usability.* The tool is usable, learnable, etc.
- *Expertise requirement.* The tool minimizes expertise requirements, especially for novice writers.

Using the above criteria, Table 1 contrasts the five types of evaluations tools — performance analyzers, usage analyzers, guideline conformance analyzers or critics, navigation

Table 1: Characteristics of existing automated web site evaluation tools.

Tool	Criteria							
	EV	**TA**	**CC**	**CtxtC**	**SE**	**A**	**U**	**ER**
Performance analyzers	✓			●	●	✓	✓	✓
Usage analyzers	●		●	✓	●	✓	●	
Guideline conformance analyzers or critics	●	●	●	●	●	●		
Navigation text analyzers	✓	●	●	✓	●	●		
Navigation simulators	✓		●	✓	●	●		

Note: Columns represent the eight ideal features of a successful tool: empirical validation (EV), time of application (TA), content consideration (CC), context consideration (CtxtC), site effectiveness (SE), adaptability (A), usability (U), and expertise requirement (ER). A tool's satisfaction of a criterion is indicated as: criterion typically met (✓), criterion potentially met (●), or criterion not typically met (blank).

text analyzers, and navigation simulators. Performance analyzers measure web server response times. Usage analyzers extract navigation patterns and other behavior statistics from log files of web page requests. Guideline conformance analyzers assess whether or not pages conform to specific guidelines; critics perform analysis and suggest ways in which to conform to specific guidelines. Navigation text analyzers assess the clarity of link or heading text with respect to locating the appropriate link for a specific information-seeking goal. Navigation simulators attempt to predict how users will navigate the site and identify potential problems.

Table 1 shows that performance and usage analyzers meet or potentially meet all but two criteria, but their influence on many design aspects like content formatting or page layout are limited. Four types of tools — usage analyzers, guideline conformance analyzers or critics, navigation text analyzers, and navigation simulators — potentially meet the content consideration criterion. As we will discuss in the next section, the current support for content evaluation is limited. All approaches potentially meet the site effectiveness criterion, but no tool can guarantee a site's effectiveness; usability tests with representative users are required.

2.1 Performance Analyzers

Performance monitoring and stress-checking tools measure web server response times for actual or simulated requests (i.e., assess how long it takes the web server to transfer a requested page and linked elements to a user's browser) (Bacheldor, 1999). They are useful for identifying performance bottlenecks, such as slow server response time, that negatively affect the usability and accessibility of a site (Wilson, 1999). In general, these tools provide little insight into the quality of the web site itself or the site's content. Hence, the tools may not be beneficial to content writers.

2.2   Usage Analyzers

Given that web servers automatically log requests, there are various web log analysis tools. Task-based analysis tools aggregate traces of multiple user interactions and produce visualizations or reports that compare users' task flows to an optimal task flow (Helfrich & Landay, 1999; Paganelli & Paterno, 2002). Inferential analysis tools support statistical analyses of site traffic and user interactions (Drott, 1998; Fuller & Graaff, 1996; NetIQ, 2002), online analytical processing and mining of usage data (Spiliopoulou, 2000; Zaiane, Xin, & Han, 1998), and three-dimensional or interactive visualizations of usage data (Chi, 2002; Cugini & Scholtz, 1999; Hochheiser & Shneiderman, 2001). Tools in the latter two classes consider web page contents in their analyses. For instance, the LumberJack tool (discussed in Chapter 7) estimates the similarity of content and uses these estimates, along with other features, to automatically identify groups of users who have related content interests and the nature of those interests (i.e., their content goals).

Usage analyzers suffer from several limitations. They require a site that is already built and in use, and, as such, they are more useful for assessing navigation patterns than design elements. Navigation patterns may provide writers with some insight about how users are reading content on a site; however, server logs are missing valuable information about users' information-seeking tasks. Server log data are also unreliable due to caching. For instance, if a user requests a page that the browser or proxy server has stored in a local cache, then the cached page is used. In this scenario, a request entry would not appear in the server's log file. Analysis of client-side data (i.e., log data captured via an instrumented web site, an instrumented browser, or a proxy server) is one way to address the inaccuracy of server log data.

Given an accurate record of how users move through the content on a site, interpretation of statistical and task-based analyses may lead to improvements in content organization. For instance, page access statistics may suggest pages that are problematic (e.g., pages that are accessed infrequently compared to other pages) and navigation patterns may suggest pages for which content can be streamlined or expanded. Considerable expertise is required to interpret and act on such results.

2.3   Guideline Conformance Analyzers or Critics

There are over 30 tools for assessing whether or not a web page or site conforms to specific usability, accessibility, HTML coding, or browser-compatibility guidelines. Available tools include: Bobby (WatchFire, 2002), WAVE (Pennsylvania's Initiative on Assistive Technology, 2001), LIFT (UsableNet, 2000), W3C HTML Validator (W3C, 2001), and many others (for an online listing, see W3C, 2002). Bobby, LIFT, A-Prompt, and a few others provide critique support (i.e., they recommend design changes). LIFT tools provide assistance with making recommended changes; one tool — LIFT — Nielsen Norman Group Edition (UsableNet, 2002) — assesses a site's conformance to accessibility guidelines that researchers developed based on studies of users who had visual and motor impairments (Coyne & Nielsen, 2001).

Only a subset of the guidelines that are embedded in these tools address issues that are relevant to web content. For instance, tools can check to see if the language of the text is identified, link titles are repeated, page titles are missing, tables are appropriately labeled, or spelling errors are present. Conforming to the tools' guidelines can potentially eliminate problems that arise, but, in most cases, the guidelines have not been validated empirically. In addition, not all aspects can or are represented as guidelines; thus, these aspects will not be evaluated. As an example, it is not possible to assess whether or not users will understand the meaning of text.

Some tools compare quantitative web page measures — such as the number of links or graphics — to somewhat arbitrary thresholds (Stein, 1997; Theng & Marsden, 1998). The WebTango Analysis Tool is one exception (Ivory & Hearst, 2002a); it compares quantitative measures on pages and sites to models developed based on evaluated interfaces. The interface models make it possible to derive quantitative thresholds for design aspects like the amount of text, links, colors, fonts, etc. to use on pages (Ivory, 2003, June; Ivory & Hearst, 2002b). The WebTango Analysis Tool can assess additional content features, such as whether the reading level is appropriate to a broad user population, the amount of text and formatting is appropriate for the page size, or the use of headings is proportional to the amount of text. A user study showed that the tool could inform design improvements.

Guideline conformance analyzers and critics are consistent with other tools like spelling, style, or grammar checkers that writers employ. Depending on the environment in which writing takes place, guideline tools (and automated evaluation tools in general), may not fit within writers' work practices. For instance, some writers may be responsible solely for content authoring, as opposed to writing web pages (i.e., HTML authoring). They may use word processors for content authoring, but automated evaluation tools are not embedded within word processors. Most tools are available online, and a few are embedded into HTML authoring tools like Macromedia®· Dreamweaver®· and Microsoft® Office FrontPage®. All tools require pages to be implemented in HTML before they can be evaluated.

2.4   Navigation Text Analyzers

Cognitive Walkthrough for the Web (CWW, Blackmon, Polson, Kitajima, & Lewis, 2002) is a critique approach that can identify potential navigation problems and provide guidance for correcting them. The approach entails the use of Latent Semantic Analysis (LSA, Landauer & Dumais, 1997), which is a theoretical approach to modeling the words that are used within a certain context (e.g., ninth grade textbooks or newspaper articles). In essence, an LSA model (referred to as a semantic space) encapsulates information about the usage of words, such as words that have similar meanings or are used together. It is possible to analyze a document or passage of text to determine the degree to which it is similar to a semantic space (i.e., uses the same types of words in the same way).

CWW uses an LSA model to contrast actual or planned web page text (headings or links) to a specified information-seeking goal (100–200 word narrative and correct link selection on the page). The LSA system computes similarity measures for the two text inputs. The authors provide similarity thresholds for three navigation problems: confusable heading or link text, unfamiliar heading or link text, and competing heading or link text. Their empirical studies demonstrate that modifying page and link text to fit within their thresholds improves usability. Other researchers are developing similar navigation text analyzers (Kaur, 2004).

Both approaches are under development and currently are manual processes; however, they represent promising future tools for writers. Similarly to essay grading systems (for a brief survey, see Hearst, 2000), these approaches could be expanded beyond navigation text to evaluate the content on a single page or across pages in a site. For instance, researchers could use the comparison approach to assess content cohesion or consistency across pages.

2.5 Navigation Simulators

WebCriteria's Site Profile[1] was the first navigation simulator developed; it used an idealized user model that followed an explicit, pre-specified navigation path through a web site and estimated several metrics, such as page load and optimal navigation times (Lynch, Palmiter, & Tilt, 1999). Several researchers developed similar navigation simulation approaches (Blackmon et al., 2002; Card et al., 2001; Chi, Pirolli, Chen, & Pitkow, 2001; Chi et al., 2003; Kitajima, Blackmon, & Polson, 2000; Miller & Remington, 2000). They developed tools to simulate information-seeking behavior by modeling hypothetical users traversing the site from specified start pages, making use of information *scent* (i.e., common keywords between the user's goal and content on linked pages) to make navigation decisions. More information about these types of tools can be found in Chapter 7.

With the exception of the approach that Blackmon and colleagues are developing, the tools require the site to be implemented for realistic evaluations. Another major limitation of the tools is that none of them account for the effects of various web page attributes, such as the amount of text or layout of links, on navigation behavior. Nonetheless, such tools could help writers to predict how users will read content on the site and possibly reveal problems that can be addressed before content writing is complete or the site is released for use. This evaluation functionality would be useful in early design stages before the site is implemented.

3 Studies of Automated Web Site Evaluation Tools

As discussed in the preceding section, there are many automated web site evaluation tools available. In this section, we are interested in the following questions:

- Are web professionals using automated web site evaluation tools? If so, how?
- How effective are automated web site evaluation tools in improving the usability, accessibility, etc. of sites?

We summarize studies that we conducted to answer these questions. We discuss tool adoption, results from two comparisons of tools, and results from a study.

---

[1] This tool is no longer available for use.

3.1   Tool Adoption

In August 2002, we administered an online questionnaire to web professionals to gain insight about their work practices, including their use of automated web site evaluation tools (Ivory, 2003; Ivory & Chevalier, 2002). (Although the study is dated, it revealed some issues that remain to be addressed, especially if automated evaluation tools are to support content writers.) Respondents included 169 practitioners (web designers, information architects/designers, content writers, usability analysts/human factors, and other roles) who had varying design expertise and work experience. Participants worked in many environments and on education, e-commerce, intranet, health, and other types of sites.

We asked practitioners about five work practices: using design guidelines/style guides, optimizing sites for fast download, optimizing sites to improve access by people who have impairments, testing sites with users, following a user-centered design/development process, and using automated evaluation tools. Over half the respondents reported that they always or often followed all practices, except for using automated evaluation tools. Only 31 percent reported that they always or often use evaluation tools. At least half the practitioners thought that the tools were helpful in creating effective sites and in learning about effective design practices; however, the majority did not think that using the tools produced sites that were better than those produced without using tools. They did not think that the tools had adequate functionality or support or that they were easy to use.

Most respondents reported using Bobby and the W3C HTML Validator guideline conformance tools (47 and 43 percent of respondents, respectively). Other tools used included WAVE (9 percent) and LIFT for Dreamweaver (9 percent). Respondents identified Bobby most often as both the best and worst tool that they had used. They stated that they selected Bobby as the best tool, because it was the only one they knew of or had used. They also thought that it provided comprehensive information, liked the multiple guidelines that it evaluates, and thought that it was relatively easy to use and pass; however, they also mentioned that it was not easy enough to use and that it did not provide adequate information.

3.2   Tool Comparisons

The preceding study suggested that guideline conformance analyzers or critics, as opposed to the four other types of tools, are most likely to be used by web professionals. We conducted two comparisons of these tools to gain additional insight about their effectiveness. The first comparison entailed determining the types of user abilities that 27 tools consider in their evaluations (Ivory, 2003; Ivory, Mankoff, & Le, 2003). We identified 10 types of diminished user abilities — mouse use (partial or no ability), keyboard use (partial or no ability), vision (partial or no ability), hearing (partial or no ability), and cognition (partial attention and partial comprehension). For each diminished ability, we reviewed each tool to determine whether or not the tool considered it in its assessments. We summarized our findings in a table that can help writers to choose evaluation tools that are most appropriate to use, based on the intended users (Ivory, 2003). For instance, most of the tools address limited visual abilities, a few address non-visual impairments, and no tools address limited keyboard use. Bobby addresses nearly all the user abilities; LIFT - Nielsen Norman Group Edition, WebSAT, and WAVE provide the second highest level of coverage of user abilities.

Although multiple tools may address a specific impairment, there may be differences in how they conduct their assessments. To better understand these differences, we used 10 of the tools to evaluate a single web page (Ivory, 2003). Our analysis of reported guideline violations revealed that they represented 45 unique errors (e.g., avoid small text, identify the language of the text, and group-related elements when possible). We inspected the web page to determine if each violation was an accurate assessment. Although we did not conduct an empirical study to confirm the validity or invalidity of violations, only 21 violations (47 percent) seemed to be valid. Inaccurate assessments were reported for issues that could not be evaluated automatically or were not automated by the tools. Results suggested that there is very little consistency in reported errors across tools. For instance, 62 percent of errors were reported by only one tool. Only 2 percent of errors were reported by 5 tools; no error was reported by more than 5 tools. Error discrepancies arise because each tool uses its own set of guidelines; there is little overlap in guidelines across tools.

3.3 Tool Efficacy Study

We conducted a final study of three guideline conformance tools — WatchFire Bobby, UsableNet LIFT, and the W3C HTML Validator — to determine whether or not designers could use the tools to improve web site designs (Ivory & Chevalier, 2002; Ivory et al., 2003). The study consisted of two phases: (1) designers used the tools to modify web sites and (2) users with diverse abilities used the original and a selection of modified sites to complete information-seeking tasks. In the first phase, nine experienced designers modified subsections of five sites in conditions without a tool (manual), with one of the three tools (Bobby, Validator, or LIFT), or with all three tools (combo). Designers were allowed 40 min for modifications in the combo condition and 20 min in all other conditions. Modifications were to address problems identified by designers (manual condition) or by tools (remaining conditions). The tools identified significantly more potential problems than the designers identified in the manual condition; however, designers made more design changes when they did not use an automated evaluation tool.

To determine if designers' changes produced different site experiences, we selected modified versions of each of the five sites for usability testing with 22 users who did and did not have visual, cognitive, or physical impairments. Results showed that the modifications that designers made to two of the sites in the manual condition improved user performance (task completion success and time), but the reverse was true for the modifications that designers made to one site in the tool conditions. Within the narrow parameters of our study, results suggest that the three automated evaluation tools were not effective in helping designers to improve web site usability and accessibility. Fundamentally, guidelines that were embedded in the tools did not examine higher-level issues that negatively limit web site use, such as page complexity or whether text is legible with the color combinations used. Such issues need to be addressed so that content writers can benefit from evaluation tools.

4 Toward Better Support of Content Writers

Although vendors and researchers did not develop automated web site evaluation tools with content writers in mind, future tools can be designed to better support this community. The first step is to understand the characteristics and work practices of writers. We need to understand how web content is produced in various settings, what tools are used, and how content is evaluated. We also need to understand the skills, training, and preferences of content writers. Furthermore, we need to identify the current barriers that they face.

We recommend a two-part study to gather data to guide the development of tools to better support writers. We suggest that initial data are collected to provide a broad overview of content writers (e.g., administer a questionnaire to diverse writers). We then suggest that researchers study web writing within the context in which it occurs (e.g., a field study with a subset of questionnaire respondents). Researchers have conducted similar studies to understand the work practices of other web professionals (Ivory & Chevalier, 2002; Newman & Landay, 2000; Vora, 1998). These studies can be adjusted and repeated with content writers.

The two-part study should provide invaluable insight about the needs of content writers and how those needs can be addressed, in particular by automated web site evaluation tools. As discussed in this chapter, current tools do not address adequately content issues. New guidelines, and possibly new evaluation approaches, need to be developed. For instance, text analysis techniques could be used to derive quantitative measures of content quality or latent semantic analysis could be used to measure content cohesion across pages in a site. The tools also need to be improved so that they are easy to use and integrated into writers' work practices. The eight factors that we discussed in Section 2 (Table 1) provide guidance for the development of beneficial tools.

5 Conclusion

We described the space of automated web site evaluation tools from the perspective of web content writers. Although many tools are available, they provide limited support for evaluating content. Research is needed to provide insight about the work practices of writers and to develop new guidelines or approaches for evaluating content. Future tools need to be easier to use and more supportive of writers' work practices than existing tools.

Chapter 9

Mining Textual Knowledge for Writing Education and Research: The DocuScope Project

David Kaufer, Cheryl Geisler, Pantelis Vlachos and Suguru Ishizaki

This chapter reviews progress on a new corpus-based text analysis technology developed at Carnegie Mellon, called DocuScope. The technology includes a pattern matcher recognizing hundreds of millions of language strings indicating micro rhetorical acts. It also includes a visualization environment that allows researchers, teachers, and students to see and explore these patterns in textual models and in student drafts. While the tool has been used for writing education, it has not yet been optimized for educational environments and its most successful applications thus far have been supporting statistics-based research in the data mining of electronic archives (including samples of student texts and writing models) for rhetorical features. The first half lays out an overview of analytic choices we have made for conducting textual research. The second half explores how the knowledge derived from the DocuScope tool can benefit writing education and the evaluation of writing curricula.

1 Introduction

Textual resources are becoming increasingly digitized over the Internet, a situation creating greater demand among textual researchers for digitized tools that can take special advantage of digitized text. This chapter describes a new technology used to support research and education involving digitized text, especially corpus-based rhetorical analysis and on-line writing education. Significantly, the mere availability of digitized texts and tools cannot replace a substantive framework for conducting textual research or delivering writing instruction, be it paper-based or electronic. The first half lays out an overview of analytic choices we have made for conducting textual research. The second half explores how the knowledge derived from the DocuScope tool can benefit writing education and the evaluation of writing curricula.

Kaufer, D., Geisler, C., Vlachos, P., & Ishizaki, S. (2005). Mining textual knowledge for writing education and research: The docuscope project. In L. Van Waes, M. Leijten & C. Neuwirth (Vol. Eds.) & G. Rijlaarsdam (Series Ed.), Studies in Writing: Vol. 17. Writing and Digital Media (pp. 115–129). Oxford: Elsevier.

2   Frameworks for Textual Research

We have long been interested in addressing questions that relate language choice and reader experience. Our research seeks to account for the wide variation in the experiences texts afford. How do the writer's small and recurring choices at the point of utterance matter to the whole text experience of the reader? Answering this question is important to rhetorical analysts who wish to understand how the plasticity of language choice affects the plasticity of responses to rhetorical situations. Answers are also important to writing educators who wish to understand the wide palette to which students must be exposed in order to master writing across a range of genres and situations.

Our research is also addressed to the kernel of rhetorical theory by exploring micro–macro connections in language design. In classical rhetorical theory, the canons of invention and style are described as separate arts. We wish to understand the deep interconnections between these arts, the extent to which local decisions traditionally associated with "style" aggregate to inform global plans associated with "invention." In what sense can micro-selections of text contribute compositionally to a text's overall genre features? Our questions focus on the constellation of language choices that provide one or another reading experience to an audience or user. Underlying this variation are what we have called "design" choices (Kaufer & Butler, 1996, 2000; Kaufer, Ishizaki, Butler, & Collins, 2004). Viewed from a theory of writing as a design activity, these design choices include, but are by no means exhausted by, the following list of decisions:

- Story-telling perspective (e.g., first-person vs. third-person),
- narrating vs. informing vs. arguing,
- subjectively tinged observations vs. "objective" referential/descriptive reporting,
- temporal orientation (past vs. present vs. future),
- writing from personal authority vs. invoking a shared authority,
- acknowledging and guiding the reader vs. leaving the reader unaddressed, and
- keeping readers in a scene or cutting across events and scenes.

What we call types or genres of writing are deeply informed by the implicit decisions writers make along these and many other choice points. Our research has sought to uncover what these implicit choice points are and the various ranges of response they afford. These choice points and responses to them cannot be uncovered by studying single texts or even single types of text in isolation. They can only be uncovered by studying any text (or type of text) alongside other texts and types as they are distributed across the language.

A member of our research group, Collins (2003) has found, for example, that detective mysteries rely on more narrative-like elements than informational or argumentative elements. But this result could not have been found by studying mystery stories by themselves, which, as a matter of fact, do contain a great deal of language associated with informing or arguing. The result was determinable only through comparative analysis, by learning that mysteries exhibit a higher proportion of textual elements associated with narrative, relative to elements associated with information and argument, than do other genres, such as government reports, instructional manuals, and legal briefs.

The need for comparative analysis led us to develop a computer-based analysis that would allow us to code language patterns across large numbers and kinds of texts. Our tool, DocuScope, is a dictionary-based text analysis tool that includes over 735 million unique patterns of English in 99 categories. Patterns can be either a single word, or multiple words including punctuation. DocuScope functions like most theory-driven text analysis tools with a predefined dictionary (e.g., Hart, 2001; Stone, Dunphy, Smith, Ogilvie, 1966). It scans a corpus of texts and counts the number of patterns found in each category. DocuScope then provides users with an interactive visualization tool for statistical analyses.

While DocuScope's design is similar to many of the existing text analysis tools, it is distinct in two ways. First, its interactive visualization environment allows users to seamlessly go back and forth between the full corpus of texts and matched language patterns in the context of a particular text. While most dictionary-based tools do not need to allow users to examine matched patterns in their local context, this is a vital feature for us since our goal is to look closely at connections between micro linguistic features and macro rhetorical effects. Second, the size of the dictionary is significantly larger than typical dictionary-based tools, many of which use less than 10,000 patterns (Klein, 2002, 2005). While typical thematic analysis might be possible with a relatively small number of language patterns, we realized in our early experiments that a much wider coverage of language patterns was critical in order to examine micro–macro connections in language design.

In the following sections, we describe the choices we made in developing our analytical framework.

2.1 Comprehensive vs. Selective Coding Schemes

Textual analysis through coding methods places the emphasis on developing systematic interpretations of streams of language (Geisler, 2004). That is, the aim is that a given run of language will be identified with one and only one category in a coding scheme. In a comprehensive scheme, all of the language in a given body of text is thus coded. In a selective approach, a search is made for specific kinds of language and only these are coded.

A comprehensive scheme requires a strong theory of the universe of phenomena being coded for because it makes the claim that it can account for all of the language in a body of text. A more selective coding scheme can be viewed as making less strong claims and being more open to evolution as text phenomenon become better understood. The approach taken here is a more selective one. Specific runs of language are looked for, runs which have a clear relationship to readerly experience. When a tech reviewer, writes, for example,

> *I'm* a big fan of Wi-Fi on laptops. (Wildstrom, 2003)

We assign the first person pronoun combined with the verb to be (*I'm*) to the category of *self-disclosure*, but other runs of language in the text — *WiFi on laptops*, for instance — are not now assigned to any category at all. Some of these runs might be added later: the phrase, *a big fan*, for instance, though not now in our analytic scheme, does appear to be systematically enough associated with a specific kind of readerly experience that we might add it later. In this sense, our analysis is open-ended, capable of evolving as our understanding increases. We do not, however, anticipate ever developing a comprehensive coding scheme for readerly experience because only some runs of language have the stability and recurrence required.

2.2   *Flexible vs. Fixed Units of Language*

A second and important decision we made in developing our approach to text analysis concerned the unit of analysis to be coded. As we have noted elsewhere (Geisler, 2003, Ch. 3), selecting an appropriate unit of language is absolutely critical for a reliable coding scheme. Most analyses use a fixed unit of language; that is, the procedure for identifying the unit will be fixed on the grain size (word, phrase, t-unit, paragraph) of the units to be coded prior to the development of the coding scheme. The same runs of language will, furthermore, be coded the same way across texts.

Such fixed units work to stabilize and systematize the subsequent coding scheme. For instance, suppose we want to code the following text with a scheme that is looking for sense objects and we come across the following run of language:

> She ate bacon and eggs while dreaming of tomorrow.

If our unit of analysis is the t-unit (a main clause plus its subordinate clauses), we would need to decide whether or not this clause contained sense objects. It obviously does — bacon and eggs are things we can put our hands on — so we could assign this to the category *sense objects*. But if another category in our scheme was *inner thinking*, we might also want to put this run of language into that category as well. Unfortunately, putting the same runs of language into two categories violates the basic rule that a given run of language will be identified with one and only one category in a coding scheme.

In an analysis with fixed units, the solution to this dilemma is to choose a smaller unit for analysis that separates the runs of language associated with different coding categories. If, for instance, we decide to segment by the clause rather than by the t-unit, our text now contains two clauses:

> She ate bacon and eggs
> while dreaming of tomorrow.

The first can be placed in the *sense objects* category, while the second can be coded as a token of the *inner thinking* category. However, if the run of language to code had instead been

> Dreamily, she ate bacon and eggs.

then, segmentation by clause would not have solved our coding difficulty. Because the *inner thinking* category now expresses itself as the adverbial, *dreamily*, arguably sharing the clause with *bacon* and *eggs*, the clause would reveal itself as too large a coding unit for adequate segmentation. At this point, traditional coding practice calls for re-evaluating the phenomenon to be coded. Normally, categories within coding schemes should represent real alternatives within the unit to which they are applied. *Sense objects* appear to be nouns and noun phrases like bacon and eggs; *inner thinking* seems to be associated with verb forms and their reductions like dreaming and dreamily. These quick appearances often hide a much messier reality. For example, *inner thinking* in English can also, like *sense objects*, be expressed in noun phrases (an apparition of, a belief in, a dream about, a commitment to). Capturing the presence of both categories across the mind-boggling variation of surface, English requires accommodating maximum flexibility in the length of words a given coding category can span and the type of surface expression a category can reference. The truth of this observation, in our view, strongly militated against a coding system relying on a fixed grain size and grammaticalized surface form. Seeking to avoid the rigidities caused by using fixed units of analysis, we ended up settling on a method that looks for the longest string it can match and then assigns that string to a category. Thus, we deal with

> She ate *bacon and eggs* while *dreaming of* tomorrow.

by assigning the string *bacon and eggs* to the *sense objects* category and the expression *dreaming of* to the *inner thinking* category. If the *inner thinking* expression was truncated to *dreamily*, we could still assign it to the category of *inner thinking*. If the word *egg* appeared in a different kind of phrase,

> She saw them *egg on* the fighters.

we could instead assign the phrase *egg on* to an entirely different category, associated with an idiomatic meaning on the order of "encouraging someone to do something that is not in their best interests or against their better judgment." Because of its negative connotations, this idiom is classified as a *negative affect*. In this way, our approach remains faithful to the principle that a given run of language can be uniquely categorized without committing to a fixed unit of analysis.

2.3 Automatic vs. Non-automatic Coding Methods

Our final choice in developing an analyzing framework was to choose automatic coding procedures. Automatic methods rely on computers recognizing a predefined input with speed and reliability (Neuendorf, 2002). Non-automatic methods rely on humans seeking to make intersubjective judgments about discrete categories of language and how they persist in streams of speech or writing. Typically, human coding has the advantage of converging on coding units that are themselves interpretative, already a layer of abstraction beyond the surface text. Automatic coding is most reliably accomplished when the coding units are less interpretative and remain closer to the surface language. Conversely, human coding, and the feasibility of intersubjective reliability degrade as the coding categories increase (grow in number), diversify (grow in qualitative difference), overlap (share common elements across categories), and rely extensively on implicit, rather than articulate, knowledge.

It may seem like a contradiction to say that computers are best at coding surface knowledge and at the same time, implicit knowledge. It is not. Consider the English string "set in," which, when used as a main verb, prompts negative news (e.g., her depression set in; but not a party set in. The example is from Channel, 2000.). Notice further that this string overlaps with millions of other potential English strings containing the words "set" (e.g., set a plan in motion, set the table) and "in" (e.g., in Paris, in regard to). Much of our early-phase rhetorical understandings of text depend upon sponging up this prodigious, diverse, overlapping, and implicit knowledge from the surface stream of text. Inasmuch as our interest was to code for this implicit stream of information, we decided to use automatic coding methods.

2.4   *Dictionary vs. Machine Learning*

There are two main approaches to building a computer program that performs automatic coding: the dictionary-based approach and the machine-learning approach. Most theory-driven text analysis software employs the dictionary-based approach, where search patterns are manually entered by human experts (Popping, 2000). One potential problem of this approach is that the bigger the dictionary becomes, the longer it takes to complete and the more potential for inconsistency and incompleteness. Thus, as we anticipated the need for an extremely large dictionary, we considered an alternative approach — machine learning.

Machine learning, an area of artificial intelligence, is a relatively new approach in automatic coding for text analysis.[1] While there are many different computational techniques within machine learning, the key idea is to make a computer program "learn" to perform coding automatically without a dictionary created by the researcher. Typically, the program "learns" by examining coding samples generated by human experts. Laurence Anthony's MOVER program (2003) and Jill Burstein's Criterion™ system (commercialized by Educational Testing Service) are good examples of the machine-learning approach. Anthony seeds his program with key words and phrases (e.g., "is a hot area of research") associated with different rhetorical moves (e.g., centrality move; Swales, 1990) in the introduction of an academic research report. Based on input, which is annotated by human experts, the program learns to classify each sentence of a new introduction text to a particular rhetorical move. Burstein and her research group (Burstein & Marcu, 2003) seed their program with annotated five-paragraph student essays. The annotation includes (a) sentence positions and the list of words associated with human annotated rhetorical structures, such as a thesis statement and (b) an RST (Rhetorical Structure Theory) tree that is automatically built by using another computer program. Their program then "learns" to identify the rhetorical structures in novel student essays.

The advantage of the machine-learning approach is to save on human dictionary building time. The disadvantage is that machines cannot literally read text, cannot penetrate the profound interaction of language and cultural practice, and thus potentially end up producing a great deal of "noisy" coding. While there are many clever techniques to reduce the signal/noise ratio of machine coding, these tools seem to work effectively only when the phenomenon being captured is well-bounded in the manner of Anthony and Burstein's programs (e.g., research paper introductions and thesis statements in five paragraph

---

[1] In text analysis, machine-learning techniques are often used in holistic analysis, such as text classification, where the primary purpose of the tool is to automate text analysis, rather than to automate coding. In this section, our discussion focuses on automated coding.

essays). In addition, a machine-learning approach requires well-defined human-coded examples to learn from. Although we had a firm high-level theory to guide our approach (Kaufer & Butler, 1996, 2000), we still had to explore and define the exact coding scheme to start this project.

This led us to explore, and finally adopt, a dictionary-based approach. Rather than to train a computer to tag English, a manual approach relies on human experts to build a large library of contiguous strings classified by rhetorical effect. In this approach, human experts sensitive to language–culture interactions explore and build the coding scheme and the dictionary. The pronoun "I" is tagged as a "first person" effect. The word "if" is associated with a "contingency" effect. These are simple examples using one word coding. However, our approach also allows for coding that can be built up over longer strings (e.g., a five-word string like "in this paper, I will" to reflect metadiscourse at the beginning of an essay). With this approach, a wide range of patterns are harvested, classified, and stored within a database; a fast string-matching program (Knuth, Morris & Pratt, 1977) runs across a target corpus of texts and annotates the patterns it finds, and counts them.

2.5 *Harvesting the Dictionary*

While a dictionary-based approach avoids the (machine learning) problem of a high-noise ratio in coding, it poses a different challenge – how to bound the coding project so that it gives some procedural meaning to "covering" the language while staying within the very limited capacities of human labor. Because of the rich combinations of word strings, it seems impossible for a human expert to enumerate all possible patterns of English that are potentially relevant to a rhetorical theory of text.

Our way of meeting this challenge was to imagine an expert "covering" the rhetorical patterns of English at the grain of contiguous word strings in three phrases. An analogy is a housepainter's covering a wall in three coats of paint. In the first phase, we focused on achieving what we deemed to be a "complete" category system for strings. Completeness of the category system was not the same as completeness of the category members (the actual strings). This first phase needed to continue for as long as our human dictionary building effort uncovered new categories for incoming strings. The phase would be concluded when we found we no longer had to invent new categories for new string input. In other words, all new tokens found in the input stream of English were covered by our existing category types.

The success of this first phase depended upon our inspecting as broad a range of English prose texts as we could find. We found our coding categories (and initial bank of rhetorical strings) from the Lincoln/Douglas debates, from student writings in a multi genre course (written journals, profiles, scenic field guides, historical narratives, exposition, popular explanation, instructions, and argument), from a 120 text digital archive of introspective fiction, character-based short stories, and essays of reminiscence, reflection, and social criticism. We took a second archive from a course on information systems. This archive contained 45 electronic documents including client proposals, design specifications, meeting minutes, documentation, focus group reports, public relation announcements, and interviews. We took a third oral-written archive from the Federalist papers, the Presidential

Inaugurals, the journals of Lewis and Clark, talk radio, song lyrics, newspaper columnists, fables of Aesop and the Brother's Grimm, the writings of Malcolm X, the 100 great speeches of the 20th century, 10 years of newspaper reporting on the Exxon Valdez disaster, and The *New Yorker.*

We divided the texts compiled into training and test samples. We coded strings from the training sample and then tested the codings on the test samples. Although we could not visually inspect every one of the strings that our string matcher matched, we built an interface that allowed us to visually inspect any of the matches made during test and improvement cycles. A "collision detector" in the software we built identified strings that were included under multiple categories, making it easy for us to keep the coding decisions mutually exclusive and providing an additional logical check on the development of our categories.

We also recruited students in writing courses as a user community providing formative feedback. We asked students to run their assignments through our software and evaluate how their prose had been tagged. We asked them to evaluate the meaningfulness, completeness, usefulness, and accuracy of our categories. Were the category names understandable? Were the category names exhaustive, or were there categories that would be useful to add? Were the categories useful to you in helping to explain how you had planned your text? Were the categories accurately applied, or were their inaccuracies in matching categories to actual strings in the input text?

The first phase of dictionary building took three years to complete. Phase 1 had focused on completeness in the coding categories rather than completeness across frequently used English. By the end of the first phase, we had cataloged 500 million unique strings of English (a fact less impressive than it seems, as it owes to the combinatorics of strings more than to our special coding process) but only 19,000 single words of English. Our categories were robust, but our system covered random texts of English very sparsely. Phase 2 assured that our coding would systematically penetrate the most frequently occurring English words. In the second phase, we applied our coding categories to the 100,000 most frequent words of English. By the end of Phase 2 (one-person year of effort), we had bumped our single word entries to 130,000 single words. This boost began to give our string libraries the feel of a genuine rhetorical dictionary of English. Despite the improvement, however, we were still sparse in 2–4 word combinations. Phase 3, completed in the summer of 2004, involved concordance dictionaries to code the most frequent 2–4 word combinations from the 10,000 or so most frequent words of English. We then turned our attention to the 75,000 most "common" words of English. Common words range in their frequency but are typically lower in frequency than the 100,000 most frequent English words. Nonetheless, common words are words considered important enough for lexicographers to include in their dictionary entries. An operational way to understand a common word is as follows: if one searches for a word on an Internet dictionary that itself searches across 100 + dictionaries of English (e.g., onelook.com), words that contain entries in at least five independent dictionaries or more are likely to be common words. From the fall of 2004 to late spring of 2005, we expanded our string libraries to include words and phrases involving the 75,000 most common words of American English.

Although our libraries of rhetorically coded English strings remain an open set, admitting of new entries, it is not too early to ask how well our categories and strings differentiate texts and genres in ways that human classifiers differentiate them? Collins (2003) investigated this question in his dissertation. Using DocuScope, he ran the software on the first half (250) of the texts from the 500 text Brown Corpus, which compiled American English of the 1960s into 15 genres. He ran a statistical procedure (factor analysis) to isolate and identify the major groupings within this sample of texts. He next tested the factors uncovered in Step 1 (using a technique called confirmatory factor analysis) to see whether the original factors discovered could explain text/genre differences in the remaining half (250) of the Brown Corpus and across 500 texts from the Freiburg–Brown Corpus, an update of the Brown Corpus using English of the 1990s.

Collins found that the original factors created by our catalog for 1960s English successfully explained the genre variation in 1960s and 1990s English. These results provided direct evidence that our dictionary at the grain size of contiguous strings separated randomized written English into genre families and subfamilies across a 30-year period robustly, consistently, and in ways consistent with human classifiers. It further provided support that style (micro-choices of individual runs of language) and invention (macro-choices about recurring constellations of text) are deeply interdependent constructs for writers of the language.

Thus far, we have focused only on the large development effort of our software without reviewing the applications that justify the time and effort. In the remainder of this chapter, we turn to applications in writing instruction.

3 Mining Textual Knowledge for Teaching Written Genres

Research on writing has often identified the educational problem with too little class time for practice and too low expectations for what student writers should accomplish. Meeting these challenges requires writing teachers to provide deeper information to students about the nature and logic of various writing topics, the nature of genre, process principles of writing, and conventions and expectations about texts both with target readers and in the larger culture.

Teachers cannot raise their expectations for students without themselves receiving support about the nature of texts and textual composition. Providing this kind of support for teachers is challenging because textual knowledge is deeply implicit knowledge (more like the design arts than math) and also vast, controlled not by the few thousand words in a student vocabulary but by the hundreds of millions of combinations of these words that any student writer can produce. For writing teachers to teach as masters, we need to give them environments that respect the nature of the knowledge they are trying to impart.

As part of our educational focus, we developed the DocuScope environment to capture scientific knowledge about the rhetorical make-up of texts within standard classroom writing assignments. We also developed the environment to provide an on-line feedback tool for students so that they can study their composing choices visually, as a painter might study fine brushstrokes in a painting. The first use of the environment — as an environment for data collection and research feeding into writing pedagogy — is already realized. The second use — as a practical product for mainstream education — remains a future prospect that we elaborate further in the conclusion. The remainder of this section describes only the first use. We illustrate how we have used the DocuScope environment to mine student model texts in order to unearth "language targets" that can be used by curriculum developers and textbook writers.

In our research, we were asked by one major textbook company to use the DocuScope tool to identify language targets for instruction in the writing samples provided by a leading fourth grade textbook. The fourth grade textbook was extremely strong in components of language (grammar, vocabulary, topic prompts) that underlie writing. Where it was lacking is exactly the focus and the strength of our approach — training in whole text (or gestalt) textual shapes, the kind of genre knowledge learned from reading and discussing large samples of drafts and their legitimate variation.

The textbook, like most writing textbooks, lacks plentiful writing models. Chapters devoting to kinds of writing contained from 0 to 3 samples at most. The paucity of samples requires students to strive for generalizations on an extremely thin reading sample. If a student is taught descriptive writing and there is only one model "descriptive" text with a very high percentage of first person, a fourth grader acts rationally to identify descriptive writing with first-person writing (however erroneous that belief may be down the educational road of a writer).

We have no objection to evaluating student writing under grading rubrics that are required by all states in America. But we do object to the idea that students be subjected to fine-grained rubric evaluation in a specific writing genre before teachers have had a chance to establish an explicit baseline of student understanding in the genre they are being tested. In simple terms, before we can assess how well a student meets a challenge, we need to establish a baseline that students understand and have had time to practice.

Without training in overall textual shapes and the legitimate way they can vary, there is a fine line between judging a low score on a rubric and judging that the student's fundamental understanding of the writing task is too impoverished for meaningful testing. Many student texts are thrown out as "Not Applicable" (and many more probably should be) in rubric testing because the student text has too much unaccounted for variation. Our approach would help reduce this problem, a problem that has hurt the credibility of rubric testing among many devoted rank-and-file teachers.

Our approach would address this gap by placing early in each chapter of instruction a unit called "The Shape of <Genre> Writing. We use statistical analysis of student models to unearth the high-level challenge of writing in said genre. The computer tool we propose (as part of the second, still unimplemented, phase of our current text mining tool) would be "trained" in each type of writing taught and could give immediate feedback whether a student draft made language selections that were "in the ballpark" of the target genre. If the answer is yes, the student proceeds to the next unit. If the answer is no, the program directs the student to samples that are especially strong in the aspects where the student's own language is lacking. The student can keep submitting to the computer until the draft falls within the ballpark of the genre on all language variables.

Using the DocuScope environment in its current form as a text mining environment, we were able to make statistical extrapolations of the few writing samples in the fourth grade writing text to find language targets for explanatory, persuasive, descriptive, and comparison writing. For example, based on a statistical sample of 1 text sample (below) extrapolated to a sample population of 1000,

> I'm so excited you are coming to visit. We'll have a great time. We can swim in the pool. Here are the directions to my apartment. Take Merrick Road North to the traffic light. Then, turn right on Planet Road. Look for the big white school building on the right. Turn left on Elm Avenue and go over the old wooden bridge. Next turn right on June Lane and go two miles. Look for the red brick apartment buildings across from the park. I live in Building D. It's the fourth building on the left, the one most closest to the pool. I'll be there. Your best friend, Mariana (p. 319).

the DocuScope tool found the following language classes statistically central to achieving explanatory writing: *first person, positive attitude, verbs of motion, relationships in space, and directing the reader*. Framed as guides for curriculum developers, the guides might read

> Based on statistical sampling of student models of explanatory writing, you might use the following to train in explanatory writing: "When you are explaining to a friend how to get to your house, you can expect to use first person, words that indicate your positive attitude, verbs that suggest motion and language indicating relationships in space from your friend's house to yours. Most importantly, you will want to make sure you use words that direct your reader so that your instructions are clear.

With more samples to explore, the language targets DocuScope finds reflects the increasing (legitimate) variation within the assignment. For example, the fourth grade text used three samples for teaching persuasive writing, one of which we reproduce below:

> Sample 3. Persuasive Writing (p. 169).
> In 1946, the International Whaling Commission (IWC) was set up to establish rules to limit whaling. Despite the rules, the numbers of whales steadily shrank. Some kinds of whales may be about to become extinct. Because of a worldwide movement to save the whales, the IWC banned all commercial whaling, beginning in 1985. But the governments of a few countries still allow their citizens to hunt whales. Whales are one of the few wild animals that are commonly friendly to humans they encounter. Many people feel that we have an obligation to preserve these intelligent and special animals. Will whales be allowed to remain to share the world with us. The choice is ours.

From this passage and two others and its built-in means to do statistical extrapolation, DocuScope found that central language targets for persuasive writing include expression of *negative aspects*, with a *future* that is *uncertain* with the writer seeking to use *reasoning to connect with readers* toward a more certain future. Each of the words in italics represents a language family within DocuScope's libraries.

In sum, as an educational tool, the DocuScope environment can extract from sample texts a rhetorical profile of the assignment along with the legitimate variation that lies within the assignment. The environment thus defines a statistical ballpark for assignments that can be valuable to curriculum designers and textbook developers if not classroom teachers.

4   Evaluating Writing Curricula

Through the statistical analysis of the rhetorical characteristics of sample texts, the DocuScope tool can, in principle, help find the rhetorical ballpark of any writing assignment. This feature yields a possible benefit for curricula evaluation. Through student samples, researchers can understand whether the high–low goals of a writing course (expressed through a course syllabus and assignment sequence) articulate with the micro rhetorical actions of students who have produced texts along that sequence. Neecia Werner and Dan Baumgardt at Carnegie Mellon are tackling this application area of the DocuScope tool. In this section, we report on a pilot assessment project, which our undergraduate students had conducted as a class project.

In this project, we invited the Director of the Freshman Writing Program (76–101) at Carnegie Mellon into our classroom to describe the high-level goals of the writing curriculum, how these goals realized themselves as a sequence of assignments, and how each assignment fit into the sequence. We learned from the Director that:

> The Goals of 76–101 are to develop freshmen's critical reading and writing skill. Students are expected to learn to summarize positions from texts, to relate positions across authors, and to come up with their own arguments based on the collective work of the authors they have read.

Functioning as consultants to the Director of the writing program, our students learned that these goals were realized through three major assignments, each written across several drafts. The assignments consisted of a written summary, synthesis paper, and finally a contributing paper. The course syllabus described each assignment's purpose as follows:

> The Summary paper is meant to give students the opportunity to restate, in the student's own words, the author's basic positions on an issue. The summary writer must look beyond what the author says and explain what the author is doing by way of offering an original position on an issue.

> This Synthesis paper is meant to give students the opportunity to compare and contrast authors for similarity and difference, agreement and disagreement. If the summary paper helps the student understand a text as an author's position, the synthesis paper helps the student understand multiple texts as a community of positions that can be evaluated.

> The Contributing paper is meant to give students the opportunity to frame their own position alongside the authors they have read and synthesized. This paper, more than the others, gives students the opportunity to present and defend their own opinions.

The Director supplied students with 25 sample essays of each assignment from an archive of previous semesters. The students used the DocuScope tool to tag the texts for their rhetorical characteristics. They then performed a statistical procedure called factor analysis to build profiles of each assignment type. By identifying each assignment type as distinctive at the micro level of rhetorical action from the two others, the student's challenge was to see if they could tell a story about the course from the vantage of student craft that confirmed the story the course syllabus sought to tell from the vantage of teacher aspiration.

The factor analysis revealed five dimensions along which to calibrate the three assignments relative to one another. The first dimension measured the extent to which the assignment involved the interactive and future oriented reasoning with a reader vs. the narrative reporting of past events. The second measured the extent to which the assignment involved directing the reader's judgment and action vs. interaction based on subjective exchanges. The third measured the extent to which the assignment required elaborating events into scenes described in time and space. The fourth measured the extent to which the assignment involved guiding the reader from left-to-right through the text and the fifth, the extent to which the assignment relied on first person commentary.

By running multiple analyses of variance (Manovas) on these five dimensions, the students were able to create unique profiles for each of the three assignments. For example, the summary papers were consistently highest in guiding the reader from left-to-right (factor 4), narrative reporting (factor 1), and elaborating events into scenes (factor 3) crossing time and space. Contrastively, they were consistently lowest among the assignments in first person commentary. These characteristics made sense to the Director of first year composition, who had taught that the summaries should guide the reader through the major lines of arguments of past writers while withholding commentary.

Factor 2 revealed extremely significant differences across all three assignments. Texts high on this factor were highly interactive with a reader, what we called reader-acknowledged. Texts low on this factor compared and contrasted the thinking of different sources without addressing a reader directly. We called texts low on this factor reader-unacknowledged. Figure 1 below plots all three assignments on this factor. As one can see, the contributing paper is significantly higher (more positive) on acknowledging readers than the summary paper, which in turn is significantly more acknowledging of readers than the synthesis paper.

The synthesis papers were consistently highest in supporting interaction based on subjective exchange (factor 2) and consistently lowest in directing the reader from left-to-right (factor 4). After some thought, the Director of Composition was able to link this micro profile to her overall syllabus. She recognized that in teaching the synthesis paper, she had been implicitly teaching students not to address a reader through a linear and singular chain of ideas; but to let the reader, mostly an unacknowledged observer, understand how a community of ideas could hatch from the collective actions of previous authors. Furthermore, she recognized that she had been asking students to build this community of ideas by creating episodes of subjective interactions between the authors (e.g., "X believes this, but Y believes that; X hold this, but Y would retort that").

The contributing papers, policy essays from sources written by the students at the end of the course, were consistently highest in future oriented reasoning (factor 1), first person commentary (factor 5), and lowest in scenic elaboration (factor 3).

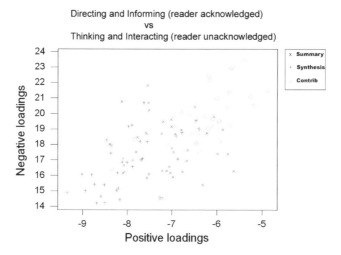

Figure 1: Three writing assignments plotted on factor (2). The X-axis measures the degree to which a text acknowledges the reader. The further right, the more reader-acknowledgment increases. Each symbol in the chart represents a single student text, coded by assignment (and genre). Note that the contributing papers (represented by 'o' or circles) dominate the papers acknowledging readers (aggregated to the right of the X-axis); followed by summaries (x) (aggregated in the middle of the X-axis) and then synthesis papers (+) (aggregated to the left of the X-axis). All differences between assignments on this factor are statistically significant ($p < 0.01$).

More importantly, the distinctive profiles of each assignment helped the Director clarify the logic of sequencing as she had. The summary papers taught how to read through a single academic argument that had been made in the past. But such preparation in reading was not sufficient preparation for writing a paper designed to carry a reader into the future. In preparation for this latter task, students had to understand that writing an academic paper requires an intermediate step, building and evaluating an inter-textual community. Students needed to learn they could create this community by composing subjective inter-actions across their sources, using the best ideas of the collective to help make their own.

With their community built and annotated for strengths and weaknesses, students were, one hopes better prepared to turn to their final assignment, focused on their first person commentary about how to move a reader (as member of a community of peers) from past to future (and problem to solution) through an issue.

5   Conclusion

With the increasing availability of electronic corpuses, including corpuses of student writing, automatic means to analyze text from a rhetorical perspective will be in increasing demand. In this chapter, we have overviewed different frameworks for meeting this demand, described a specific system that we built as a result of the choices that confronted us within the space of these frameworks, and overviewed some applications of our system, notably using student samples both to evaluate and improve writing instruction and writing curricula itself. Areas of further work in this line of research involve exploring if automatic learning methods can profitably extend the textual knowledge found by human experts, and on-line tutors to teach advice about genre to students.

Earlier we had mentioned that the successful uses of the DocuScope environment in education thus far has been in research in support of the development and testing of curricular materials related to writing. Our review of educational applications in this chapter has consequently focused primarily on these uses. We also mentioned our interest in entering a second phase, using the DocuScope environment to create practical products for direct use in writing pedagogy. These products would directly interact with teachers and students in embedded classrooms. One product would be an interactive web-based tool that would help teachers understand their own writing assignments. Teachers would submit to a DocuScope web site archives of writing produced by students per writing assignment. The web site in turn would automatically generate a "written report," outlining for the teachers the major rhetorical strategies used in each assignment and a comparative analysis of whether, and how, these strategies significantly differed from assignment to assignment. Teachers could use this tool for evaluating their own writing curricula in the way we described for 76—101 above. A second application would be an interactive coaching system designed directly for classroom use. In this context, DocuScope would need to be "trained" to recognize the rhetorical strategies associated with "successful" writing on a teacher's given assignments. The student would then submit drafts to the DocuScope web site and get feedback whether these strategies were being followed. While the environment would have a prescriptive component, the major educational aims would be less prescriptive than many automatic essay graders. The aim would focus on helping students learn to recognize and carefully describe rhetorical strategies. Rather than leaving "good writing" a prescriptive black box understood only by the machine, the idea would be to leave it to the intelligence of students to learn how the rhetorical strategies of effective writers (a matter of description) corresponds to (or not) the prescriptions of "good writing."

Chapter 10

Visualizing Patterns of Annotation in Document-Centered Collaboration on the Web

Henrry Rodriguez and Kerstin Severinson Eklundh

Sharing documents with others and getting comments on them are frequent activities for most authors. This is especially true while revising a document. We present Col·lecció;[1] a Web-based, asynchronous, groupware tool that supports sharing and annotation of documents in small or medium-sized groups. Each document is associated with its own space for commenting, in which a text-based dialogue can be formed among the participants. A site in Col·lecció is called a domain, and consists of a collection of documents and a set of comments in connection with each document. Case studies of the use of the system have shown that a domain is often complex as a discourse environment, as the system supports several parallel document discussions. We present a visualization model, Domain Interactivity Diagram (DID), as an aid for analysing patterns of annotation and referencing in these dialogues. This model is especially adapted to document-centred discourse, and highlights the role of the author in communication about a document. One aim of the DID is to show the extent to which a participant has focused on each document and which documents he/she has commented on. A more ambitious aim has been to support coherence in the discourse developed within a domain.

1   Introduction

Although writing is to a great extent a solitary activity, there are parts of almost any writing process that involve sharing and collaboration. This is especially true while revising a document. Sharing document versions and getting comments on them are frequent activities for most authors. In many cases, comments are made by someone who is not a co-author of that particular document, such as a colleague, a tutor, or an external reviewer.

---

[1]The earliest version of this system was called Domain Help System (DHS) presented in Rodriguez (2003).

Rodriguez, H., & Severinson Eklundh, K. (2005). Visualizing patterns of annotation in document-centered collaboration on the web. In L. Van Waes, M. Leijten & C. Neuwirth (Vol. Eds.) & G. Rijlaarsdam (Series Ed.), Studies in Writing: Vol. 17. Writing and Digital Media (pp. 131–143). Oxford: Elsevier.

A commentator might have very different purposes with his/her comment: to review the content of an early text version in order to change it, to design the layout of the document, to discuss ideas for a better understanding of the topic treated in the text, etc.

An author may benefit from getting feedback from different commentators. This, however, could imply a sharing and distribution effort for both the author and the commentators. Furthermore, this activity is more complicated when more than one document is part of the process of getting feedback. Commentators might be discussing a set of documents as part of a common project or task. A common practice would be to discuss the documents one by one in a face-to-face meeting. This discussion could have two levels: one level that is specific to the document in discussion, and the other related to the general discourse, including all the documents commentators have already discussed or will be discussing. To support such a discussion in a distributed, asynchronous, text-based form is a complex task. It would be of interest to have the possibility for authors and commentators to engage in a dialogue in which these two levels could be supported.

2   Using the Web for Collaboration among Writers

During the last decades, there has been an increasing interest within the field of Computer-Supported Cooperative Work (CSCW) to design computer support for collaborative writing. Research efforts in this area have included basic taxonomies for collaboration (e.g., Sharples et al., 1993; Baecker, Nastos, Posner, & Mawby, 1993) as well as a number of research prototypes supporting various parts of a collaborative writing task (e.g., Prep: Neuwirth, Kaufer, Chandook, & Morris, 1990; Quilt: Fish, Kraut, & Leland, 1988). In spite of these efforts, collaborative writing systems were rarely used outside of research laboratories before the advent of the World Wide Web. Some studies suggested that writers lacked a common infrastructure for collaboration around documents, and therefore they tended to resort to individual tools, using only email to exchange text versions and comments (Dourish & Bellotti, 1992).

Due to its accessibility and ubiquitous nature, the Web is a powerful infrastructure for mediating shared objects (e.g., Web documents) and broadcasting of text-based messages (e.g., comments) as part of collaboration (Munro, Höök, & Benyon, 1999). These aspects are important for the process of revision in writing, and have been supported in certain groupware systems (BSCW: Appelt & Busbach, 1996; SEPIA: Haake & Wilson, 1992; GROVE etc.: Ellis, Gibbs, & Rein, 1991). However, so far there have been few efforts to design collaborative environments that writers can use for sharing and communicating about their texts, and in which both levels mentioned above — document specific and project — are supported.

In this chapter, we present Col·lecció; a Web-based, asynchronous, groupware tool that supports sharing and text-based annotation of documents in small or medium-sized groups. Each document is associated with its own space for commenting, in which a text-based dialogue can be formed among the participants (e.g., authors and commentators). A site in Col·lecció is called a domain, and consists of a collection of documents and a set of comments in connection with each document. The set of comments on a particular document may form a dialogue. That is, several parallel dialogues are going on in a domain.

We also present a visualization model, Domain Interactivity Diagram (DID), as an aid for analysing patterns of annotation and referencing in these dialogues, both to other comments and to other documents in the system. This model is especially adapted to document-centred discourse, and highlights the role of the author in communication about a document. These tools have a potential use as social navigation aids for users (Erickson et al., 1999), helping them to decide what to read and which items to comment on, based on others' activities. Another aim of this model is to show the extent to which a participant has focused on each document and which documents he/she has commented on. A more ambitious aim has been to support coherence in the discourse developed within a domain (see Severinson Eklundh & Rodriguez, 2004).

3 Col•lecció in Brief

Col·lecció allows members of a group to form a collection of Web documents, on which comments can be made in parallel. The set of comments could evolve into a dialogue among participants, aligned with the document, and serves as a communication channel throughout the reviewing process (see Rodriguez, 2003; Figure 1).

Technically, Col·lecció is a Web-based tool that runs in an ordinary Web browser supporting JavaScript. Col·lecció lets users add Web objects in a shared space. Although there are many types of Web objects, we have focused on HTML and XML files. Col·lecció also allows users to link comments to these Web objects (Web documents hereafter). These comments are shared within a group and can be used to establish a dialogue among the members.

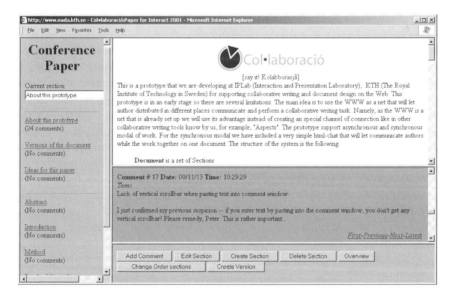

Figure 1: Browser layout running Col·lecció.

Col·lecció's interface is divided into two vertical frames. The left frame provides an *Index of contents* consisting of hypertext links labelled with descriptive titles. The links can be to any document on the Web. They can be grouped under a topic label or by the name of the user who added the links. The right frame is divided into three horizontal frames. The *Content frame* shows the Web document.[2] The *Comment frame* shows the comments that have been attached to that Web document. The *Command frame* contains the four button commands: *Add URL*,[3] *Add Comment, Delete URL*, and *Show last events*. When the Add URL button is clicked, a window pops up, presenting a form where the member enters the URL of the Web document that is about to be included in the domain and a descriptive title for the link. The Add Comment button calls up a separate window with a form where the member can make a comment. The Delete URL button deletes the current item from the Index of contents that was shown in the Content frame. These actions are immediately implemented, thus making the updated Index of contents or new comments available when another user enters the system.

When the "Add comment" button is clicked, the Add-Comment Window of the system pops up. This window is divided into two vertical frames. The left frame shows the Web document that the user has selected from the Index of contents followed by its comments, if any. This lets the user view the comments in case he/she needs to refer to a previous comment. In this way the system supports a dual context for the annotations, including both the Web document and the past comments. The right frame presents a text box where the user can write the comment.

When a comment is submitted, a notification email is sent to the person who added the Web document. This is used as an awareness mechanism. Awareness in teamwork, generally, refers to co-workers' ability to perceive and understand the activities of others as a context for their own work (Baecker, Dimitrios, Posner, & Mawby, 1993). We have experimented with different modes of email awareness, distinguished by *to whom* the notification email is sent and *the content* of this email. These design issues are thoroughly discussed in Rodriguez and Severinson Eklundh (2005). Another way of promoting awareness in the system is through the "comment counter" that tells the users how many comments have been made on a document. Finally, a more general form of awareness is the Show last events button. It presents an activity report, which shows the changes that the shared space has gone through, including when and who made the changes.

Col·lecció has similarities to the system WebAnn (Bernheim et al., 2002), which supports shared annotation of Web documents. WebAnn, however, supports threading of comments. Another difference is that WebAnn allows comments to be associated with a particular part of a document, such as a word or paragraph, whereas the Col·lecció links a comment with the entire document. This difference has consequences for the evolving communication. In a comparative study where WebAnn was used along with a traditional discussion board system (Bernheim et al., 2002), it emerged that the discussions in WebAnn were more concerned with specific points in the papers discussed.

---

[2]As an alternative, the system can show the Web document in an independent window larger than the Content frame.
[3]The system indeed can add any Web object, e.g., a picture, a movie, a document by using the URL of the Web object. Therefore, we have decided to use Add URL instead of Add document.

4 Data Collected in Case Studies with Col•lecció

Comments exhibit referential complexity. They may contain references to the current document, to previous comments, and to other documents and comments in the domain. Many comments are also made about the Col·lecció system itself through a special dialogue space reserved for questions about the system. The extent to which these kinds of references actually occur depends on the particular context of the dialogues, the purpose and nature of the collaboration, what aspects of the documents are being negotiated, etc.

In order to explore such referential patterns of annotation in detail, we have analysed a corpus of data from two case studies in which Col·lecció was used for discussion in an educational context. Each participant had submitted a short essay (about one page) about a personal experience of group collaboration with technology as an introductory assignment for a university course. The participants (20 men and 10 women) were 4th year students in computer science or engineering, specializing in human–computer interaction. The assignment included reading and responding to other students' essays in Col·lecció during a period of approximately two weeks.

The material collected includes data from five consecutive versions of the course (Rodriguez, 2003). The two sets of data we shall focus on here are CSCW00 and CSCW01 (see Table 1). In those case studies, students in a course were asked to write an essay on the topic "Collaboration with and without computers". The essays were then distributed, shared, and discussed using Col·lecció. The domain CSCW00 consisted of 13 documents and 95 comments. CSCW01 consisted of 17 documents and 67 comments. In total, the material analysed here contains 30 documents and 162 comments, where each document is authored by one of the participants in the discussion.

The purpose of the assignment was both that the students should get feedback on their own experiences of collaboration as expressed in the document they had submitted, and that they should interact with each other by sharing and discussing these experiences. This double purpose is reflected in the nature of the resulting discourse, in which contributions contain references to both documents and previous comments.

We applied a coding procedure to analyse the modes of reference in these data. Two judges read the documents and the discussions, and assigned each comment one or more codes according to the comment's way of referencing previous comments and documents. For example, a coding for a certain comment could be [D, K1, K3], meaning that it contained

Table 1: Commenting references to the document (D), to previous comments (K) and to both (DK) in the two sets of data.

	D	DK	K	Doc X	Total
CSCW01	46	18	25	6	95
CSCW02	29	17	20	1	67
Total	75	35	45	7	162
%	46.3	21.6	27.7	4.3	100

three identifiable references: one to the current document, one to the first comment in the same dialogue space, and one to the third comment in the same dialogue space.

Table 1 shows the distribution of comments in the general categories D (reference to the document), K (reference to the previous comments), DK (both references occur in the comment), and Doc X (references to other documents in the domain). It is clear from these results that the discussions as a whole exhibit a pattern of dual reference: they both address the content of the documents and they are also interactive, i.e., comments refer back to other comments. In other words, the participants regularly respond to each other's comments while also addressing the content of the documents.

The degree of activity varied a lot among participants, with the number of postings by one person ranging from 0 to 15 comments during the task (mean = 5.17; median = 4). An interesting factor is the number of comments that an author makes within the dialogue space of his or her own document. It is reasonable to expect that authors want to monitor the discussion on their own essay and respond to the comments made. However, only 17 out of 30 discussions actually contained a response from the author to other participants' comments, and there were many cases of direct questions to the author that remained unanswered. A possible explanation is that the author considered the assignment completed and did not enter the system in spite of the fact that the comments made on the document were continuously sent to him/her by email to support awareness.

In Severinson Eklundh and Rodriguez (2004), the referencing patterns used in these discussions are described in more detail, including the linguistic strategies used to connect to previous contributions in a dialogue. These were of particular interest because the Col·lecció system does not support threading of comments.[4] This means that the users must find their own strategies of linking to a previous element in a conversation, which in this case sometimes led to ambiguous references or incoherence in dialogues.

5   Visualization of the Discussion in Col•lecció

The case studies confirmed that certain domains are complex as a discourse environment, due to the multiple contexts of documents and comments to which participants refer in their comments, and the fact that several, parallel dialogues are formed in the course of a collaborative task. We have created a visualization tool, DID to help clarify the conversational activity exhibited in Col·lecció. The purposes have been partially explorative: to assess the interactivity and referential relationships within a particular domain, and as a tool for comparison between different discussions in this regard. However, we believe that visualizations like the ones we are using might also be helpful to participants themselves as optional coherence tools. This would increase the accessibility of the discussion space,

---

[4]In standard email and news reading software, the coherence of a discussion is usually supported by a threading mechanism, which emphasizes the reply-to relationship and shared subject between messages. The reason for not including such a mechanism in Col·lecció was that the main purpose of the system was to support communication about shared documents. Each comment is expected to be oriented towards a particular document, and longer dialogue threads are not expected to occur. This design choice and its implications are discussed in detail in Rodriguez (2003).

and thereby its "social translucence" (Erickson, 1999), i.e., the degree to which other people's activities are immediately available and visible to a user.

One aim of the visualization of a domain is to help participants to get an overview of the general character of a discussion at a glance, before reading. For example: Which was the document that was most commented on in the domain? Was the document discussed by many of the participants? Did the author of the document participate in the discussion? The answer to these questions might help the user to choose her reading strategy. Moreover, a participant could assess a comment according to what is known about the author of the comment in relation to the task. For example, knowing whether a participant has read the other documents in the domain or not, would help to assess his/her point of view about the document.

We designed DID to take the characteristics of conversations actually occurring into account. For example, in the cases analysed, only 5% of the documents ($N = 30$) had more than 10 comments; no more than 10 members took part in the discussion of one document; 95% of the comments were no longer than 200 words; and 50%, 68%, and 80% of the comments were submitted within one, two, and three days, respectively. It is important to note, however, that in another use context, the information in a domain could diverge from the one that we had in mind when the DID was designed.

The DID presents a domain at two levels. The first level, the *Panorama View*, is a general overview of the domain; the second level, the *Document Interactivity View* (DIV), focuses on the discussion of a single document. In both views, each participant in a domain is assigned a colour, and all comments or documents are presented in that colour. With this information it is easy to see how each person has spread out his/her activities among the different discussions. As a social navigation feature (Munro, Höök, & Benyon, 1999) this may both support coherence and promote the group's discussion when the number of participants increases. For example, a reader could benefit from reading all the comments by a particular person. However, it could be a problem to distinguish between colours when the number of participants increases, and therefore other means to identify users are also necessary.

5.1 Panorama View of a Domain

The Panorama View is generated automatically by the system (see Figure 2). It presents:

(1) The list of participants and his/her respective colour.
(2) A pop-up menu that offers quantitative information about the domain such as the number of participants, the number of documents included in the domain, the number of comments made to the documents, the number of words in all the comments, the average number of comments per document, and the time the discussion lasted.
(3) A bar chart. Each entry on the *x*-axis represents a document and is labelled with Doc *n*, where *n* is the sequence number in which the document appears on the *x*-axis. The position of the document on the *x*-axis can be defined by different criteria, e.g., by the number of comments received, by the date in which the document was included in the domain, or by the number of different participants who made comments to the document. The *y*-axis presents the number of comments that each of the documents in the domain received. The bars in the chart are built up by coloured blocks, each of which represents a comment.

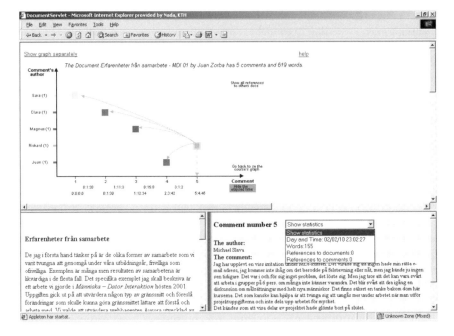

Figure 2: Panorama view of a domain generated by DID.

(4) A menu list. Each option of the menu is formed by the following items: the label Doc
n, the name of the author/responsible, and the title of the document as it was presented
in Col·lecció. For example, *Doc 10: Ana Ferrer: A case of an unfortunate collaboration*. The selected option takes the users to the Document Interactivity View, a more
detailed representation of the corresponding document (see Section 5.2).

From the Panorama View we could grasp the following information: In relation to the participant we could answer how many participants took part in the discussion and their names.
The frequency in which a colour appears corresponds to the activity of a particular participant in the discussions.

In relation to the document that is discussed, the size of the bar indicates the extent to
which a document has been discussed. If the bar is rich in different colours, the document
has been discussed by many of the participants. Observe that using these parameters, documents could be compared.

In relation to the discussion, the Panorama View shows the amount of discussion that will
be found in the domain and how active the whole group was. The order in which the documents are presented on the *x*-axis can give a general idea of the discussion. If sorted by number of comments in the document, it tells the distribution of the discussion along the different
documents presented in the domain. That is, it is easy to focus on those documents that were
extensively commented on, or those that were not discussed at all. If ordered by the number
of participants in the discussion of a document, it is possible to focus on those documents
that attracted more involvement among participants.

5.2   The Document Interactivity View

To reach the DIV, users select from the menu list presented in the Panorama View. Once the user has requested a document, a new layout is displayed. The upper frame presents the Document Interactivity Chart (see Figure 3), which shows the time sequence in which comments on this document have been received and the reference connections between the comments and the document. To generate the Document Interactivity Chart, the help of an analyst (a person) is needed who will create the code so that the links between the comments could be generated by the DID.

The bottom frame is divided into two vertical frames. The left frame displays the Web document that has currently been selected by the user. The right frame presents the text of the comment that the user might select from the document interactivity graph. The purpose of the bottom frame is to support navigation within the text-based communication associated with a document. It also gives some support for "rebuilding" the context in which the comment was made as the document in question is presented.

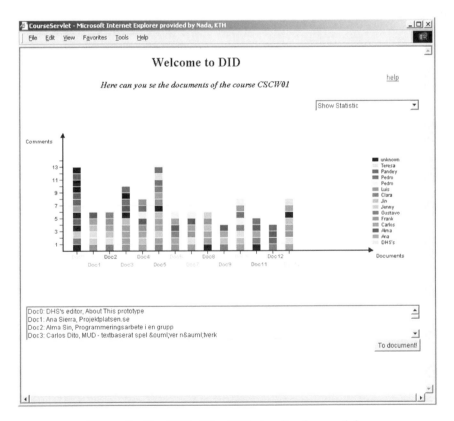

Figure 3: The DIV of the DID visualization module.

5.3   The Document Interactivity Chart

The Document Interactivity Chart is a two-dimensional view of the comments and participants found in a discussion of a document. The *x*-axis (the baseline) represents the document under discussion and shows the time sequence in which the comments on the document were received. On the *y*-axis, we have the names of those who made at least one comment in the discussion of the document in question, and within parenthesis the number of comments made by him/her. This number is used to sort the list. The closer a participant's name is to the baseline, the more comments he/she has posted in that discussion. However, this principle has one exception. The author's name is always part of the list and it is placed closest to the baseline regardless of whether he/she took part in the discussion.

If a comment (represented as a coloured square) makes direct reference to the selected document, a perpendicular dotted line is drawn from the comment to the baseline. If a comment makes reference to a previous comment, this is represented by a line and an arrow that links the comments in question. These links can be used to identify conversational threads within the discussion, and altogether, they show the interactivity of the discussion around a particular document.

As with the Panorama View, with the DIV we could grasp some information. The *y*-axis allows the reader to see at a glance how many members participated in the discussion of this document and who were the most active. As the comments are presented in chronological order, it is possible to see when the activity of the participant occurred, at the beginning, at the end, or during the whole discussion. As the author of the document in question is always placed closest to the baseline, one can easily see how the author has participated in the discussion about his/her document. It shows different response strategies chosen by participants. For example, participants might respond in one comment to several comments, or post a separate comment for each response.

About the discussion as a whole, the Document Interactivity Chart could give helpful information. For example, having a glance at the baseline and seeing how often it is intersected by a perpendicular line provides an easy way to determine the extent to which the discussion has indeed been focusing on the document in question. Also, the network of links that are formed between the comments is an indicator of the referential relationships among the comments. Therefore, one can say whether a discussion has been active or passive regardless of the number of comments.

About a particular comment, we can find out when the comment was made in relation to the other comments. The incoming arrows pointing to a comment indicate that the comment has been referenced by subsequent comments. Therefore, it could be possible to determine the degree of interest attracted by a particular comment. The outgoing arrows from a comment indicate which previous comments it makes reference to, for example, a reply. Therefore, the number of incoming and outgoing arrows of a comment might indicate the effect that the comment had in the whole discussion.

6   Examples of the Use of a Domain Interactivity Diagram

In this section we will present and discuss some examples of graphics that the DID system generates. The aim is to show in practice how this tool might be used. In the first section we show the Panorama Views of one domain. In the second section we show some examples of the DIV. The data used to generate the graphics is taken from the case study CSCW01.

To illustrate the use of the diagrams generated by DID we will focus on the following hypothetical scenario: Carlos is interested in the topic "Collaboration with and without computers". Luis, a friend of his who used Col·lecció in one of these discussions, informs Carlos that he can find information about the topic in the domain. Carlos decides to explore and read the material in order to learn more about the topic, but he does not have much time for this. He finds the DID system and uses it to explore and read the documents in the domain.

6.1 Using the Panorama View

In this case, the Panorama View, presented in Figure 2, displays the order in which the documents were included in the domain.[5]

At a glance it is possible to say that all the documents in the domains have been commented on. The time restriction might influence the reading strategy that Carlos might choose. One possible way would be to read those documents that had the most comments. The number of comments received by a document could reflect the interest that participants showed for the document; therefore, it might indicate whether the document is worth reading. Furthermore, Carlos could learn not only from the document content but also from the discussions around the document.

All the documents in the Figure 2 domain have got at least four comments, which could mean that thorough discussions can be found in that domain. Carlos noticed that Luis was part of this group. Also, it can be seen that Luis has commented several times and on almost all the documents in that domain. If Carlos compares this Panorama View with another domain in which the same topic was discussed, the view might help him decide which of the domains he would select.

6.2 Using the Document Interactivity View

For simplicity, let us say that Carlos is interested in those documents which presented at least three comments. Figure 4 shows two Document Interactivity Charts selected by Carlos.

Carlos can see that the discussions in the documents he selected refer to the document content in question several times. If we compare Figure 4A and B in relation to the links between the comments, we could say that the comments in Figure 4A are more closely related to each other that the ones in Figure 4B. A clear sign of this is that even the last comment made in the discussion makes reference to the very first comment that initiated the discussion in Figure 4A. Of them all, the unique comment sent by the author, closest to the baseline, in Figure 4A looks interesting or controversial as it is linked to all the other comments in the discussion. This might indicate that it is worth reading.

---

[5]One document included in the domain was designed to get feedback on the tool from users; the first place in the Panorama View was reserved for this document and labelled by Doc 00.

From Figure 4A and B, Carlos can observe that in these two documents, participants have taken part in the discussion of the documents, and the author has participated in them. Participants in the discussion of Figure 4A posted only one comment in the discussion. That was not the case for the discussion held in the discussion represented in Figure 4B. The author of the document and one of the participants sent three comments each within the discussion in general. The author of the document was not the only one who replied to a comment. In all the examples a participant who was not author of the document in discussion replied to another participant's comment (e.g., Figure 4A, comment #6). For the discussion in Figure 4A, Luis posted only one comment in the middle of the discussion in terms of sequence. Carlos also observes that Luis was more inter-

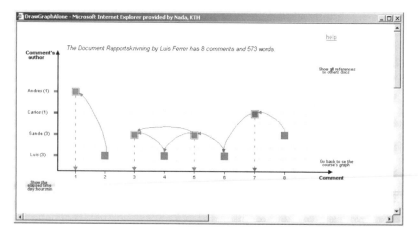

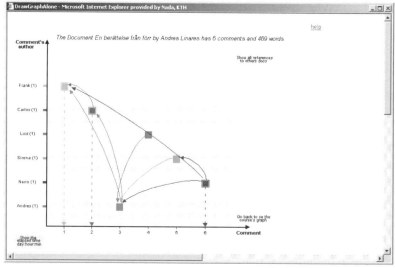

Figure 4: Two document interactivity charts generated by DID.

ested in the discussion of his own document (Figure 4B): Luis took part in the discussion from the very beginning until almost the very end and, his replies were made promptly.

The author in Figure 4A participated only once which could indicate, at first glance, that this author was not concerned about the discussion. However, this could just be the result of the when-to-reply strategy that the author of the document adopted. The author could reply as soon as possible after a comment is posted (see Figure 4B or wait for further comments to appear, see Figure 4A). The response could refer to a single comment (see Figure 4A, comment #2, 4, 5) or to multiple comments (see Figure 4A, comment #3, 6; Figure 4B, comment #5).

6.3   Remarks

We have limited the discussion here to just the visual cues that the system gives. The DID system offers other interactive possibilities (e.g., statistical information) that we have not taken into account to describe the possible interpretations that Carlos might make of the pictures.

A comment can also make a reference to the content of another document in the domain, or to a comment made on another document. As this is a rare case in our data, it is not included in the visualizations here, but there are conventions covering this case in the system.

As with any other graphical model, users will get much more out from the graphics generated by DID as he/she learns to use this representation. The aim is to enable the user to make inferences about interaction patterns from a quick view of the graphs.

7   Summary and Design Implications

We have developed graphical representations, both of an entire domain and of a particular dialogue around a document, that give an at-a-glance view of the participants' activity and clarify the structure of discussions. These visualizations, however, have so far only been used as research tools and part of them require manual work by an analyst to produce. A central issue for future research is if and how a graphical representation could be automatically created when a reply comment is posted and used as part of an active coherence mechanism for users. Such a capability could both preserve the document-focus of the environment and provide for increased interactivity.

So far, these representations have had the limitation that only one aspect of a participants' activity is visible, namely, the creation of a new document or an annotation. A remaining problem is how to give a more complete picture of the activities in a domain, including how users navigate among the documents and their dialogue spaces. We are currently working on different ways to represent and visualize the overall participation of a group in the course of a collaborative task. This will include overviews of recent actions, concurrently present users, patterns of navigation, and reading.

The use of Col·lecció as well as the DID visualization merits further investigation as they represent a new approach to the reviewing process in collaborative writing. Many issues remain to be studied in relation to how collaboration around document is affected by the use of these tools. Generally, we believe that the use of visualization tools to help the interpretation of online document discussions is a promising area for future research.

Chapter 11

Online Study of Word Spelling Production in Children's Writing

Jean Noël Foulin and Lucile Chanquoy

In the area of spelling, empirical findings largely come from analyses of spelling responses, mainly misspellings. By contrast, online studies of spelling production are rare, in adults as well as in children. Yet online examination of spelling production could provide decisive information about the cognitive processes underlying spelling production and spelling development in children. The first section of this chapter considers some issues regarding spelling management and spelling acquisition, the investigation of which requires online explorations of spelling production. In the second section, we report a temporal study whose purposes were to examine how children manage written spelling production and how the learning of word spelling affects spelling production. French-speaking fourth-graders were required to spell 48 words whose frequency and orthographic structure had been manipulated. Each word was to be spelled twice, before and after the children had been explicitly taught how to spell the words. Spelling latencies and spelling transcription times were recorded by means of a digital graphic tablet connected to a PC. The data were analyzed for the first spelling session, and then a comparison was made between the two spelling sessions. Results are discussed in the framework of a dual-route spelling model.

1   Introduction

We already know much about spelling skills, and the greatest part of this knowledge comes from off-line studies of spelling responses, mainly spelling errors (Frith, 1980; Rieben, Perfetti, & Fayol, 1997). Despite the growing amount of work in the domain, online studies of spelling production in adults (Bonin, Peereman, & Fayol, 2001; Glover & Brown, 1994; Kreiner, 1992, 1996) as well as in children (Rittle-Johnson & Siegler, 1999; Steffler. Varnhagen, Friesen, & Treiman, 1998) remain the exception. The reason is

Foulin, J.N., & Chanquoy, L. (2005). Online study of word spelling production in children's writing. In L. Van Waes, M. Leijten & C. Neuwirth (Vol. Eds.) & G. Rijlaarsdam (Series Ed.), Studies in Writing: Vol. 17. Writing and Digital Media (pp. 145–152). Oxford: Elsevier.

both methodological, the recording of writing activity is time-consuming, and theoretical, the temporal data in writing production are multidetermined and therefore puzzling to interpret (Foulin, 1995). Yet a more comprehensive understanding of the cognitive processes involved in spelling skills might be gained from online approaches. In the first section of this chapter, we consider some issues regarding spelling management and spelling acquisition, the investigation of which requires online explorations of spelling production. The second section reports a temporal analysis of spelling production in children, which we have carried out by the means of a digital tablet, to illustrate how the online study of spelling activity enlarges the understanding of spelling acquisition.

2   Spelling Production: Temporal Organization and Cognitive Management

The necessity of online study in spelling first arose with regard to skilled adult spellers. Although investigating spelling responses in adults is far from being fruitless (Holmes & Carruthers, 1998; Tainturier & Rapp, 2000), the very low rate of errors in good spellers requires an examination of the temporal features of spelling production in order to investigate linguistic and psycholinguistic variables which may influence spelling proficiency. For example, Glover and Brown (1994) have shown that spelling-production times in adults were affected by word phonographic consistency, whereas spelling accuracy was not. Likewise, Orliaguet and Boë (1993) found that the temporal organization of spelling production was influenced by the morphological structure of the word being spelled. Furthermore, temporal variations during spelling activity may be interpreted as reflecting variations in the amount of attentional resources devoted to spelling processing. The analysis of the time course of spelling production may thus shed light on the speller's strategy, that is, how spelling processes are managed and attentional resources are allocated during spelling production (Alamargot & Chanquoy, 2001; Fayol, 1999). Analyses of the effects of word frequency and phonographic consistency effects on spelling production times revealed that two spelling procedures, addressing (lexical retrieving) and assembling (phonological encoding), are involved in combination in adult spelling (Bonin & Méot, 2002; Kreiner, 1992, 1996). Temporal variations in spelling activity also suggested that adult spellers make cognitive strategy choices while facing spelling constraints. For example, a problematic grapheme inside a word can be processed either during latency (i.e., before word transcription), or in parallel with the transcription of precedent letters, or even at the moment this grapheme is to be spelled (Orliaguet & Boë, 1993).

Online studies are particularly interesting with regard to the investigation of spelling development. Spelling acquisition is not only a matter of progressing in accuracy and orthographic knowledge, but also in efficacy and procedure choice. Spelling procedures are more effective in older children than in younger children, and older spellers are faster than younger spellers (Rittle-Johnson & Siegler, 1999; Steffler et al., 1998). When words are correctly spelled, only temporal data can shed light on gains in speed and automation that affect successive productions of the same word as spelling develops. Temporal data are also requisite for exploring the developing strategies, which underlie children's progress in speed and accuracy. Beyond gains in general cognitive processing and handwriting speed, increasing effectiveness of spelling production may be explained by changes in spelling management: on the one hand, the execution of these procedures becomes more rapid; on the other hand, slower procedures, such as assembling, are progressively replaced by more effective procedures, such as addressing and analogy (Rittle-Johnson & Siegler, 1999). Such procedural evolution speeds up the spelling production while it reduces the demands in cognitive resources.

The understanding of individual differences in spelling level raises similar issues. Along with spelling acquisition, differences in spelling accuracy decrease with successive school grades and spelling levels (Sprenger-Charolles, Siegel, Béchennec, & Serniclaes, 2003). Here again, the temporal study of spelling production could reveal individual differences in attentional resources and/or spelling management, regardless of whether or not spellers are distinguishable in spelling accuracy. Online measures would not only differentiate the successive levels in normal spelling development but would also contribute to explain the relative slowness and overloading of unskilled spellers in comparison to skilled ones (Martlew, 1992).

While supplying information about the overall cognitive management of spelling processes, online studies can furthermore provide more fine-grained data relative to the management of sublexical orthographic units (e.g., graphemes, syllables, morphemes). The letter-by-letter analysis of the temporal course of word transcription gives information about the way children adapt the transcription speed to spelling constraints (Chanquoy, Foulin, & Fayol, 1990). It also makes possible the examination of issues relating to the nature and size of orthographic units in order to understand how children compose words while spelling and how the functional status of such units changes as spelling skills develop. For example, from their study of typed spelling in elementary school children, Steffler et al. (1998) reported that letter position affects keystroke latencies. Latencies that were shorter within a consonant cluster than in other positions suggested that children processed consonant clusters as a simple orthographic unit. Latency analyses also showed that different spelling procedures were associated with different temporal patterns. More precisely, addressing reflected more regular and flatter letter-by-letter latencies than assembling.

To summarize, online investigations have already supplied substantial and encouraging results about the cognitive architecture underlying spelling skills, both in adults and in children. Undoubtedly, the continuous record of temporal organization of spelling production reveals valuable information describing more completely the cognitive management of spelling and how this management changes with spelling acquisition. Extending the corpus of online data appears to be a critical step in research into spelling, mainly with regard to the typical written spelling mode. The next section presents an online study of spelling production in children, which confirms that the temporal analysis of spelling activity is helpful to achieve insight into the development of spelling skills. Moreover, such a study illustrates that the use of a graphic tablet as a digital tool is of primary interest in this area.

3   Temporal Analysis of Children's Spelling Production

The purpose of the study was to investigate two issues: first, how children manage written spelling production or, more precisely, how they deal with spelling constraints in real time;

second, how the learning of word spelling affects spelling production times and spelling management.

Children had to spell to dictation the same words twice, before and after they were taught the spelling of each word. This study design was considered to be a relevant framework for investigating the longitudinal changes in spelling production, which were assumed to accompany the improvement of word spelling knowledge.

Word frequency and word phonographic structure, which are known to influence both spelling accuracy and spelling production times (Kreiner, 1992), were manipulated. These two variables were used to investigate the involvement in children's spelling of the addressing procedure, which is sensitive to word frequency, and of the assembling procedure, which is sensitive to word phonographic structure. Manipulating these factors may help us understand what procedures and strategies children use while spelling, and how spelling management evolves when children progress in their knowledge about word spelling.

In the first production, high-frequency words were assumed to be spelled through addressing and low-frequency words through assembling. Accordingly, spelling latency and production time were expected to be shorter for high-frequency words than low-frequency ones. Temporal data were also expected to reveal an interaction effect between word frequency and word structure on spelling production time. In the second production, we assumed that the improvement of word spelling knowledge, due to word learning, would influence online spelling production, but in a different way according to word frequency. In high-frequency words, as children became still more familiar with word spelling, addressing would become more rapid and close to automatic. In low-frequency words, given that the learning of word spelling might contribute to the formation of word-specific orthographic representations, an acceleration of spelling production was also expected, considered this time as a consequence of the procedural transition from assembling to addressing. Overall, we predicted that the interaction effect between word frequency and word structure observed on spelling production times during the first session might disappear during the second one.

4   Method

The participants were 27 ten-year-old French-speaking children attending grade 4. Only the products of the 18 children who had made the fewest errors in the first session were analyzed. It follows that these children may be more skilled spellers than their classmates.

Children had to spell 48 five-letter words mapping three phonographic structures: 16 consistent CCVCe (or CVCCe) words including a consonant cluster (e.g., *brave* [brave], *sucre* [sugar], *brute* [brute], *sacre* [coronation]); 16 CVV*Ce words including an inconsistent vowel digraph (e.g., *danse* [dance], *fauve* [wild beast], *reine* [queen], *laide* [ugly]); and 16 CVVCe including a consistent vowel digraph (e.g., *boule* [bowl], *toile* [cloth], *moine* [monk], *louve* [she-wolf]). Each word type was represented by eight high-frequency words and eight low-frequency words (Lété, Sprenger-Charolles, & Colé, 2004). All words were chosen to increase the probability of accurate responses in the first session.

Children had to spell to dictation the same words twice, before and after they had learned the spelling of each word. The second part of the experiment took place about three months after the first one. In the last month preceding the second session, children participated in six tutorials during which they were taught the spelling of each word. They also had to write them several times. Word spelling accuracy was assessed in the middle and at the end of the tutoring period. Each spelling session took place on two consecutive days. Words were presented in four blocks, with four words from each word type included in each block. Several presentation orders of the blocks and of the words within each block were used among the children.

In each session, spelling responses and spelling productions were recorded by means of a digital tablet (digitizer Wacom A4 UD-1212R) connected to a PC (see Figure 1). Using a pressure-pen, children wrote on a sheet of paper placed on the graphic tablet (a piece of carbon paper was positioned under the writing paper to obtain a visual imprint of handwriting). All movements and pauses of the pen produced during spelling activity were recorded to an accuracy of the nearest millisecond, together with their spatial coordinates. Temporal and graphic data were monitored by a software program, which was responsible both for the word-by-word recording of data and for the replay of the written activity (G-studio: Chesnet, Guillabert, & Espéret, 1994).

The words to be spelled were first recorded on audio files by a male speaker. The computer controlled the auditory presentation of the words, which were dictated, one by one, through two loudspeakers placed in front of the child. The child initiated the word dictation by pressing with the pen on a specific space on the tablet. The temporal data were recorded from the onset of word dictation to the raising of the pen at the end of word transcription. This technique made it possible to directly obtain two main temporal parameters for each spelling production: spelling latency, which corresponds to the duration which elapses from the start of word dictation to the beginning of word transcription on the tablet; and transcription time, which corresponds to the duration which elapses between the beginning and the end of word transcription.

Figure 1. The digital tablet connected to the PC.

5   Results and Discussion

Table 1 presents mean spelling latency and transcription time as a function of word frequency and word structure, during the first and the second spelling sessions. Two 2 (word frequency: high and low) × 3 (word structure: CCVCe, CVV*Ce and CVVCe) × 2 (session: first and second) analyses of variance were computed with repeated measures on all the factors, for each dependent variable. Only the main results are reported here.

Analysis of spelling latency in the first spelling session revealed the effects of word frequency, of word type and of the interaction between these two variables. Spelling latency was, as expected, shorter for high-frequency words than for low-frequency ones. The interaction between word frequency and word structure revealed that word structure affected spelling latency only for low-frequency words: CVVCe words were spelled faster than CVV*Ce and CCVCe words, and CVV*Ce words were spelled the most slowly. In the light of previous results (Kreiner, 1992; Rittle-Johnson & Siegler, 1999), a plausible explanation of these results is that high-frequency words were spelled through addressing and low-frequency words were spelled through assembling. This interpretation was substantiated by the analysis of spelling transcription time. Indeed, the word structure affected spelling transcription time of low-frequency words: CCVCe and CVV*Ce words were written more slowly than CVVCe words. Conversely, this variable did not influence high-frequency words transcription time. Such findings suggest that high-frequency words were managed differently than low-frequency words during word transcription. In contrast with the structure management of high-frequency words, the structure management of low-frequency words was not achieved when children began to write down the word, and continued over the course of transcription. However, the absence of a word frequency effect on transcription time is an apparently conflicting result. A first possible explanation is that, in children, the cognitive cost of the sole word transcription abolishes the word frequency effect. Another hypothesis concerns the contribution of addressing and assembling to

Table 1: Mean-spelling latency and spelling transcription time in milliseconds (and standard deviation) as a function of word frequency and word structure in first and second spelling session.

	Spelling latency		Transcription time	
	S1	S2	S1	S2
CCVC*e*				
High frequency	1859 (*313*)	1654 (*369*)	4263 (*919*)	3987 (*919*)
Low frequency	2178 (*644*)	1634 (*367*)	4288 (*984*)	3721 (*839*)
CVV*C*e				
High frequency	1848 (*369*)	1699 (*376*)	4209 (*822*)	3815 (*995*)
Low frequency	1971 (*446*)	1583 (*392*)	4312 (*882*)	3925 (*909*)
CVVC*e*				
High frequency	1876 (*343*)	1517 (*280*)	4133 (*692*)	3834 (*659*)
Low frequency	1774 (*303*)	558 (*357*)	4030 (*698*)	3700 (*851*)

spelling production in children. As assumed in adults (Kreiner, 1996; Tainturier & Rapp, 2000), both procedures may not be completely independent but may have a combined influence during the course of word spelling. Contrasting high- and low-frequency words, as in this study, could hide the effects of a joint or interactive intervention of both procedures during word spelling production. The functional combination between assembling and addressing would probably be more apparent if word frequency represented a continuum (Bonin & Méot, 2002). Finally, word frequency counts may not be relevant measures in spelling research because they imperfectly match how children have really experienced words in writing (Kreiner, 1996).

Comparison of overall spelling production time (i.e., spelling latency and transcription time) according to word structure showed that CVVCe words were easier to spell than CVV*Ce and CCVCe words, which did not differ. Simple consistent words are processed more rapidly than inconsistent and complex ones because resolving spelling problems requires both following a decision-making procedure and inhibiting alternative responses. In children, additional processing seems to take place during both latency and word transcription. Finally, word structure affected either spelling production but not spelling accuracy (e.g., between CCVCe and CVVCe), or spelling accuracy but not spelling production (e.g., between CCVCe and CVV*Ce).

The comparison of temporal data across the pre-learning and the post-learning spelling sessions shed light on how spelling management evolved with word spelling knowledge. The most revealing findings were the decrease in spelling production times, which affected both spelling latency and spelling transcription time. Analysis of spelling latency showed that children began the transcription faster in the second session than in the first one, regardless of word frequency and word structure. Likewise, the analysis of transcription time showed that children wrote down the words more rapidly in the second session than in the first one, once again regardless of word frequency and word structure.

Another main finding concerned the effect of word frequency and word structure in each session. Whereas, in the first session, both variables significantly influenced spelling latency and, only for word structure, spelling transcription time, they were largely noninfluential in the second session. If it is hypothesized that, during the first session, high-frequency words were retrieved from the speller's lexicon, the decrease in latency during the second session suggests that spelling practice may still improve the execution speed of addressing. Word spelling would be retrieved from the lexicon more rapidly because practice improves the quality of word-specific orthographic representations. The decrease in transcription time for high-frequency words during the second session, in comparison with the first one, might support the same explanation: better word-specific orthographic representations enhance the lexical retrieval that, in turn, elicits a faster and possibly automatic word transcription. Such findings appear to be relevant data regarding the issue of the automatization of word spelling production.

As far as low-frequency words are concerned, the disappearance of the word structure effect on both spelling latency and transcription time during the second session suggests that they were now spelled through addressing, regardless of their type. The learning of word spelling might result in the formation of word-specific representations and a change in spelling procedure, children using addressing instead of assembling. A more fine-grained analysis of word transcription might reveal different letter-by-letter temporal patterns between the two sessions and presumably more regular temporal patterns in the second session (Steffler et al., 1998).

To summarize, this study showed that both spelling latency and spelling transcription time are sensitive measures of spelling cognitive processing in children. Several findings allowed a larger comprehension of how children deal with spelling information in real time. First, the temporal organization of spelling production in the first session revealed that children manage spelling constraints both before and in parallel with the word transcription. Then, the variations affecting the temporal parameters of spelling production across the two sessions confirmed that children's cognitive management of spelling takes place in both latency and transcription periods. Finally, the results suggested possible interpretations of how children use spelling procedures and become skilled and automatic spellers.

6   Conclusion

The parallel examination of spelling production times and spelling responses makes possible a better understanding of cognitive processes that underlie spelling production. The digitalizer appears to be a powerful research tool in investigating the temporal organization of written-spelling production. The use of a digital tablet has strong advantages when compared with alternative methodologies. The written spelling task makes it better suited for research involving schoolchildren than either typing or oral spelling tasks. The typing task presents obvious problems when used with children or adults who are not experienced typists. The digital tablet methodology is also less cumbersome and time-consuming than the videotape recording of written-spelling activity. The latter requires the uninterrupted attention of the examiner during recording and presents great difficulties in measuring spelling production times precisely.

Furthermore, analyses confined here to macro temporal parameters can be extended to sublexical parameters since the digital tablet also provides within-word information about pause and handwriting activity. Studying temporal data at a sublexical level, namely pause duration and handwriting speed, would allow for investigating local strategy choices made by children while transcribing words.

Despite the advantages brought out by the use of a digital tablet, online studies of spelling production face two persistent problems. The first is that collecting and analyzing temporal data from writing production is still very time-consuming. The second problem concerns the difficulty of unambiguously interpreting temporal data in terms of cognitive processes or strategies. We hope that advances in theoretical models of spelling and in experimental designs will allow future studies to overcome these obstacles.

Chapter 12

Digital Tools for the Recording, the Logging and the Analysis of Writing Processes

Introduction, Overview and Framework

Kirk P.H. Sullivan and Eva Lindgren

This subchapter provides an introduction to the possibilities and limitations of digital tools for recording of writing processes, a comprehensive framework in which the digital tools that are explained further in the subchapters 2–5 are integrated and a critical perspective to the characteristics of the tools, their usage and related automatic analyses.

1 Introduction

Spelman Miller and Sullivan (2006, forthcoming) in their introduction to keystroke logging stress the widespread calls in the literature for a comprehensive theory of writing that takes account of the interconnected cognitive, textual and socio-contextual dimensions of writing. *Digital tools for the recording of writing processes* can play a part in the shaping of such a comprehensive theory of writing.

Before considering how digital tools for the recording of writing processes can contribute to the evolution of writing theory, it is necessary to define what digital tools are, what they record and what they do not record. Without this framework it is not possible to assess the contribution to the shaping of a comprehensive theory of writing made by the research using digital tools that is presented by four research teams in the subchapters 2–5 of this chapter.

Sullivan, K., & Lindgren, E. (2005). Digital tools for the recording, the logging and the analysis of writing processes: Introduction, overview and framework. In L. Van Waes, M. Leijten & C. Neuwirth (Vol. Eds.) & G. Rijlaarsdam (Series Ed.), Studies in Writing: Vol. 17. Writing and Digital Media (pp. 153–186). Oxford: Elsevier.

2   Why the Digital Tool?

Research into how humans interact with their computers can be viewed as one of the stimuli for using digital tools to record text evolution or writing in a digital medium. The question of how the human computer interface could be improved drove much of the early development of the tools that registered users' interactions with computers. Writing researchers saw the advantages of using the computer to record the writing process over the use of the video recorder, think-aloud protocols or retrospective verbal reports.

Video recording has been used to study writers' behaviour among others (Matsuhashi, 1981; Williamson & Pence, 1989). Video recording affords the researcher the possibility to repeatedly visually observe how a recorded pen and paper or word processor composition evolved. Such recordings require that the researcher manually translates the video recording into a protocol of information that indicates aspect of the writing process such as textual revision, and pause position and duration.

Video recording coupled with researcher transcription currently facilitates, as Strömqvist, Holmqvist, Johansson, Karlsson, and Wengelin (forthcoming) point out, a time resolution of no greater than 40 ms as video recording offers a time resolution of 25 pictures/frames per second. Such a time resolution affords neither accurate duration measurements nor a realistic time resolution for conducting a pause analysis. However, digital tools for recording of the writing process afford a time resolution that facilitates accurate pause analysis.

The potential of computer keystroke logging for precise time registration of keystrokes was realised in the mid-1980s by Bridwell-Bowles, Sirc, and Brooke (1985) and Bridwell-Bowles, Johnson, and Brehe (1987), who reported on a series of studies on word-processor writing at the University of Minnesota in which the program 'Recording Wordstar' was used. Since then a range of keystroke logging software programs for different platforms and with different functionalities have been produced. These include JEdit (Cederlund & Severinson Eklundh, n.d.; Severinson Eklundh & Kollberg, 1996), Keytrap (Van Waes & Van Herreweghe, 1995), Inputlog (Leijten & Van Waes, 2005a), Scriptlog (Strömqvist & Karlsson, 2001), and Translog (Jakobsen, 1999).

3   Characteristics and Limitations

The possibility of exact time registration of each interaction made by the writer in the word-processing environment is afforded by using the computer to record and pipe to a computer file all keystrokes, mouse actions, cut and paste actions that a writer makes during writing along with the time of each action. The resultant log-file makes for computer script-based analyses of the data possible.

Examples of how the keystroke log can be automatically analysed can be found in Kollberg (1998) and Wengelin (forthcoming). Kollberg presented a computer-based method for studying and representing text composition called S-notation; this method forms the basis for the research presented by Perrin (Leijten & Van Waes, this volume) and also used as the basis for the revision analysis module for Inputlog (this volume). Wengelin demonstrates how corpus linguistics methods can be applied to keystroke logged data to examine pause behaviour during writing.

As with all data analysis that a researcher undertakes, the researcher applying a computer script to a keystroke logged data file needs to be aware of the limitations of the data collection approach and of the analysis limitations of the particular analysis they are conducting. When the researcher has written the computer script comprehension of the limitations is often inherent. However, when using the automatic analyses that are available in digital tools for studying writing processes the researcher needs to spend time making sure that the limitations of these automatic analyses are understood before being applied.

One example of an automatic analysis module available for analysis of a computer keystroke is the revision analysis statistics module available in Trace-It (Kollberg, 1998). The revision analysis statistics provided by Trace-It present the number of revision at various levels, e.g., word, phrase and sentence. The researcher needs to understand the algorithm's definition of these levels; it is not certain that a manual analysis by a linguist would produce the same results. Further the researcher needs to be aware that typographical errors are included in these revision statistics and interpret these statistics with this in mind. Moreover, the researcher needs to make it clear to the reader that they are aware of the limitations. One example of research conducted using Trace-It's automatic revision analysis statistics module where from the paper it is not clear if impact of typographic errors has been taken into account or not is that of Thorson (2000).

Automatically produced quantitative data can result in research that on the surface is well motivated and well conducted, yet without an understanding of how the quantitative data was produced and automatically analysed; the resultant conclusions may be based on fundamental flaws in the interpretation of the data analysis. It is, therefore, paramount that the researcher using automatic analysis functions in keystroke logging programs, or using scripts that they have written themselves, make it clear to the reader how they have dealt with aspects such as typographical errors and that the limitation of the data analysis script is understood and accounted for in any conclusion drawn.

A limitation of most current computer keystroke logging programs is that they only log interactions with one program at a time. That is, beyond logging that a writer is not interacting with the program being logged, or that the mouse has moved outside of the program being logged, interactions between the writer and other programs, such as a web-browser or Excel, are not logged. A similar limitation, that would remain when keystroke logging programs are able to log interactions with more than one program at the same time, is that the computer keystroke logging program can only record interaction with the computer. It cannot, for example, reveal anything about pen and paper mind mapping prior to formal text production or the pen and paper doodles and other peripheral activities, such as looking up things in books or papers, made in parallel with the formal text production on the computer. These limitations delimit and frame the interpretation of keystroke logged writing sessions.

To record pre-writing, pen and paper map creation, and pen and paper peripheral activities a digital tablet or a digital pen can be used in conjunction with a computer keystroke program. These tools have not yet been developed to synchronise with keystroke log programs. Until they are, video recording is needed if the researcher wishes to maintain a synchronised timeframe between these digital tools. Video recording is also demanded if the researcher wishes to track the writer's use of other programs and the use of books and papers. By combining a video recording with keystroke logging and a digital pen or tablet would provide the researcher access to both an overview of the peripheral activities and to a keystroke log with high-time resolution. The different data sources would need to be linked together by the researcher.

An approach to linking data from various digital and non-digital sources using Geographic Information Systems was posited in Lindgren and Sullivan (2002) and is outlined in more detail in Lindgren, Sullivan, Lindgren and Spelman Miller (forthcoming). Andersson et al. (this volume) present another approach to linking and presenting data from two digital media, namely eye-tracking and keystroke logging.

The recent discussions in the literature around how to link, or layer, data from more than one source or form of analysis have grown out of the strengths and limitations of the data collection and analysis approaches used for studying writing processes. No single approach affords access to the entirety of the writing process. Without video recording it is impossible to have access to the peripheral pen and paper activities and keystroke logging only provides the researcher with high time resolution data describing the writer's interaction with the computer. The limitations associated with keystroke logging are presented by Andersson et al. as one motivation for linking eye-tracking and keystroke logging. They argue that this combination provides a window on the interplay between perception and production in writing. For example, keystroke logging does not afford the researcher information about where the writer is looking when pausing.

Obtrusive observational approaches such as video-recording and eye-tracking can make the writer feel observed. This can result in the writer behaving differently. Such processes can be reactive.

Similarly, when authors are asked to verbalise their thoughts during writing, the writing process is affected. In a similar fashion to being video recorded the writers are continually reminded that they are being observed. Moreover, the method places extra cognitive demands upon the writer who has to simultaneously write and talk about writing. Janssen, Van Waes, and Van den Bergh (1996) found changes in pause time when using the think-aloud method and Sleurs, Jacobs, and Van Waes (2003) that the items verbalised were those of focal attention and not automated actions.

Computer keystroke logging is less reactive in that it operates in the background of the word-processor being used and does not continually remind the writer that they are being observed. Another approach that leaves the writer feeling unobserved during writing is the retrospective interview. In this method, writers are interviewed about their writing after they have completed their texts. From a writing process research perspective cf. didactic perspective, the researcher is never sure if the writer remembers or constructs new explanations of their composition process. (See Levy, Marek, & Lea (1996) for a discussion of how to use this approach to affect.)

When writers translate their ideas into texts this tends to occur in an environment with which the writers are familiar. The familiarity of the setting, the office, the home, the train to work, the pen, the laptop and the word processor are diametrically opposed to the research setting that is often used for writing research. Perrin (this volume) examines, keystroke logging writing in a natural work environment, that of the journal. However, by doing so he is unable to control as many variables as can be controlled in an experimental setting. His natural research is as delimited in its validity as the experimental-based writing research, but in different ways. Each of the following five subchapters of this chapter present a digital tool for recording writing processes. Each of them achieves something that the other does not. For example, the research using CAMTASIA and CATMOVIE reported by Degenhardt (this volume) achieves platform transfer and permits the writers to compose in their preferred word processing environment. Yet, neither CAMTASIA nor CATMOVE generate a log-file for later quantitative analysis.

4 Conclusion

The study of writing using digital tools not only has a role to play in the shaping of a comprehensive theory of writing that would be able to account for the situation described at the beginning of this paper, but also a role to play in the development of new didactic approaches to the teaching of writing and the encouraging of language awareness (see Lindgren, 2004, 2005; Lindgren & Sullivan, 2003; Sullivan & Lindgren, 2002). Thus, when reading the research presentations in the subchapters 2–5 consider both the research implications and the didactic implications of the research tools for writing processes that are presented.

Logging Writing Processes with Inputlog

Luuk Van Waes and Mariëlle Leijten

In this subchapter we describe a new logging program, called Inputlog. Most logging tools are either developed for a specific computing environment, or not adequately adapted to the current Windows environment. As such, they cannot be used for writing studies in which 'natural' writing and computer environments employ commercial word processors. This was the main incentive to develop a new logging tool, i.e., Inputlog. This program consists of three modules: a data collection module that registers on line writing processes on a very detailed level; a data analysis module that offers text and pause analysis; and a play module that enables researchers to review the writing session. The functional description of Inputlog is complemented by two examples of research studies in which the program was used. We wind up the chapter with a preview of the plans for further developments.

1   Introduction

The basic concept of most logging tools that have been developed is more or less comparable (Sullivan & Lindgren, in this volume; or for a review, see Sullivan & Lindgren, in preparation). All keystrokes and mouse movements during a writing process are logged and stored for later processing. This continuous data storage does not interfere with the normal usage of the computer, creating an ecologically valid research context. At a later stage, the logged data can be made available for further analysis, either within the program environment itself or as exported data in statistical programs such as SPSS or SAS. Depending on the research question, researchers can choose to analyze different aspects of the writing process and the writing behavior by combining, for instance, temporal data (e.g., time stamps, or pauses) with process data (keystrokes or mouse movements). The data collection (and processing) can be performed much faster and more accurately by means of the computer, than it could ever be done manually.

At the moment most logging tools are either developed for a specific writing environment, or not adequately adapted to the current Windows environment. As such, they cannot be used for writing studies in which 'natural' writing and computer environments employ commercial word processors (e.g., MSWord or WordPerfect). This was the main reason to develop a new logging tool, i.e., Inputlog. In this chapter we present a short description of the functional characteristics of Inputlog. Next, two research studies are presented to illustrate the use of the program. We conclude the chapter with a preview of the further developments of the program.

Van Waes, L., & Leijten, M. (2005). Logging writing processes with Inputlog. In L. Van Waes, M. Leijten & C. Neuwirth (Vol. Eds.) & G. Rijlaarsdam (Series Ed.), Studies in Writing: Vol. 17. Writing and Digital Media (pp. 158–165). Oxford: Elsevier.

2   Characteristics of Inputlog

For the development of Inputlog we were able to fall back on the functionality of two existing programs: JEdit and Trace-it on the one hand (Severinson Eklundh, 1994, 1996; Severinson Eklundh & Kollberg, 1996, 2003; Kollberg, 1998), and ScriptLog on the other hand (Strömqvist & Malmsten, 1997). JEdit and Trace-it are suitable for Macintosh personal computers. JEdit only logs data in an in-house developed limited word processor. ScriptLog also mainly logs in a limited word processor that was developed for research purposes (i.c. mainly writing experiments with young children). Trace-it features an extensive revision module, while ScriptLog combines logging data with recorded eye-tracking data (Andersson et al., this volume).

As mentioned above, most logging-tools cannot be used for writing studies in which professional writing in an ethnological business environment is studied. Professional writers almost always employ commercial word processors like MSWord, mostly in a Windows environment. Existing logging tools up till now are mainly developed to operate in experimental settings, which was problematic for our writing research in which we studied professional writers in their own environment. Another impetus for the development of Inputlog has been a study on the influence of speech recognition on the writing process. For this study we observed the writing processes of 20 participants who used speech recognition software during their day-to-day work in their professional business contexts (five observations of approximately 30 min per participant; see Leijten & Van Waes, 2005b). Because it was not possible to register keyboard input in combination with speech mode data with any of the existing logging tools, the process data had to be analyzed manually. To collect the writing process data, or should we say speech recognition data, we combined two digital observation instruments: a digital screen cam (i.c. Camtasia; see Degenhardt in this volume) and a digital sound recorder (i.c. Quickrecord). The study showed that the chosen observation instruments and analyzing methods did enable us to analyze and describe the specific speech recognition writing processes, but the data analyses were very time-consuming.

Inputlog was developed to give in to these objections. It consists of three modules that should assist researchers in the collection and analyses of online writing processes in a Windows environment: a record, a generate and a play module. In short, the logging process is organized as follows. The first step is the activation of the recorder itself. To identify a particular writing session that is going to be logged, the user defines certain characteristics using a set of (predefined) variables and then starts the recorder. By default MS Word will be started to create a writing environment that is familiar to most writers. From then on, the writing process will be logged as it evolves on the screen. At the end of the registration the output data are saved in a source file, a so-called IDF-file. The data of this file can be used either to generate analyses files, or as an input for the playback module. The analyses files are the result of several conversions of the data in the source file, and enable researchers to analyze the modus data, the pause data, and the text data on a more aggregated level. Finally, the playback module enables researchers to replay the writing session exactly as it was registered, or speed up to the researcher's preference. Furthermore, the playback module is also used as an intermediate facilitator for the revision analysis (under development).

The three main steps in the logging procedure are now described in more detail. Depending on the researchers' objectives, certain options in the modules will be more appropriate than others.

Step 1: Record the data of a writing session in MSWord. Before a new session is started the researcher can first specify the file information and the identification data for a specific session. This information will be included in all the analysis files that will be generated based on the session source file, facilitating the identification of each writing session. The file that will be generated in the recording session has the extension *.idf, which is added automatically. This file will be used as an input for the generate and play functions (cf. infra).

Each logging session can be identified by a maximum of 10 variables (six predefined and four user-defined variables). These variables should enable the researcher to identify a writing session in detail.

Step 2: Generate data files for statistical, text, pause and mode analyses. In the generate module of the program, analysis files can be generated on the basis of a source file that was recorded in a previous logging session. In other words, any IDF file can be opened at any time to generate data output files for specific analyses. Inputlog 1.4 offers four different analyses:

(1) *General logging file*: a spreadsheet with a basic log file of the writing session in which every line represents an input action (letter, function, mouse click, or movement); for every input action the session information is stored together with an identification of the input, the time stamp, the pausing time that followed it, and — for a mouse operation — the *xy*-value of the screen position.
(2) *Statistical analysis*: a spreadsheet with basic statistical information on the writing session such as the session information, some basic data about the written text (product and process), pausing behavior and the use of the different writing modes.
(3) *Text analysis*: a plain linear text in HTML format with the complete linear production of the text including mouse movements and other activities; extra options allow for the production of a linear output in which the writing activities are divided into periods (time periods of *x* seconds) or intervals (number of intervals in which the writing process is to be divided).
(4) *Pause analysis*: a spreadsheet with analyses of every non-scribal period; the threshold for the pauses can be set to 1, 2, or 5 s as a standard or to any user-defined level.
   Two other analyses are under construction for the next release:
(5) *Mode analysis*: a spreadsheet with information about the distribution of the writing modes (keyboard, mouse, speech technology) that were used as an input device during the writing session.
(6) *Revision analysis*: a spreadsheet with a basic analysis of the number, the level and the kind of revision that has taken place during the writing session.

Step 3: Play the recorded session at different speeds. A recorded writing session can be replayed using Inputlog. Again, the IDF file is used as a source file for the replay. To verify the information labels of the file that is selected for a play back session, all defined variables of the session identification appear in the dialog box on the left side of the screen. The writing session can be replayed at different speeds.

3   Usage

To illustrate the possible usage of Inputlog, we briefly discuss two fragments of writing processes taken from experiments in which we have used the program as a logging device. The first experiment concerned a more technical writing experiment that focused on the working memory requirements necessary for error detection in the 'text produced so far' (Leijten, Ransdell, & Van Waes, 2006); the second example is taken from a case analysis of a writer producing a bad news letter.

3.1   The Text Produced So Far and the Use of Working Memory

An experimental setting was set up to assess the memory load during the 'text produced so far' interaction in the text production phase. The design included the most frequently occurring error types found in a case study of professional writers that were using speech recognition for the first time to write business texts (Leijten & Van Waes, 2005b). In the example at hand, we selected two text fragments in which a sentence with large speech recognition errors is corrected. The errors that occurred in the text produced so far were considered as major because the number of characters that differed from the intended text was more than two. Besides, the selected errors could only occur in speech recognition.

The task in the experiment consisted of a set of sentences that was presented to the participants to provide a context. In Figure 1, an example of a correct and an incorrect sentence is given (see sentence 2). After every sentence (1) the participants had to click the 'ok' button, to indicate that they had finished reading the sentence. A sub clause of the previous sentence was then presented as text produced so far (TPSF) in a subordinate causal structure (2), and the participants were prompted to complete the sentence (3) on the basis of the context provided earlier (1).

The participants could either prefer to correct the errors first and then complete the sentence, or to complete the sentence first and then correct the error. In case, for this sentence 83% of the participants preferred to complete the sentence first and correct the error afterwards. Figure 2 shows the linear output of the writing session of two participants that used another writing strategy. Pauses longer than 1 s are included in the output; texts are in Dutch.

Correct
1. Because the height was not indicated, the pick-up truck drove by the underpass.
2. The pick-up truck drove by the underpass,
3. because the height was not indicated.

Incorrect
1. Because the height was not indicated, the pick-up truck drove by the underpass.
2. The **picot trug** drove by the **underparts**.
3. because the height was not indicated.
Dutch "De **heeft week** reed onder de **brief** door, want de hoogte was niet aangegeven."

Figure 1: Examples of correct and incorrect sentences in the TPSF experiment.

sentence completion → error correction (83%)	error correction → sentence completion (17%)
[MwC.910,701-391,348] [McLeft]	{2.66}[McLeft][MwC.910,711-149,347]
de hoogte was niet aangegeven {2.19}	[McLeft] *[MwC.149,347-375,355]*
[MwC.491,352-145,346] [McLeft]	[BS 9]ftruck {1.6} [MwC.372,357-
[BS 9]	269,340] [Mselect]
eftruck {1.27}	[MwC.270,340-342,341]
[RIGHT 17] [DEL 4]	[BS 4]
ug <1.17>	ug <1.81> [RIGHT 15]
[MwC.165,335-933,699] [McLeft]	de hoogte stond niet aangegeven <1.25>
	[MwC.348,338-884,695] [McLeft]

Figure 2: Example of linear output of a text fragment generated by Inputlog. Remark: MwC, mouse movement without click; McLeft, mouse click left; Mselect, selection of text by mouse; BS, backspace; right 17, arrow right 17.

In these examples of two short writing fragments, different writing strategies can be distinguished. The first writer prefers to continue completing the text first, before correcting the mistake in the TPSF. He positions his cursor after the first segment (TPSF; cf. *xy*-value of left mouse click) — without a significant previous pause — and then completes the sentence. After the sentence is completed he pauses for 2.19 s. He then positions the mouse after the incorrect word and deletes it by using the backspace key. Next, he navigates through the text by pressing the right arrows key and deletes the second error. Finally, he has a short pause before he continues to the next sentence. The logging of the writing session of the second participant reveals a different pattern. He pauses before he starts writing and then positions the cursor behind the error to correct this first. After correcting the second error he completes the sentence.

In the analysis of the research data presented here, we were mainly interested in a description of the interaction with the text produced so far. Differences in writing strategies can be related to both individual differences and to error characteristics in the TPSF. This short example illustrates how the detailed process information that is generated by Inputlog provides a basis for analyzing writing strategies that are no longer visible in the final written product.

3.2   *Pausing and Revision Behavior in Writing Bad News Letters*

In Figure 3, we show the linear text representation of a writer producing a bad news letter in which he declines an offer to deliver a keynote address for an international conference. We were especially interested in the process characteristics of the writing episode that concerned the wording of the bad news itself. As we know from the literature on this issue, the strategic considerations to make the bad news as acceptable as possible for the reader are crucial in the perception of the message (and may also determine the future interpersonal relation with the reader).

The writer needed about 10 min to finish the letter of about 130 words. The replay function of Inputlog was used as a stimulus for a retrospective thinking aloud protocol. Figure 3 shows the sequential linear output (periods of 30 s) of a fragment that illustrates the writer's strategic considerations at the beginning of the second paragraph.

150 sec	{8.44} Presenting a {1.33} paper to {2.36} this group {3.66} [CTRL+LEFT 1] {1.02} quality {1.8} [END] {1.03} deserves a {1.53} thor
180 sec	ough {1.39} and {2.42}time {1.19} [BS 4] {1.66} comprehensive effort {2.13}.{3.61} Of course, [BS 12]. {1.02} Obviously {2.90}
210 sec	, such an effort {2.03} requires {5.55} a lot of [BS 8] {1.05} considerable [BS 12] time. {4.84}
240 sec	However, {1.34} my schedule {2.66} [CTRL+LEFT 4] {1.28} [DEL 10] M [END] {2.38} is fully comm{1.77}itted to a
270 sec	writing project {2.30} {7.17} [CTRL+LEFT 7] {2.16}

Figure 3: Linear output of two fragments of a writing process in which a bad news letter was produced.

The fragment shows a very fragmented and staccato writing process that starts off with a long pause of more than 8 s in the beginning of the second paragraph (announcement of the refusal). In the production of about 30 words, there were 28 pauses longer than 1 s, which is substantially more than in the previous period when the introductory context of the letter was written. About half of the time in this fragment is used for pausing, showing the time attributed to careful and strategic formulation. An interesting example of such a strategic consideration is the revision that takes place after 4 min (240 s segment). The participant starts the sentence with 'However', but two words later he rereads the beginning of the sentence and realizes that this contrastive connective announces the bad news in a too early stage of the paragraph. Therefore, he decides to delete the connective to neutralize the context of this argumentative sentence.

Again, this example shows that process logging enables researchers to analyze writing processes from different perspectives enriching possible interpretation based on text analysis. Other observation methods, like recording (retrospective) thinking aloud protocols, might complement the acquired data.

4   Further Development

To facilitate a broad usage of Inputlog, the program is put at the disposal of the research community for free, provided that reference is made to Leijten and Van Waes (2005b). The users' feedback is very important for the evaluation and further development of Inputlog.

We have identified four important niches that may increase the applicability of Inputlog, especially in the domain of writing process research. In the near future we would like to further develop the following (in order of priority):

(1) *A module for logging speech recognition events.* To facilitate the integration of speech recognition input, Scansoft added a new API to their latest professional version of Dragon Naturally Speaking 8.1, which enables us to integrate the dictated text with the data logged by Inputlog (for more information, see Leijten & Van Waes, in press). The implementation of speech recognition will stimulate research on the effect of this new technology on the writing process (of both professional writers and writers with learning disabilities).

(2) *A module for revision analysis*. In the revision analysis we would like to produce an output analysis in which different characteristics of in-process revisions are described, e.g., the number of revisions, type of revisions, level of revisions, number of words and characters involved in the revision operation, as well as the location of the revisions in relation to the point of utterance. To define revisions we have developed an algorithm and a set of rules. At the moment we have predefined about 50 sets of rules to test the algorithm for deletions and substitutions. However, after the testing phase, the rules will have to be extended and further tested to cover a more complete range of revisions.

(3) *A module for progression analyses (basic and extended)*. So far, the development of the text in Inputlog is represented in the linear text analysis. To visualize this textual development we would like to extend Inputlog with two graphical representations of the text progression, a basic and a more extended one. In the basic progression analysis we would like to visually represent the number of characters that are produced at each moment during the writing process taking into account the characters that are deleted at that stage. This basic progression analysis is based on writing strategies researched by Perrin (2003; this volume); the extended representation is inspired by Lindgren, Sullivan, Lindgren, and Spelman Miller (2006). They use a Geographical Information System (GIS) to visualize and summarize the writing process. GIS enables researchers to analyze different subprocesses of the writing process by selecting representative variables. The graphical representations are not static, but they allow a researcher to interact with the data at different levels and to move back and forward between the data and their representation.

(4) *A module for integration with Morae*. Morae® is a macro-oriented observation tool developed by Techsmith (www.techsmith.com). It is our intention to complement the data of Inputlog with logging data of Morae, which is mostly used for usability research. This program captures, for instances, changes between programs on a higher level and registers, for instance, the URL-addresses of websites that are accessed during a writing session. Just like Inputlog it also logs very detailed timestamps, which should enable us to integrate the additional data registered by Morae into the output of Inputlog. For the observation of writing processes during which the participants combine MSWord with other programs especially, this integration opens new perspectives for further analyses.

In addition to these developments, we will pay special attention to the further development and optimization of the existing modules. Furthermore, the compatibility with different versions of the Windows operating systems and the Office environment will require constant attention. Finally, the integration of our logging data with data from eye-tracking observations is also on the agenda (see also Andersson, this volume).

5   Conclusion

In this paper we have briefly described the main characteristics and the functionality of Inputlog. The program differs from other keystroke logging programs in that it is not limited in its usage to a self-designed word processor. It is primarily developed to log writing processes in MSWord (Windows environment).

Inputlog offers three main functions — record, generate, and play — enabling the researchers to collect very detailed data about a writing process and to prepare some basic analyses for further study. The replay function allows for a review of the writing process and it can also be used as a stimulus for a retrospective thinking aloud protocol. For more detailed information about the use of the program we refer to the help file and the detailed description on the program's website www.inputlog.net.

To increase the applicability of Inputlog we would like to further develop the program by adding new modules. Four new components are planned: a module to log speech recognition events, a module for revision analysis, a module for progression analyses, and a module to integrate macro-level data recorded by Morae. We hope to report about these further developments soon.

Acknowledgment

We would like to thank Wesley Cabus, Ahmed Essahli, and Bart Van de Velde for their excellent work in programming Inputlog.

Combining Keystroke Logging with Eye-Tracking

Bodil Andersson, Johan Dahl, Kenneth Holmqvist,
Jana Holsanova, Victoria Johansson, Henrik Karlsson,
Sven Strömqvist, Sylvia Tufvesson and Åsa Wengelin[1]

This subchapter describes the successful development of a new methodology for studying on-line writing. The text-logging tool ScriptLog has been combined with the eye-tracking technology iView X HED + HT, in order to enhance the study of the interplay between writing, monitoring and revision. Data on the distribution of visual attention during writing help determining to what extent pauses are used for monitoring. The complexity of the experimental settings, and the expertise needed for interpreting the eye-tracking data make this a method suitable mainly for laboratory settings. The chapter also introduces an analysis tool that merges data from ScriptLog and iView and thus helps the researcher to organise and analyse the vast amount of data produced.

1   Introduction

The aim of this chapter is to show how keystroke logging can be combined with eye-tracking, to enhance the study of writing processes in subjects of different ages and with different writing skills.

Producing a text involves an interplay between several mental processes, such as planning, encoding, monitoring and revision (e.g., Hayes & Flower, 1980). Production-rate data derived from keystroke logging offer a window on these processes. In our previous research (e.g., Wengelin, 2002; Strömqvist, Nordqvist, & Wengelin, 2004), we have explored this window by means of ScriptLog (Strömqvist & Karlsson, 2001), a tool for research on the online process of writing, which we are continuously developing. ScriptLog keeps a record of all events on the keyboard (i.e., the pressing of alphabetical and numerical keys, cursor keys, the delete key, space bar etc, and mouse clicks), the screen position of these events and their temporal distribution (the time that elapses from one keyboard event to the next). From a ScriptLog recording of writing activity you can analyse not only the final edited text with its lexical and grammatical aspects and global content structure, but also the 'linear' text (see example in Figure 1) with its temporal patterning, pauses and editing operations.

---

[1]Authors in alphabetical order. Corresponding author: Åsa Wengelin, Lund University.

Andersson, B. et al. (2005). Combining keystroke logging with eye tracking. In L. Van Waes, M. Leijten & C. Neuwirth (Vol. Eds.) & G. Rijlaarsdam (Series Ed.), Studies in Writing: Vol. 17. Writing and Digital Media (pp. 166–172). Oxford: Elsevier.

```
Swe:
<RETURN>Mitt på bilden finns det också
<2.021>kor<3.031> <4.210>som är bruna och
vita<14.351>.

Eng:
In the middle of the picture there are also
<2.021>cows<3.031> <4.210>that are brown and
white<14.351>.
```

Figure 1: Example of a linear file.

Many of these patterns, however, are ambiguous with respect to different interpretations. For example, keyboard inactivity, just like silences in speech, can be indicative of the process of planning the continuation of the text. But keyboard inactivity may also be indicative of reflection and the monitoring of text already produced. In this context, additional data on the distribution of visual attention in the writer can serve a disambiguating function (Holmqvist, Johansson, Strömqvist, & Wengelin, 2002).

In order to forward this line of investigation, we have combined the keystroke logging program ScriptLog with the eye movement technology iView X HED + HT. Our proposed methodology provides a powerful yet non-intrusive way of getting closer to the text-writing subject. The methodology provides a particularly valuable window on those phases of the text-writing process, which necessitate visual feedback, namely, instances of monitoring and revision demanding that relevant parts of the emerging text actually are read. The present paper explains the technical aspects of our method in greater detail as well as an analysis tool that assists the researcher in analysing the vast amount of data produced by keystroke logging and eye-tracking. We also present a detailed example of our analyses of a text fragment from a writer participating in one of our experiments.

2 Our System: Scriptlog + SMI iView

An eye-tracker is simply a device to measure where people are looking. There are several eye-tracking technologies, but this text will only discuss infra-red video systems. In order to use an eye-tracker in combination with ScriptLog, several parameters need to be considered.

First, you need to consider which kind of data you are interested in. *Video data* show the field of view of the writer with a small circle indicating the point of gaze. The video may also contain sound. Video is typically used for the presentation of the recording situation. Furthermore it can be used for retrospective interviews; i.e., the video is shown to the writer immediately after the data collection and the writer is interviewed about his writing and visual behaviour. However, videos are very time consuming to analyse and to code for quantitative analyses.

Data coordinates are much easier to work with, but more difficult to collect. Basically, coordinates presume a coordinate system with dimensions. The writer's computer monitor is a good candidate for a coordinate system. It must be noted, however, that the eye-tracking coordinates of the monitor will differ from the pixel coordinates of the monitor itself.

Assuming that a translation between the two coordinate systems can be made, a second problem arises: The eye-tracking data refer to the screen as it looked at the time of writing. If we want to know which word the writer looked at a specific time, ScriptLog must be able to reproduce the screen *exactly* as it looked at the time of writing.

Writers do not look exclusively at the screen. Most writers spend a considerable time looking at the keyboard. Eye-tracking data should include fixations on the keyboard, which could be part of the coordinate system of the monitor, or be a plane of its own (as in our set-up). When the task is to write about a picture, it is interesting to know when and where the writer looks at the stimulus, and that calls for a third plane.

To record data coordinates in a coordinate system of the stimulus, either a remote eye-tracker or a head mounted eye-tracker with head tracking can be used. A remote system requires the writer to sit very still while writing and, therefore, we chose to use a head mounted eye-tracker with head-tracking (SMI iView X HT). An eye camera and a scene camera are placed on a bicycle helmet worn by the writer. On top of the bicycle helmet, there is a magnetic sensor that keeps track of the head in 6-D: position and direction. The eye-tracker calculates a vector for the gaze direction that emanates from the eye (in the head). The head position and direction together with the eye direction allow for a real time calculation of the position where the combined eye–head vector hits the monitor plane, or the keyboard plane or the stimulus picture plane.

In order for this to work, the environment in which the recording takes place must be measured. This needs to be done only once, in advance of a series of recording sessions. A simple type of virtual reality model of the monitor, keyboard and picture is created, which tells the eye-tracker their positions in space, and what extension they have. Since data are recorded in the co-ordinate system of this virtual model, the keyboard, monitor and stimulus picture may not move away from the measured position. Consequently, we have fixed all these planes to the table, and indirectly to the floor.

It is important to place all planes within as small a visual angle as possible. An eye-tracker covers approximately 60° of visual angle for a writer who does not turn his/her head. If the writer looks further away, data will be partially lost.

When all the coordinates systems are in place, we are able to get precise data on where the writer looks. But we also want to know *when* she/he looks at the monitor, in order to, for instance, find out whether she/he looks up at the monitor more often when she/he has just concluded a clause than when she/he has concluded a word. Synchronisation of data in our system is achieved by letting ScriptLog send a start signal to the eye-tracker when a ScriptLog recording is started.

When the system is set up, a recording typically starts by placing the helmet on the writer and adjusting the camera. The writer is then asked to sit down by the keyboard in the recording environment. On the monitor, 13 calibration points are shown in a certain sequence, and the writer is asked to look at the points in that order. The eye-tracker analyses the video signal of the eye in each position and builds an interpolation matrix that allows us to get precise data also between points. The interpolation matrix resulting from the calibration is specific to the writer's individual eye; and calibration should be made at least once for each recording.

A calibration of the scene camera follows immediately. This procedure allows the eye-tracker to output video in parallel with data coordinates. The recording then starts.

In order to achieve high data quality, careful positioning of the eye camera is necessary before calibration and recording. If the writer uses glasses or lenses, the reflexes from infrared light in these may cause disturbances. Lighting conditions must be chosen with care. It is also advantageous to have filtering options on the eye video processing in the eye tracker. Settings for the eye video processing may have to be monitored continuously for some subjects. For each writer and each text, the eye-tracking part of our set-up outputs

- An MPEG-2 video of the visual field with overlaid gaze cursor, timestamp and sound.
- A data file which gives the following data for every 20 ms: plane number, gaze coordinates in the coordinate system of that plane, head position and head orientation, eye position and time.

3   Data Analysis: An Example

As was mentioned earlier one type of output from a writing session with ScriptLog is the *linear file*. The linear file presents every event during a writing session, and includes pauses of any minimum duration defined by the analyst. An example of a linear file produced during a picture elicitation experiment is shown in Figure 1.

This linear file shows that the writer paused four times while writing this sentence, but it does not tell us anything about *what* the writer did in those pauses. We will now proceed to show how additional information about gaze behaviour can help us refute hypotheses about what was going on during the pauses in the production of this text fragment.

For the analysis of the interaction between writing and gaze behaviour, we have developed an analysis tool, inspired by the so-called multimodal time-coded score sheets developed by Holsanova (2001). The tool is used for the analysis of temporal and semantic synchrony in picture viewing and picture description. A merged time-coded data file produced by ScriptLog and iView provides a visual representation of the verbal and visual flow. This representation gives the analyst an enhanced picture of the writer's attention processes: which objects or areas were scanned visually and which objects or areas were described in writing at a certain point of time? The tool provides an overview of how the writer's attention was distributed between the stimulus picture, the keyboard, the computer monitor and elsewhere during the writing session. In addition we have implemented what we call a writing filter, which specifies a person's writing activities. Let us discuss an example.

The text fragment in the example was produced by a female university student, who participated in an experiment where the task was to describe a detailed picture from a childrens' book in writing. During the first 12 minutes of the writing session the writer has given an overview over the picture's main characters and their activities and described the animals and plants present in the picture. She is just about to start the last quarter of her picture description where she will focus on minor details.

The linear file (Figure 1) shows that she has just made some revisions to her text and started a new paragraph (<RETURN>). The first sentence in the new paragraph is "Mitt på bilden finns det också kor som är bruna och vita." ('*In the middle of the picture, there are also cows that are brown and white'.*) A first glance at the linear file reveals that her writing is interrupted by pauses. Let us turn to the visual presentation format in Figure 2 to find out how her visual attention was distributed.

The visual presentation format consists of five horizontal synchronised tiers. The tiers enable us to analyse how the visual attention is distributed over the areas in the writer's

Figure 2: Multimodal time-coded score sheet of keystroke data and eye-tracking data combined.

experimental environment during the writing session (on the screen the tiers are shown in different colours to facilitate the analysis).

In the presentation format time progresses from left to right. The bottom (first) tier contains the stream of keystroke-logged text writing where the distance between the keystrokes shows the writing speed (the shorter distance between the letters the faster the writing). The second tier from the bottom defines writing activities (based on a changeable predefined pause criterion; here 1 s). The third, fourth and fifth tiers represent the distribution of the subjects' visual attention during writing. The grey slots in the third tier mark time when the subject was looking at the keyboard, the slots in the fourth tier when she was looking at the screen, and the fifth tier finally when she was looking at the stimulus picture. We can also observe the flow of simultaneous perception and production, e.g., when the subject is looking at the keyboard while writing (intersection of the second and third slots) or when the subject is looking at the monitor while writing (intersection of the second and fourth slots). Another advantage is that we can determine with greater accuracy what happens in a pause, e.g., whether the person is scanning the picture, re-reading her own text or looking for a key on the keyboard.

The fragment shown in Figure 2 reveals that the subject — after a pause — begins a new sentence with quite constant speed: "Mitt på bilden finns det också [...]" 'In the middle of the picture there is also [...]' In the beginning of this sentence, the subject tends to look at the keyboard whereas later on, she mainly looks at the monitor when writing. Before naming the objects and writing the word "kor" 'cows', this person stops and makes a short pause (2.02 s) in order to revisit the stimulus picture. She may, for example, be checking whether the cattle in the picture are cows, bulls, calves or perhaps sheep. After the visual information gathering is accomplished, she finally writes "kor" 'cows'. After writing this, she distributes her visual attention between the screen and the keyboard without writing anything but a space. In the linear file (Figure 1) this is shown by the pauses <3.031> and <4.210> between which she presses the spacebar. She then finishes the sentence by writing "som är bruna och vita" 'that are brown and white'.

Our analysis tool can be used as a point of departure for various kinds of analyses, such as:

- correlation studies between for example pause durations or pause locations and gaze behaviour;
- comparative studies of visual attention between different groups, such as experienced–inexperienced writers, or good–poor writers; and
- qualitative case studies, for example of how writers integrate semantic information gathered from text and from picture during writing, text revisions and editing.

Further research along the lines presented here will help determine the nature of this interplay and how it is shaped by different kinds of subjects and different kinds of writing tasks.

4 Some Concluding Remarks

To sum up, the combination of keystroke logging and eye-tracking provides a powerful and highly accurate means for the analysis of the dynamic interplay on-line between production and perception during writing. This complex interplay has hitherto been little studied. A great advantage with the use of eye-tracking for this purpose is that we can draw upon the knowledge generated by the vast body of reading research generated by the 'eye-tracking community'. The method is also relatively unintrusive. The drawbacks of the method are that it is complex and takes a lot of equipment and expertise to use it. It is, therefore, more suitable for lab studies than for example a classroom study. Moreover, while the combination of keystroke logging and eye-tracking can provide reliable data on when reading is going on, and perhaps also give some indication about the processes in other pauses, other methods may be more suitable for tracing other cognitive processes in writing. However, the combination of keystroke logging and eye-tracking could easily be combined with yet another method such as concurrent or retrospective protocols, in order to enhance data interpretation.

Progression Analysis: An Ethnographic, Computer-Based Multi-Method Approach to Investigate Natural Writing Processes

Daniel Perrin

Progression analysis was developed to investigate digital writing processes at the workplace. It is a multi-method approach with respect to its methodology and examines writing processes at three levels: the work situation by means of interviews and observations, the writing process by means of computer logging, and writing strategies by means of event-specific retrospective verbal protocols. Progression analysis has been used primarily to investigate journalistic writing, but is now being applied more widely in writing research.

1   How are Texts Produced in Natural Contexts?

What exactly do journalists do when they write? In 1997, the Swiss Federal Office for Communication (BAKOM) commissioned a qualitative and explorative investigation of journalistic writing in print, radio, TV, and on-line news offices. Before the study could begin, an ecologically valid method had to be developed to investigate writing processes at workstations: the writing processes had to be accessible from a number of relevant perspectives but not be affected by the data collection.

Progression analysis was developed and applied for the first time within the framework of the BAKOM research project. Data on writing processes were obtained from 40 workstations in media newsrooms and evaluated as case studies (Perrin, 2001, 2005a, 2005b, 2006). Additional corpora on journalistic writing have since been collected, and current research projects are using progression analysis to investigate writing in other domains[1] as well, such as in academia and industry.

One of the first case studies in the BAKOM-corpus is that of the *Weltwoche* in which the editor RS writes a reportage in German for the Swiss weekly broadsheet *Weltwoche* about snowboarders preparing for the winter Olympics. The data were obtained at the end of

---

[1]Domain here means a bundle of similar contexts for language behavior, within institutionalized frameworks as well as with typical settings, roles, norms, tasks, illocutions, themes, and varieties. Adamzik, Antos, and Jakobs (1997) provide an overview of domain-specific writing; an operative summary is offered, for example, in Lehnen and Schindler (2003).

Perrin, D. (2005). *Progression analysis: An ethnographic, computer-based multi-method approach to investigate natural writing processes. . In L. Van Waes, M. Leijten & C. Neuwirth (Vol. Eds.) & G. Rijlaarsdam (Series Ed.), Studies in Writing: Vol. 17. Writing and Digital Media (pp. 173–179).* Oxford: Elsevier.

1997. In the meantime, RS has changed professions and released the data for publication. In this chapter, the *Weltwoche* case study serves as an example to illustrate the methodological approach.

2   Progression Analysis as a Multi-Method Approach

Progression analysis refers to an ethnographic, computer-based multi-method approach with which data can be obtained on three levels. Before writing begins, details about the work situation are elicited with interviews and participatory observations (2.1); during writing, movements are measured with computer-based recordings (2.2); after writing, the repertoire of writing strategies is deduced with data-supported retrospective verbal protocols (for more details, see Perrin, 2003).

2.1   Work Situation: Question and Observe Who Writes and Why

Before writing begins, progression analysis determines the writing situation and the writer's experience through interviews and observations. Important factors include professional socialization and economic, institutional, and technological influences on the work situation as well as the specific writing task that the author must accomplish. All of these factors are part of the real world and at the same time part of the mental representation that an author has of the world and that motivates his actions.

For the *Weltwoche* example, the extract from the situational analysis would be: the *Weltwoche* is (at the time of data collection) the leading Swiss German-language weekly newspaper, a bylined newspaper. According to the comments by the editor RS in a preparatory interview, it orients itself to a demanding readership: infotainment is not desired. As indicated further on, this programmatic statement by RS contradicts some of his writing strategies.

2.2   Writing Movements: Measure What Happens during Writing

During the writing process, progression analysis records every writing movement in a logging program that runs in the background behind the text editor. In the larger investigations with progression analysis, the logging programs run behind the text editors that the writers usually use, for instance behind the user interface of the news editing systems. The logging follows the writing process over several workstations and does not influence the performance of the editing system. The software is custom-made for each news editing system. It records all the keystrokes as timed actions related to text entities and writer identification. The output can be transformed automatically to S-notation.

In order for the logging to have as little effect on the writing staff as possible, the researcher lets time and forgetfulness take their toll. First he obtains permission for the research procedure and installs the software, and then the computer starts logging data that are not used immediately for research purposes. Only after a certain waiting period does the researcher begin to collect and evaluate the data.

Example 1 is an excerpt of a logging file taken from the *Weltwoche* case study. The first sentence in this example was produced in five revision steps, as described below. At the beginning, RS just writes NA. In the first revision step, R1, he deletes the A and then writes without interruption until Teutsch_. In the second step, R2, he deletes the blank space after Teutsch and writes Teutsch-Pils,_. In step R3, the comma after Pils is replaced by _und. In steps R4 and R5, Race office becomes Race office Zelt and then RS finishes the sentence with telefonieren mit dem Handy. Five text versions in sequence can be considered the intermediate products of the process (see example below; translations in italics).

(R0) NA

(R1) Nach dem Rennen hängen sie alle im dick verrauchten Race office herum, kippen Tee oder ein Teutsch_
  *After the race they all hang around in the smoke-filled race office, sipping tea or a Teutsch_*

(R2) [...] Race office herum, kippen Tee oder ein Teutsch-Pils,

(R3) [...] Race office herum, kippen Tee oder ein Teutsch-Pils und

(R4) [...] Race office Zektherum, kippen Tee oder ein Teutsch-Pils und

(R5) [...] Race office Zelt_herum, kippen Tee oder ein Teutsch-Pils und telefonieren mit dem Handy.
  [...] race office tent, sipping tea or a Teutsch pilsner and making calls on cell phones.

These steps can be more concisely represented in the so-called S-notation (Kollberg & Severinson Eklundh, 2001), which is produced automatically from the logging data. Wherever the writing is interrupted to delete or add something, S-notation inserts the break-character $|_n$ in the text. Deleted passages are in ^{n}[square brackets]^n, later insertions in ^{n}{curly braces}^{n}. The numbers ^{n} and $_n$ indicate the order of the steps. The first eleven steps of RS's writing process are shown in S-notation in example the below.

^{7}[ghghghdghggh gfgfgfgbgzf↵
↵
↵
↵
↵]$^7|_8$ ^{8}{Die rote^9[S$|_9$]^9,^{10}[o$|_{10}$]^{10} Sonne verkriecht sich hinter dem Berg, }$^8|_{11}$ ^{11}[ ]^{11},^{6}{↵
↵
↵
↵}$^6|_7$
N^1[A$|_1$]^{1}ach dem Rennen hängen sie alle im dick ver-rauchten Race office ^{4}{Ze^5[kt$|_5$]^{5}lt }^{4}herum, kippen Tee oder ein Teutsch^2[_$|_2$]^2-Pils^3[,$|_3$]^3 und $|_4$ telefonieren mit dem Handy.$|_6$

Translation: The red sun creeps behind the mountain, after the race they all hang around in the smoke-filled race office tent, sipping tea or a Teutsch pilsner and making calls on cell phones.

S-notation simplifies the detail analysis of the writing event; the broader pattern, by contrast, is traced in a progression graph. It indicates how the writer moved with the cursor through the developing text. The temporal sequence of revisions in the writing process is represented on the ordinal scale of the *x*-axis; the spatial sequence of revisions in the text product is on the *y*-axis, also ordinal. In the example, revision 3 is the third in the writing process but its result is at the end of the text product, in position 11.

Represented in this way, the revisions describe a two-dimensional graph of text progression. In the extreme case, $n(x) = n(y)$, and the graph is a straight line from the upper left to the lower right, representing a linear writing process without any jumps within the text. By contrast, RS does not move linearly in his first 11 steps. He writes the end of the text (revisions 1–3), revises it (4–6), and then adds the beginning (7–11). The graph shows a zigzag movement or, smoothed out, a wave (Figure 1).

2.3   *Writing Strategies: Record How Authors Explain their Actions*

After the writing is over, progression analysis deduces the repertoire of an author's writing strategies. Preferably immediately after completing the writing process, authors can view how their texts came into being on the screen, either in real-time or in slow motion. While doing so, they continuously say what they did when writing and why they did it. An audio recording is made of this event-specific retrospective verbal protocol (Prior, 2004; Leander & Prior, 2004).With respect to the example, RS's remarks about two of his revisions are as follow (see example below; translated from the German transcript).

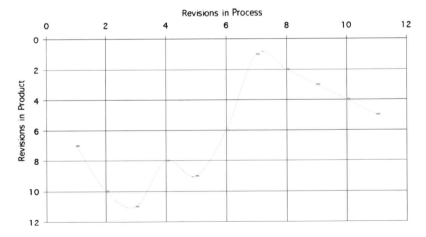

Figure 1: Progression graph: first the end, then the beginning of the text is written.

(V1)   Now I'm moving something around. I always make sections
       and blocks; this is more obvious later. And then I put
       in white space and stuff. And then there are chunks
       that might be moved around later. Oh, I just moved
       something down, too, because I knew that it stays at
       the bottom. (WW(I).6, translation)

(V2)   Now I had an idea once and thought I would start with
       the red sun. Ah, that is just what appeared in the
       paper. The red sun. That's because it also started in
       the evening. I thought it would be funny to start with
       the sun, which disappears. (WW(I).8 6, translation).

In this extract of the verbal protocol, RS talks about moving sections of text and grad-ually discovering and developing an organization to his text (V1). As well, he explains his reasons for the spontaneous beginning (V2). Such explanations of strategic actions in the writing process derive a semantic structure of the format X•Y, where X represents the action, • a logical relationship, and Y an argument: "I do X because Y is true" or "I do X to achieve Y". In these terms, the two strategies used by RS can be expressed as:[2]

(S1)   Keep individual "chunks" separate that "might be moved
       around later".

(S2)   Just start with an idea because it is funny.

This third level of progression analysis opens a window into the mind of the writer. The question is what can be recognized through this window: certainly not all and only the con-siderations that the author actually made, but rather the considerations that an author could have made in principle and that he is able to articulate, based on his language awareness. These considerations represent a significant portion of the repertoire of writing strategies. Progression analysis places these in relation to the other findings.

Writing strategies here refers to the reinforced, conscious, and therefore articulable ideas of how decisions are to be made during the act of writing so that the writing process or text product has a great probability of taking on the intended form and fulfilling the intended function. By *writing process* is meant the process of production of a written text. The writing process begins when a prospective author realizes what the assignment is and ends when the author passes the text on.

3   Results: Recurrence in One and Several Cases

RS starts his writing process in such a way that he can constantly implement his flashes of inspiration. He does not follow the chronology of events, the standards of a particular

---

[2]A reduction of the analytical content to the propositional content (cf. Perrin 2001, 18ff) is one possibility for analyzing verbal protocols. It creates categorizable answers to the question of what the individuals under inves-tigation are talking about and includes an interpretation of metaphors, something that Schmitt (2003) addresses. If the analysis should include how the individuals talk about their writing, then more complex discourse analyt-ical techniques must be used, building on ethno methodological principles.

genre, or the routine of an established production process. Much more, he seeks his own dramaturgy for both the process and the product. The search for a suitable form, the circling toward a main focus, and the combinatory play with parts of the text and comments are expressed in the data on the writing process.

RS worked on the text for four days in eight stages. In between, he abandoned the writing process completely: he did sports, went into his garden, or switched workplaces and continued in the office what he had started at home. "With sufficient distance and a fresh view of things, it flows much easier now." In each of the eight stages, he loaded the previously written text on the screen to serve as a new starting point, and in the progression analysis each of the stages shows different characteristics.

In the fourth stage, for example, RS works from the top and the bottom, jumping back and forth, toward the middle of the text. He shifts his focus of attention and moves whole sections of text — until a key position when he has a protagonist say that a medal at the Olympic games would signify the end of freedom for snowboarding: "the end of thinking independently" (revisions 371–374, translation from German). Then he expands his previous story by adding a long passage at the end and revises the beginning (Figure 2).

With his writing strategies, RS radically subjugates the text to his main "focus", to his dramaturgical idea, and to his story. In doing so, he also alters the statements of his sources. This begins with the usual journalistic considerations of how spoken comments should be represented in writing: RS talks here about "condensing" the sources' comments. Above and beyond that, though, he puts words in the mouths of his text protagonists that are plausible but "invented". He formulates strategies for the development of the text function as follows.

(S10)   Compress statements, "condense things for people" (WW(IV).355.q).

(S11)   Formulate citations in such a way "that it still sounds like speech" (WW(VIII).81.r).

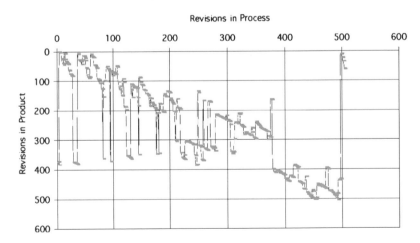

Figure 2: Progression graph of the fourth stage: RS works from the top and bottom toward the middle of the text.

(S12)   Have someone "say something" even though "it's invented", something that this person "might or might not have said here" (WW(IV).274.p).

(S13)   Put words in a protagonist's mouth (WW(IV).259.o).

(S14)   Decide whether "one lets people say something themselves" or "one says it oneself" (WW(VIII).81.s).

The observed writing movements and verbalized strategies allow us to assume considerable dramaturgical extravagance. The revisions and strategies even indicate that RS invents comments and attributes them to his sources for the benefit of his literary production (Häusermann, 2001; Luginbühl, Baumberger, Schwab, & Burger 2002). This contradicts RS's programmatic claim before the writing process that infotainment is not wanted in the *Weltwoche*. Such insights can only be obtained with a multi-method approach such as progression analysis.

Evaluations of the BAKOM corpus have made possible elucidation of such phenomena as how coherence problems develop in texts, how the writing of experienced and inexperienced journalists differs, and how journalists handle emotions and original ideas or recontextualize statements from source texts. To allow a broader investigation of journalistic writing processes, all writing at all the workstations in the newsroom of a large daily newspaper has been logged for two years.[3]

Outside the domain of journalism, progression analysis has been applied in explorative studies on academic writing (Boschung & Gnach, 2003). At the time of the present article, the integration of progression analysis into two national research projects is being prepared. One focuses on technical writing at universities and the other on writing in media-pedagogical projects. In this way, progression analysis will be introduced to other research communities for discussion.

---

[3] Coherence problems are described in Perrin (1999), experience in Perrin (2001), emotions in Perrin (2006), recontextualization in Perrin (2005a), and ideas in case studies of journalistic writing in Perrin (2005b). A research project statistically evaluating the full survey of the Swiss daily newspaper Tages-Anzeiger is in preparation.

CAMTASIA and CATMOVIE: Two Digital Tools for Observing, Documenting and Analysing Writing Processes of University Students

Marion Degenhardt

CAMTASIA and CATMOVIE are two digital tools that can be used for observing, documenting and analysing the writing processes of university students. CAMTASIA, a screen-recording program, is able to create movie files from any action on a Microsoft Windows desktop. It does not interfere with the writing processes of the students. CATMOVIE is a research tool for understanding learning and instruction, in particular for the analysis of videotapes of school lessons. For writing researchers it provides a graphical user interface for encoding the movies recorded with CAMTASIA.

    Both tools and their use in a current writing research project are described and discussed. Distinctions relative to other digital tools in writing research are also noted. Based on an analysis of the advantages and disadvantages of the tools and experiences from a current research project, recommendations for their use in further projects are provided.

1   Introduction

We discuss two digital tools for observing, documenting and analysing the writing processes of university students. With CAMTASIA[1] one can record and observe the writing processes, while CATMOVIE[2] supports the professional analysis of the data. A method using both tools for writing process analyses is presented in this article. In order to evaluate the tools for writing research, a current research project will be introduced, which is based on the writing process model of Hayes (1996) and the paradigms of "action research". The latter means bringing "together action and reflection, theory and practice in participation with others" (Reason & Bradbury, 2001, p. 1), with the aim of improving the student's practice, based on a substantiated theoretical background.

---

[1] http://www.techsmith.com (July 5, 2005).
[2] Author: Prof. Dr. Klaus Peter Wild, University of Regensburg (Germany).

Degenhardt, M. (2005). Camtasia and Catmovie: Two digital tools for observing, documenting and analysing writing processes of university students. In L. Van Waes, M. Leijten & C. Neuwirth (Vol. Eds.) & G. Rijlaarsdam (Series Ed.), Studies in Writing: Vol. 17. Writing and Digital Media (pp. 180–186). Oxford: Elsevier.

First, a short description of the tools and the original context in which they were developed are given. Next, we focus on their special benefits for writing researchers. This includes a short comparison with other tools that are also described in this volume. Finally, some examples show how the tools were used in the current research project, and what further conclusions may be drawn from these experiences.

2   CAMTASIA

CAMTASIA is a screen recording program that creates a movie (avi-file) from any action on a Microsoft Windows desktop. It runs in the background after it has been started and, if the program is used correctly (cf. 2.1), it does not interfere with the writing process itself.

CAMTASIA is a commercial product of TechSmith, and was not intended originally for research purposes. According to TechSmith it is suitable for many different uses, e.g., recording software demonstrations, recording lectures, creating online tutorials, recording seminars on a CD-ROM, and so forth.

Even though CAMTASIA was not explicitly developed for research purposes, it provides many useful features for researchers. The short list below focuses only on those features that are valuable for observing the writing processes. They are:

- The region on the screen, which has to be recorded can be defined easily. The options are: full screen, only one window, or a fixed rectangular region.
- The video frame rate is adjustable, with a maximum of five frames per second.
- Audio data can be integrated, either during the writing process or afterwards.
- It is possible to replay the recorded movies at different speeds.

From our practical experiences with CAMTASIA in a writing research context, we recommend customising certain default parameters (2.1). In addition, the advantages, as well as the disadvantages, of the use of CAMTASIA compared with other tools should be carefully considered (2.2).

2.1   *Recommended Pre-Adjustments*

Colour depth   The default parameter for the colour representation is usually "true colour" (16/32 bit). Since a high value of the colour depth does not have much influence on the quality of the data recorded in a writing process, but requires significant computer resources (slowing down the working process with CAMTASIA), we recommend the use of only 256 colours.

Framerate (fps)   It is recommended to take only one or two frames per second. Experience with the current research has shown that two frames per second gives enough information to retrace the writing process, and at the same time does not encumber processor resources. Higher frame rates do not lead to a better understanding of the documented writing process.

2.2   *CAMTASIA Compared with Other Tools*

Compared with other tools used for documenting writing processes, CAMTASIA has specific advantages, as well as disadvantages. These are presented below:

Advantages:

- CAMTASIA runs in almost all Microsoft Windows environments and is unaffected by the settings of the operating system level or the word processor. The latter is a very important difference to Inputlog (Leijten & Van Waes, this volume), which requires exactly the same computer settings for recording and replaying the data.
- In contrast to logging tools, like ScriptLog (cf. Andersson et al., this volume), CAMTASIA is not limited to a custom-designed word processor. Rather, it permits the use of all writing software.
- CAMTASIA allows the utilisation of more than one program, or file, in parallel. This enables the students to integrate earlier written text modules, or figures from other files, in their current products. They may also search elsewhere for relevant information, e.g., in the WWW, or in separate files. Such activities are commonplace while writing in computer environment, and should therefore be taken into account.
- As noted earlier (cf. Section 2.1), CAMTASIA does not interfere with the writing process itself: It runs in the background, the students do not feel observed, and they can work in their familiar writing environment.
- CAMTASIA is inexpensive and is easy to handle. It can, therefore, be used by the students themselves to document and analyse their individual writing processes and/or discuss them with others. All have been successfully done within our research project (cf. Section 4).
- Since the movies recorded by CAMTASIA have to be encoded afterwards, the codings can be very individual and user specific. There are no restrictions imposed by CAMTASIA — everything that can be seen on the screen during the writing process can be analysed afterwards. Thus CAMTASIA — in combination with CATMOVIE (see below) — is very appropriate for detailed qualitative analyses with small samples.

Disadvantages:

- The recordings of the writing processes with CAMTASIA give minimal information about what the writers do when they are not using the computer. An extra movie perspective, an observing person (cf. Leijten & Van Waes, 2003), or additional eye-tracking data (cf. Andersson et al., this volume) would compensate for this deficiency.
- Statistical calculations are possible only after the data are encoded. The encoding process entails significant extra efforts.

3   CATMOVIE

CATMOVIE is a tool for research on learning and instruction, in particular for the analysis of videotapes of school lessons. Unlike CAMTASIA, CATMOVIE is not a commercial product.

In fact, it has been developed explicitly for research purposes.[3] However, in order to use CAT-MOVIE, a licence for the statistical software package SPSS of SPSS Inc. is needed.

CATMOVIE provides a graphical user interface for encoding the recorded movies, that integrates a movie player and several different data input fields. All elements of the user interface must be defined by the user beforehand. Hence, everything can be adapted to the very special individual needs of a single user.

Before starting the work with CATMOVIE, three types of files have to be prepared: The *movie and/or audio files*, which will be analysed, an *SPSS data file* and a *CATMOVIE job file*, which creates the specific user interface.

- The *movie files* must be provided in MPEG or AVI format (which can be read by ActiveMovie), whereas the *audio files* must come as WAV or MP3 files.
- In the *SPSS data file,* all the variables needed for the analysis must be defined. The time unit for the encoding steps[4] must also be determined. A tool for easily creating the SPSS data file is included in CATMOVIE.
- In addition to the names of the movie and/or audio files and the name of the attendant SPSS data file, the *job file* (file extension .cat) contains information about the appearance, size, location and amount of all integrated elements of the user interface, e.g., the movie-windows, the data input tools (buttons and text fields) and the font-type, -size and -colour of almost all textual elements. A sample code of the job file is shown in Figure 1.

Creating the job file for the first time can be especially intricate. But on the other hand, it allows flexibility in making individual adjustments, e.g., defining the size of each element, defining the variables in terms of a particular category system and creating space for all sorts of comments one wants to add on certain sequences.

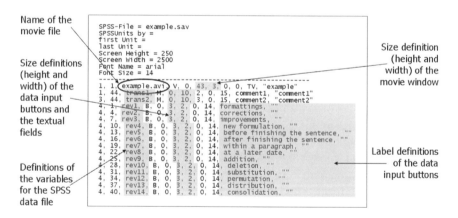

Figure 1: Sample code of the job file, which defines the user interface shown in Figure 2.

---

[3] A detailed description of the program, including a manual, can be found under www.catmovie.de (July 5, 2005).
[4] For example: If different encodings should be possible every other second, which is recommended for the analysis of writing processes, the time unit should be 1 second.

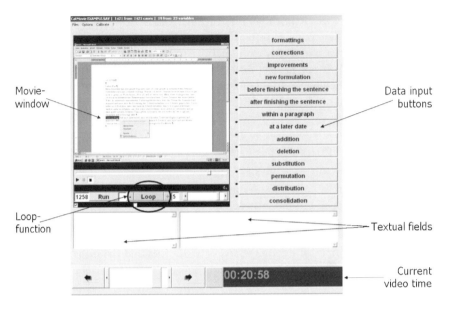

Figure 2: Example of the created graphical user interface.

Figure 2 shows the graphical user interface that is created by the code of the job file explained above. It is just an example for demonstration purposes, since normally the size of the data input buttons would be much smaller and the size of the movie-window much larger.

Before starting the encoding procedure, the CATMOVIE job file and the attendant SPSS data file have to be synchronised in a calibration process. But from then on, all data inputs and other comments made on the created user interface are automatically documented in the SPSS data file (a necessary condition for further statistical calculations).

4   CAMTASIA and CATMOVIE in the Current Research Project

4.1   Short Description of the Study

The aim of the current study, where CAMTASIA and CATMOVIE came into operation, is to investigate the writing processes of students at the University of Education in Freiburg (Germany). The main focus is on tasks like composing summaries of research articles, or talks which have been read or heard beforehand, writing commentaries to drafts in preparation, and most important, writing several drafts of the same writing task. The time required to complete the different tasks usually ranged from 15 to 45 minutes. The writing processes have been recorded with CAMTASIA.

Since qualitative analyses are intended, the random sample of 15 students is quite small. Besides a detailed description of the writing processes, the learning styles of the students have been identified (Kolb, 1984; Honey & Mumford, 1992). An investigation of assumed interrelations between the learning style and the writing process data of the students is also in preparation.

To ensure that the gathered data are valuable for the researcher and the students (an important condition for "action research"), the recordings took place in natural situations with real tasks that the students had to fulfill as part of their ongoing lectures.

4.2 Data Analysis

The recorded data have been analysed by both, the researcher and the students.

The students watched the CAMTASIA recordings privately, marked interesting or critical sequences during their own writing processes, and reflected on them alone, and/or discussed them together with fellow students, the lecturer and the researcher. Additionally, some students focussed on and investigated their own writing process in term papers, based on the recordings done by CAMTASIA and learning diaries among other things.

Of course the data have also been analysed by the researcher.[5] Therefore a job file in CATMOVIE was created which contained all relevant variables (see Section 3) and was connected to the attendant SPSS-file. Then the movies were encoded as well as commented at all important sequences. These comments are an essential part of the qualitative analyses. All marks and comments were automatically transferred to the SPSS data file. The subsequent statistical analyses are unfortunately beyond the scope of the present paper.

5   Conclusions

The properties of CAMTASIA and CATMOVIE allow the definition of very individual research criteria and a combination of different data types, which are indispensable for qualitative analyses. Unlike logging tools, CAMTASIA supports field studies of student's writing processes in their accustomed writing environment. No limitations of a special word processor that has to be used, or certain required computer settings, are imposed. Hence, the students do not feel observed and the data collection has no impact on the writing process itself. CAMTASIA is easy to handle and is inexpensive. Students can use it on their own, which enables "action research" in a very real sense: Students can reflect on and investigate their writing processes by themselves and they become engaged partners in the research process.

On the other hand, the analysis process is time-consuming, since statistical calculations are only possible after an intensive encoding procedure. Therefore, CAMTASIA recordings are not practical for quantitative analyses of large random samples. Rather, it should be considered that the qualitative analyses of data recorded by CAMTASIA can result in a detailed description of important episodes within writing processes, e.g., revision episodes (Kollberg & Severinson Eklundh, 2001). In turn, these descriptions should prove to be useful for the further development of more quantitative-orientated tools like Inputlog, as Leijten and Van Waes pointed out in their paper (this volume).

---

[5] This process is still in progress, thus not completed as yet.

In conclusion, the decision to use any of these tools, logging tools or screen recording tools, is highly dependent on the research interest and the design of the study. If one requires a research tool only, or quantitative analyses of large random samples are intended, logging tools are probably the optimal choice. To do qualitative analyses, develop new categories for analysing writing processes, or integrate the student's investigations of their own writing processes, CAMTASIA in combination with CATMOVIE is preferable.

Section IV:

Writing in Online Educational Environments

Chapter 13

Tools, Language Technology and Communication in Computer Assisted Language Learning

Petter Karlström, Teresa Cerratto Pargman and Robert Ramberg

In this chapter, we discuss the use of Language Technology (LT) (e.g. spelling and grammar checkers) in tools for Computer Assisted Language Learning (CALL). Attempts in merging research from LT and CALL were popular during the 1960s, but has since stagnated. We argue that this state of affairs is unfortunate, and that it has several causes: technology not living up to expectations, a single-minded focus on either communication or on linguistic forms in language teaching and framing computer systems for learning as "tutors" instead of "tools." Following brief introductions to Computer Aided Language Learning and LT, we provide a framework for designing "tool"-based systems, and argue that these tools should be used in a communicative setting while simultaneously training linguistic forms.

1 Introduction

Computer Assisted Language Learning (CALL) is an interdisciplinary and still young research area. Before the emergence of computers in teaching (pre-1960s), technology in language learning took the form of language laboratories. These were based on the then-popular, "audio-lingual" learning methods that emphasized spoken over written language. Teaching via these laboratories was conducted in a highly structured manner, in the form of conditioning and habit-forming exercises.

With the introduction of mainframe computers, new possibilities for using technology emerged. An important change from earlier teaching machines was in attempting to go beyond behaviorist audio-lingual paradigms, for example by providing grammatical explanations to learners.

Karlström, P., Cerratto Pargman, T., & Ramberg, R. (2005). Tools, language technology and communication in computer assisted language learning. In L. Van Waes, M. Leijten & C. Neuwirth (Vol. Eds.) & G. Rijlaarsdam (Series Ed.), Studies in Writing: Vol. 17. Writing and Digital Media (pp. 189–198). Oxford: Elsevier.

However, the advent of microcomputers in the 1980s coincided with the rising popularity of "acquisition"-oriented language learning theories. These theories emphasize unconscious "acquisition" over conscious "learning" and innate abilities over learned ones. Chapelle (2001, Chap. 1) notes that much of CALL's history was labeled "learning" oriented, and that it was consequently lost.

Since its foundation, CALL has seen a multitude of systems, but too little in terms of scientifically conclusive results. The field has witnessed an imbalance between development and evaluation of systems. One of the possible reasons for this is the variety of methodologies used (coming from areas such as linguistics, computer science, second-language learning/acquisition and pedagogy), as well as the multiple possible foci to choose from when evaluating CALL systems (the technological system, the learning process, the language, etc.). Chapelle (2001) makes the important observation that methodologies for CALL evaluation are critical for further research, but that they are too often neglected. Methods for the evaluation of CALL systems should be both judgmental and empirical, and based on criteria elaborated within the research field of second language acquisition (SLA).

Nevertheless, fields other than SLA, such as technology, may still be relevant areas of inquiry in CALL (Salaberry, 1999). The area is interdisciplinary, and benefits from research in developing systems as well as research on how languages are learned. While the evaluation of CALL systems certainly is a very important activity in CALL research, the question of what to evaluate remains. Computers are becoming a pervasive part of life, including learning and teaching. With no specific knowledge on how we should design CALL systems, there would be no reason to give CALL any special treatment within the more general field of SLA.

Arguably, this may not be a problem, if one has low expectations in technology that aims to solve specific problems. We believe that this point of view contains missed opportunities. Computers are multi-purpose tools, and there may be yet unknown uses of the computer specifically for the purpose of language learning. It should be in the interest of the CALL community to investigate issues in the development and design of interaction in CALL systems as well as principles for their evaluation.

Systems that are designed for language learning contain explicit or tacit models of how that learning is supposed to take place. Among researchers having debated design questions in CALL, Levy (1997) discusses the role of computers in teaching and learning and makes a distinction between the computer as a "tutor" and the computer as a "tool." This distinction, taken from the area of Computer Aided Instruction and applied on CALL, points out a fundamental difference among systems for learning. Systems in the "tutor" category act as a replacement teacher, and take control of the learning process. Systems based on this model contain "knowledge" that is supposed to be transferred into learners' brains. "Tool"-based systems, on the other hand, do not "teach" the learner but provide her with resources and opportunities for learning, more often than not in a classroom context.

Some currently popular tool-based views put an emphasis on collaboration and communication between students, who then co-construct knowledge. Several communicative approaches are under way, for example those in Network Based Language Teaching, as suggested by Warschauer and Kern (2000).

Skehan (2003) takes task-based instruction as the starting point in the design of CALL. The author distinguishes between learning stages, which call for the design of different tasks to be performed by the learner. The tasks chosen may thus be supported by different forms of technology. Skehan's suggestion is to use internet technology to collect learning materials, for tasks involving reading.

Holland and Kaplan (1995) present a framework for the design of CALL that emphasizes the use of Language Technology (LT). Examples of implementations of LT that may be well known to most computer users are grammar and spelling checkers, as seen in, for example word processors and e-mail applications. Other implementations include automatic filtering of unsolicited e-mail ("spam"), automatic keyword extraction and automatic text summarization.

Several authors request renewed efforts in LT for CALL. For instance, Salaberry (1999) calls for further research in LT for CALL because "technological sophistication is actually behind what L2 teachers would like to accomplish." Borin (2002) provides several suggestions for use. LT may be used for selecting appropriate texts for reading in a second language, for helping teachers correct student essays and free-form exam questions, and as a generic toolkit used in authoring tools for student writing.

In the context of writing, Borin (2002) notes that some of Chapelle's (2001) list of desirable functions in a CALL authoring system may be tackled in the domain of LT: Estimating task difficulty, analyzing learners' linguistic output, analyzing the language of objects (written, text, audio and video), supporting objects ordered in a database, gathering process-oriented data, supporting a structure for a learner model and authoring learning conditions could all contain an LT component.

Using LT in CALL systems is not unproblematic. Research in LT strives to implement technology that analyzes language as completely and accurately as possible. The current state of the art is quite useful (albeit far from entirely trustworthy) for first-language writers. Regarding second-language writers, using LT is more problematic. Knutsson, Cerratto Pargman, Severinson Eklundh, and Westlund (2006, forthcoming) show that second-language writers find inaccurate output from LT applications difficult to judge.

Improving LT is one side of the coin concerning the problem of developing adequate CALL systems. The other side concerns design of learner interaction, i.e. how the interaction between the user and the system should be designed for the purpose of second-language learning.

Holland and Kaplan (1995) affirm that use of LT in CALL has stagnated, and that "The challenge for the remaining systems is to find ways to reduce the uncertainty of Natural Language Processing (NLP) analyses, *or to help students deal with it.*" (our emphasis). There is a need to put effort into questions regarding design of second-language learning/computer interaction.

Our approach is grounded in a developmental perspective on language learning that emphasizes on the mediating role that any artifact might play in a learning process (Wertsch, 1998). The sociocultural perspective presupposes that one conceives of language and other sign systems in terms of how they are part of and mediate human action (Säljö, 1996).

We believe that the mediating potential of LT used in the context of learner/teacher–learner interaction, rather than student–tutor interaction presents interesting opportunities for second-language learning. The pedagogical rationale for our approach lies in what has been called "focus on form" in SLA.

2   Focus on Form

There is a perennial discussion on the importance or non-importance of grammar in the language curriculum. The discussion is one of the most critical in the research field of SLA. At the heart of the issue is the question whether language learning and teaching should be focused on meaning and communication, or on linguistic forms. In other words, whether to focus on the learner's language socialization or on language as an object for learners to study (Long & Robinson, 1998).

Long and Robinson list three options in language teaching, each being used in different teaching methodologies. The first is labeled focus on formS. The capital S in the name for this option has become a naming convention to distinguish it from linguistic forms in general. This option treats language as an object to be taught. The syllabus, then, consists of information about the language being taught. Student exercises are designed for training certain linguistic forms.

Several flaws in formS focused teaching are noted by Long and Robinson. For example, the needs of learners may be overlooked. Worse, scientifically proven language-learning processes may be ignored or be replaced by explicitly or tacitly behaviorist models of language learning that have been shown to be less effective, and limited.

The flaws in formS-focused language learning led several SLA theorists to abandon focus on formS in favor of an "equally single-minded" focus on meaning. Advocates of extremely meaning-focused standpoints claim that language learning takes place incidentally or implicitly. For example, the controversial "input hypothesis" introduced by Krashen (1985) calls for a need for "comprehensible input," while learner output, as well as any focus on formS, is regarded as superfluous.

Apart from Krashen's unclear and often criticized notion of "comprehensible input," there are other faults with a pure focus on meaning. It is insufficient for full competence, and learner progress is slower than in a syllabus, which also teaches formS. This has lead some SLA theorists to conclude that too much focus on grammar leads students to learn *about* language, while too much focus on communication has adverse effects on students' progress in learning the new language (e.g. Skehan, 2003).

Focus on form (FonF) is a middle way between the two extremes. It incorporates grammar, while keeping communication on the learners' agenda. A syllabus with focus on form does presumably not contain synthetic language exercises. Instead, like in meaning-based pedagogy, it teaches other subjects. However, unlike purely meaning based methods, "focus on form"-based methods "overtly draw students attention to linguistic elements as they arise incidentally in lessons whose overriding focus is on meaning, or communication." (Long, 1991). There are varying views on how to achieve this attention. We suggest that using LT is one possible way.

3   Language Technology

The distinctions between domains in LT are not always clear-cut. Here, we have chosen to use the term Language Technology in a broad sense, to describe technology that in some way analyzes, produces, or modifies natural language. Two other terms in use are

Computational Linguistics and NLP. The latter two are often used in a more narrow sense, to describe specific techniques or technological engines.

Being a core subject in LT, techniques from NLP may be used in several different forms of language software. As previously mentioned, grammar and spelling checkers are perhaps the most successful commercial applications. Also, NLP technology can serve as a key component in machine translation or multimodal systems that support several different modes of human–computer interaction, such as speech, pointing and clicking, body language, etc.

Research in LT overlaps with artificial intelligence (AI). AI in general also concerns other requisites for what may arguably be labeled "intelligence" in computer applications. These other requisites include knowing, reasoning, planning, learning and other tasks performed by the human brain. Philosophically speaking, these tasks may or may not be separable from language, but this is a point not delved into here.

Historically as well as presently, AI and NLP are branches on the same research tree. Jurafsky and Martin (2000) and Russell and Norvig (2003) devote the first chapter of their respective surveys to historical overviews. While the former book concerns NLP (including speech) and the latter concerns AI, their historical accounts overlap, showing the common ancestry of the two research areas.

NLP is traditionally divided into four large sub areas: *Morphology (words), Syntax (grammar), Semantics (meaning)* and *Pragmatics (language use)*. These are of course also large sub areas of general linguistics as well as LT. *Phonetics* may also be included, if one sees NLP as concerned with speech as well as text. Also *discourse* is sometimes seen as an area separate from pragmatics.

In *Morphology,* the automatic processing of words (or more precisely morphemes), we find applications such as spell checking, dictionaries and searching.

In *Syntax*, the relationship between words is under scrutiny. This is needed in grammar checkers as well as in rudimentary dialogue systems.

Touching on the subject of AI, *Semantics* concerns meaning, which implies at least some kind of knowledge of the world, or a particular domain thereof. This is perhaps most obviously needed in would-be intelligent agents that interact with users by means of language.

While intelligent agents belong to the AI area as well as LT, there are more specific uses of semantic knowledge in LT. It is for example used to disambiguate meanings of words, such as the word "bank" or split compounds (a common error in written Swedish), thereby improving on grammar and spelling checkers.

Semantics does not suffice to completely describe language, because language is not used merely to state facts about the world. As famously observed by Austin (1962) and Wittgenstein (1958), language is a form of human action, rather than a way for humans to describe the world. *Pragmatics*, then, concerns the use of language. Discourse analysis and dialogue management are covered in pragmatics, thus, the level of analysis in pragmatics lies not only in individual utterances, but also on an inter-utterance or inter-sentence level. Pragmatics is needed to understand meaning not disambiguated by semantics, including, but by no means limited to, phenomena such as metaphors and irony.

There is a plethora of methods and techniques used in each of these areas of NLP. One major scientific problem, common to all areas and methods in NLP, is coverage. In other words, it is difficult to build NLP systems that can analyze language input (or produce language) both correctly and completely. This is, of course, a major research problem in its own right, even when disengaged from specific applications such as CALL.

4   Language Technology in CALL

CALL systems present extra difficulties in coverage when using NLP. First, the language output from learners is more difficult to process automatically than output from native writers. Second, non-native speakers have difficulties in judging the output from the NLP system.

Holland and Kaplan (1995) see two major limitations in using NLP in CALL. These are aptly labeled *formality* and *fallibility*. The problem of formality concerns the inherent focus on formS in NLP, and how to merge this with communicative approaches in the language curriculum. The problem of fallibility is the problem of linguistic coverage, in other words that LT-engines are not fault-proof.

Low coverage has two ramifications. First, some ungrammatical constructs will be accepted by the NLP engine, while some grammatical constructs will not. Therefore, some learners are confused by NLP engines. Second, the NLP engine will be affirmative in its reports, thereby instilling a false sense of certainty in some users. In other words, the uncertainty of using LT in educational settings is in part related to the existence of false alarms generated by the program, and the limited recall of important linguistic constructions in the learners' texts (Knutsson, Cerratto Pargman, & Severinson Eklundh, 2004).

Leaving these issues unattended may be part of the reason that teachers and SLA researchers are unimpressed by advancements in LT. Technology that can simultaneously instill extraneous confusion and false certainty is clearly sub-optimal for a learning environment.

To discuss these problems, Holland and Kaplan (1995) provide a framework for design decisions in "intelligent," tutor-based CALL. Holland and Kaplan's framework is a layered one, consisting of decisions on different levels: *Context of Use, Student–Tutor Relationship, Tutoring* and *NLP*. As seen in the layer names, a tutor model is assumed in their framework. Since a tutor must somehow teach the student, it is assumed that NLP techniques can be used for implementing "intelligence" in the tutor, as well as for analyzing students' language.

To our knowledge, Holland and Kaplan's (1995) framework has not been extensively discussed by CALL designers using NLP technology. We find this unfortunate because decisions made in each of the layers have ramifications on pedagogical and usability concerns, whether or not those were foreseen by implementers.

Pedagogical concerns are, of course, at the center of attention in SLA-oriented frameworks and guidelines. As we have argued, there is also a need for technology and interaction-centered design, informed by SLA theory. There is a need for a theoretical frame, similar to Holland and Kaplan's, to discuss tool-based approaches to building applications for language learning.

5   Discussion

The framework presented by Holland and Kaplan (1995) is NLP-centric, and directed toward an audience in technology. The problems tackled by the framework are the aforementioned difficulties in formality and fallibility. Suggested solutions to these problems are approached by means of design decisions in each of the layers.

A fundamental design decision in Holland and Kaplan's framework lies in choosing to build a tutor. We believe that this decision may come somewhat naturally to researchers in NLP and LT, because of its closeness to AI, and the obvious uses for "computational" semantics and pragmatics. However, a complete tutoring system presupposes "strong" AI, that closely, if not completely, matches human intelligence.

Whether "strong" computer intelligence will ever be developed is a heavily debated question. Two famous arguments criticize the common assumptions in "good old-fashioned" AI, that intelligence is equivalent to symbolic processing, and that it therefore does not matter whether a brain or a machine performs that processing.

Dreyfus (1992) pointed out, among other things, difficulties in formalizing everyday knowledge, and traced these difficulties back to fundamental flaws in assumptions on what everyday existence actually is. The arguments drew on Heidegger's philosophy, which, in simple terms, treats everyday existence as the most basic way of being, one that cannot be exhaustively explained by being divided into categories or rules.

Searle (1980) criticizes the "Turing test," which is meant to be used to measure success in AI systems. Searle's "Chinese Room" thought-experiment points out the absurdity of the test itself. In simplified form, ascribing "intelligence" to a symbol-processing system is compared to ascribing knowledge of a language to someone with access to only a dictionary and grammar.

These two are, of course, critiques against old paradigms in AI research. New techniques have arrived, and the area has seen some progress, at least in sub-domains. However, the question of strong AI remains moot. The practical issue in CALL is what consequences to draw from limitations in AI.

Since strong AIs do not yet (if ever) exist, a common approach is, as Holland and Kaplan (1995) suggest, limiting the computer intelligence to manageable "microworlds". However, even AI in microworlds fails in behaving in ways people judge as "intelligent" in the everyday meaning of the term. There are, of course, weaker forms of AI, for example, those implemented in computer games. These may very well be useful in systems for learning, but here we take a different approach to the design problem.

Recalling Levy's (1997) terms, we propose an approach building on tools rather than tutors. This eliminates the need for strong AI, albeit several problems in semantics remain (e.g., disambiguating words). Intelligent CALL may be seen as NLP-based CALL incorporating semantics and/or pragmatics. From this, it does not follow that what must be implemented is a tutor. Instead, semantic and pragmatic knowledge may simply be used to improve on the NLP engine's language analysis and language production.

In order to discuss CALL tools using LT, we will take some liberties with Holland and Kaplan's framework and introduce some important changes. The changes we suggest stem from the following observation: Each of the layers in the framework concern issues in human–computer interaction, while the problems of formality and fallibility are specific to NLP. We suggest broadening the framework to more generally concern human–computer interacion.

The first of the proposed questions lies in Holland and Kaplan's assumption of the NLP engine as containing "knowledge to be taught". One important feature in the "focus on form" approach is the students' own communication. Students may learn things not known by the system, for example by inputting new "knowledge" into the system or by observing errors made by the system. Further, it is not clear why only one student at a time should interact with the system. Two or more students frequently collaborate on ordinary learning tasks. There is no reason to exclude collaborative tasks when using computers for learning language.

In order to reflect focus on form and tools in the framework, the names of two of the layers should be changed. We extend the "student–tutor relationship" to all systems, yielding a "student–system relationship." Instead of "tutoring," we propose the more general term "interaction." With these changes, the layers more clearly concern human–computer interaction in a general sense.

The "NLP" kernel of the framework is tightly knit to the view of the system as "tutor" because NLP is related to AI. The decision on what technology to use has already been made, albeit partially, in the framework. However, tools are not dependent on NLP in the way tutors are. Instead, we envision using several different technologies when constructing tools. In order to include other technological possibilities, we propose to change the kernel to the more general term "technology." Technology may be of any kind deemed useful for CALL, such as multimedia, networks, NLP, etc. It may also be a combination of different technologies.

This broad framework may be used to make design decisions in layers concerning *Technology, Interaction, Student–System Relationship* and *Context of Use* (Figure 1). Having introduced these changes in the framework, we will describe a specific approach incorporating NLP and other technologies (see Table 1).

Since focus on form concerns bringing students' attention to linguistic formS while working on a communicative task, we consider using NLP for highlighting formS. The communicative task, then, may vary. Network-Based Language Teaching is certainly one possible way to learn by communicating. Co-located classroom exercises are another. The

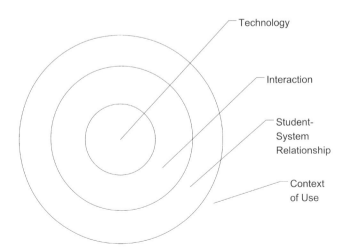

Figure 1: Framework for designing tools for CALL (adapted from Holland and Kaplan (1995)).

Table 1: Suggested design decisions in tools.

Layer	Formality	Fallibility
Context	Design explicitly for a pedagogical context where focus on form is used. This choice favors communication with an intermittent attention to formS over synthetic and formal exercises.	Conceptualize the CALL application as a tool (instead of a tutor). While this does not solve the problem entirely, at least it removes demands on LT being used to implement strong AI in the application.
Student–System Relationship	Provide opportunities for real occasions of language use with the tool. Authoring assignments can provide opportunities. Writing and editing collaborative documents on the Web is one suchoccasion, and sharing a computer to write in a co-located classroom setting is another.	While the LT engine may instill false assumptions in students, this can hypothetically be mitigated by collaboration. Student discussion concerning the tool may help in detecting errors made by the LT engine, and thus learning the engine's limitations. This would mean that flaws in the engine could conceivably be usedin order to learn about the language in question.
Interaction	Provide several modes of interaction with the LT engine, ranging from implicit to explicit. For example, it is possible to provide feedback by highlighting and explaining errors, as done in grammar checkers for first language writers. It is also possible to highlight and explain linguistic information, such as word classes, clauses, inflection, etc.	If documents are edited collaboratively, there will be feedback from more sources than only the LT engine. In other words, students will need to make linguistic decisions concerning their own output, as well as output from other students, the teacher, and the NLP engine.
Technology	Let the LT engine be formal. Instead, extend the engine, for example by incorporating semantics and pragmatics, as also suggested by Holland and Kaplan (1995).	Improve the LT engine specifically for learners. Incorporate several different LT engines in order to get statistical LT-engine will yield results different from a rule-based one, and a "concordancer" showing examples of language use may be helpful where a syntax checker fails.

choice of either of these two ways of communication yields different collaborative tasks for students to participate in.

For example, one of the tasks we are currently evaluating is a co-located one, where students are asked to reconstruct a text. A text is read aloud for them, and they are asked to summarize what they have heard, in pairs. When doing this, they use an NLP-augmented word processor. Another possibility would be to use an NLP-based tool in network systems. These could be synchronous, chat-based systems, or asynchronous systems for collaboratively editing documents.

These suggested systems are, of course, very different in practical use, and raise more issues in pedagogy and usability than delved into here. We have discussed how formality and fallibility in LT for CALL may be mitigated in tool-based, communicative approaches. That is to say that we believe that LT is useful in "focus on form", and that incorporating LT into either online environments or systems for co-located collaboration is at least a partial solution to the problem of formality/fallibility.

In summary, we have argued for using LT in CALL, and that problems perhaps stem from a focus on single-user tutor-systems and leaning too heavily on either grammatical forms or on communication. In our argument, we have examined a framework for design, suggested by Holland and Kaplan (1995). We have analyzed this framework, and modified and broadened it in order to discuss specific issues in implementing *tools* rather than *tutors*. In using the framework, our suggestions are grounded in the "focus on form" perspective in language learning, and in collaboration between students.

In our current work, we are investigating how appropriate these design decisions are for learners of Swedish as a second language. We hope that explicit design decisions may be helpful in reintroducing the use of LT for learning purposes, and that the future will bring a large variety of CALL systems following different designs.

Acknowledgments

We are grateful to Ola Knutsson for fruitful discussions and valuable comments. This research was funded by the Swedish Research Council (VR).

Chapter 14

Rethinking Instructional Metaphors for Web-Based Writing Environments

Mike Palmquist

Since the early 1980s, writing theorists and instructional designers have envisioned digital "writing environments" that would support writing processes. This work has informed the development of word-processing tools now used routinely by writers. Conspicuously missing from the design of these environments, however — at least from a teacher's perspective — is attention to instruction. Their designers seem to have assumed that writers would bring sufficient knowledge and experience to the composing process to write their documents. In this essay, I argue that an ideal writing environment would provide student writers with immediate access during composing to relevant instructional materials and feedback tools. I review the design of earlier digital writing environments, develop a theoretical framework that supports the integration of instruction into writing environments, describe Colorado State University's Web-based instructional writing environment, discuss current and planned research on the environment, and consider implications for future development of such environments.

1 Introduction

Since the 1980s, instructional software for writers has been shaped strongly by what might be termed a "common-denominator approach." Faced with the variety of pedagogical theories informing instruction in writing classrooms — among them current traditional (Berlin, 1987; Young, 1978), expressivist (Elbow, 1973; MacCrorie, 1970; Murray, 1972), cognitivist (Bereiter & Scardamalia, 1987; Flower & Hayes, 1980, 1981; Hayes, 1996), social constructionist (Berlin, 1987; Bizzell, 1982; Bruffee, 1984, 1986; Faigley, 1986), postmodern (Gale, 1996; Faigley, 1992; Fairclough, 1992; Schilb, 1991), cultural studies (Berlin, 1996; Sidler & Morris, 1998), and post-process theories (Kent, 1999; Trimbur, 1994) —

Palmquist, M. (2005). Rethinking instructional metaphors for web-based writing environments. In L. Van Waes, M. Leijten & C. Neuwirth (Vol. Eds.) & G. Rijlaarsdam (Series Ed.), Studies in Writing: Vol. 17. Writing and Digital Media (pp. 199–219). Oxford: Elsevier.

developers of instructional software for writers have tended to focus on practices common to the majority of these classrooms. The result has been software that supports practices such as brief lectures, class discussion, collaborative idea generation, student–teacher conferencing, peer and teacher feedback on writing, textbook-based assignments, and out-of-class writing assignments.

In this chapter, I suggest that a primary focus on supporting dominant instructional practices has worked against the development of innovative instructional software for writers. By choosing to focus our development efforts on feature sets that support widely used instructional practices, we have, for the most part, perpetuated the instructional *status quo*. More important, we have not fully considered how advances in information technologies might inform our instructional practices.

Below, I report on efforts to use an alternative instructional approach — a studio approach — as a basis for the development of instructional software for writers. Developed as a result of our studies of technology-supported writing classrooms (Palmquist, Kiefer, Hartvigsen, & Godlew, 1998; Kiefer & Palmquist, 1996a,b), our studio approach views the writing classroom as a place where writing is not only discussed, but carried out, an approach that contrasts with the more traditional treatment of the writing classroom as a place where writing is treated primarily as an object of discussion and analysis. This instructional approach carries with it a number of implications about classroom practice and, by extension, about the design of instructional software for writers. In the following, I review the development of instructional software for writers since the 1980s, consider work on digital environments for writers, trace the development of Web-based resources for writers, and report on efforts to develop a Web-based writing environment for student writers. I conclude by considering the implications of work on this environment for writers, teachers, and developers of similar environments.

2   Instructional Writing Environments

In the early 1980s, as personal computers began to infiltrate writing centers and writing classrooms, scholars began to consider how they might extend word processing and computer-aided instruction (CAI) software to create a more supportive environment for writers and writing students. This work was made possible by the visionary contributions of earlier scholars, such as Vanevar Bush (1945, 1967), whose Memex is widely viewed as the inspiration for work on hypertext systems; Douglas Engelbart (Engelbart & English, 1968), whose work on hypertext, windowing systems, pointing devices, and ARPANET led to current computer operating systems and the Internet; and Theodore Nelson (1965, 1974), a hypertext pioneer who is credited with coining the term "hypertext." It was also made possible by early work in CAI for writing instruction by scholars including Hugh Burns, (1980, 1984), Burns, Culp, and George, (1980), Friedman, Von Blum, Cohen, Gerard, and Rand, (1982), Von Blum and Cohen (1984), Holdstein (1983, 1984), Kriewald (1980), Neuwirth (1984), Dawn and Ray Rodrigues (1983, 1984), Rosaschi (1978), Schwartz (1982, 1984), Selfe and Billie Wahlstrom (Selfe, 1984; Selfe & Wahlstrom, 1979, 1983), and Wresch (1982, 1984). For a review of CAI for writing, see Palmquist (2006).

Initial attempts to create instructional writing environments focused largely on integrating existing word-processing technologies with CAI software. WANDAH (Writers Aid and Author's Helper ; Friedman et al., 1982; Von Blum & Cohen, 1984) was a notable example of an early writing environment, as was DRAFT (Neuwirth, 1984). DRAFT, which integrated "conventional text editing facilities with tools to help writers with invention, arrangement, and style" (p. 191), came closest to current conceptions of an instructionally oriented writing environment, but it was not widely adopted. WANDAH, which was marketed commercially as HBJ WRITER, was characterized by McDaniel (1986) as "a rare early development that supported ... integration, surrounding an easy-to-use word processor with prewriting, planning, proofreading, and revision aids." McDaniel pointed as well to ACCESS and WRITER'S HELPER as examples of integrated writing environments:

> ACCESS, a writing "environment" developed at the University of Minnesota, supports the integration of writing-aid programs with WORD-STAR and also offers utilities that a teacher can use to construct writing exercises and assignments and communicate with students about their writing, WRITER'S HELPER is also one of these integrated packages that works with BANK STREET WRITER and some other word processors.

Despite their promise, these programs were not widely adopted. In 1987, Frase argued for the creation of more robust environments that would take advantage of writing tools — "online dictionaries, thesauruses, and encyclopedias" (p. 220) — and computer networks. "We have the technologies to address the needs of writing teachers, students, administrators, testers, and researchers," he wrote. "But all these resources have scarcely touched education in America, and they will continue to pass the classroom by until educational environments are structured to coordinate and integrate these resources" (p. 220). Similarly, in 1990, Carlson expressed her surprise that, despite the potential flexibility in the design of writing tools based on computer technologies, "most computer-aided writing (CAW) software available today is based on a model derived from writing with traditional tools" (p. 95).

Throughout the early and mid-1980s, software supporting writing instruction focused largely on helping teachers, who typically made decisions about software adoptions, pursue their curricular goals. As such, the software served largely to replicate, in an online environment, teaching methods used for many years in writing classrooms. Most CAI software, for example, extended the worksheets used in many writing classrooms for purposes ranging from reviewing grammar and mechanics to generating ideas to revising essays, while most style checking software, such as WRITER'S WORKBENCH (Kiefer & Smith, 1983, 1984; Kiefer, Reid, & Smith, 1989), was used to supplement (or even to replace) face-to-face tutoring or handbook review.

By the late 1980s and early 1990s, spurred by the success of hypertext programs such as Apple's HYPERCARD and Eastgate Systems' STORYSPACE, scholars began to consider the role such tools might play in instructional writing software. Programs developed for student writers that incorporated hypertext tools included Learning Tool (Kozma & Van Roekel, 1986; Kozma, 1987) and TEXTVISION (Kommers & De Vries, 1992). Reflecting on his work with this type of tool, Kozma (1991a) argued for the need to go beyond word processing:

> Certainly word-processing programs help writing by automating some of the more burdensome aspects of text production and revision. Features such as inserting, deleting, and moving blocks of text are likely to account for the findings that students who use word-processing programs write longer compositions, have fewer errors, and make more revisions (Hawisher, 1988, 1989). However, these features have little to do with the formulation of plans, the retrieval and organization of knowledge, or the evaluation of the emerging text: those cognitive processes least prevalent among novice writers.

Kozma argued that student writers were likely to benefit from tools that corresponded "more directly to cognitive components of the composing process," such as idea organizers, style and grammar checkers, planning and revising prompts embedded within the writing software, communication packages that support peer review, chat, and email, and "artificially intelligent writing environments" that support composing processes and facilitate the analysis of drafts. To test this argument, Kozma (1991b) studied student writers as they composed using computer-based outlining tools, spatial organizers, and rhetorical/topical prompting. He found that students did more planning when using idea organizing tools (as opposed to using a word processor alone) and even more when prompts were built into the tools.

Despite the strong theoretical support mustered for the use of hypertext-based writing tools for students, these tools would not have a significant impact on the composing processes of most student writers. In contrast, the growing use of network communication tools and the development of large file sharing networks would lead to significant changes in the way students composed. Two early projects, one that did not move beyond the proposal stage and another that had a relatively brief run, offer insights into the theoretical motivations of early developers of network-based instructional software for writers.

In 1987, Richard E. Young and Christine Neuwirth, members of the rhetoric faculty at Carnegie Mellon University, proposed the development of an instructional writing environment informed by an alternative pedagogical metaphor (Neuwirth, 1989; Young & Neuwirth, 1987). Their proposal to the Buhl Foundation, submitted in 1987 and resubmitted in 1988, called for the creation of a network-based environment based on a distributed instructional metaphor. The proposal laid out an ambitious alternative to the then-current approaches to writing instruction, calling for an environment that would provide real-time connections between writers seeking assistance and other writers who were logged onto the network, delayed feedback on drafts through electronic mail and commenting programs, and access to instructional software that could have been used independently of course curricula. Although the Buhl Foundation chose not to fund the proposal, it provided a theoretical framework for network-based writing support that mirrors the framework adopted by many Web-based OWLs (online writing labs).

In 1989, at Colorado State University, a similar initiative was undertaken by Dawn Rodrigues and Kate Kiefer. The Electronic Writing Service (Rodrigues & Kiefer, 1993), like the environment proposed by Young and Neuwirth, called for a distributed approach to instruction in which students could request interaction with writers and tutors, request instructional materials via electronic mail, and submit drafts for style and grammar analyses from the WRITER'S WORKBENCH program housed on a UNIX server. Rodrigues and Kiefer described the Electronic Writing Service as "a 'virtual reality,' a place where students can 'talk' in writing to one another or to a tutor, a place where they will also be able to locate appropriate writing software to help them with a writing assignment in any of their courses" (p. 223).

This shift to a focus on network computing was also reflected in software developed in the mid-1980s to support collaboration. Early commenting programs included COMMENTS (Neuwirth, Kaufer, Keim, & Gillespie, 1988) and PROSE (Kaplan, Davis, & Martin, 1987). COMMENTS was integrated into the network system used at Carnegie Mellon University, where it was developed, while PROSE relied on file sharing (often literally the exchange of diskettes). The first version of the DAEDALUS INTEGRATED WRITING ENVIRONMENT (Butler, Carter, Kemp, & Taylor, 1988) was also developed at this time. Running on a local area network (LAN), the program provided access to CAI, a limited word processor, a spell checker, and real-time chat. Programs such as these would lead, by the mid-1990s, to a set of sophisticated LAN-based groupware programs that supported document sharing and communication among writers and teachers. These included ASPECTS, which supported concurrent editing of documents and real-time chat (Amdahl, 1992); COMMONSPACE, a program based on the PREP EDITOR developed at Carnegie Mellon University (Neuwirth, Kaufer, Chandook, & Morris, 1990), which supported commenting and real-time chat (Tucker, 1996); Norton CONNECT.NET, which integrated Microsoft Word and its commenting tools into an environment that supported public and private chat, paper submission, and limited class management tools (Woodlief, 1997); and DAEDALUS INTEGRATED WRITING ENVIRONMENT, which provided features comparable to Norton CONNECT.NET (Sands, 1997).

Despite the promise of these programs, only DAEDALUS INTEGRATED WRITING ENVIRONMENT continues to be distributed and developed. The growing sophistication of word-processing tools and the availability of key features within Web-based classroom management systems, such as WebCT and BlackBoard, appear to have reduced the attractiveness of this type of commercial software. The development and assessment of these programs, nonetheless, contributed in important ways to our understanding of how to provide digital support for writing students, including strategies for integrating instructional content into composing tools; requesting, providing, and working with comments; using network communication tools to support writing instruction; and integrating spelling, style, and grammar checking tools into word processing programs.

3   Writing Environments for Professionals

A second strand of software development relevant to instructional writing environments focuses on the development of tools for professional writers and writing teams. Unlike the classroom-based metaphors that influenced the development of instructional writing environments in the 1980s and 1990s, the metaphors that shaped the development of these digital writing environments tended to be of writers, individually and in groups, facing specific composing tasks. Most often, the developers of digital writing environments turned to cognitive models of writing, such as the theoretical models that emerged from the work of Hayes and Flower (1980, 1981), Hayes (1996), and Bereiter and Scardamalia (1987), to conceptualize those tasks. John Smith (1994), for example, observes in his introduction to *Collective Intelligence in Computer-Based Collaboration*:

> From the beginning, we believed that if we could understand more clearly the cognitive process of writing, then we should be able to build computer systems consistent with that process. That is, if we could identify key-mental activities that comprise expository writing, then we should be able to build corresponding features into our computer systems to support and, we hoped, enhance those same activities (p. ix).

Work on digital writing environments for professionals focused on two primary questions: How can writers work with information? How can writers work together? The first question was informed by work in hypertext, network file systems, and emerging tools for working with multimedia content, such as images, audio, video, and animation. The second question was informed by work on communication tools and emerging database models that supported locking and versioning of documents. While the instructional writing environments developed for writing students tended to focus primarily on CAI, word processing, chat, spelling, grammar, and style checking tools, the writing environments targeted at professional writers (and writers working in professional settings) focused more heavily on storing, managing, and working with information, and on supporting communication and document sharing among writers who might be collaborating on a project.

One of the first digital writing environments for professional writers, the aptly named Writing Environment (WE), was developed by Smith and his colleagues at the University of North Carolina. WE reflects a strong focus on information management. Influenced strongly by early work in hypertext, it had four modes: network mode, which supported exploration using nodes and links; tree mode, which supported hierarchical structuring of ideas and information; edit mode, which allowed editing of nodes; and text mode, which provided a linear view of nodes and supported editing for coherence (see Figure 1). Development on WE began in the mid-1980s (Smith, 1987; Smith et al., 1987) and continued into the early 1990s (Lansman, Smith, & Weber, 1993; Smith & Lansman, 1989, 1992).

Another early digital writing environment, Brown University's INTERMEDIA (Garrett, Smith, & Meyrowitz, 1986), reflects a similar focus on information management. Built largely as a hypertext editor, it was used primarily to support the development of complex hypertext documents. Initially, INTERMEDIA provided a text processor, graphics editor, timeline editor, image viewer, and 3-D model viewer. By the time it reached the end of its development phase, INTERMEDIA offered tools for working with audio, video, and animation and provided access to an online dictionary. It also provided limited support for collaborative writing through its implementation on a shared file system network and an annotation tool.

In the 1990s, the focus on hypertext shifted to a focus on hypermedia. Denley, Whitefield, and May (1993) describe a database-driven collaborative writing environment that supports

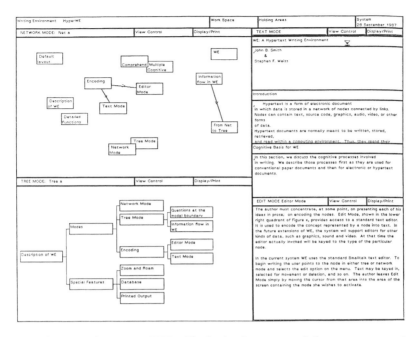

Figure 1: Writing Environment (WE). Clockwise from upper-left corner: network mode, text mode, edit mode, and tree mode.

the development of multimedia documents and allows browsing of text, graphics, audio, and audiovisual objects stored in the system's database. SEPIA (Structured Elicitation and Processing of Ideas for Authoring); (Streitz, Hannemann, & Thuring, 1989), offered support for the creation of argumentative hypertexts, allowing writers to work in activity spaces dedicated to content, planning, argument, and rhetorical considerations. Collaborative tools allowed writers to simultaneously view and edit files consisting of text, images, audio, and video. Annotation of files was accomplished by linking to a new file containing a comment.

The influence of hypertext technologies on the development of digital writing environments is also seen in several programs designed to support work with notes, among them NOTES (Neuwirth, Kaufer, Chimera, & Gillespie, 1987), NOTECARDS (Trigg & Irish, 1988), INTERNOTE (Catlin, Bush, & Yankelovich, 1989), AQUANET (Marshall & Rogers, 1992) and MILO (Jones, 1993). Notes, developed at Carnegie Mellon University, provided both a general tool for working with notes and three task-specific tools for summarizing and synthesizing: Summary Graph, Synthesis Grid, and Synthesis Tree. Although it was available on the university network, NOTES did not see widespread use by writers. Instead, it was developed largely to test the efficacy of task specific tools for writers as opposed to the more general tools found in environments such as WE (Neuwirth & Kaufer, 1989). MILO, developed around 1990, provided collaborative support for notes-based writing projects. MILO allowed writers to create notes containing both text and graphics, link notes, and view notes as a graphical tree, as a linear indented outline, or in their order of creation. MILO also provides a search tool and a spell checker.

A key concern informing the development of these systems was how best to represent information, and in particular the emerging text of documents, on screen. Even when working with comparatively larger screen sizes and resolutions, computer monitors fell far short of the flexible workspace offered by a large desk or an office floor. This posed problems with what has been described by Severinson Eklundh, Fatton, and Romberger (1996) as a "local perspective." Some developers, such as Streitz and his colleagues (1992) and Marshall and Rogers (1992), addressed this problem by allowing representations of notes or nodes to extend beyond the available screen view. Severinson Eklundh and her colleagues experimented with a program they called PAPER, which provided a view of a document as a set of pages. Their purpose was "to provide a writing environment that both gives a sufficient global view of a document and supports the writer's spatial memory" (pp. 138–139). In a manner similar to many notes-type programs, PAPER allowed writers to stack pages on top of each other and to reposition pages by dragging them across the screen.

To address the second key question informing work on writing environments for professional writers — how can writers work together? — designers turned to network communication tools, such as chat, email, and video conferencing, and database technologies that allowed advanced control of documents. Key issues faced by these designers included choice and implementation of communication tools, negotiation (or imposition) of roles among members of a collaborative team, representation of annotations, document control and versioning, revision tracking, and document merging.

Chat, shared views of documents, and, less frequently, audio or video conferencing were used to support communication among authors in many collaborative systems. SEPIA (Streitz et al., 1992) was among the more ambitious collaborative writing environments, employing shared browsers, notification of users currently working on a shared project, voice conferencing, and video conferencing. SASSE (Baecker, Nastos, Posner, & Mawby,1993) allowed collaborators to work concurrently on shared documents in a What You See Is What I See (WYSIWIS) editor, determine who was actively involved in an editing session and which parts of the document they were editing, and create text and voice annotations.

The roles adopted by — or assigned to — members of a collaborative writing group were a key issue explored by designers of collaborative writing environments (Miles, McCarthy, Dix, Harison, & Monk, 1993). Ultimately, the debate focused on whether to assign roles through software, through social interaction, or through some combination of the two. In a report on their work with the PREP EDITOR, Neuwirth, Kaufer, Chandook, and Morris (1994) observed that factors affecting writers' roles involved "activities such as agreeing to enter into communication and negotiating its form, allocating access to resources, and agreeing on commitments" (p. 148). As they reflected on challenges facing them and the work they would pursue, they noted:

> We see our work as split between increasing the technological potential of group interaction and harnessing this potential to satisfactory communication outcomes. Down this second branch, we expect to find some technological solutions, but many social ones as well. Cultures define hundreds of regulatory devices in face-to-face interaction to monitor social behavior.

We are still in the earliest stages of establishing cultures for group exchange over networks (p. 151).

Writing a year earlier in his introduction to *Computer Supported Collaborative Writing*, Sharples (1993) characterized the challenges facing designers as a mix of technological issues and social realities:

> Those of us who wish to design software for the support of collaborative writing must tread very warily. If we rush in proffering out shared editors, coordination tools and negotiation support systems then we are, at best, likely to be ignored or, at worst, seen as a Trojan Horse of new technology intruding into the writer's world of formal agreements and structures, and informal alliances, unacknowledged collaboration and tacit social support (pp. 4–5).

Although role assignment was explored in a number of early environments (e.g., Garrett, Smith, & Meyrowitz, 1986), the consensus that emerged among developers was to rely most heavily on social negotiation of roles. In part, this consensus resulted from the recognition that roles within a collaborative group can change quickly. For example, a reviewer might be asked, in a real-time exchange, to begin editing a document. If the software restricted that person from editing the document and none of the collaborators currently working on the document were able to change the restrictions, time would be lost.

Designers of collaborative writing environments also addressed issues related to document annotation. Questions focused on how best to display annotations (e.g., as links, as marginal comments, as the equivalent of footnotes) and differences in annotation modality (e.g., voice versus text). Wojahn, Neuwirth, & Bullock (1998) studied alternative representations of comments, finding that annotation interfaces affected "the number and types of problems about which collaborators communicate" (p. 456). Neuwirth et al. (1994) investigated the effects on writers of written and spoken annotations, finding that writers found the "greater expressivity of the voice modality" useful for all but low-level editing issues (p. 51).

The growing sophistication of databases allowed designers of collaborative writing environments to coordinate the changes made by multiple authors to shared documents, providing a solution to a long-standing problem, articulated in 1986 by Garrett et al.:

> If a hypermedia system is to be useful for cooperative work it must provide ways for multiple authors to read, link to and from, and even edit the same set of documents, while also allowing authors to protect their work from unauthorized access or changes. At its simplest this functionality could be implemented in a system where authors have sequential access to documents. However, it would be more useful for cooperative work within a fully networked environment where multiple authors would have simultaneous access to documents (p. 171).

Systems such as SEPIA and SASSE used databases to control a range of actions by writers, among them synchronizing changes to a shared document (Olson, Olson, Mack, &

Wellner, 1990), saving versions of the document (Miles, McCarthy, Dix, Harison, & Monk, 1993), and locking all or parts of the document (Baecker, Nastos, Posner, & Mawby, 1993; Streitz et al., 1992). Databases also supported flexible display of documents, such as hierarchical outlines and webbed representations of linked documents in hypertext and notes-based systems and alternative views of annotations. By using databases to associate information, rather than to save documents as single files, designers were able to provide flexible displays of the document and save multiple document states. When needed, these states could be compared, inadvertent changes could be discarded, and information could be recovered from earlier versions of the document.

Work on digital writing environments for professionals has had a significant impact on the "environment" used most frequently by student writers, the modern word processor. Leading word processors routinely include spelling and style checking, drawing tools, revision tracking and commenting tools, and linking tools. Some word processors also employ limited forms of versioning. In addition, most are integrated into network environments, supporting email and Web browsing, among other communication tools. Specific writing environments, such as the PREP EDITOR, which is the foundation for COMMONSPACE, have been marketed as instructional writing environments. Other instructional writing environments, such as ASPECTS, drew heavily on the shared editor and synchronous communication tools that emerged from this body of work.

Despite these contributions, however, work in this area has had limited impact on the education of most writing students. In part, this reflects the experimental nature of many early writing environments, most of which served primarily to explore possibilities or to prove a concept. In part, it reflects the decision to develop many writing environments on high-end Unix systems rather than on the operating systems more commonly used on personal computers. And, in part, it reflects a reluctance on the part of many writing teachers to accept the theoretical foundations shaping the development of early writing environments. Kemp (1992), for example, argued that the cognitive models underlying these environments have worked against their widespread adoption for instructional purposes.

It might also be that the metaphor underlying these environments — that of the professional writer, working alone or collaboratively, often on hypertextual documents — is inconsistent with the metaphors informing most writing courses: a novice asked to learn about writing concepts and processes through discussion and then sent out of the classroom to apply those concepts and processes to the creation of essays. If so, the most important contributions of these environments to the development of instructional writing environments may lie in what designers have learned as they have considered such issues as how to support information management, co-authoring, and document review.

4   Web-Based Support for Writing Instruction

The Web has emerged as an important source of instructional support for writers and writing teachers. Since Purdue University's OWL (online writing lab) moved from its home on Gopher to the World Wide Web in 1994 (OWL Fact Sheet, 2005), a large number of writing centers, writing-across-the-curriculum programs, and composition programs have established presences on the Web. For a more detailed history of this movement, see

Palmquist (2003). The majority of OWLs have used the Web to provide access to instructional materials, to schedule online or face-to-face meetings between writers and writing center tutors, to support online review of drafts, and to publicize services offered by writing centers and writing programs.

By 1996, more than 100 OWLs had established a Web presence. Lasarenko's (1996) review of 93 OWLs indicated that they ranged from OWLs that served primarily to announce the services available from campus writing centers to those offering handouts and links to other online resources to "Full-Fledged" OWLs, which offered "a complete set of online services, including online manuscript submission and feedback." Johnson (1996) observed that these OWLs also offered "a local publishing environment for student writers of electronic texts" and made "a pointed philosophical mission of redefining traditional notions of academic literacy."

Despite the rapid movement of OWLs to the Web, a number of scholars, among them those most involved in spurring that movement, urged caution. Harris and Pemberton (1995), for example, warned that offering online tutorials offered significant challenges to the designers of OWLs:

> Attempting only to replicate familiar face-to-face tutorial settings in an electronic, text-oriented environment can lead to frustration and to defeat as OWL planners find themselves unable to simulate all characteristics of effective tutorials. Instead, it is important to recognize that OWLs can have a number of very different configurations — configurations that take advantage of the strengths of online environments and that work with, not against, both local conditions and writing center theory (p. 145).

Hobson (1998) cautioned that some of the online instructional practices associated with OWLs were inconsistent with the pedagogical principles and philosophies informing most writing centers. Hobson called attention in particular to a reliance on worksheets, drills, and guides to form, as well as what he saw as tacit encouragement of writers to work in isolation. Crump (2000), similarly, observed that the online support offered at that time by most OWLs, whether in the form of instructional materials or online interaction with writers, was "still very limited in terms of scope and shape" (p. 225).

Since Crump's observation, a number of OWLs have provided more sophisticated instructional support for writers and writing teachers. The Purdue OWL (http://owl.english.purdue.edu) offers resources on a range of writing topics and is considering a move toward a database-driven content management system. The Wiki-based OWL at Texas A&M University Corpus Christi (http://falcon.tamucc.edu/wiki) supports writing and writing-intensive courses and offers significant resources for collaboration among teachers and students. The largest OWL, at Colorado State University (http://writing.colostate.edu), offers more than 27,000 pages of content for writers and writing teachers, ranging from instructional guides to annotated links to database-supported tutorials.

In addition to OWLs, important Web-based support for writers includes the development of online textbooks, such as *Paradigm Online Writing Assistant* (http://www.powa.org/), the *Writer's Handbook* at the University of Wisconsin Madison's OWL (http://www.wisc.edu/writing/Handbook/index.html), and *College Writing Online*, by Joe Moxley (2003), which is available by subscription from Longman. In addition, Web-based resources such as the University of Antwerp's CALLIOPE (Computer Aided Language Learning in an Interactive Online Pedagogical Environment) (http://www.calliope.be) offer suggestions for new directions in support for writers (Jacobs, Opdenacker, & Van Waes, 2005). CALLIOPE, which is implemented using a content-management system, is based on a problem-based approach and segments instructional materials into theory, practice, and case.

The Web has also provided a foundation for several instructional writing environments, including La Console d'ecriture, TC3, and ScienceWRITE. La Console d'ecriture (Bisaillon, Clerc, & Ladouceur, 1999), targeted at French secondary students, focused on poetry, informative texts, and adventure stories. It operated in a learning and a writing mode and provided pedagogical scenarios for student writers. The learning mode provided a "detailed description of the writing process" (p. 200) and offered access to five cognitive activities as well as explanations, examples, and practice. The writing mode provided a word processor, spell checkers, and idea generators, as well as a terminological extractor and document management software. TC3 (Text Composer, Computer supported & Collaborative) was developed to support argumentative writing among Dutch secondary school students (Erkens, Kanselaar, Prangsma, & Jaspers, 2003). A groupware program which provided access to Internet resources, it was based on an earlier instructional writing environment, Collaborative Text Production, developed in the mid-1990s (Andriessen, Erkens, Overeem, & Jaspers, 1996). The system provides four windows (two private, two shared): Information, Notes, Chat, and Shared Text. It also provides two planning tools, one for diagramming and the other for outlining, as well as a help function. Science WRITE (Greene et al., 1998) is a Web-based instructional environment that builds on Bereiter and Scardamalia's cognitive model of composing (1987), as well as on their procedural facilitation model (1982), combining explicit textual instruction with example texts and exercises that build on each other. Students can work interactively through the modules, which focus their attention on both content and rhetorical situation.

The Web is also the home to larger, institutional efforts to support writing instruction. Web-based course management systems that have been developed for use in writing courses include SyllaBase (http://english.usu.edu/Document/index.asp?Parent = 6451), which is being developed at Utah State University by a group of writing teachers (Buchanan, 2000), Critical Tools (http://www.albany.edu/~critical), which was developed through the Computer Writing and Research Lab at the University of Texas at Austin, the Speakeasy Studio & Cafe (http://speakeasy.wsu.edu/studio/), which is being developed at Washington State University, and TOPIC (http://ttopic.english.ttu.edu/), which is being developed at Texas Tech University. SyllaBase should be of particular interest to writing teachers. Unlike course management systems such as WebCT and BlackBoard, which attempt to emulate a class taught on the lecture model, SyllaBase emulates instruction that typically takes place in writing classrooms. The instructional metaphor informing it, as a result, is more closely aligned with that of the writing teachers who might use it. TOPIC (Texas Tech Online-Print Integrated Curriculum), in contrast, represents a significant departure from most writing curricula. The system supports an instructional approach in which one group of teachers provides classroom instruction while another evaluates and responds to student writing (Kemp, 1999). A database-driven Web application, TOPIC

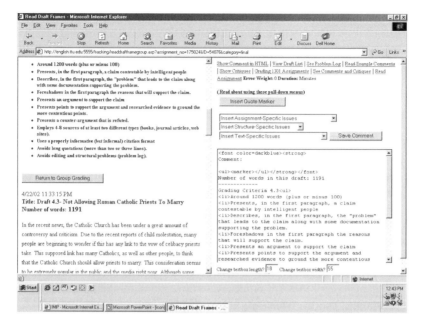

Figure 2: TOPIC grading page. Source: http://ttopic.english.ttu.edu/manual/grading_page.htm.

manages the submission and review of essays written by students enrolled in Texas Tech writing courses (see Figure 2). TOPIC also provides course management tools for students and teachers, descriptions of writing assignment, and related instructional materials, including online textbook materials.

The majority of Web-based instructional resources developed for writers and writing instruction have been informed by the dominant metaphors that inform most writing courses. Systems such as Science WRITE, CALLIOPE, and TOPIC, however, are based on instructional metaphors that differ, in degrees ranging respectively from moderate to extreme, from those dominant metaphors. In the next section, I discuss a Web-based writing environment, the Writing Studio, that is also based on an alternative instructional metaphor, that of a "writing studio."

5   A Database-Driven Digital Writing Environment with an Instructional Focus

In August 2005, Colorado State University announced a major upgrade to its OWL, Writing@CSU (http://writing.colostate.edu). The updated site allowed writers to create password-protected accounts in which they could save work created through the site. The site provided access to composing tools, commenting and document exchange tools, communication tools (including chat, blogs, and discussion forums), a course management system, and instructional resources including writing guides and interactive activities. The revision marked the site's transition from a standard OWL, which provided access to information about writing and the teaching of writing, to a Web-based instructional writing environment shaped by the metaphor of the student writer at work.

5.1   Development

The Writing@CSU project began in 1991, when faculty at Colorado State University began planning a campus-wide writing environment to replace the earlier Electronic Writing Services (Rodrigues & Kiefer, 1993). In 1993, using the name, "Online Writing Center," it was released as a hypermedia application available through the University's wide area network. In 1996, the Online Writing Center moved to the Web. By May 2005, the site, which had been renamed in 2001 to Writing@CSU, had more than 60,000 static pages and additional dynamic pages and had received more than 2.4 million visits in the previous year.

In 1999, faculty associated with development of the Writing@CSU Web site had recognized that, although it was providing a significant set of resources to writers and writing teachers, the nature of those resources was similar to those that had long been used in writing classrooms. The hypertext writing guides available through the site, some with more than 500 pages of content, could be characterized as enhanced textbooks. The interactive tutorials were similar in form and content to worksheets that had long been assigned in writing courses. Similarly, resources such as curricular materials, guides for teachers, and annotated model texts had clear analogues in the print world. Essentially, the site was providing a rich set of resources that served largely to support the instructional *status quo* in the University's writing and writing-intensive courses. Indeed, despite significant investments in technology-based writing instruction in our department over the past two decades, the overall approach used in our courses reflected classroom-based practices that would be recognizable to a writing teacher from the 1970s or 1980s.

Work on a previous project had convinced us, however, that technology-supported writing instruction would be more successful if it were based on an instructional metaphor that focused on the student writer in the act of composing. That metaphor emerged from the Transitions study (Palmquist et al., 1998), an exploration of computer-supported and traditional writing classrooms in which we found that the presence of networked computers in a writing classroom was correlated with strikingly different attitudes among students and teachers toward the use of writing during class meetings. Briefly, we found that students in traditional writing classrooms resisted writing during class and their exchanges with classmates were more likely than not to be off topic. In contrast, we found that students in the computer-supported classrooms were more receptive to writing during class, more likely to talk about their writing with teachers and classmates, and more confident in their writing skills at the end of the term. Most important, we found that student writers seemed to learn best when they could ask a teacher or classmate for advice and feedback *as they composed*.

We characterized the instructional interactions we observed in the computer-supported writing classrooms as a "studio approach" to writing instruction because the behaviors we observed seem more similar to classes held in an art studio, where teachers and students discuss work in progress, than to a typical writing class, where writing is discussed and then out-of-class work is assigned. Our conception of the writing classroom as a studio is consistent with visions of writing classrooms articulated by several scholars, many of whom predate the widespread use of computer and network technologies (Grego & Thompson, 1996; Phelps, 1992; Platt, 1991). As such, we are making no claims about the novelty of our instructional approach. We suggest, however, that this approach can be used not only in face-to-face instructional settings, but also in electronic settings — and, perhaps more important, that it can provide a powerful metaphor to guide development of instructional writing environments.

In 2001, we developed a prototype Web site that attempted to use a studio approach to support the teaching and learning of writing (Fogelson, 2002, May; Kiefer & Barnes, 2002; Palmquist, 2002, March, May). The Writing Studio, which was designed to be part of the larger Writing@CSU site, allowed writers to access instructional resources, communicate with and receive feedback on writing from teachers and other writers, access tools that supported elements of the writing process, and save their work for later access. The Writing Studio was initially designed as a collection of "rooms," each of which could focus on a particular genre, discipline, or course. Our first room, based on instructional materials developed by Mackenzie Fogelson (2002) as part of her master's project and implemented using Macromedia ColdFusion, Microsoft IIS, and Microsoft SQL Server, supported secondary students working on informative writing assignments. The Writing Studio provided a password-protected environment in which student writers could learn about, compose, ask questions about, share drafts of, and save their informative writing assignments (see Figure 3). The room was developed as a single application that allowed navigation among modules that guided students through the process of choosing a topic, planning a writing project, drafting the project, and revising and editing the project. An instructor's guide was provided.

In summer 2002, we created a second prototype that simplified the user interface, provided multiple navigation options, and implemented an expanded set of instructional materials, communication tools, and composing tools. Key changes included a drop-down menu running across the top of all pages in the Studio; implementation of a discussion forum and chat system; implementation of a writing center draft-submission tool; WYSIWYG drafting, note-taking, and bibliographic citation tools; and the ability to download or email work completed in the Studio. The instructional modules used in the first prototype were enhanced through the use of a WYSIWYG editor, linked tutorials, annotated example texts, and video-based discussions of relevant composing processes by experienced writers and teachers (see Figure 4).

Subsequent enhancements to the Writing Studio during 2003 and 2004 included the addition of commenting tools, a course management system, new composing tools, and a video-based help system. The commenting tools allow writers to request comments from writers, teachers, and writing center tutors and to make comments on work completed by writers who grant them access to their project portfolios. Reviewers can notify writers by email that comments had been made on their work. In addition, "comments" icons in instructional materials and composing tools alert writers that feedback is available, allowing them to view and manage comments as they compose.

The course management system adopted the approach pioneered by the developers of SyllaBase — using the writing classroom, rather than the lecture classroom, as the basis

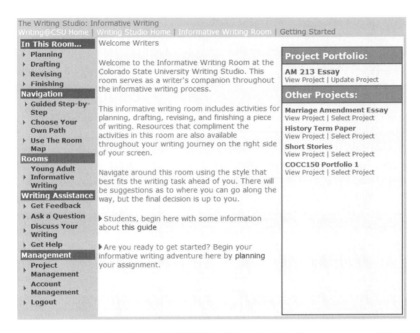

Figure 3: A page from the Informative Writing Room in the first prototype of the Writing Studio, Spring 2001.

for the design of course management tools. The course management system allows teachers to create and manage classes and to view and comment on student work. Teachers can display calendars, course syllabi, assignments, course materials, related links, and relevant instructional materials on the Writing@CSU site. The course tools also support communication via electronic mail, discussion forums, chat, blogs, shared file folders, and a grade book. Teachers can manage class rosters, set commenting access rights among students, assign students to groups, keep notes about their course in a teaching notebook, modify the appearance and content of the course page, and manage co-instructors, among other options. Although the overall set of tools is similar to that of course management systems based on a lecture-class metaphor, the assumption that they will be used to support writing classes shaped numerous decisions about which tools to include and how they would be designed. For example, teacher commenting tools are provided while test and quiz tools are not. Similarly, to support journaling, students can "publish" their blogs to a class's blogs page.

The new composing tools included an ideas tool, an outliner, a "Work at a Glance" tool, and a blogging tool. The ideas tool provides a space for recording ideas and information related to a writing project. "Ideas" can be categorized and linked. The outliner supports the creation of an outline and supports links to source citations, notes, and ideas. The "Work at a Glance" tool allows writers to view all work they have completed on a writing project as they work on a draft. It provides a centralized information management space that supports drafting and revising processes (see Figure 5).

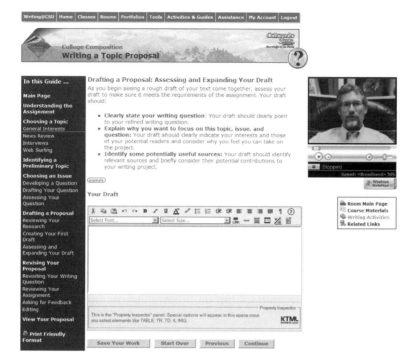

Figure 4: A Writing Studio practice guide, ca. 2003.

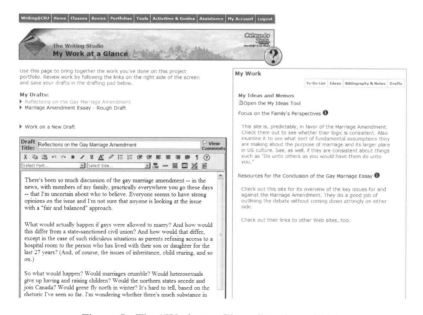

Figure 5: The "Work at a Glance" tool, ca. 2004.

In summer 2005, following assessments that involved analysis of site traffic, interviews with teachers and students, informal usability testing, and a formal usability study conducted at the University of Twente in the Netherlands (Van Craaikamp, 2005), the site's developers decided to merge the Writing Studio and the larger Writing@CSU site. The decision reflected the recognition that the login required to access instructional materials was discouraging writers from viewing instructional content housed within the Studio. It also reflected a desire to redesign both Writing@CSU and the Writing Studio to account for the results of the usability tests, which indicated the desirability of a reduced set of navigation tools and the creation of a unified look and feel across the site. The redesign resulted in a smaller Web site (total pages were reduced from roughly 60,000 to roughly 27,000, largely by shifting older pages to another site) with simplified top-level pages (see Figure 6) and a new classification of instructional resources. The "rooms" have been replaced by Writing Collections and the disparate collection of materials previously found in individual rooms have been integrated into the larger set of writing guides, activities, and demonstrations. Writers are now asked to login only when they attempt to access resources that will require them to access customized content (such as a course page) or to save work (such as a composing tool or

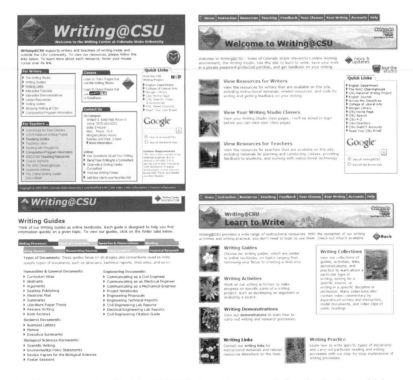

Figure 6: Changes to the Writing@CSU site. From top left, clockwise: old home page, new home page, new top-level page, and old top-level page.

an interactive activity). The redesigned site also makes greater use of a database to individualize access to materials on the site and to control the appearance and behavior of pages on a user-by-user basis.

5.2 Current Status

Access to the Writing@CSU site is unrestricted, allowing its use by writers and writing teachers regardless of their affiliation with Colorado State University. Following the announcement of the availability of the Writing Studio course management tools in December 2004, teachers at more than 30 educational institutions began evaluating its use to support their courses. By December 2005, the number of user accounts on the system exceeded 20,000.

Current plans for expanding the services offered by the site include

- strengthening partnerships with other higher education institutions, both in the United States and abroad;
- developing collections, composing tools, and instructional materials for primary and secondary students;
- increasing instructional resources for writing-intensive courses across the curriculum;
- developing or adapting composing tools that support graphical representation of information and flexible positioning of text passages on a screen;
- developing a portfolio publication tool that will allow writers to present their work to external audiences;
- enhancing the blogging tool to support syndication; and
- developing alternative entry pages for the site and "skins" for the course management system for a range of writers, from young learners to specialized communities of learners.

Long-term plans include integrating leading word processors into the site's composing tools (or, should that prove impractical, replacing the HTML editor we are currently using with an XML editor that would support greater customization) and enhancing the site's collaborative tools to support real-time document sharing and group writing projects. Potential projects include exploring the use of artificial intelligence to support collaborative interfaces — software that collaborates with a writer — as Babaian, Grosz, and Shieber (2002) have done with Writer's Aid, a program that uses writer's plans and past behaviors to partially automate bibliographic searches.

5.3 Future Research

Current research projects include ongoing, informal usability testing of the site and a classroom study of the use of the Writing@CSU site to support the teaching and learning of writing in computer-supported and traditional classrooms. A fall 2005 study of classes taught by 10 instructors at Colorado State University is currently underway. Student attitudes toward writing, technology, and the use of the Writing@CSU site (with particular emphasis on the composing tools, course management system, and interactive instructional materials) are being assessed through surveys and interviews. Writing and online behaviors are being assessed through classroom observation, usability testing, analysis of Web site usage, and analysis of writing produced for the course. Instructor behavior and attitudes are being assessed through interviews, classroom observation, and informal usability testing. Instructors in the study represent a range of teaching experience and attitudes toward using technology. We intend to follow the instructors' use of the Writing@CSU site across two academic terms. We also intend to carefully assess differences in the use of the site in the two classroom contexts.

Future research will involve assessment of the use of Writing@CSU site in primary and secondary classrooms, periodic usability testing (both formal and informal), and continuing analysis of the site's traffic.

5.4   Limitations

The Writing@CSU Web site is a work in progress. Key limitations include its reliance on a WYSIWIG editor that is not compatible with all browsers, problems with making comments on specific regions of a document, and incomplete implementation of composing tools. The current WYSIWIG editor works with Internet Explorer 6.x and higher, Mozilla 1.4 and higher, and browsers based on the Mozilla core. We have implemented a browser check that alerts users if they enter the Studio with an unsupported browser. The warning is given only at the beginning of each session and can be disabled. The comments tool does not support-linking comments to a specific passage of text. Currently, all comments are made at the level of the document. This is not a significant problem for memos and notes, but it poses challenges for commenting on drafts and other longer documents. Writing@CSU does not currently offer a graphical hypertext linking and display tool, such as those found in earlier writing environments, nor does it offer a drawing tool. In addition, the bibliographic citation tool generates a "working" bibliography that must be checked by writers for accurate formatting of entries.

6   Conclusions

The Writing@CSU Web site offers an example of an instructional writing environment based on a pedagogical metaphor that differs from that commonly used in writing classrooms. The articulation of an ideal learning situation — in this case, that of a student writer who has access to relevant composing and researching tools, relevant instructional materials, and feedback and advice from classmates and a teacher — has informed our development of the site. Working from this metaphor, we have developed an instructional writing environment that provides writers with support for the full range of composing, communication, and information-management processes they face as they engage in a writing task. Work by a wide range of scholars over more than two decades has laid the foundation for such an environment, but shifts in technological capabilities and changes in the kinds of documents writers are asked to create continue to redefine the ideal.

The instructional approach that led to the creation of the Writing Studio and the Writing@CSU Web site has potential for enhancing students' writing skills. It also has potential advantages for teachers of writing and writing-intensive courses. By providing access to instructional materials and composing tools that support students as they learn to write — whether that writing be general activities such as summaries and reviews of literature or more discipline-specific activities such as engineering design reports, chemistry lab reports, and business letters and memos — we can significantly reduce the effort faculty might otherwise make to develop materials of their own. By developing communication and document management tools that support feedback on student writing, we can support out-of-class peer review and increase teachers' options for providing response. By creating support materials for faculty — including Web-based guides on integrating writing activities into courses, guides that provide direction on reducing the time needed to provide substantive responses to student work, and model course curricula and materials — we can further reduce the effort disciplinary faculty need to expend to use writing activities and assignments in their courses.

Our observations of instructors working with students in computer-based classrooms suggested an alternative approach to writing instruction, one that departs in significant ways from that used in most writing courses. When student writers compose in isolation, their instructional resources are typically limited to information obtained through a textbook or course notes. When student writers compose in an instructional learning environment such as the Writing@CSU Web site, they have access to a far wider range of instructional materials. In addition, through network communication and commenting tools, they have the possibility of obtaining feedback on their writer in far less time than would be the case if they had to wait for the next class or an instructor's office hours. The development of instructional writing environments based on pedagogical approaches that differ from the dominant approach of class discussion followed by students writing in isolation offers an intriguing alternative to computer-based instructional materials that maintain the pedagogical *status quo*.

Chapter 15

Approaching the Skills of Writing

Per Henning Uppstad and Åse Kari Hansen Wagner

The present chapter investigates theoretical perspectives on how to combine new information about on-line measures with end-product features. An attempt is made to delimit traditional approaches to writing, which focus primarily on aspects of the end product. In order to outline an alternative, it is suggested how writing and cognition can be operationalized and how awareness and automaticity are intertwined in writing. A pilot study of three 11-year-old bilingual pupils is used as an example of the theoretical and methodological questions raised in this chapter. This example shows how pupils exploit their pausing time differently, and how on-line measures add information to the profile drawn from end-product measures. The chapter presents a model for the skills of writing. This model is considered to be a hypothesis, which is testable by further use of the on-line measures described in the present chapter.

1 Introduction

New technology has provided new information about the process of writing. The aim of this chapter is to discuss how to combine this new information with traditional analyses of written texts. A very important methodological question in this new research on writing is to decide what emphasis to put on the end product on the one hand and on the writing process on the other. A valuable goal for such work should be to find causal relationships — explanations — between process and product (Levy & Ransdell, 1996). The present chapter is based on the claim that the basic assumptions made in mainstream linguistic and psychological theory are not well suited for solving this task (Tønnessen, 1999b). By "mainstream" is here meant the heritage from the coupling of linguistic formalism and cognitive psychology, which is considered to have given rise to cognitive science in the 1960s (Gumperz & Levinson, 2006). Our approach is based on a coupling of connectionism and linguistic functionalism (cf. Uppstad, 2006). In the present chapter, it is claimed that a "common sense of text" has been challenged over the past decades, resulting in new

Uppstad, P.H., & Wagner, A.K.H. (2005). Approaching the skill of writing. In L. Van Waes, M. Leijten & C. Neuwirth (Vol. Eds.) & G. Rijlaarsdam (Series Ed.), Studies in Writing: Vol. 17. Writing and Digital Media (pp. 221–235). Oxford: Elsevier.

knowledge about writing. However, it remains unclear how these different approaches relate to a unified conception of the skills of writing, resulting in reductionism of different kinds. This situation provides us with a number of normative descriptions, but few explanations. Therefore, descriptions of different aspects of writing should be treated as hypotheses concerning the skills of writing. In order to be able to change skills, we need explanations. But first of all, we need a methodology for going from descriptions to explanations.

In this chapter we suggest a model for the skills of writing. This model contrasts with important aspects of the common sense of text, and it has the potential to combine various insights gained from the different approaches to writing. It is based on the theoretical insights formulated as thinking-for-writing (Strömqvist, Nordqvist, & Wengelin, 2004) and a nuanced understanding of skill (Tønnessen, 1999a). The benefit of doing so is twofold. First, we acquire a theoretical basis for how on-line measures relate to writing and cognition. Second, we acquire a tool for balancing two important aspects of human functioning, namely awareness and automaticity. The outcome of the chapter is an example of how the balance of end-product features and on-line measures can be operationalized. A pilot study of three bilingual pupils is used as an example of some of the theoretical and methodological questions raised in this chapter.

2   The Writing Process: Contrasting Views

For the case of understanding, let us draw a parallel between the issues of text and of law and justice. In the legal field, we have what we may call a common sense of justice, which influences most aspects of institutionalized justice. People's opinions about right and wrong are relevant to the legislative and judicial powers, both concerning the coherence and interpretation of the law and concerning the equal practice of the law. We also know that the common sense of justice is incomplete for the domain of law and justice; but still, it cannot be fully disregarded.

It is tempting to claim the existence of an analogous common sense of text. This notion could be useful when we want to highlight aspects of text construction that do not correspond to such a common sense of text. Further, it is required in order to argue in favour of a conceptual space for on-line measures in the study of writing.

The essential part of the common sense of text has been inherited from classical rhetoric (Levy & Olive, 2002). A highly influential part of this heritage is the focus on the functions of texts as well as the speaker's more or less intellectual construction of a speech. The rhetorical ideals of text construction were for the speaker to touch emotionally, to instruct and to please the listener. A valuable aspect of rhetoric — at least in its dynamic epoch — is the attention directed towards language and linguistic choices likely to be successful in actual speech. According to this position, success in speaking is evaluated according to the agreement of intention and effect. In the course of history, as rhetoric was institutionalized by the Church — e.g., in scholasticism, — rhetoric became formalized and static. The unhappy outcome was the maintenance of the formalistic focus but the loss of the pragmatic source for the rhetorical work. This tradition has had a huge impact on how the process of text writing is considered up to our own time. We could say that the history of rhetoric has nourished what we may call the common sense of text, and that reflections on text are oriented along the axes of the rhetorical tradition. In our case, two assumptions forming part of the common sense of text are highly pertinent:

- First, speech and writing are nothing but genres of text construction. This implies an identical or similar basis for the processing of spoken and written texts. In the history of rhetoric, insights taken from speech were transposed to the domain of writing without any important distinctions being made between speech and writing. For our approach, this is unfortunate, because on-line measures in writing are interpreted within the same framework used for the production of spoken language.
- Second, text construction is mainly a conscious enterprise. This implies that constructing a text amounts to carrying out the intellectual work of choosing the words that fit the subject matter and, further, arranging these words and the text in a convenient way. All in all, it is a matter of problem-solving and choice in order to bring about the fulfilment of the speaker's intention. For our approach, this point of view is unfortunate because it does not differentiate between awareness and automaticity in text construction.

It is our claim that we need to clarify these two assumptions in order to proceed in exploring the relationship between process and product.

The early focus on creative writing in the 1960s is a clear case of opposition to the focus on the final product in the research and teaching of text construction. In fact, this approach was a reaction to the rhetorical idea that text construction is primarily an intentional enterprise in which meaning is something we have before we start formulating a text. Furthermore, it was a reaction to the formalistic approach to text construction. Indeed, the early focus on creative writing highlighted the non-intentional aspects of writing, but it has been criticized for exaggerating the focus on the creative process. In short, this approach is in clear opposition to the second assumption of the common sense of text, but it makes no important distinction as regards the first assumption mentioned above.

The works of Vygotsky and Bakhtin (Bakhtin, 1986; Vygotsky & Cole, 1978; Vygotsky & Kozulin, 1986) have generated many interesting contributions to the study and conception of writing, placing the arena of meaning in a social context. According to this position, meaning is not intentional in a strict sense, because it is always second to the social context (Kostouli, 2005). And owing to its social foundation, text construction cannot be primarily a matter of conscious problem-solving, either. This aspect raises the pertinent question of how these insights can be coupled with aspects of choice and problem-solving.

Cognitive approaches stand in contrast to the common sense of text in their focus on the process of writing. These approaches have focused on and identified strategies in writing, derived from "think-aloud protocols" (Bereiter & Scardamalia, 1987; Hayes & Flower, 1980; Smagorinsky, 1994), and they are grounded in cognitive psychology and may provide a record of some aspects of the conscious part of the writing process. Still, what is left open is how "processes" and "strategies" should be understood with regard to awareness and automaticity.

In the broader context of cognitive psychology, the study of temporal measures and pauses in both speech and writing has been gaining attention (Levy & Olive, 2002; Levy & Ransdell, 1996). The different approaches taken in this context tend to be compatible with what Schilperoord (2002) calls a "basic theory of language production processes": "This theory posits four types of cognitive processes operative in text production: planning text and retrieving information from memory; formulating information that is retrieved; monitoring the text produced so far; and repairing already produced text." (Schilperoord, 2002, p. 71). He further states: "Almost any cognitive theory of production I know starts from this distinction" (p. 71, note). However, the "processes" of the widespread "basic theory" are problematic in an empirical sense, in that they presuppose the existence of separate processes. It is also difficult to see how these "processes" can be treated as good — i.e., falsifiable — hypotheses, given the following statement: "In principle, any interpretation attributed to a pause should be based on the basic theory" (Schilperoord, 2002, p. 75). Another point to be made is that the notion of "process" in cognitive psychology is claimed to be highly normative, and that "process" as a biological/physiological notion is mixed up with mental issues without any plausible explanation of how — or if — this is possible (Tønnessen, 1999b). As a consequence, the status of the notion of "process" — and therefore the basis of the "basic theory" — is highly vague and uncertain. Another characteristic of cognitive approaches to writing is the equation of production processes for spoken and written language. This is shown implicitly in Schilperoord (2002), where generalizations regarding pauses in written language are made on the basis of a speech corpus. In this sense, recent literature on writing shows that cognitive approaches tend to concur with the two above-mentioned assumptions inherent in the common sense of text, although they have qualified the second one in an important way.

The above-mentioned positions contrast with and extend the common sense of text by emphasizing aspects of text construction that have not been focused on earlier. But a major question still remains: can these aspects of the skills of writing be combined and operationalized without committing reductionism? The problem of reductionism can be illustrated by the well-known oriental parable of the blind men searching for a runaway elephant, where some got hold of the trunk while others got a grip of the tail; what they had in common was that they all claimed to be able to describe the elephant. Similarly, in focusing on one part of the object of study we risk overemphasizing the importance of this specific part without considering the object of study in its entirety. One major challenge when approaching the skills of writing is the question of how the different aspects of writing relate. In our view, the common sense of text is relevant to the study of writing. However, our claim is that we need to elaborate a platform for the study of writing that also contains plausible and testable positions concerning the two pertinent assumptions of the common sense of text. Among the contrasting views, cognitive approaches go far in focusing on both process and product. However, cognitive approaches also tend to concur the most with the two assumptions. What is more, Gumperz and Levinson (1996) claim that the rise of the cognitive sciences in the last part of 20th century is partly due to an interplay of linguistic formalism and cognitive psychology. In this sense, cognitive approaches are maintained both by a rich tradition of rhetoric and by a powerful combination of mentalistic approaches in psychology and linguistics (Uppstad, in press). This paradigm is strong, although its empirical foundation in both linguistics and psychology has been questioned.

The present approach does not concur with the assumptions of this paradigm; instead, it is oriented towards linguistic functionalism and connectionism. This is not simply a matter of choice, but is guided by high standards of empirical science. In the following, we will outline how various features of the skills of writing can be combined in a way that involves a minimum of introspection and reductionism. The objective of this chapter is therefore to outline an alternative model for the skills of writing — a model that should be treated as a hypothesis. In the next section, this model will be elaborated in two steps, which constitute alternatives to the two pertinent assumptions of the common sense of text. The first step represents a differentiation between speech and writing based on functional linguistics. The second step, which incorporates the insights of the first, represents a nuanced understanding of skill elaborated as a synthesis of behaviourism and cognitivism, based on the framework of connectionism.

2.1 First Step: Thinking- for-Writing

The common sense of text has no operationalized differentiation between writing and speaking when it comes to cognition. Most differentiations are philosophical and relate to the text as a finished product. We suggest that the study of on-line measures should rely on a model where cognition is not abstracted away from the actual mode of communication: speaking versus writing. This argument is empirical, because the assumptions made about cognition in connection with writing may then be exposed to data. Otherwise, "cognition" will be too vague a concept to meet the standards of the empirical science of writing. From the viewpoint of the common sense of text, on-line measures do not make sense. First, in this tradition it is not clear if or how written language is systematic in a temporal way. Second, on-line measures are considered only as more or less random aspects of the path leading to the final text. While the cognitive approach has made these aspects more nuanced, it still retains the basic assumptions.

In other words: we need to reshuffle the cards and find out how the different aspects of writing are related, and further to find out how the on-line measures fit in with a series of arguments concerning the skills of writing. Dan I. Slobin's theory of thinking-for-speaking (Slobin, 1996) focuses on how the speaker is influenced by the particular language he or she is using, thus concluding that this thinking-for-speaking is different in the world's languages. The title of Slobin's (1996) book chapter clearly shows the operationalization present in his perspective: "From 'thought and language' to 'thinking for speaking' ". Strömqvist et al. (2004) extend this position by means of the notions of thinking-for-writing and thinking-for-signing. According to their reasoning, the various modes of communication impose very basic constraints on cognition (see also Chafe's (1994) notion of "adaptation" in this context). What is more, the constraints of on-line communication are highly different in speaking, writing and signing. In spoken communication, there are strong constraints of on-line processing, resulting in a high production rate and few pauses. In writing, however, neither a lower production rate nor more and/or longer pauses hamper communication. Taken together, the approaches of Slobin (1996) and Strömqvist et al. (2004) may provide a powerful differentiation between speech and writing with regard to cognition. According to this differentiation, on-line measures become relevant as systematic effects of the specific constraints on writing. There is still a need to interpret these measures, but the major progress is found in how on-line measures are central to the skills of writing. Like thinking-for-speaking, thinking-for-writing is considered to be language-specific. In a sense, this means that the relationship between writing and cognition is, at the same time, both relativized (from a universal perspective) and operationalized.

2.2   Second Step: The Notion of Skill

Having established a differentiation between speech and writing with regard to cognition, we now arrive at the challenge of how to evaluate awareness versus automaticity in writing. This challenge is part of the conceptual work of relating on-line measures to other aspects of writing, for instance the "think-aloud protocols" of Hayes and Flower (1980). Our approach relies on an understanding of writing as a skill as described by Tønnessen (1999a), who maintains that a skill involves both automaticity and awareness. Common to activities in connection with which the term "skill" could be used is that they all have to be carried out with some cognitive participation. "In both the learning and the performance of a skill our cognitive faculties are engaged (cf. for example: Colley & Beech, 1989; Ericsson & Smith, 1991). It is difficult to say precisely what the cognitive participation consists of, but we know it is there when a task is done better consciously than unconsciously." (Tønnessen, 1999a). Skill is therefore seen as the flexible combination of automaticity and awareness. An important point here is that awareness and automaticity can hardly be assessed or evaluated separately; according to Tønnessen (1999a), the belief in such separability is a major weakness of assessment tools for dyslexia, which are based on cognitive psychology. This nuanced understanding of "skill" also implies that the balance of automaticity and awareness is not static in the language learner (or in any person possessing or acquiring any skill), but rather in constant change. By considering writing as a skill, we will stress that the basis for the study of writing must be the dynamic interplay of automaticity and awareness. Focusing on either part only will lead to reductionism: "The demands made on cognition vary from skill to skill, but the cases where a practical skill needs explicit theoretical knowledge or understanding are comparatively rare." (Tønnessen, 1999a). This also means that on-line measures are intertwined with and therefore relevant to other aspects of text construction. According to Tønnessen, the notion of skill is best conceived as a sound synthesis of behaviourism and cognitive psychology. While behaviourism turned out to be too mechanistic, cognitive psychology became too intellectualistic, and this leads Tønnessen to ask: "Does this mean that two important aspects of decoding have to be described by two different schools of psychology? Are two basically incompatible theories of learning being used to describe and analyse the decoding process? If so, is there any way of uniting these two factors under the same concept of learning?" (p. 92). His answer is that such unity is possible in the framework of connectionism. This position provides important perspectives on how primarily intellectual approaches – such as the rhetorical tradition and cognitive approaches to writing (Hayes & Flower, 1980) — can be related to approaches focusing on creative writing (Elbow, 1973) and to approaches with a social focus, inspired by the works of Bakhtin and Vygotsky. The danger lurking in all this is reductionism, and we should constantly question componential approaches to what writing is: "A skill consists of both performance and awareness, but is more than the sum of these parts." (Tønnessen, 1999a).

In many important aspects, we consider the writing process to be similar to the reading process. When it comes to awareness, even very able writers — as well as readers — need a certain amount of more automatized monitoring when writing simple texts (Tønnessen, 1999a). With more advanced tasks, for instance naming and referring, the writing process demands a more conscious steering (Tønnessen, 1999a). Different tasks locate the writing process on a continuum ranging from monitoring to steering, where every point along the continuum represents a combination of automaticity and awareness. Even at the end-points, it is never a matter of automaticity only or awareness only; the two aspects are always inter-twined in different ways: "Automaticity, then, is not the goal, but rather achieving a flexible combination of automaticity and cognitive participation" (Tønnessen, 1999a).

We have now presented a model for how on-line measures can be combined with other important factors of text construction. What still remains is to outline how we can relate these measures to aspects of the end product. This enterprise corresponds to the claim made by Strömqvist et al., who "believe that the coupling of on-line studies of linguistic behaviour and the flow of discourse in both speech and writing with analyses of linguistic information encoding will pave the way for a richer and more fruitful scientific investigation of the production, perception/understanding, and acquisition of language" (Strömqvist et al., 2004, p. 369). In order to find such a coupling, it is suggested that both end-product and on-line measures should be considered as important features of the skills of writing (Levy & Ransdell, 1996). However, to be able to explain writing behaviour, our model focuses on writing and not on texts that have been written. On-line measures should not be conceived simply as pathways leading up to the end product — such a conception of "process" represents only a slight modification of the common sense of text.

The investigation of temporal aspects of writing may reveal certain basic prerequisites for producing good texts. It is possible to identify temporal patterns that relate to different groups of writers (Levy & Ransdell, 1996; Wengelin, 2002; Wengelin & Strömqvist, 2005). The point here is not to establish isomorphy between patterns and cognitive functions, because that may very well result in pure introspection. We cannot know the relationship between patterns and cognitive functions, and therefore, in order to ensure their hypothetical character, patterns should be seen as no more than patterns. Rather, what we should do is to identify patterns of writing behaviour — based on on-line measures — and relate them to groups of writers who, say, write better texts than other groups of writers. This clearly amounts to extensive work, but nevertheless this is how to proceed if we want to explore the skills of writing and not only aspects of text. Based on this reasoning, it is hypothesized that profiles of writing behaviour can be identified and related to the evaluation of the end product. Temporal patterns show both the rhetorical work of text construction and processes in a biological/physiological sense. We cannot easily separate these, but we can observe how writing unfolds in real time and what comes out of this effort at the end. We believe that our model is well suited for this enterprise. With regard to the complex interplay of biological processes and rhetorical work, we may further ask whether assessment of reading comprehension can support the exploration of different writing profiles. Such questions touch upon the deeper relationship between reading and writing as well as upon the question of whether creativity in writing and reading is fundamentally different from automatic behaviour. According to our position, it is not.

In this section, we have argued for a model for the skills of writing whose theoretical preferences differ from those of mainstream linguistic and psychological theory in writing research. It is argued that this approach meets high standards of empirical science and that it contributes to a platform for studying the process–product relationship in individuals. This model suggests solutions to two controversial issues of the past century: the relationship between spoken and written language (cf. Linell, 1982) and that between automaticity and awareness (cf. Tønnessen, 1999a).

In order to show how these theoretical arguments can be applied in practice, we will turn to an example of bilingual pupils' writing in two languages.

3 An Example

Our example is drawn from a pilot project on bilingual literacy focusing on the writing behaviour of three pupils in their two languages.

3.1 Subjects, Tasks and Procedure of Analysis

The pupils in this study, called Heidi, Susan and Carla, were all 11 years old when the project started, all were born in Norway and all of them are bilingual in English and Norwegian. One year before the project, they had also all participated in the international PIRLS study (see Mullis, Martin, Gonzalez, & Kennedy, 2003), which assesses reading literacy in the national language (in our case Norwegian), where they spread out nicely above and below the international mean score (Carla: 609, Susan: 543, Heidi: 484; international mean: 500). What is presented here is the writing experiment included in the pilot study (Wagner & Uppstad, 2005). The pilot study was undertaken to explore aspects of the relationship between thought and language in bilinguals writing in Norwegian and English, in order to form more precise hypotheses about this relationship. We will first outline the method and design of the writing experiment and then go on to discuss some features of this experiment. Finally, we will show how these features illustrate our theoretical position.

The pilot study has an overall design of texts written in a specific order (see Figure 1). In total, the example consists of twelve texts, four by each pupil. The on-line measures are derived from recordings of these twelve texts. This design enables assumptions and predictions to be made about a hypothetical bilingual pupil whose strongest language is considered to be Norwegian. Upper-case letters in the figure indicate a major effort, while lower-case letters indicate a minor effort; "major" and "minor" effort here refer to the fluency observed, which is taken to indicate that some contexts are easier to perform in than others. In the pilot study, the design incorporated rather precise predictions of effort in performance, where Condition B was thought likely to be the most demanding (see Wagner & Uppstad, 2005).

The three pupils are all bilingual girls, with English and Norwegian as their two languages. The first two texts were written at the end of the fifth grade (when the pupils were eleven years old), and the last two were written six months later. All of the pupils attend Norwegian schools and all of them follow the ordinary syllabus of English as a

June 2002		December 2002	
Condition A: Norwegian	Condition B: English	Condition C: English	Condition D: Norwegian
THINK	THINK	think	think
write	WRITE	WRITE	write

Figure 1: Design of the study: for the group of pupils, Norwegian is considered to be the strongest language. Upper-case letters indicate a major effort while lower-case letters indicate a minor effort (Wagner & Uppstad, 2005).

foreign language. The texts were written in ScriptLog (Strömqvist & Karlsson, 2001; see also Andersson et al., this volume), an advanced computer tool for key-logging that enables the study of on-line writing. The program has a specific module for designing writing experiments, and in our case we set up a picture-elicited writing task using The Space Story (Nordqvist et al., 2002, Nordqvist, Leiwo, & Lyytinen, 2003).[1] The Space Story is designed specifically for 10-year-olds and consists of eight pictures telling the story of a space adventure. The pupils click through the pictures, one at the time; they are not allowed to go back to the previous picture. They always see the whole text that they have written, and they can revise it at any time. Each pupil's four texts were written in a specific order (see Figure 1): At the first session (June 2002), the pupils first wrote their story in Norwegian (A). Then, after a 5-min break, followed the second recording, where the pupils wrote about the same pictures, but this time in English (B). At the second session (December 2002), they wrote the same story again, but then they first wrote in English (C) and then in Norwegian (D). The fact that the pupils thus produced texts based on the same pictures four times will naturally have lead to a decline in effort. The pupils were told that they could use as much time as they wanted on writing, and we emphasized that they were not supposed to translate the story in the second writing. They all knew that they participated in a research project, and we told them to perform at their very best. However, they also knew that the project was voluntary and that the texts were not going to be judged by their teacher.

3.2   *Results and Discussion*

In the pilot study, we used lexical diversity as an end-product feature. Lexical diversity expresses the ratio of the number of different word types and the total number of words, and it is measured by means of VOCD (Malvern & Richards, 1997), a measure that also

---

[1] For further information about The Space Story, please visit the project pages of "Early language development, early literacy and dyslexia", www.jyu.fi/fennicum/wriproject/jld/ index.htm

takes into account differing text lengths. Although there are methodological problems involved in comparisons of lexical diversity across languages owing to typological differences, we believe that the differences between English and Norwegian in this respect are truly minimal. Consequently, the patterns of lexical diversity combined with on-line measures across the four conditions may give us information about aspects of thinking-for-writing in the bilinguals' language profiles. With regard to end-product features, the pattern of lexical diversity was validated by means of a traditional qualitative text evaluation performed by six adults with extensive experience of texts. It is, however, an empirical question whether the VOCD measure can in fact be the benchmark called for by Levy and Ransdell (1996).

We see (Figure 2) that the measure of lexical diversity decreases for all three pupils between the first and the second text; the effort is greatest when the picture series is unfamiliar. We also notice a difference between Susan and Carla on the one hand, whose lexical diversity is always linked to the order of the languages, and Heidi on the other hand, whose lexical diversity is linked to the specific language (Norwegian always has a higher diversity, regardless of the order of the two languages).

When it comes to on-line measures, we have focused on pausing time in writing. The notion of on-line measures refers to transition times between events on a keyboard, in which temporal patterns of writing activity can be studied. Pauses are studied by means of ScriptLog, and a pause is here defined, in all contexts, as a stop lasting 5 s or more. In research using key-logging, a 2-s criterion is most often used (Strömqvist, Holmqvist, Johansson, Karlsson, & Wengelin, in press). While a 5-s pause may thus seem rather a long stop, it should be noted that these pupils' keyboard skills are not at the expert level, and a 5-s pause is clearly distinct from their average transition times between letters. By means of this definition of a pause, we believe that what we capture are transition times that concern primarily the more steering-related aspects on the awareness–automaticity continuum. Our interest lies in how these aspects relate to different layers in the process of writing for different pupils. We believe that this is an important point concerning the flexible combination of automaticity and cognitive participation. However, it should be

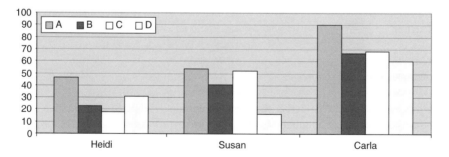

Figure 2: Lexical diversity: the vertical axis indicates the VOCD measure according to Malvern and Richards (1997) and the horizontal axis indicates the order of recordings for the three pupils (Wagner & Uppstad, 2005).

remarked that our approach represents only one aspect of the huge material of on-line measures provided by key-logging tools.

Figure 3 shows how much time each pupil spent on pausing in relation to total writing time. We notice that Carla's four texts are more equal in pausing time than the other two pupils' texts. What is more, Carla's pausing pattern is associated with recording order, as is her lexical diversity, whereas Heidi's and Susan's pausing patterns follow language in the sense that their English texts always have the largest amount of pausing in each session. However, the figure gives us only the overall pausing time; it does not say anything about what the pupils actually do when pausing. In the pilot study, we therefore defined three main pause contexts:

- Micro contexts, which include pauses made inside words and pauses related to correction of the latest word written.
- Macro contexts, which include pauses made before a major delimiter (full stop, question mark), pauses made after a major delimiter and pauses related to correction of something other than the latest word written.
- Pauses made between words.

These three contexts were defined based on an analysis of six different pause contexts, among which five were defined by reference to traces of some specific event and one was defined by the absence of such traces. The function of this latter type of pause context is most unclear, as we have no logged traces of what the pupils were doing. Nevertheless, this context is clearly distinguished from the other contexts and certainly involves cognitive participation in searching for words in general among poor writers and for convenient words among skilled writers. We expect to find differences between stronger and weaker writers as regards these different pause functions (see Wengelin, 2002).

Heidi's most prominent pauses (Figure 4a) are probably those related to the two texts written first in each session (Conditions A and C), and the pause context is associated with the function of planning a new sentence. We consider this to be a general pattern, due to the work of elaborating the narrative plot in a text. Susan's most prominent context (Figure 4b) is the one between words, which is associated with both English texts. Carla's texts

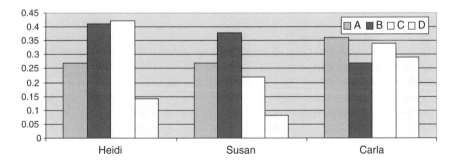

Figure 3: Overall pausing time: the vertical axis indicates the proportion of the total writing time devoted to pauses, and the horizontal axis indicates the order of recordings for the three pupils (Wagner & Uppstad, 2005).

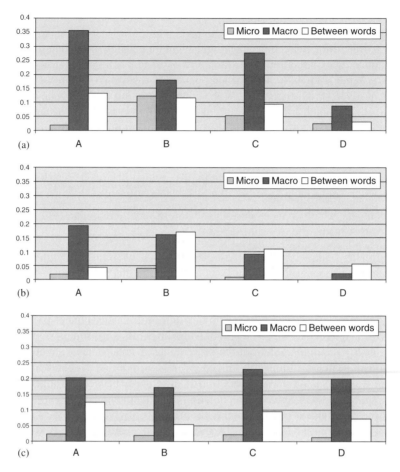

Figure 4: (a) Heidi's pause contexts (b) Susan's pause contexts and (c) Carla's pause contexts: the vertical axis indicates the proportion of the total writing time, and the horizontal axis indicates the different pause contexts in the four recordings (Wagner & Uppstad, 2005).

(Figure 4c), in fact, reveal no clear prominent pause contexts; the only possible candidate is the time spent on macro corrections in one of the English texts (Condition C). Across all three pupils, even when we look at some specific pause patterns, we see that they apparently exploit their pausing time differently (For a more detailed analysis of these profiles, see Wagner & Uppstad, 2005). With regard to diversity, a strong pupil, such as Carla, seems to benefit from her pausing; she probably searches for the appropriate word or phrase and thus obtains a high level of lexical diversity. The weaker pupil, however, will search for words in general, with low diversity as a consequence (Wagner & Uppstad, 2005).

From the analysis above, we have hypothesized that pausing time is associated with different phenomena. First, Carla's pausing time is longest in the first text in each session (Conditions A and C). Heidi's pausing time, on the other hand, is longest each time she writes in English. Second, the three pupils exploit their pausing time differently, as indicated by the lack of correlation between lexical diversity and pausing time.

However, the comparison of on-line measures and end-product features is not our primary concern. Instead, our primary interest is how to deal with cognitive participation in writing, because we believe that this issue needs clarification in order for us to proceed in discussing the relationship between process and product. Without such clarification, we will easily end up focusing on aspects of finished texts and lose sight of other important aspects of the skills of writing. Therefore, the on-line measures are not secondary to aspects of text; rather, on-line measures and aspects of texts are equally important features of the skills of writing. The distribution of pause contexts in the three pupils (Figure 4a–c) is interpreted as indicative of how different pupils' writing behaviour is differentiated with regard to aspects of steering. In Heidi's case, the indications of steering in micro contexts in her English text are interesting as regards her skills of writing. Likewise, the fact that the amount of pausing time in the three pause contexts differs across the conditions is interesting with regard to her bilingualism. When it comes to Susan (Figure 4b), she writes without corrections and without extensive planning. Her overall pausing time is also much shorter than that of the other two pupils, which indicates that she writes in a rather fluent way. Still, this fact does not necessarily mean that she is a skilled writer. In her case, the indications of steering in the pause context between words may represent an important feature of her skills of writing. Concerning Carla (Figure 4c), there are only minor differences between the conditions, specifically a longer pausing time in the first recording of each session, probably owing to the unfamiliarity of the plot. Besides this fact, Carla seems to do the same things in every context, and comes across as a skilled writer in both languages. The regular pause patterns throughout her four texts are a strong indication of her well-developed writing skills, with regard to both automatic and creative aspects of writing.

We believe that these examples show how temporal measures point to important basic insights concerning thinking-for-writing (Strömqvist et al., 2006). We also consider that the temporal patterns found in our pilot study — though limited — indicate that talking of "strategies" in a more intellectual sense is rather remote from what the skills of writing are really about. We believe that these patterns should be interpreted from the viewpoint of an understanding of "skill" as the good combination of automaticity and awareness. This is a point that becomes evident in, for example, Heidi's bilingualism, but it is considered to be of equal relevance to monolinguals learning written language.

4   Conclusion

In scientific studies of the skills of writing, we consider it a major goal to reduce introspection and reductionism. In this chapter, we have so far suggested that reductionism can be reduced if we focus on how different approaches to writing may be combined. Introspection can be reduced if we leave the intellectualistic or cognitive approach to writing, and focus instead on the important interplay of awareness and automaticity.

Still, these reflections only hint at the direction we should take. Without a clear scientific procedure, they are simply some interesting points of view. In approaching the skills of writing, we need a procedure in order to achieve our ambitious goals. The major tasks of science concern understanding, description and explanation, and the procedure followed in approaching the skills of writing should be differentiated according to these three domains. Importantly, the domains of understanding, description and explanation cannot be separated, because they interact. Still, however, they should be differentiated. We claim that the lack of such differentiation is part of the reason for the reductionism that can be identified in some scientific studies of writing. With the notions of thinking-for-writing and skill, we believe ourselves to be able to discern between matters of description, explanation and understanding in a fruitful way: Thinking-for-writing enables us to make testable descriptions of writing associated with cognition. The important interplay of awareness and automaticity encompassed by the notion of skill belongs primarily to the domain of explanation.

In approaching the skills of writing, researchers should be conscious of which domain (understanding, description or explanation) they are focusing on at different points of time. We believe that the confusion of these domains hampers both progress in research and success in teaching. The domain of understanding is primarily about the immediate experience of a phenomenon, involving empathy. The domain of description is primarily about the logical coherence of conscious knowledge, with an emphasis on cognitive/intellectual abilities. The description is not objective, owing to subjective limitations in the use of language and in perception. The domain of explanation is reserved for causal relations. The units of description should not be used *a priori* in the causal explanation, in order to avoid circular explanations. In our case, the patterns of on-line measures concern primarily the domain of description. These patterns are hypothetical constructs, which relate to the domains of both understanding and explanation, but without being fully valid in either of them. This clearly indicates how the domains cannot be separated, even though they must still be differentiated. When these patterns are used in explanations, their hypothetical character cannot be overestimated. If differentiation is not maintained, what we will get are descriptions disguised as explanations. Such a situation will be fatal to teaching. When we emphasize the interplay of automaticity and awareness, we raise questions of the common denominator of the skills of writing. At the same time, we also raise the question of the relationship between the skills of reading and writing. These questions are highly related to matters of explanation. Reading and writing performance can be described differently, but the question is whether they can be explained in similar ways.

We should note that the coupling of on-line measures and end-product assessment is primarily a matter of description, not of explanation. Levy and Ransdell (1996) highlight the importance of finding causal relationships — explanations: "[I]t would be important to know whether this relation is causal or merely correlational. If it is causal, then possibly with a sufficiently clever methodology, it should be feasible to intervene in the writing process, nurture the appropriate pattern, and thereby enhance the finished work" (p. 159). Our contribution to such a methodology is a model for the skills of writing that has a potential for explanation and avoids introspection. The connectionist position maintained by Tønnessen (1999a) represents a framework for explaining how patterns come about, in a way that cognitive psychology and folk psychology never could. In teaching writing, both understanding and explanation are required. The teacher must focus on aspects of writing that can be understood, and further reflect on explanations in order to provoke change and progress. As for researchers, their scientific enterprise is continuously to differentiate between — not separate — the domains in order to gain new insights and ensure the quality of the research. Following the pathway outlined here, this amounts to keeping temporal patterns as hypothetical patterns in descriptions without connecting them directly to cognitive functioning. This indirect, hypothetical relationship is what lies in the notion of skill, where awareness cannot be separated from automaticity.

In this chapter, we have argued for the relevance of temporal patterns in text writing. These patterns are descriptive, and the question of this chapter is how to relate them to the process of writing. In our effort to approach the skills of writing, we have exemplified how to conceive of cognitive participation in writing. This is first done by drawing on the position of thinking-for-writing (Strömqvist et al., 2004), which provides a basis for the description of central aspects of the skills of writing. This theoretical position further opens for a nuanced conception of "skill" (Tønnessen, 1999a) in order to explain central aspects of the skills of writing.

It may be questioned whether we need a theoretical platform that may appear as additional to mainstream theory. As an evaluation criterion, one may investigate the risk of circularity, introspection and reductionism in the different platforms. Such flaws of science are proposed to be identifiable in the lack of differentiation concerning description, explanation and matters of understanding.

Section V:

Social and Philosophical Aspects of Writing and Digital Media

Chapter 16

Bilingual Literacy and a Modern Digital Divide

Sarah Ransdell, Naheel Baker, Gillian Sealy and Carol Moore

The increasing social, economic and linguistic disparities among American students has consistently been a critical issue in education. As the role of digital technology continues to gain importance within the educational system, these inequalities have intensified to an even more obvious extent. This is evidenced by the substantial number of children in the South Florida region who are especially at risk for academic underachievement because they and their schools experience a "digital divide" caused by complex factors. The current digital divide is not simply about economic resources, but it is instead a combination of several factors: how computers and other digital resources are used in school and in the home, if and when they are available; how economic conditions interact with language use and background; and the under-representation of the Spanish language among Internet sources.

1 Introduction

1.1 Definitions of Digital Divide

In this age of increased computer accessibility and affordability, there continues to be a digital divide separating people along social, economic and linguistically diverse lines. Originally, the term "digital divide" was reserved for what was primarily an economic divide. Those with technological resources could use them for writing and other forms of instruction, while those without, simply could not (Warschauer, 2003a). A modern digital divide is defined here as a persistent separation among those who have adequate computer resources, including social resources, such as support staff, teacher training, and scheduled upgrades, and those who do not (i.e., Kling, 1998; Warschauer, 2003a, 2003b). A working definition must include social, economic and linguistic factors that account for the divide.

Ransdell, S., Baker, N., Sealy, G., & Moore, C. (2005). Bilingual literacy and a modern digital divide. In L. Van Waes, M. Leijten & C. Neuwirth (Vol. Eds.) & G. Rijlaarsdam (Series Ed.), Studies in Writing: Vol. 17. Writing and Digital Media (pp. 239–252). Oxford: Elsevier.

This research will discuss these factors as they relate to parent educational attainment, computer usage at home and school, levels of income among various ethnic groups and the technological obstacles faced by those who speak some form of non-standard English in southeastern America. Social characteristics include level of education of the parents and values about computer use in the home and school. Economic factors encompass family income levels that continue to vary among ethnic and language groups. Linguistics factors refer to the use of Standard English in the school and students for whom Standard English is not the primary language in the home. Hawisher and Selfe (this volume) show, in their case by qualitative data from non-Western societies, that literacy practices are increasingly embedded within complex social and cultural systems. Even though we present quantitative data from an urban region of America, we too find such complexity, as well as the persistence of a digital divide. The purpose of the chapter is to describe the concept of a digital divide, discuss what is known about a modern digital divide, and identify research questions that remain to be addressed, especially as they are related to writing and digital media.

1.2   History of the Concept of Digital Divide and Its Refinements

There are many "divides" that characterize modern societies (Lee & Bean, 2004). Kling (1998) has conceptualized the digital divide as having a technical aspect referring to availability of the infrastructure, the hardware and the software, and a social aspect referring to the skills required to manipulate technical resources. Keniston (http://web.mit.edu/~kken/Public/papers1/Language%20Power%20Software.htm) further distinguishes four social divisions: those who are rich and powerful and those who are not, those who speak English and those who do not, those who live in technically well-established regions and those who do not, and those who are technically savvy and those who are not. Keniston also stresses the importance of the part played by the cultural hegemony of Internet-dominant languages. The present study will focus primarily on the first two sources of social division, those for whom socioeconomic, and linguistic differences persist. The dominance of English on the Internet will also be included in an analysis of the factors affecting a digital divide in South Florida.

Most recently, the term "digital divide" is being replaced in some areas by the term "digital equity" (i.e., Solomon, Allen, & Resta, 2003; Warschauer, 2003b). The term digital equity suggests a rebalancing of the equation that keeps disadvantaged groups, those who are poor and non-native speakers of English, from taking advantage of all that digital media can do to improve literacy. For example, Solomon et al. use the term digital equity in the context of providing practical suggestions to teachers for creating powerful learning environments. The present study looks at the factors impeding progress toward such equity in the South Florida region of America.

1.3   The Research Problem: Bilingual Literacy as a Neglected Factor in the Digital Divide

Knowledge and use of digital technology has been found to magnify existing inequalities within schools and society (Warschauer, 2003a, b) and especially among bilinguals

(Ransdell, Brown, & Baker, 2005). In many parts of the world, bilingualism offers an economic and cultural advantage; however, bilingualism in America can often mean just the opposite, particularly for recent immigrants. For example, impoverished schools in South Florida often have high percentages of bilingual students who speak English at school, but heritage languages, such as Spanish, Portuguese and Haitian-Creole at home. In the Broward School District in South Florida, nearly 20% of children were found to be limited English proficient (LEP) in schools with higher populations of childhood poverty, and only 10% were LEP in schools with more economically advantaged children (Ransdell et al., 2005). Ransdell et al. have recently found that childhood poverty is the best predictor of school-level writing and reading performance. LEP status was no longer predictive of literacy when economic disadvantage was considered in a multifactor model.

The question of bilingual literacy is then directly tied to social and economic, as well as linguistic factors. In this research, we document how poor bilingual children are increasingly disadvantaged by a modern digital divide. This divide is more complex in nature and can no longer be explained by merely separating those who have computers from those who do not, which was the norm at the end of the 20th century when personal computers debuted (Kling, 1998; Warschauer, 2003a, 2003b). Less affluent bilingual students are doubly disadvantaged by the impact that their economic environment can have on their opportunities for computer literacy advancement. Poor children who do not speak Standard English at home have teachers who are less well trained in digital technology than economically advantaged children who speak Standard English as their native tongue. Bilingual children also notice that their heritage languages, particularly Spanish, are not as prevalently heard or used outside their family life and this impression is echoed in relation to linguistic use on the World Wide Web (WWW). These factors will undoubtedly affect the ability of children to take advantage of reading and writing technology that has become increasingly available to those on the "positive" side of the divide (i.e., MacArthur, this volume; Palmquist, this volume).

In Southern California as in South Florida, bilingual children are more likely to attend less affluent public schools than their monolingual peers. Thirty percent of children in low socioeconomic status (SES) schools in Southern California were found to be non-native speakers of Standard English, while less than 10% were non-native speakers in high SES schools (Warshauer, 2003a, b). School SES has traditionally been defined as a composite of parent educational attainment and occupational status at the child level; at the school level, it is defined as the percentage of children receiving free or reduced lunch in the school, as well as family income and house values within the school neighborhood (Hecht & Greenfield, 2001; Hogan, 1972). Without question, an environment of poverty remains one of the most substantial risk factors to school performance (Evans, 2004). As a group, children from lower SES backgrounds are more likely to have difficulty in developing academic skills when compared to children from higher SES backgrounds, especially during the elementary school years (Hecht & Greenfield, 2001; Hecht, Burgess, Torgesen, Wagner, & Rashotte, 2000; Hogan, 1972). But it is not impoverishment *per se* that can lead to limited use of computer technology. Warschauer (2003a) found that while computers were available in poor schools, they were less well integrated with literacy instruction, teachers were less well-trained to use them, children did not have computers at home, and computers and Internet resources were consequently less valued than in more affluent schools. Of course, the argument can be made that this lack of training is a result of the economic conditions of the neighborhood, which affects school finances and ability. So, the integration of technology could still arguably be a result of general poverty. For new teachers, the ability to take additional courses that emphasize the use of technology within the curriculum may also be restricted as a result of finances. The lack of computers at home for students is also a result of finances in the home. Ransdell et al., however, found that it was the poverty of the child rather than school expenditures that predicted writing and reading in their study of over 250 elementary, middle and high schools representing 270,000 children.

SES is more likely to be an important predictor of bilingual literacy than it is for monolingual literacy. Ransdell and Wengelin (2003) have found that bilingual children in South Florida were reliably poorer in English vocabulary, but similar in other measures of literacy, such as English writing quality and reading comprehension. Sixty-seven percent of the variance in bilingual children's writing quality was accounted for solely by SES and grammar awareness. No significant variance was attributed to SES in the monolingual children's writing quality, even though SES was widely distributed in both groups. The full model included most known predictors of literacy, such as phonological awareness, grammar awareness, receptive vocabulary, reading comprehension, writing fluency, home literacy, and SES. Furthermore, bilingual status alone did not account for variance in English writing quality when these other variables were taken into account. Despite a high percentage of bilingual children living in relatively impoverished circumstances, these children were as able to create high-quality English writing as their monolingual peers. This result, suggests that bilingualism may bring positive benefits that can offset low vocabulary and low SES, such as language richness or sociolinguistic status (Ransdell & Nadel, 2005) and precocious metalinguistic awareness (Arecco & Ransdell, 2002; Bialystok, 1988; Ransdell & Arecco, 2001).

In attempting to disentangle language richness from poverty in South Florida, Ransdell and Nadel found evidence for the predictive power of a new measure called sociolinguistic status or SLS. They found that one aspect of SLS, tolerance to languages that are perceived to have a negative status, such as Haitian-Creole, was positively correlated with English writing quality among both monolingual and bilingual college students. The study involved asking students to respond to hypothetical scenarios about the use of languages other than English. Students that expressed tolerance, especially to Creole, were found to be better writers. This correlation is provocative because it suggests that students of roughly equal English language instruction have stronger skills if they are more accepting of bilingualism, regardless of whether they are bilingual or not. The influence of economic factors, SES, and linguistic factors, SLS, to bilingual literacy will need to include a much wider view of possible correlates than in past research. Research must also situate the bilingualism within its geographic and cultural context. We present three reports from archival web-based searches that highlight Florida's modern digital divide and demonstrate the under-representation of Spanish among Internet sources.

1.4   Importance of the Problem

Public schools in the United States are facing a series of changes related to ethnic and linguistic demographics, technological utilization, and academic accountability, all of which will have an affect on student academic performance. The bilingual population in

America is on the rise, and this is especially apparent in parts of the country where Spanish-speaking families are likely to emigrate, such as Florida, Texas, New York, and California. In South Florida, the number of bilingual students in the BSD continues to increase at a rapid rate. According to the 1990 US Census Bureau, 17.3% of the population in Florida spoke a language other than English at home, with Spanish the predominant home language. By 2000, this percentage was 23.1%. At the same time the increasing numbers of bilingual children begin school in South Florida, computers and Internet-based resources have become more ubiquitous as learning tools in the classroom. An additional trend is that schools are being held more accountable for academic performance than in previous years. The consequences of unequal access to digital technology and human resources are many.

1.5   *Relation of the Problem to Writing and Technology*

Since accountability of public schools is on the rise, and is now including measures of writing to existing standardized measures of reading and math skill, it is even more important to acknowledge and understand how the digital divide contributes to technological advances in teaching writing. On the one hand, digital media can serve to "democratize" access to literature, writing tools and tutorials, and information databases that can assist young writers. But there is growing evidence that the digital divide is increasing rather than decreasing. The focus of the present research is to highlight limits to widespread access to digital materials for assisting writing instruction and show that they are not just economic, but social and linguistically based as well.

Next, we illustrate resource differences among South Florida school children as revealed in three web-based archival reports. The first archival report is specifically about web-based information pertaining to the modern digital divide in Florida. The second report is about the kinds of linguistic, social, and economic factors that are highlighted in websites in our school district in South Florida. The third report highlights the under-representation of the Spanish language on the Internet. Following these reports, we provide some conclusions about encouraging bilingual literacy and reducing the digital divide as well as discuss some remaining research questions.

2   Method and Results of the Present Study

The present study employs archival data endorsed or conducted by a government or independent agency in the US. Sources included the National Center for Educational Statistics, the US Census Bureau, the Annie E. Casey Foundation and the US Department of Commerce. Much of the data initially collected focused on economic factors and neglected social factors involved in the divide. In fact, as mentioned earlier, the term "digital divide" was first coined to refer to the simple lack of computers in schools serving poor children relative to those serving economically advantaged students. This definition proved to be problematic since computers appear in equal numbers among diverse schools, but resources and training do not. Further specific data relating to Florida, and South Florida in particular, was limited with regard to bilingual literacy and the use of non-standard English.

2.1   Findings Regarding Florida's Digital Divide

Among Florida children, 9% or 289,000 do not have a phone in their home, thereby pre-cluding Internet access. These children are poor, often non-standard speakers of English whose parents are not well-educated. In Florida, 44% of households do not own a home computer and 47% do not have Internet access. The national average is similar at 43% and 49%, respectively. There are 7.1 students for every Internet connected computer in Florida public schools and 7.9 in schools with high poverty areas. The national average is 6.8 and 8.1, respectively. While school computers are available, computer training is not. The result is that teachers have the resources needed to integrate technology within the curricula but lack the ability. Just as in Warschauer's finding in California (2003a), the divide is not a simple matter of "haves" and "have nots". In 18% of Florida's public schools, half of the teachers report being no better than "beginners" when asked about computer proficiency. This percentage increases slightly to 19% of Florida's high poverty schools with half saying they are only beginners, so there is no real divide in terms of teacher experience, most are under-prepared (US Department of Commerce, 2002).

The implications for including socioeconomic and linguistic factors in explaining the digital divide offers a revealing perspective. For example, the modern digital divide is increasing more among some groups, such as speakers of non-standard English, including Hispanics, American and foreign-born Blacks, and others. While school use is roughly equivalent across these groups, home use is not. According to a US Census Bureau Current Population Survey (2001), school use of computers ranges from 75% in schools where the average family income is under 20,000 USD (16,500 EUR) to 85% where the income is 75,000 USD (61,800 EUR) or more. However, there is a drastic difference in home use within those same ends of the spectrum, 31% in the under 20K and 89% in the over 75K. The numbers are very similar when using parent educational attainment rather than income. Parents with less than a high school credential have children who use computers only 23% of the time at home and 69% in the school. Parents with a graduate education have children who use computers 89% at home and 84% at school. Ethnicity records show that white children use computers at home 77% of the time and at school, 84%. Black and Hispanic children use computers at home only 41% on average, while schools provide computer instruction to them about 75% on average. Both Black and Hispanic children are also much more likely to speak something other than Standard English in the home. It is increasingly clear that social, economic and linguistic circumstances correlate with, and perpetuate, the continuing divide forming a coalescence of factors that need to be better understood. The diversity of children within South Florida's Broward School District (BSD) is illustrated by archival web-based data, which is discussed in the next report.

2.2   Findings Regarding the Broward School District's Digital Divide

With more than 265,000 students in the 2004 school year, the BSD is the sixth largest school district in the nation. An English for Speakers of Other Languages (ESOL) annual report for 1998–1999 stated that in the BSD, LEP students came from 147 different coun-tries and spoke 107 languages. LEP students then accounted for 12% of the total student population. Nearly another 25% were estimated to be bilingual, but not LEP. Data from the 2000 to 2001 school year shows that 21% of all children were considered LEP and another 30% were considered English proficient bilingual, meaning that the district had a total of about 120,000 total bilingual students in 2000–2001. In the 2002–2003 school year, 428 schools and 246,928 school children were represented in the BSD. In all 37% were white, 22% Hispanic, 36% African American, 3% Asian, and 2% multi-racial. No data pertaining to language background were available from this site.

The adjacent district to the south, Miami Dade, is the fourth largest school district with approximately 338,417 students (smaller only than Los Angeles, Houston, and Detroit) and an even larger percentage of LEP, bilingual, and poverty-stricken students. In the BSD, 37% of all children were eligible for a federal program, which provides subsidized nutrition to poor children. Free and reduced price lunches are available to students for whom family income is determined to be below 17,500 USD (14,400 EUR) a year. In short, approximately 120,000 children in the BSD speak a language other than, or in addition to, Standard English at home, and approximately 100,000 children live in poverty. Although not all bilingual children live in poverty, there is a substantial overlap between economic and language factors.

Students who are bilingual in South Florida are more likely to live in poverty than their monolingual peers because of the influx of recent immigrants from war-torn or politically unstable regions in the Caribbean, as well as Central and South America. Familial connections here in America are often the only way of rising from poverty. The primary focus of this research was to gather information on (LEP) students and Free/Reduced Lunch (FRL) students (a federal marker of poverty) in the BSD. LEP students are defined as those whose home language is one other than English and whose English proficiency is below the average English proficiency level of English speaking students at the same age and grade. There are also large numbers of bilingual children whose English proficiency is at grade level, but these children are not considered in this report.

This archival research looks at existing web-based information that is available, with particular attention to the following search phrases: Broward County elementary schools, Florida LEP students, Free/Reduced Lunch students in Broward County, LEP students in Broward County, and low SES schools in Broward County. The purpose of using this particular set of phrases was to define language and economic factors that a typical web search would reveal. The language factor focuses on students with LEP and the economic factor on FRL status. This research presents information on how LEP and FRL students are characterized within the school system based on web information.

This report is based on school, government, and state-sponsored organizations with web-based information from 1998 to the present. The search revealed numerous sources, but only those that specifically focused on information pertaining to bilingual elementary school students will be discussed. The report includes state-sponsored evaluations and reports, such as the National Clearing House for English Acquisition, reports from professional meetings, an ESOL status report, and various other school data. The report is organized around the terms used to search on the web. Each section of this review focuses on LEP and FRL Program students in general, and gives a brief summary on results that were available from the search phrases used.

2.3   Findings using the Search Term "Broward County Elementary Schools"

The search phrase "Broward county elementary schools" produced numerous web results but only five are described here. One website contained archived information pertaining specifically to the BSD. The site noted that in 1999–2000, there were more than 239,960 students, and 12,575 instructional staff with students from 159 countries within the BSD. When this is compared to ESOL data for 1998–1999, an addition of 12 countries can be seen in the following year. These data did not give the percentage of LEP or low SES students or grade levels in the BSD. However that information was available from another site, which noted that in 2000–2001, there were 35,407 or 10.7% LEP school children in the state of Florida.

The official home page of the BSD was one of the most inclusive and informative sites consisting of either information or links on various school assessment outcomes, program evaluations, research studies and annual school surveys among others. The site allows individuals to obtain the name and location of the closest available school(s) to their home and provides a link to that school(s) website address. Information regarding school calendars and district reports as well as other information pertaining to the school district could also be found. District reports include FCAT test results and school diversity characteristics, which contain ethnicity, LEP, FRL and ESE data by school, among other detailed information. Although some of the information on this site was available in the three most common home languages other than English, Spanish, Portuguese, and Haitian-Creole, information about LEP students was only available within the specific school's information.

2.4   Findings using the Search Term "Florida LEP Students"

In the state of Florida, 6 countries account for 81% of the state's LEP population and 3 languages account for 93% of the state's LEP population. The countries are United States, Cuba, Puerto Rico, Haiti, Nicaragua, and Mexico. The two predominant languages are Spanish and Haitian-Creole. The percentages of LEP students were arranged by district, level of proficiency, country of origin, and students' program participation level. The Florida School Indicator's Report was also accessible and provides LEP percentages for each individual school within the various Florida counties. It also provides comparative information regarding LEP percentages, among other factors, between districts. For example, in the 2002–2003 school year 10.7% of students in the BSD were listed as LEP while 24% of Dade County students were classified as LEP. For the 1998–1999 school year; the BSD was listed as having 20,091 LEP students, which was 8.9% of the total enrollment of 225,619. In 2000–2001, there were 35,407 LEP students, or 10.7% of the total of 254,517. That school year, 14% of LEP students were reclassified as English Proficient. Seventy-five percent of Florida's LEP students were Spanish speakers, 12.5% were Haitian-Creole, and 2.2% were Portuguese.

2.5   Findings using the Search Term "FRL Broward"

The results for the search term "FRL Broward" yielded only one website that contained information that was useful to this report. A PDF file entitled "Title 1 in Florida Schools

2000/2001 School Year," comprised a 16-page report on the Broward County School District and was compiled by the Florida Department of Education, Bureau of Equity, Safety, and School Support, Title 1/Migrant programs. Title 1 is the name of the federal entitlement for children living in poverty. The Title 1 report covered the 2000–2001 school year and contained data on preschool through 12th grade students in Title 1 programs within the state of Florida. Individual reports were available on 67 districts. It was noted that Title I school-wide programs were those in which 50% or more of the students were eligible for Free or Reduced Price Lunch. Eligibility for the FRL Program is determined by income level of the family using the Federal poverty guidelines set by the US Department of Health and Human Services. These guidelines classify a family of four with an income below 17,500 USD as being in poverty. The report listed student percentages by race, ethnicity, LEP, exceptional student education, and FRL eligibility. In fiscal year 2000, the national school lunch program served 227,539,159 lunches in Florida. Migrant children were included in these data, which identified 0.68% of children as migrants in the Title 1 program in Broward County, 21.44% were identified as LEP, and 30.25% speakers of languages other than English. The percentage of LEP students who did not participate in Title 1 programs was 22.67%. Overall, 37% of the total school population was eligible for the FRL program in 2000.

2.6 Findings using the Search Term "LEP Students in Broward County"

The search term "LEP students in Broward County" generated a very large number of websites, files and reports that contained information pertaining to LEP students and their situation in Broward County. A listing of 2003–2004 low-performing schools and their Title 1 school improvement plans was available for access. For example, a report from the school board for one low-performing school in south Broward outlined the school's objectives and accountability report data. The school community was profiled and included 7.9% LEP and 69.8% FRL students. A report from the ESOL on Broward County School District 1998–1999 school year reported that Broward county LEP students came from 147 different countries and spoke 107 languages. The report listed the percentages of the five native languages that made up 90% of the district's LEP population. Spanish consisted of 55.40% of the LEP student population: Haitian-Creole: 25.71%; Portuguese: 5.94%; French: 1.83%; and Chinese: 1.14%. An additional listing of the percentages of the 12 countries that accounted for 86% of the district's LEP population was also found. Several other files and reports listed the low performing schools in the district. One of these reports showed that in 1999 only 4 of the low performing schools in Florida received a "C" or higher (on a scale of F the lowest and A the highest), this number has since increased considerably to 88 in 2003.

This search also led to a 2002–2003 report that contains a plan to increase the participation of underrepresented groups in gifted programs in the BSD, an initiative known as "Plan B". Its policy is determined by a combination of the LEP and SES student information. The targeted population was LEP and low SES groups. According to a district gifted membership survey, in October 1991, there were no FRL or LEP students in any gifted program. By October 2001 there were 1156 (1.18%) FRL students and 293 (0.08%) LEP students in gifted programs throughout the district. The goal, as stated by the district plan, is to increase by 5% the number of students within each targeted group by 2004. In an effort to increase awareness of the gifted program's demographics, professional workshops have been offered to better understand the characteristics of giftedness in the underrepresented groups. Parents and members of the general community are able to nominate students via nomination forms that have been translated into Spanish, Haitian-Creole, French, and Portuguese. Clearly, policy makers recognize the need for better understanding of the interaction among language and economic factors in predicting school performance, however, there continues to be a need for further research. The next archival-based report highlights a different, but related, issue. The predominant language spoken by non-native students in the BSD is Spanish. While many people speak and use Spanish at home, at school, and in the workplace, Spanish language text is not well-represented on the Internet or other computer sources. This means that children who speak Spanish have little recourse but to consider it a language mainly for home use. Our SLS data (Ransdell & Nadel, 2005) suggest that these children would do better in English language coursework if they had a stronger sense that Spanish were valued in technological arenas as well as at home.

3   The Under-Representation of Spanish on the WWW

The advent of the Information Age and its subsequent technological advances has yielded substantial improvements in the areas of communication, globalization, and knowledge acquisition. However, access to these improvements may be contingent on English speaking ability while disregarding the needs and/or preferences of speakers of other languages. This report uses various sources of data in conjunction with independent Internet web searches to analyze the status of bilinguals in relation to Internet usage. In particular, the ratio of Hispanic websites to English websites and the Internet preferences of Hispanic households with Internet access will substantiate the existence of an under-representation of websites in alternate languages.

3.1   Findings

This report utilizes data obtained from the US Census, the Thomas Rivera Policy Institute, and Global Reach 2000, in conjunction with an independent website search regarding the availability of websites catering to Spanish speakers. In particular, the ratio of Hispanic websites to English websites was studied in order to substantiate the existence of a linguistic under-representation.

The Thomas Rivera Policy Institute, TRPI, is a research establishment devoted to the study of issues that affect Latin Americans within the US In their Latino Internet Content Study: Findings from Focus Group Sessions, the TRPI found four impediments to Internet use by Latinos. These obstacles included: (1) lack of Internet knowledge and subsequent intimidation of use, (2) lack of computers, (3) lack of Spanish language websites, and (4) lack of Latino-directed content. Barriers 3 and 4 exemplify the need for more websites that cater to speakers of other languages. The TRPI study conducted in May of 2000 contacted self-identified Latino individuals in five major areas: Los Angeles, New York, Miami, Chicago and Houston. Of those participants, 35% used Spanish as their primary language in the home, 45% primarily used English, and 20% considered their home language use to be bilingual. Home language use was correlated to Spanish language website use as more than half of the participants stated that they currently visit "Latino and/or Latin American-oriented" websites. In terms of language preference, 63% preferred English, 12% favored Spanish and 25% favored bilingual access. When the focus was directed toward Miami participants 48% of the respondents preferred Spanish websites in contrast to 27% of respondents in the Los Angeles market. Miami had the highest percent of Latinos preferring to navigate the web in Spanish or bilingually, 19% and 29%, respectively. Overall, Latinos that primarily speak English at home had a clear preference for English web surfing at 88% compared to only 2% for Spanish language websites and 10% bilingual.

One of the drawbacks of the archival data was that it did not provide a wealth of information on Internet use and availability of Hispanic websites within areas that were highly concentrated within a Hispanic population. To examine that particular hypothesis, a web-based study was conducted on the frequency of Spanish language websites in South Florida. The study was conducted utilizing the yahoo advanced search engine because it allowed for the restriction of results by both language and country. The search consisted of entering 30 commonly used search phrases with "South Florida" included in the search phrase. The advanced feature was used to limit search results to the .org, .com, .gov, and .edu domains. Results were further limited by language (English only websites and then Spanish only websites). A second search was conducted using the same phrases while excluding "South Florida" from the phrase, and a third search included entering a Spanish translation of the aforementioned phrases. All results were obtained from regular website hits.

The results from the first search yielded 98% more website hits across domains for all search terms in the English language when compared to Spanish sites, which yielded 2% or less for each phrase. This result was consistent with the findings of Global Reach 2000, which showed that while 7.2% of Internet users are native Spanish speakers, only 2.4% of all WebPages are available in the language. To increase the number of website hits available in Spanish, the inclusion of the "South Florida" phrase was omitted from the second search. The results remained consistent with the first search. In the third and final portion of the study, the search terms were translated and entered in Spanish. With three search phrase exceptions, results remained consistent with the previous searches. The exceptions were health (salud), news (noticias), and politicians (político) with noticias receiving more hits in Spanish than English within the ".org" domain. The most interesting finding was obtained by comparing search results between the English search terms limited to Spanish websites and the translated Spanish searches. 77% more Spanish language websites can be found by using a Spanish search term rather than an English term.

Overall, the archival and web-based studies show that there continues to be an under-representation of Spanish language websites throughout Spanish-speaking regions, which is only partially sensitive to language background concentrations within those areas. As a result, an evident gap remains between ethnic groups in relation to Internet availability, usage, and online navigational ability. The pervasive use of computers and the Internet within almost all aspects of society has made knowledge and access to its features a necessity in the modern industrialized world. Since the Internet is frequently used for research and work related purposes, linguistic limitations in the area could potentially impede professional and educational success. Social, linguistic, and cultural considerations must be made and reflected in websites in order to eliminate this under-representation. Suggestions for further research include expanding the languages to be studied, limiting participants to bilingual Hispanics (or other language), use of Spanish or alternate language search engines to obtain website results, a limitation of the study to particular areas with high ethnic concentrations, and an examination of the potential link between participant language preferences and availability (or lack thereof) of the language on websites. The issue of under-representation is particularly important in terms of the potential impact that the nearly monolingual availability of Internet content can have on students throughout the US school system. Furthermore, when Spanish language websites are discovered, they are more likely to come from Spain or Latin America than from the US, making them less usable for obtaining regional information and services.

4   Encouraging Bilingual Literacy and Improving the Digital Divide

Children are among the poorest Americans. In 1997, there were 35.6 million people living in poverty and 14.1 million of them were children (Arnold & Doctoroff, 2003, US Census). While over 17 million people now call Florida home, an increasing number live in poverty and do not speak Standard English at home, especially in urban South Florida. Poverty strikes with particular vengeance in the form of a modern digital divide. Most poor children do not have access to, nor do they or their families value, digital technology at home. Access at school is frequently limited by poor teacher training, which minimizes the use of technological resources within the curriculum, thereby minimizing student contact with technological mediums. At home, Spanish may be the language of choice. However, when children see that Spanish is underrepresented on the WWW, they may make attributions that Spanish is not a "world language" and that it is valueless outside of the home. Previous research on sociolinguistic status has shown that if children are intolerant of other languages, or see those languages as being inappropriate because of their limited use in the printed media, TV, and especially Internet resources, then both bilingual and monolingual children were less likely to do as well writing in English (Ransdell & Nadel, 2005). Students who read only in English on the web will tend to see English as the language of literacy, the school, and the workplace. This inhibits bilingual literacy in a way that reduces school success, especially given that bilingual children often are economically disadvantaged. Exposure to multiple languages, especially in print, encourages the early development and command of metalinguistic awareness, which in turn, improves reading and writing skill (Bialystok, 1988). Bilingual literacy should then be encouraged, especially through digital technology sources.

4.1   Encouraging Bilingual Literacy

The results of the present archival web searches suggest the following ways of encouraging and enhancing bilingual literacy. First, we should recognize that while a digital divide does exist, it is different from the one that occurred in 20th century America. The divide is not about the amount of computer hardware and Internet connections available in schools; instead, it is about the impact of poverty on the ability to reinforce technological knowledge that has been gained in the classroom, outside of the school setting. The value placed on technology within poor and bilingual homes is also lower, as many low SES homes do not have computers, and a large number do not even have a telephone line. The digital divide is also about the lack of computer training available to teachers in impoverished and middle class public schools. Second, it should be acknowledged that when comparing bilingual and monolingual children, especially in South Florida, one must be aware of the complex interaction among economic conditions and bilingualism. Bilingual children tend to come from low SES homes and therefore reports of monolingual advantage may be simply those of economic advantage. Third, the under-representation of Spanish in WWW sites can lead bilingual children to believe that Spanish is a "home" language. Children will not benefit from the potential gains in metalinguistic awareness when the two or more languages that a child possesses are not used in both speech and writing.

4.2 Improving the Digital Divide

A recent report from the Children's Partnership and the Digital Divide's New Frontier Project on Low-Income and Underserved Americans makes several suggestions for improving the modern digital divide. Underserved Internet users seek more "life information". Life information, especially for school-age children, is about online tutorials for different software programs they may be using in their school, tutorials that show the kinds of research information they may not realize they can find on the Internet, as well as other types of homework assistance. Students who are non-native speakers of English need online translation tools, English practice, and English for Speakers of Other Languages (ESOL) assistance. Older students and their family members would especially like more information in their native language about federal, state, and local government services, taxes, and transportation, in addition to local cultural and educational events.

4.3 Outstanding Research Questions

The following recommendations for future research stem from this research report. Native and non-native speakers of English alike recognize a diglossia exists. That is, English is the language of school and some other language, most likely Spanish or Creole, is increasingly the language of home in many families living in South Florida. Both monolingual and bilingual students should realize that language use is dictated by need, not necessarily discrimination. Bilingual students need to value their home language and encourage their family members to learn and use both of their languages in each context and to exchange languages when they can and see the need to do so. School-based research should include detailed demographic information about economic resources and bilingual status in order to evaluate the impact of digital technology and other teaching tools on writing and other academic outcomes. Researchers should realize that the relationship between bilingualism and poverty is often dramatic. Any researcher reporting evidence of the impact of language background or linguistic instruction on academic skill must consider the moderating effects of economic, social and linguistic context. Research on digital media and writing will be especially influenced by a digital divide that exists in some, if not most, geographic regions.

Research suggests that practical information available on the Internet will be especially effective in drawing those who typically do not use digital sources for information. Future research should directly address the rise of practical information linking school resources to those that might prove useful to home users. Other research should explore avenues for free or reduced cost Internet access in after school or library settings for those currently underserved by digital technology. Explicit research into current barriers to participating in increasingly pervasive digital technology should focus on why some technologies are readily assimilated, i.e., the use of ever sophisticated cell phones, while others are not.

Technology used in the American school setting and on Internet sites is almost always in English. Future research will need to explore the ramifications of bilingual language usage patterns when designing studies of the impact of digital media on writing and other domains of academic instruction. It might even be profitable for both bilingual and English-speaking monolingual students to discover uses for multiple languages and dialects in the world and in the classroom. The lines between school and classroom can be softened when digital technology, and the training necessary to use it, are available to larger numbers of students and their families. For example, research could directly compare the impact of digital media as part of in class activities with teacher assistance, with and without out class homework exercises that can be accessed from free local sources. Local sources, both those that are classroom based but after school and those in regional libraries, must reflect the language and socioeconomic conditions of their constituents. When local sources are made readily available, they will stand the chance of making a positive impact on both monolingual and bilingual literacy.

Finally, the dire ramifications of persistent unequal access to digital technology should be made clear. It should be kept in mind that unequal access includes the integration of digital technology with traditional technology, and sustained, effective teacher, staff, and student training, especially in areas that have high concentrations of non-native speakers of English and poverty. Research will need to track the progress of the digital divide and find out if patterns of unequal access can be reduced through integration of computer resources in multiple languages and in school and home activities. Studies of the efficacy of increased teacher training, and increased value placed on digital resources, human and otherwise, should be part of the research agenda of all educational studies that hope to keep up with changes in digital media and writing in the 21st century.

Acknowledgments

The authors would like to thank Richard Coff, Eva John, Katerina Nadel, Luuk Van Waes and two anonymous reviewers for comments on earlier drafts of this chapter.

Chapter 17

Literacies and the Complexities of the Global Digital Divide

Cynthia L. Selfe and Gail Hawisher with Oladipupo (Dipo) Lashore and Pengfei Song

In this chapter, we discuss the literacy narratives of coauthors, Dipo Lashore and Pengfei Song, who grew up a world apart, but who attended school in the United States for undergraduate and graduate studies and became increasingly immersed in learning digital literacies. Our goal is to demonstrate the importance of situating digi tal literacies, and writing more generally, within specific cultural, material, educa tional, and familial contexts that influence — and are influenced by — their acquisi tion and development.

1 Introduction

In recent years — and especially in connection with incursions by the United States into Afghanistan and Iraq — sociologists, economists, and technology scholars along with non-governmental organizations, such as the United Nations and the World Bank, have begun to pay increasingly close attention to the global digital divide, the disparity between people who have access to and use of computer technologies, computer networks, and the special-ized technological education needed to maintain a digital infrastructure and those who do not.[1] Although the relationship among technology, literacy, poverty, and human devel-opment are depressingly complex, the primary impetus for this work is the recognition that computers and other digital technologies may help bring about change – especially in regard to improving the environment for the acquisition and development of writing and

---

[1] See especially Internet in Iraq: Limited, Appreciated (2001), Norris (2001), Castells (1998), *Human Development Report 2001: Making New Technologies Work for Human Development* (2001), and the World Bank (World Development Report, 2002) for further discussion of what has come to be called the global digital divide.

Selfe, C. & Hawisher, G. (2005). Literacies and the complexities of the global digital divide. In L. Van Waes, M. Leijten & C. Neuwirth (Vol. Eds.) & G. Rijlaarsdam (Series Ed.), Studies in Writing: Vol. 17. Writing and Digital Media (pp. 253–285). Oxford: Elsevier.

literacy, increasing people's access to knowledge, and connecting them with others who have similar interests and needs. Information technology, in other words, can be a "critical tool" for advancing human development (*Human Development Report 2001: Making New Technologies Work for Human Development*, 2001, p. iii).

The timing for this recognition is no accident. Scholars have observed that two simultaneous shifts — the computer revolution and increasing globalization — have converged to create a new network age, characterized by computer networks that span continents and geopolitical borders (*Human Development Report 2001: Making New Technologies Work for Human Development*, 2001). These two processes, globalization and technological innovation, are mutually reinforcing, that is, technological innovation speeds globalization, and globalization rewards countries with high-tech industries. It is noteworthy, for example, that in 67 of 68 countries accounting for 97% of the global industrial activity in 1985–1997, high-tech production grew more than twice as fast as total production (*Human Development Report 2001: Making New Technologies Work for Human Development*, 2001, UN, p. 31).

In part, this disproportionate growth occurs because new companies, research development, and corporations come together in centers of innovation that are supported by massive concentrations of computer networks and equipment. Such centers not only attract scientists but also universities, corporations, and research labs. Unfortunately, high-tech centers — like technology in general — are not evenly distributed around the world. By generating money and resources, they also attract money and resources, thus adding to a global digital divide. Thirteen of these high-tech hubs are located in the United States, 16 in Europe, nine in Asia, and two each in South America, Africa, and Australia (*Human Development Report 2001: Making New Technologies Work for Human Development*, 2001, p. 38).

More important, however, is the suggestion in many of these recent reports that innovations related to information technology have the potential to benefit literacy, poverty, and "human development" on a global scale because they support educational efforts, help eliminate "barriers to knowledge and participation," increase "access to information and communication" within and across cultures; and provide a fertile environment for scientific research that depends on collaboration and the rapid exchange of information (*Human Development Report 2001: Making New Technologies Work for Human Development*, 2001, p. 32).

The dynamics of the relationship among technology, literacy, poverty, and human development remain difficult to identify and are overdetermined. Indeed, the nations that might benefit the most from technological innovation are in the worst position to exploit it. In Chile, for example, e-mailing a 40-page document to Kenya, costs "less than 10 cents" while "faxing it [costs] about $10, and sending it by courier $50" (*Human Development Report 2001: Making New Technologies Work for Human Development*, 2001, p. 30) — this in a country with only eight computers for every 100 people, 141 secure servers in the entire nation (*World Development Indicators 2002 database*, 2002, "The Information Age"), and 21.2% of its population living below the poverty line (*World Development Report 2003*, 2003, p. 236). Similarly, in sub-Saharan Africa, a region with an average of seven computers for every 1000 people (*World Development Indicators 2002 database*, 2002, "The Information Age"), only one in every 250–400 people has access to the Internet. This compares to a world average of about one in every 15, a North American and European average of about one in every two, an average of one in 30 for Latin America and the Caribbean, one in 250 for South Asia, one in 43 for East Asia, and one in 1666 for the Arab States (*African Internet Connectivity — A Status Report*, 2002, "The Current Status of the Internet in Africa").

Even more alarming, statistics documenting the relationships among computer access, literacy and education, patterns of regional poverty, and human development, describe an embarrassingly persistent — and even growing — Global Digital Divide[2] (see also Ransdell et al., this volume):

- 94% of all Internet users live in the 40 richest countries in the world (*Facts and Figures 2000*, 2000, p. 31)
- More than three-quarters of Internet users live in high-income OECD (Organisation for Economic Cooperation and Development) countries, which contain (only) 15% of the world's people (Human Development Report 2001: Making New Technologies Work for Human Development, 2001, p. 40)
- "30% of Internet users have a university degree." (Facts and Figures 2000, 2000, p. 31)
- Internet use is clearly concentrated (along the axes of wealth and education). In most countries, Internet users are predominantly better educated and wealthier. In Bulgaria, the poorest 65% of the population accounts for only 29% of Internet users. In Chile, 89% of Internet users have had tertiary education, in Sri Lanka 65%, and in China 70% (Human Development Report 2001: Making New Technologies Work for Human Development, 2001, p. 40)
- "It would cost the average Bangladeshi more than 8 years' income and the average American just one month's salary to purchase a computer." (Facts and Figures 2000, 2000, p. 31)
- "Telecommunications and Internet costs are particularly high in developing countries. Monthly Internet access charges amount to 1.2% of average monthly income for a typical US user compared with 614% in Madagascar, 278% in Nepal, 191% in Bangladesh and 60% in Sri Lanka." (Human Development Report 2001: Making New Technologies Work for Human Development, 2001, UN, p. 80)

These statistics indicate the complex relationships that exist between the rise of the information society, the uneven diffusion of technology around the world, and the global

---

[2]According to bridges.org, a South African organization dedicated to promoting "effective use of information and communications technology (ICT) in developing countries to improve people's lives": the use of information technologies is increasing across the board — in access rates, in content, in e-commerce, e-governance; almost regardless of ethnicity, age, gender, etc ... Unfortunately though, in most categories the relative gap between countries and groups is increasing ... . The numbers of PCs, amount of internet bandwidth, number of telephone main lines, mobile phones, and other information technologies are slowly rising for all countries, but the "information have" countries are growing fastest, thus widening the divisions ... . In terms of Internet hosts, the relative gap is increasing — the gap between North America and Africa was a multiple of 267 in 1997, by October 2000 it was 540. The entire African continent has 0.25% of all Internet hosts, the majority of which are in South Africa, and the overall percentage is decreasing. Nonetheless, the total numbers of users in all areas is increasing (*Spanning the Digital Divide: Understanding and Tackling the Issues*, 2001, p. 29).

digital divide. This relationship can be further illustrated by case studies that help us understand *how* peoples' literacy practices and values are shaped by — and shape — their ability to access and use computer technologies, and *how* people's literacy practices and values shape — and are shaped by — the global digital divide. Case studies can also help illustrate what happens when the prevailing patterns *don't* hold true — when, for instance, students in our classes from Nigeria, China, or Chile seem entirely at home in communicating online or when students born in the US come to the university knowing little or nothing about writing and reading and composing online.

2   Background

To help supplement the picture provided by statistical studies, this chapter offers two case studies of digital literacy acquisition: one focusing on a young man from Nigeria and the other on a young man from China. With these two cases, we hope to illustrate some of the complexities entangled in the concept of a "digital divide." We also hope to encourage researchers to consider a wider constellation of factors influencing both technology use and literacy. These cases illustrate that people other than those often named as the primary users of the new technologies (e.g., North Americans or western Europeans, who are English-speaking, white, and relatively affluent) can — and do become digitally literate (Selwyn, 2003). Later in this chapter, we discuss the fact that today's Internet is less Anglophile in makeup than earlier 20th century versions of the Internet.

   This chapter continues the process of reporting on a series of digital literacy narratives that we have collected from people in the US (see Selfe & Hawisher, 2004; Hawisher & Selfe, 2004) and abroad, many of the latter coming to the United States for tertiary-level study. The goal of this research is to extend our earlier studies of those born in the US to find out more about why and how people from around the world acquire and develop digital literacies.[3] We are also interested in how these literacies intersect with people's education and everyday lives.

   Part of the motivation for this research goes back to 1998 when we were inspired by an outstanding talk Brandt (2001) gave on her impressive oral-history literacy project. In listening to her speak about why some people in the US during the 19th and early 20th century had been able to acquire, or not, literacy practices as they are more generally defined, we realized that we were uniquely positioned to find out more in our own times about the acquisition of *digital literacies.*

   Shortly thereafter, we began a relatively large-scale study to identify how and why people in the United States acquired and developed (or, for various reasons, failed to acquire and develop) digital literacies between the years of 1978 and 2003 (Selfe & Hawisher, 2004; Hawisher & Selfe, 2004). We wanted to document the period during which computers first found their way into — and altered — people's lives before the cultural memory of this

---

[3]By digital literacies, we mean the practices involved in reading, writing, and exchanging information in online environments, as well as the values associated with such practices — cultural, social, political, and educational. For us, the term differs from computer literacy in that it focuses primarily on the word literacy — and, thus on communication skills and values — rather than on the skills required to use a computer.

important era faded entirely (Zuboff, 1988). Given this context, we also believed that it would be important to analyze the information we collected within the larger contexts of the historic, political, economic, and ideological movements that occurred during this period. And we wanted to reconcile, to register, and to bring into intellectual correspondence this series of perspectives — the macro-, medial-, and micro-levels — in the interest of obtaining a more robust, multidimensional image of digital literacy acquisition and development. More recently, we have shifted these stories out of the United States and have collected some 30 literacy autobiographies of individuals from Egypt, Taiwan, Bulgaria, Norway, Nigeria, and the People's Republic of China, among them (Hawisher & Selfe, in press-a,b), in the hope of studying digital literacies more globally. In conducting the life history interviews for our earlier US study, we had realized that our focus in some respects was too narrow — that if we really wanted to learn about the connections between computer technology and reading and writing in the 21st century, we needed to bring other people and other countries into our field of vision (Hawisher & Selfe, 2000).

From this research, we have selected the case studies of two international students attending Michigan Technological University: Oladipupo Lashore, a 20-year-old undergraduate student in Electrical Engineering from Lagos, Nigeria, and Pengfei Song, a 24-year-old Ph.D. student in Biochemistry, from Linqu City, in Northeast China (see appendix for international interview protocol on the Sig Writing Publications (prepublications and archives): http://www.sigwritingpublications.org/). We have focused on *only* two cases not because we consider them representative of any larger populations, but rather because we believe that close and extended attention to the details of personal narratives can help supplement and complicate our existing understanding of the information society (Castells, 1996), and the digital divide — that it can help shape this understanding from the granular perspectives of individuals. By looking through the eyes of these two young men, we seek a clearer picture of how macrolevel phenomena like the information society and the digital divide are situated — how they function at a particular period of time, in particular places in the world, and within the concrete lived experiences of two families and two individuals.

We have selected these two *particular* cases because both young men — while they are from different countries — have grown up during a period essentially coincident with the invention of the microcomputer. Both were born after 1977, a date which provides a reasonable starting point for examinations of the information society; they were in elementary and secondary school when the term "digital divide" first came into use in 1993;[4] and they were in college or preparing for college when the same term was mentioned in United Nations Press briefings in 2000.[5] Focusing our exploration on this important period of time,

---

[4]Although no one seems to know exactly when this term was coined, the best estimates are sometime in 1993: According to the Benton Foundation, the term was first used in discussions of the National Information Infrastructure (NII) Advisory Council by former President William Jefferson Clinton ca. 1993 (Fostor & Borkowski, n.d.).

[5]See, for example, the remarks of Harri Holkeri (2000), the then President of the UN's General Assembly, states that: Information and communication technology has an important role in managing globalization and as a vehicle for development. Helping to bridge the digital divide by making information and communication technology a servant of development is one of the challenges ahead. No one should be denied access to knowledge. http://www.un.org/ga/president/55/closing.htm

we believe, can help deepen understandings of the rise of the information society and its relationship to the digital divide at one key point in history.

In presenting the case studies of Dipo and Pengfei, we recognize that it is difficult to understand their literacy narratives without also understanding something about the complex relationships among language, technology, and culture. The high-tech expansionism characterizing the US and western Europe during this period of rapid technological development supported not only the globalization of markets and new transnational economic formations, but also the increasing exportation of Western culture and the "globalization of discursive practices" that "increasingly flow across the boundaries of culture and language" as Schoffner (2000) explained. Of particular concern to scholars during this period was the growing dominance of English. A frequently cited anecdote in discussions of this problem came from speeches given by US Vice President Gore (1994):

> Last month, when I was in Central Asia, the President of Kyrgyzstan told me his eight-year-old son came to him and said, "Father, I have to learn English."
>
> "But why?" President Akayev asked.
>
> "Because, father, the computer speaks English."

Comments like Gore's prompted Lockard (1996) to articulate concerns about the linguistic imperialism of English:

> English is local; cyber-english is global. A superdominant English specifically intrinsic to a computer-mediated technology base, cyber English has rapidly come to serve as a transmission belt for "free market" ideologies … . The colonial pursuit … has historically relied on over-languages to endorse a politics of subordination … . Viewed as a stage in this historiographic continuum, cyber-english is the latest extension of a centuries-long drive towards extinction of small tribal languages and consolidated expansion for a few languages of power.

Few doubted in the late 20th century that English had cornered the Internet.

It was within this dynamic technological and cultural context, then, that Dipo Lashore and Pengfei Song were born, grew up, and acquired both their conventional literacies and their digital literacies. Their stories, we believe, provide a valuable snapshot on the complexities of the digital divide for literacy and technology researchers in the 21st century.

3   The Story of Dipo Lashore

Dipo Lashore was born in the University Teaching Hospital in Lagos, Nigeria, on 27 May 1984, one year after General Mohammed Buhari took command of the Nigerian government, in a move characteristic of the political upheavals marking the country's history

Figure 1: Dipo Lashore.

from 1966 to 1999 (see Figure 1) (*Chronology of the Struggle for Stability and Democracy: allAfrica. com*, 2000). As Dipo recalled:

> I was born into military rule until May 29, 1999 when the Civilian Government was sworn in. There was oppression of the civilian by the military. The press was not free to publish the truth. There was no accountability in the management of the country resources. All the infrastructures were completely neglected and mismanaged. Electricity was epileptic, water supply was almost non-existence and communication was at its lowest development. Before I left Nigeria all these are being addressed by the new civilian administration. News reaching [me] confirms that things have started improving.

The third child of five in his family, Dipo's ethnic heritage is Youruba, and despite his country's troubled circumstances, he was fortunate to grow up in a family whose economic situation, as he described it, was "comfortable." His father, who had planned well for the emergence of the information society was a "Computer Marketing Manager as well as a Computer Engineer," and his mother, a "Chartered Accountant." Both parents were the first generation in their respective families to pursue advanced educations, an accomplishment achieved only with tremendous effort:

> My grandfather went to elementary school and can read and write. My grandmother did not go to school. My father has [degrees in] OND, HND Electrical & Electronics Engineering. B Sc. (Second Class Upper) in Business Administration. M Sc. (Marketing). My mother has [degrees in] OND & HND in Accounting and has professional certificate in Accounting

by a body called ICAN (Institute of Chartered Accountants of Nigeria). I remember when my father and mother were studying for the examination my father will be away for weeks only come back on weekends while my mother studied late in the night. She used to go to lectures and come back very late when we must have been sleeping.

With this background of intellectual and professional accomplishment, Dipo's parents both recognized the importance of schooling for their children. As he observed:

> My dad and mum value education a great deal … . All my brothers and sis-ters are made and encouraged to go to school to read and learn. My dad would tell me that I should try to strengthen myself to do the rigorous work of reading and that the end of the hard work will be greatly rewarding.

> My father and mother ... read at home. They read newspapers journals and [the] Bible. At times they do office work as well. For the purpose of studying for their examinations they use to read a lot ... . I could remember them stay-ing [awake] late into the night while studying. I could still remember my father staying away in the university because of [the] need to work undisturbed.

> [My parents would say,] "Your writing tells much about who you are so write well." and "Education: Is the greatest asset you can give a child."

Dipo was given formal instruction in English as soon as he began to attend elementary school, and he was also encouraged informally to develop his skills at home by his parents:

> I was taught or instructed with English right from my Nursery school, but I can't exactly remember when I began to combine the alphabets together to speak English. I would probably say that I started speaking English when I was in Primary one, in elementary school, although I initially made gram-matical blunders in my speech but I was encouraged to continue speaking English, especially when my father talked to me with English.

> If you include the Alphabet ... as "writing English", then I can boldly say that I started writing English in 1987, at my Nursery school, Onward Nursery and Primary school, Orile-Iganmu Lagos in Nigeria.

For Dipo, whose informal literacy education had begun at home, school was both a pleasure and a challenge. He considered his elementary school, for example,

> a nice place to get qualitative education. I really enjoy[ed] it because it was there I was motivated to always try to get to the top. I was taught discipline and morality here. It was a big school where we also do various sporting activities like running, etc.

> I liked Mathematics best because it involved tasking the brain and also mak-
> ing calculations which have only one answer that you will need to get. I liked
> English (essay writing) least because it involves being judge[d] on what has
> been written down on a topic and this never has one exact answer, therefore,
> one is unsure of what one is going to get based on one's piece of writing.

In his English classes, Dipo learned, "how to write or make essays, how to answer Comprehension passages and knowing the meaning of some complex words." In addition, he "wrote essays for competitions," although he could not remember qualifying for any prizes or honors in such arenas.

It was also in elementary school that Dipo first came into contact with computers — machines he considered wonderful because they provided an environment for playing new kinds of games. As he tells the story:

> Actually, I came in contact with computers at elementary school when we
> were ... taught the use of computers even though we did not use it often. But
> when I had the chance of being near any computer, I will like to go and play
> only games on it because that was what I thought computers were mainly
> made for. It was "Pac man" I usually enjoy playing ... . [I]f my friends ...
> had access to computers, they would prefer playing games on it.
>
> Because of the way I enjoyed playing games on computers, I thought at first
> of being a computer scientist. But later, changed my mind to ... Electrical
> Engineering ... . My entire family liked using computers; my brothers use
> it to do their architectural assignments as well as some other engineering
> homework.

In 1994, Dipo left elementary school and moved on to secondary school, one year after Moshood Abiola, a Muslim Youruba, won a nationwide presidential election and was forced to flee the country by the military ruler, Major Ibrahim Babangida. This highly charged event sparked a nationwide prodemocracy strike that ended only when the Chair of the Joint Chiefs of Staff, General Sani Abacha, stepped in, reformed the current politi-cal situation created by the former military ruler and formed a civilian Interim National Government (ING). General Abacha, also arrested Abiola, charged him with sedition, and jailed him. In the face of these ongoing political struggles, the Nigerian economy suffered. Although more than $200 billion in oil had been extracted within Nigeria, for example, the per capita income remained at $300 (*Chronology of the Struggle for Stability and Democracy: allAfrica. com*, 2000).

Such events, while disruptive to the nation as a whole, figured less centrally in Dipo's life because he was attending a well-known boarding school in Badore, Nigeria. As he recalls the experience:

> It ... [was] a very big school where I learnt to read more on my own than
> depending on teachers. It was a boarding school and we have time to go to

class to listen to what the teacher had to say for the lecture, time to go and eat at the dining hall and also time to do some schoolwork (like cutting the grass) and also, time for sporting activities.

[I studied] Mathematics, English, Social Studies, Business Studies, Yoruba Language (my native tribe language), Igbo Language (another native tribe Language), Introductory Technology, Further Mathematics, Physical Education and some other ones which I cannot remember now were studied by me in my Junior Secondary school. Social Studies, Business Studies, Igbo Language, Introductory Technology and Physical Education were removed and substituted with Chemistry, Biology, Physics, Technical Drawing and were taught in my Senior Secondary school.

To support his son's intellectual efforts and to encourage his emerging interest in computers, Dipo's father purchased a computer in 1998, when his son was 14 years old:

My father works in a computer company called Data Processing Maintenance & Services (DPMS) Limited, formerly called IBM World Trade in Nigeria. He decided to buy a computer for the family ... to expose the family to computer education. My father encouraged us by bringing a colleague in his office to teach us.

The computer was bought for about $1,000.00. My father told us that it would be deducted from his sales commission.

The first thing we learn[ed] was playing games. Later we started to use it to draw. Mum use to do her office work, i.e., accounting using Excel. We learn how to type with it. Later we learn how to load programs into it. We also use it to play music. We slot some textbooks CDs to play it contents. We use it to write letters. My brother who is studying architecture used it for aided design.

Since my dad bought a computer for the family use, ... [he] has been continuously encouraging not only me, but the entire family on making the profitable use of computers and not only on playing games all the time.

Using the computer was my best hobby. If I am not eating or reading then I will be on the computer. My parents at times intervene when I struggle with my senior brothers to use the computer. On most weekends that my parents slept I normally woke up very early to work on the computer.

By the time that Dipo graduated from high school in 2000, the political struggles in Nigeria had stabilized under the leadership of democratically elected Olusegun Obasanjo who reinstated the country's new constitution, drafted in 1976, and directed the transition to a civilian government with parliamentary and presidential elections. At this point,

Nigeria began serious efforts to revitalize its economy (*Chronology of the Struggle for Stability and Democracy: allAfrica. com*, 2000), and, as the time had come for Dipo to apply for a university-level education, his family considered sending him to Great Britain. As he remembers:

> My family never thought of sending me to USA for my education. It came by accident. My father went to collect UCAS form just for a trial to send me to UK. A friend saw him with the form and convinced him that it is cheaper to read in USA than in UK. This is how my father started making inquiries. I registered for TOEFL and SAT coaching lessons and the examinations. I did them and passed. This explains my doing my degree program in USA today.

> My family thought the idea of being in the United States was something wonderful and significant. They thought it was a place of real comfort compared to Nigeria. They think that life in the United States is far better than life in Nigeria. They would think that anyone in the United States is enjoying [life].

In 2002, Dipo was accepted at Michigan Technological University at the age of 19 and enrolled as an Electrical Engineering student, becoming one of 582,996 international students and 4499 Nigerian students to study in the US that year — 70.7% of them attracted to careers in computer studies, science, engineering, and other high-tech disciplines (*International Students 2002 — Data Tables*, 2002).

At the university, Dipo made friends easily and extended his own digital literacies. As he explained:

> My friends believe that the computer ... help[s] them to be able to do their work well and efficiently. For instance, it helps them to be able to print out their documents; they can use it to watch various kinds of movies. They can also use it to listen to music, book their flight tickets from the internet, make series of presentations and so on. They admire the use of computers a lot and for my American friends, there is no day that they do not use the computer.

Dipo, himself wrote e-mails to his parents and sisters, and contributed to the listserv of the African Students Organization. At the time of our interview, he had experience in downloading science fiction movies from the Web, visiting chat rooms, completing assignments for classes online, making PowerPoint presentations, creating poetry web pages, sending online greeting cards, doing research on the Web, downloading software from the Internet, working with his own digital photography online, and playing games like *FIFA 2002*, and *Need For Speed* in digital environments. When asked whether or not he was working with global information systems, CAD-CAM, simulation software, or 3-D rendering packages, and whether he was making movies, Dipo's response was, "not yet".

In terms of his digital literacies, Dipo noted:

> I would say that even though reading or writing in computer-based environments ... contributes to the challenges/problems I face when writing, I have come to like and embrace the use of computers ... . Making use of Microsoft Word to correct little mistakes I make along the way when typing out my homework is what I consider of great help because all one need[s] ... to worry about is the organization of one's writing. With the use of computer, one could make a lot of researches on different readings that could help bolster one's writing strength. One could even research into different readings so that one can know a lot about the topic one is meant to write about, thereby enabling one to make a wonderful, outstanding and superb writing.

Had Dipo remained in Nigeria for his collegiate education — had his family not been able to afford sending him abroad, had they not had the connections and the wherewithal to pursue this option — he would have had to develop his digital literacies within a very different cultural ecology. In 1996, for instance, when Dipo was attending high school and preparing for his university study in the US, Nigerian universities were able to offer most students only limited access to computer networks for the purposes of communication. As Alabi (1996) reported:

> Within Nigerian Universities, 63% ... reportedly communicated by messengers/couriers ... only 1% of respondents ... communicated by e-mail within their university communities ... . Electronic mail access was reported by only 3% of respondents." ("Case Study," 16.1.4)

In 2003, as Dipo himself observed, Nigeria had begun the long process of building a computer infrastructure, and some things were changing in his home country. However, it was also clear that such a process would be a long one. A case study of one Nigerian University, completed in 2003, indicated that only 8.2% of respondents had access to a computer in the university library, which "suffered from a low level of connectivity" and "restrictions placed on the use of this facility," while 45.2% had access to these machines in cyber cafés (Jagboro, 2003, "Access to the Internet, Table 2"). Today Nigeria continues its efforts to provide a more adequate computer infrastructure to bolster its struggling economy with mixed success.

4 The Story of Pengfei Song

Five years Dipo's senior, Pengfei Song was born 20 January 1979 on a farm near the small village of Yinjiahe in the People's Republic of China at the same point in history that his country established formal diplomatic relations with the United States (*A Timeline of China*, n.d.), and the first fully assembled microcomputers began rolling off factory production lines in California (see Figure 2).

Figure 2: Pengfei Song.

Pengfei describes his birth in terms of family lore and the government's attempt to control population:

> I was born in my maternal uncle's kitchen because I was not supposed to be born due to the population plan. My mother didn't dare to go to the hospital as she might be forced to do an abortion.

His family, as he described it, lived in a very rural area of China and "had very little money." As he tells the story,

> Everyone was poor at the time, but we were poorer since my parents had to support both us and the in-laws. I remember when I was a third grade student, we were asked to subscribe the "Elementary Student's Newspaper" for like 40 cents a semester. I was the only one who could not do it. I did not actually even ask my parents for the money since I did not want to add even a little bit to their already heavy burden.

> We lived in a three-bed room house with a big patio. We had our own well, own vegetable garden. We had chickens, rabbits, pigs and quails. The bathroom is a hut where the pigs lived. We had lots of trees in the yard. We used the trees to make furniture. We also made food from the leaves of the elm trees and the flowers of the Chinese scholar trees. Most of the time, hand-washed clothes were hanging out on a string to let them dry. [Here] is a picture I made a year ago.

To give a general sense of his home in Yinjiahe, Pengfei sent the following drawing and photo (see Figure 3).

Figure 3: A house in Yinjiahe.

He noted:

> Twenty years ago, when I was a kid, everyone was living in a house like the
> one in ... [this] picture. The corn stems leaning against the wall are for the
> kitchen fires. I think my house was a lot more beautiful ... .

> My elder sisters needed to go outside to cut grasses to feed the rabbits and
> the pigs, to catch grasshoppers to feed the chicken, to help fertilizing and
> harvesting the crops and sometimes to help with cooking. We used mostly
> dry stems of the corn, the soybean, the wheat to make a fire for the kitchen.
> Our furnace was made of mud. We had our mill to make flours. Many
> times, my sisters and my mom would stay up late grinding the corn around
> the mill.

Pengfei's parents, although poor, were nonetheless supportive of their children's literacy — albeit in very different ways. His mother, Yun Wang, had no formal schooling or
instruction in reading and writing — having been born in the same turbulent year that
Chiang Kaishek lost the battle for mainland China and fled to Taiwan; and that Mao
Zedong, who proclaimed the People's Republic of China, became the chair of the com-
munist party, joined forces with Zhou Enlai (the newly appointed Premier), and entered
Tibet. Yun Wang's childhood — coincident with Mao's national collectivist project and
China's Great Leap Forward (*A Timeline of China*, n.d.) — left her little time for formal
education. These momentous events did not prevent her, however, from sharing her family's great esteem for both literacy and education. As Pengfei tells her story,

> My mother was born in 1949. When she was ready to go to school, the
> Land Reform Movement started in China. Because of her paternal uncle
> being a landlord (He was shot to death when my Mum was 5.), she was

deprived of the right to go to elementary school. When she finally got a chance, she was already 14 years old. She said she went to the class once, and she felt stupid since she was so much taller than her classmates and she decided at the time not to go there again. Indeed, she didn't go and she is almost illiterate. But even if she knew how to read, she wouldn't be able to teach the children since we were so poor at the time and she had to do all the farm work as well as making handicrafts to sell to support her four children and her in-laws.

My mother sang to us. She memorized several articles written by Chairman Mao (which was made to songs). ... My mom ... [also told] us like whose son in the village had been admitted by the college, whose daughter was chosen by the best high school, etc. We all admired them and wanted to be good students.

My mother, thinks education to be very very important. She married my father because my father was then a teacher teaching my mother's brother and sister. My mother knew that one did not have to do farm work if he or she knew how to read and write. In the Chinese history, it has always been the educated people who ruled. She wanted us to be good students and could be at least a teacher after school.

She could not teach us how to read and write, ... My father would not teach her and she was busy. She had been a construction woman, a dustman sweeping the streets, and finally an officer inspecting the city sanitation ... but her encouragement and her tears did the thing ... . She now feels very proud of us since all of us had been excellent students.

Pengfei's father, Dechang Seng, was born in 1946, a year after the end of World War II, a conflict that saw the death of 20 million Chinese citizens. As Pengfei observed, his father

was the first child in his family. He has 3 brothers and a sister. At the age of 17 when his youngest brother was just born for a few months, his [Dad's] father died due to the poor medication at the time. Although an excellent student in his class, my father decided to quit school and start working to support the whole family. His fame of getting the first prize in a county-wide writing contest easily earned him a position in a local high-school. A few years later, he became a news-reporter writing articles for the government. During that time he published many articles on the national papers and he even published two of his own books. He is a really smart guy.

But since he broke the policy of the population plan (I was the fourth kid.), he had a very hard time getting promoted. He had been working in a city 4 miles away from where we were living ever since I was born. But since we had no vehicles, we didn't see each other except on the Sundays ... .

> My father ... [was] so busy those years that he did not pay much attention
> to us. But I do remember I was once playing truant and was caught by him.
> I got a good beat[ing]. It was the only time that my father had beaten me.

While the family lived in the country, Pengfei noted, his education was limited by both
circumstances and economic resources. As he noted:

> [N]one of my little buddies went to the kindergarten. Actually I had never
> seen a playground slide, a seesaw, or a swing until I was 7 years old ... . At
> the age of 5, I had a chance to go to a preschool which we called "Yu Hong
> Ban" (literally, it means "class to cultivate the red-army children"). But
> since we were poor and many other children did not go either, my parents
> decided that I could wait for another year ... .

> My formal education started in 1985 in a village elementary school. My
> class teacher herself was a farmer too and she taught us Chinese,
> Mathematics and Science. The classroom was made of mud and the stu-
> dent-tables were made of cement. We had to bring our own stools. In win-
> tertime, each of the kids was asked to bring a bundle of firewood, so that
> we could keep ourselves warm. Though there were not many types of
> equipment, we still had lots of fun. We used whatever we had (rocks, bones,
> vegetables) to do experiments to help learn the text. But there were no
> classes like arts, music, or physical education.

In 1986, however, when Pengfei was seven, his family moved to Linqu City, about six
miles away. There, he was able to attend a larger school:

> ... I started with a new school, which was a lot better. The first thing that
> surprised me was that the Class teacher (Chinese teacher too. Usually the
> Chinese teacher is the class teacher) required us to speak in Mandarin when
> reading. The second were all those classes of arts, music, and physical edu-
> cation. I remember the first time when I attended the music class, my
> teacher asked me to sing a song and I was wondering what a song was. My
> mother had been singing all the time at home, but I never knew that it was
> called "song" till then.

At home, Pengfei's reading was limited to his school textbooks and to an occasional
novel smuggled into the house by his older sister, who was coming of age in a period when
100,000 prodemocracy students and workers protested in Beijing's Tiananmen Square during Deng Xiaoping's administration (*A Timeline of China*, n.d.):

> [There was] nothing much to read around the house. My father had several
> books about world literature, but I found them to be very abstract and bor-
> ing. He also had lots of books written by Karl Marks, Lenin, etc. I hated

them too. I read mostly my textbooks. I got more reference books to read as a teenager since my sisters got some. I didn't even buy my textbooks. I just use[ed] my sister's books.

I also read my first novel at this period "How the Steel was Tempered". One of my sisters was a big fan of martial-art novels like "Crouching Tiger Hidden Dragon". My father hated it and burned all those novels that she borrowed. But that "How the steel was Tempered" was not burned.

It was at his new school in Linqu that Pengfei started his study of English, an effort he grew to love:

In my sixth grade, when I was 12 years old, we started learning English. I did not know almost anything about [it]. I was very fortunate to have a teacher who just graduated from the college and spoke mandarin during the class. Her pronunciation was perfect, thus I did not get too much bad influence called "Chinese-accented English" ... .

My three sisters like English too. I guess I liked it because my parents do not know anything about it. My father knows some Russian, but very little. He never encouraged me to learn English, but I liked it from the very beginning ... . On the first test after we have learned all those 26 letters and some words, like "bee, bed, apple, bag", I got a perfect mark. The teacher did not praise me, but I was proud of myself and loved English more ever since.

During the summer vacation of 1993, my sister borrowed a book called "New Concept English" from a rich classmate of hers. She liked it very much, but she did not have time to read it before it was the time that she must return it. Thus she asked me to copy the book for her since I had no homework that summer. I agreed and started copying the [entire] book. There were about 300 short English articles and hundreds of new words for me. However, I finally finished it. In that fall I started my senior high school ... . I noticed ... how [much] better my English was than the others. There were more than 700 students in my grade, and I always got the highest score for English.

There was once a national English contest for senior-3 students. My English teacher encouraged me to try and I got a much higher score than the senior-3 students. However, my English teacher never praised me. In the class, I was always ready to answer her questions and I guess she was not happy that I did not give the other students a chance. But honestly, I did not realize it. I loved it so much that I thought I was the only student.

Pengfei noted that many of his scholastic achievements were accomplished within a context of extremely strict discipline. As he remembered,

> The teachers in the junior high school would punish the students if he/she talked in the class while the teacher was out. All teachers in the school beat the students. One of my teachers once knocked my classmates head to a piece of glass on the table. The glass cracked and my classmate got blood on his head.

When asked if his school was segregated by religion, or race, or gender, Pengfei noted, "No. The teachers beat the girls almost in the same way as the boys."

Given his excellent scores in English, his growing love of Mandarin poetry and literature, his hobbies of broadcasting, painting, and singing, and his success in math and science courses, in 1996, the year before Deng Xiaoping died, the English left Hong Kong, and the new Premier Jiang Zemin unveiled a plan to privatize state-owned industries, Pengfei was accepted at Tianjin University, the oldest university in China. At this point in history, China's economic vigor had begun to show itself and the country was playing an increasingly active economic role in global marketplaces. In fact, the gross domestic product, in China, was growing faster — at about 10% a year — than that of any other nation in the world (*A Timeline of China*, n.d.).

In looking back on this optimistic time of national growth, Pengfei described his performance in most classes as "average," although he admitted that he excelled in the study of English. As a Chemical Engineering major, he studied scientific English, and

> started to keep an English diary a week after I entered college since I was told by a senior student that it would help improve my English. It was hard at the beginning to write it since I felt there was not much to say, but once I have been keeping it for a month or so, I could not stop writing. Sometimes, I would write a diary of eight pages long. I checked my old diaries I kept at the time last year when I went back to China and I found lots of mistakes. But I could tell that my English at the last page was a lot better than that at the first few pages. I kept the diary for two years.

Pengfei also enjoyed practicing his English in conversational situations. A bridge across one of the lakes on the Tianjin University campus had become a meeting place for students who wanted to practice their language skills in a conversation setting, and it became known as "the English Bridge." Pengfei noted that he liked the English bridge because he could converse "in the open area where one can feel the cool breezes," and added, "I do not like indoor Conversation[al] English." As he remembered:

> There was an English bridge ... at the time on campus every Saturday evening. It was a place that all the English lovers go practicing the oral English. I have been keep going there until it was banned. If it rained, we would talk in raincoats or under umbrellas. If it was cold, we would put on lots and lots of coat and jump to keep our feet from being numb.

I would talk there with different people until I was the last one who stayed there. The time I went back to the dorm, the janitor of the dorm would have already locked the door. I knocked for a long time and he would not open it. I went back to the building hoping that I could call my roommates out to open the door but they were fast asleep. I finally found a way to climb onto the second floor where I lived through a bathroom window.

The bridge was banned two years after because of an accident that happened there. I had been so angry that I sent a letter to the president of the university. He replied me, but he did not reopen the bridge. I felt empty and could not sit still when Saturday evenings came. I walked on the road, I talked to myself in English to myself. I was once thought crazy by some of the people and I was. I started to bother those over-sea students on our campus. Most of them were from Africa and their mother tongue were not English but they knew it. It is not allowed for the Chinese students to enter their building, but I found a way to sneak there. I had a friend from Guinea, but he would prefer to speak Chinese to me. Not long from then, I came to know another place that people could practice oral English. It was about 20 minutes ride on bicycle. I started going there every week till I graduated in 2000.

It was also at Tianjin University that Pengfei first encountered computers:

I had never seen a computer until I went to college. We were using Apples for freshman to do some Fortran programming for one of the computer course ... . The university thought it is necessary for us engineering students to learn a scientific programming language using the computer. I was 17 then. Freshman. They gave lectures and exams. The computer lab was locked most of the time and we could not touch the computer when the lab was over. We were not allowed to try any new things since they thought we would screw up the computers. [My access was] 2 hours per week when I was a freshman. No access for sophomore year and junior year.

By 1999, Pengfei had begun frequenting Internet cafes in order to complete applications for graduate programs in the United States:

I started to go to the internet bars to send emails to US because it is cheaper and faster than sending out an application through mail ... . I learned to use Word when I started the US university application [process] in 1999, then for my thesis paper. I used Note pad mostly. I had to learn [myself]. There was no encouragement from anyone. Everyone was learning to use ... [computers] at the time.

These same Internet cafes, Pengfei noted, were partially responsible for China's rapid entry into the global information society:

It was not easy before 1998. But now there are internet bars everywhere. Surfing the internet is no longer the rich college student's privilege. There are training classes everywhere to teach you how to use it. All you need to do is to pay them money. China is developing fast as far as computers are concerned. Now my father has a computer and we chat on the internet. One of my sisters has a computer too. The other two sisters are planning to buy one.

Educational and economic factors ... made this possible. Everyone knows now that computer is a powerful tool for people of our generation. If you do not know how to use a computer, you are considered almost illiterate and will lose lots of working opportunities.

By 2000, Pengfei had been accepted into a graduate program in biochemistry at Michigan Technological University and had been awarded a teaching assistantship at that institution, becoming one of 547,867 international students and 59.939 Chinese students to study in the US that year (*Open Doors 2001 — Data Tables*, 2001).

At the university, Pengfei continued to develop and expand his range of digital literacies. By the spring of 2003, six years after he first saw a computer, he was using these machines to write email to friends, family, professors, and employers; conduct research for his classes; download Chinese folk music and videos and software programs for his research; chat in real time; work on his digital photography; design presentations and advertisements for events; prepare PowerPoint presentations; study Spanish; send web-camera videos to his parents; make greeting cards; and play computer games.

As he described his interests,

Most of my Chinese friends are computer geeks. They learn programming and everything. ... [One] friend knows where to download everything for free from the website. I always ask him when I have a question. He would also tell me what website is not safe to download. My strategy is to ask my friends to go to the chat rooms. I know a freebie website which is really cool.

Pengfei's family now owns a computer as well,

My father bought the computer with my eldest sister's help. My eldest sister's brother in law is the owner of a computer shop and gave my father a good bargain. He bought it a year [ago]. I told him that I could talk to him for free (saving the telephone bills for me.), I could let him see me using a webcamera. [The computer cost] $600. That's like half a year's income of my father.

My father still only uses the computer for chatting with me and for surfing the internet. My sister is learning to use all the office files and other multimedia applications.

As Pengfei observed about his own increased computer use,

> There's no other choice. You have to do your homework on the computer ... .
> I think the US system is forcing people to learn how to use computers ... .
> I do not know what to do without a computer. I am not going to [know] what
> is happening in the world without the internet.

Despite his own accomplishments and his family's successful entrée into the information society, Pengfei also recognized that technology was still far from evenly distributed in his own country:

> Older citizens, people living in the countryside, people that has little education and people who work mainly as a labor[er] do not have access to computers. Since most programs are English directed, it is difficult for those people to learn how to use [computers]. Also, they may not realize how powerful the computer is or they simply do not have money to buy one.

> Computers are considered to be a luxury by many people. In my opinion, there is almost no sex or race discriminations in China. (Maybe in very few of the far-away mountain villages, girls are discriminated.) But if you are poor, you can't buy a computer. Usually inland people have less access to computers since they are poorer.

In Pengfei's China older people and those who live in rural areas often have less access to information technologies.

5   What these Case Studies Suggest

These two cases represent only an initial effort to help illustrate the story of digital literacy and the digital divide in a global context — and, clearly, they provide only limited perspectives and uneven information about these larger phenomena. We recognize, for instance, that both people presented here have achieved a high degree of digital literacy — and that some people would consider them success stories in connection with the digital divide. We also recognize, however, that many other young men — and women — in Nigeria, in China, and in the US and western Europe, for that matter, have not had the same opportunities as Dipo and Pengfei (Katz & Aspden, 1998; Selwyn, 2003; Drori & Jang, 2003). Our aim here is not to underestimate the seriousness of the digital divide or to suggest that hard work and determination — alone or as isolated factors — can help individuals and their families close this gap. They cannot. This recognition, however, does not diminish the value of the first-hand accounts told here. On the contrary, each of the literacy histories is richly sown with information that can help those of us studying literacy and its relation to information technology situate ongoing research in specific cultural, material, educational, and familial contexts.

In focusing on Dipo's and Pengfei's stories, we hope to foreground the conditions that both contribute to and detract from people's successful encounters with literacy. For us, the value of these accounts is that they present, in abundant detail, everyday literacy experiences that can help all of us — educators, policy makers, and researchers — better understand the many factors associated with the global digital divide.

The two cases we have included here help illustrate many of the observations we have drawn from earlier studies on information technology and the global divide and underscore the importance of ongoing research. Here, we identify just a few observations that Dipo and Pengfei's stories help illustrate.

Observation #1: *We can understand literacy as a set of practices and values only when we properly situate these elements in a particular historical period and cultural milieu, and within a cluster of material conditions — these contexts constitute an ecology of digital literacy that functions both locally and globally; that shapes micro-, medial-, and macro-levels of experience for individuals; and that is shaped by factors and effects at these same levels.*

The work of contemporary literacy scholars — Street (1995), Gee (1990), Barton (1994), Graff (1987), and Brandt (2001) — remind us that we cannot hope to understand any literacy until we understand the complex social and cultural systems — both local and global — within which literacy practices and values are situated. Hence, we cannot hope to understand digital literacy — in Nigeria, China, or the US and western Europe — with simplistic references to a global digital divide; and we cannot represent digital literacy solely through statistics that provide the numbers of computers in different countries. Further, the definition of both *literacy* and *digital literacy* are far from stable over time, so we must also examine the practices and attendant values of digital literacy within a specific set of historical circumstances.

As these two cases illustrate, then, the ways in which individuals from various nations acquire and develop digital literacy — or are prevented from doing so — depend on a web of factors: among just a few of them, income, education, access and the specific conditions of access, geographical location, and support systems. Within any given nation, many of these factors depend, as well, on technological infrastructure, a critical mass of skilled engineers and scientists, investment in education and educational technology, political stability, and technology policy *(Spanning the Digital Divide: Understanding and Tackling the Issues*, 2001). Because of this complex relationship between literacy, computer technologies, and *development* (both *human development* [6] as measured by health, education, and standard of living; and *national development* as measured by large-scale economic factors), statistics can reveal only part of the story, only part of the intricate ecological framework within which literacy is both shaped and shapes the lives of humans. It may be for this reason that individual case studies of digital literacy are so

---

[6] The United Nations measures human development along three basic dimensions: "a long and healthy life, knowledge, and a decent standard of living" (*Human Development Report 2001: Making New Technologies Work for Human Development*, 2001, p. 253). These human development dimensions are further complicated — in the United Nations' annual Human Development reports — by factors such as life expectancy, poverty, illiteracy, per capita income, gender and income equity, access to health services and resources, and educational attainment.

valuable — these personal narratives are capable of demonstrating the many ways in which micro-, medial-, and macrolevel factors shape, and are shaped by, the lived experiences of real people.

Dipo's case, for instance, provides a good example and illustrates the complex ways in which, and levels at which, opportunities to acquire and develop digital literacy are related to class and income, education, geographic location, and political policy, and technological infrastructure, as well.

According to the United Nations' *Human Development Report 2001*, for example, Nigeria — which has a "human development index" (HDI) ranking of 136 out of 182 — also has an income inequality score of 50.2 on a scale of 100 (with 0 representing perfect equality) (pp. 182–184). Nigeria also has a national adult literacy rate of 62.6% (p. 176). In terms of technology, World Bank data indicate that Nigeria averages 6.6 personal computers per 1000 people, as compared to a global average of 78.3 (*World Development Indicators 2002 database*, 2002, 5.10 "The Information Age"). To situate this number in a continental context, a recent report on African Internet efforts, reported that 1 in 130 Africans had access to a PC in 2002, and 1 in 160 used the Internet (*African Internet Connectivity — A Status Report*, 2002, p. 1). As that report explained,

> In Africa, each computer with an Internet or e-mail connection usually supports a range of three to five users. This puts current estimates of African Internet users at 5–8 million outside of North and South Africa. This is about one user for every 250–400 people compared to a world average of about one user for every 15 people, and a North American and European average of about one in every two people (*World Development Report 2003*, 2003). Figures for other developing regions in 2000 were 1 in 30 for Latin America and the Caribbean, 1 in 250 for South Asia, 1 in 43 for East Asia, 1 in 1666 for the Arab States. (*African Internet Connectivity — A Status Report*, 2002, "The Current Status of the Internet in Africa")

Within this context, it is clear that the unusually stable microlevel economic situation that Dipo's family was able to provide and the professional paths that his parents had chosen were key factors in his own ability to acquire and develop digital literacy. It is also clear that such a situation is *not* available to many Nigerian citizens. This microlevel environment within which Dipo developed digital literacy was made possible, in part, by his father and mother's commitment to completing their own schooling, the home instruction they had been able to provide him in digital literacy practices and values, and their decision to locate the family in the city of Lagos. Further, the decision Dipo's parents made to pursue their own advanced educations anticipated a number of factors at a medial level: among them, the increasingly heavy demand for professionals in information technology and accounting in Lagos; the increasing stability of the local political situation; the growth of the city as an information technology center; and the increasing concentration of scientific and engineering expertise which made the city an unusually attractive location in Nigeria. Dipo's ability to acquire digital literacy was also affected by macrolevel trends: among them the growing global reliance on digital networks, the increase of e-commerce, and the increasing pace of technology innovation. These factors and trends of course, cannot be located simply at one level of effect — the microlevel decision that the family made about the schools Dipo would attend was influenced by their recognition of the increasingly important role that technology was playing in a global arena, as was Dipo's own choice of major in college. Similarly, Dipo's microlevel choices about cultivating technologically savvy friends and his personal determination to participate as fully as possible in the online environments available to him was also shaped, at least in part, by macrolevel patterns of technological innovation.

In turn, Dipo's own digital literacy shapes the ways in which he exchanges information with his family in Nigeria, the expectations he will have for his own children's education, their own educational opportunities and expectations, his personal definition of literacy, his professional qualifications as a computer scientist, and his eventual contributions to the technological infrastructure of his home country. Similarly, his own decisions — to purchase a computer, to download music, to play games in online environments — especially when these are multiplied by similar decisions that other individuals make, shape global and national rates of technological change, contribute to the concentration of digital resources and expertise, and help create national and global expectations for literacy, education, and personal opportunity.

As a 1996 Report of the African Information Society concluded, digital literacy exists within overdetermined systems that are constituted at many levels:

> Every facet of ... basic rights is dependent on telecommunications. Such basic rights of the individual as the right to life, the right to personal liberty and dignity, the right to free expression and information, and the right to free movement, all of which enhance the quality of life of the individual, are facilitated by telecommunication. (Alabi, 1996, 1.1.4)

Thus, the role of computers and telecommunications' technologies have assumed a huge role in delivering not only the educational promises associated with digital literacies, but also with everyday opportunities necessary to lead a better life on every level.

Observation #2: *At this point in history, although many factors affect people's ability to acquire and develop digital literacy, geography and location — because they are linked with other social formations at numerous levels, and because their effects are often multiplied and magnified by these linkages — often exert more force than other factors in shaping a national ecology for digital literacy.*

One key factor in people's opportunities to develop digital literacy has to do with where they are born, live, and are educated. As the United Nations notes,

> The global map of technological achievement ... shows huge inequalities between countries — not just in terms of innovation and access, but also in the education and skills required to use technology effectively. (*Human Development Report 2001: Making New Technologies Work for Human Development*, 2001, p. 3)

At a macrolevel of effect, Pengfei's home country of China, for instance, has 0.1 Internet hosts per 1000 people as compared to 179.1 in the US, 120 telephone lines per 1000 people as compared to 993 in the US, and an average of 6.4 years of schooling among the population of citizens aged 15 and above in comparison to an average of 12 in the US (*Human Development Report 2001: Making New Technologies Work for Human Development*, 2001, pp. 48–51). Similarly, China was able to spend only 2.3% of its gross national product on public education in 1995–1997, while the US spent 12.2% (*Human Development Report 2001: Making New Technologies Work for Human Development*, 2001, pp. 170–173). These factors and many others make the geographical location of a person's birth a significant factor in determining the extent and frequency of opportunities they will have to acquire and develop digital literacy.

Within a country, geography matters as well. Pengfei's very different microlevel and medial experiences in a rural school in the small village of Yinjiahe, in a larger school in the small town of Linqu, at Tianjin University, for example, illustrates how uneven technological diffusion may be between rural and urban environments, as well as between nations. Such unevenness can also be documented in statistical terms:

> In China the 15 least connected provinces, with 600 million people, have only 4 million Internet users — while Shanghai and Beijing, with 27 million people, have 5 million users. (*Human Development Report 2001: Making New Technologies Work for Human Development*, 2001, p. 40)

Dipo's case also illustrates the uneven diffusion of technological opportunity in urban and rural environments. At a media level of effect, Lagos, his hometown, boasts one of the highest concentrations of technology in Nigeria, in part because of its population density. As Feyt and Edelmuller (2000) point out,

> Nigeria's Internet market comes mainly from Lagos among the young urban elite, the oil-based communities of Port Harcourt and Warri, and the cities of Abuja and Kano ... whilst in other areas access to the Net is considered a luxury.

Outside of such large cities, as a recent report on the status of African Internet connectivity indicates, opportunities are far more difficult to come by:

> Irregular or non-existent electricity supplies are a common feature and a major barrier to use of the ICTs, especially outside the major towns ... . In response to the high cost of Internet service and the slow speed of the web, and also because of the overriding importance of electronic mail, lower cost e-mail only services are continuing to attract subscribers ... . Due to the relatively small number of people who can afford a telephone line, let alone a computer, public access services are very much in demand in the urban areas. As is most evident in Nigeria and Senegal ... there is a rapidly growing number of kiosks, cyber cafés, and other forms of public Internet

access, such as adding PCs to community phone-shops, schools, police sta-
tions and clinics which address low-income levels by sharing the cost and
maintenance of equipment and access. (*African Internet Connectivity — A
Status Report*, 2002, "The Current Status of the Internet in Africa")

Thus, where one lives locally and globally exerts a profound influence on the number
and kinds of available opportunities to develop digital literacies.

Observation #3: *Wealth — because it is linked with other social formations at
numerous levels, and because its effects are often multiplied and magnified by these
linkages — often exerts more force than other factors in shaping a national ecology
for digital literacy.*

Both Dipo's and Pengfei's stories remind us as well that wealth is also directly related
to digital literacy and the opportunities that individuals have for acquiring and developing
digital literacy. In Dipo's case, his family's microlevel economic circumstances — which
were determined by the salaries his mother and father earned — meant that he had access
to a computer in his home while growing up. As Feyt and Edelmuller (2000) point out, this
situation is relatively rare in Nigeria:

The average cost of the Internet for an annual subscription is N82,000,
approximately $1000, "proving prohibitive for the average Nigerian." The
same subscription fee in Europe and the USA would have an average cost
of only $150. 35 times less than that of Nigeria, and salaries which are at
least 10 times greater than the African average ... . This is obviously having
an adverse effect on the spread of the Internet in Nigeria, as only the elite
[are] able to afford connectivity fees, whilst most of the population who live
in rural areas is unable to afford such a luxury.

Further, the fact that Dipo's family could pay tuition for private schools that had
resources for learning and practicing digital literacy also had an impact on Dipo's opportunities to develop digital literacy. As Alabi noted in a recent report on the availability of
computers in Nigerian schools:

Of the 18.7 million students enrolled in schools, less than 2 million have
access to formal computer activities except in a very few private primary
and secondary schools ... which are elitist in their setups and charge fees
ranging from N20,000 to N250,000 per annum compared with an average
of N500 per annum charged in public schools. (4.2.1)

Dipo had privileges in schooling about which most young Nigerians can only dream.
Pengfei's claim that "if you are poor, you can't buy a computer" reminds us that wealth
also matters in China. Income inequality in China — the range between the richest and poorest segments of society — is essentially equivalent to that within the US, with China scoring
40.3 on the United Nation's scale of 100 (0 representing perfect equality) and the United

States scoring 40.6 (*Human Development Report 2001: Making New Technologies Work for Human Development*, 2001, pp. 182–183). As a nation, however, China is much poorer, ranking of 87 out of 138 developing countries in terms of human poverty (*Human Development Report 2001: Making New Technologies Work for Human Development*, 2001, p. 149) and with a gross domestic product per capita of approximately 10 times less than that of the US.

As a nation with limited monetary resources, China has also had proportionally less to spend over the crucial years of the information revolution on computers, on research and development (*Human Development Report 2001: Making New Technologies Work for Human Development*, 2001, pp. 52–55), on tertiary education (pp. 170–173), and on computer infrastructure in schools (*World Development Indicators 2002 database*, 2002, 5.10 "The Information Age") than has the United States. At the same time, the average monthly charge for service providers in China is $7.00 while in the US it is $5.00 (*World Development Indicators 2002 database*, 2002, 5.10 "The Information Age").

Within this context, as Pengfei's own experiences point out, access to computers in China is often limited to those with sufficient wealth or shared in public spaces like Internet cafes or university settings, and many students seek an education abroad in order to gain the kind of access to digital communication environments they desire. Thus, although the United Nations has placed China among countries described as "dynamic adopters of technology," it has also given that nation an overall rating of 0.299 on the Technology Achievement index. The United States, in comparison, is classed as a technology "leader" and rated at 0.733 (*Human Development Report 2001: Making New Technologies Work for Human Development*, 2001, indicator, p. 48).

Observation #4: *Education and computer skills — because they are linked with other social formations at numerous levels, and because their effects are often multiplied and magnified by these linkages — often exert more force than other factors in shaping a national ecology for digital literacy.*

Both these case studies indicate that the overall level of education and computer skills within a nation also matter a great deal in relation to its citizens' opportunities to acquire and develop digital literacy. As the United Nation's Human Development program explains:

> Skills matter more than ever in today's more competitive global market ... . Developing countries cannot simply import and apply knowledge from outside ... . [E]very country needs domestic capacity to develop technology's potential benefits and to adapt new technology to its needs and constraints."
> (*Human Development Report 2001: Making New Technologies Work for Human Development*, 2001, p. 37)

In this context, Pengfei's observation that China was making speedy progress in terms of technology ("China is developing fast as far as computers are concerned"), the rapid deployment of computer technology within his family, and his own experiences in increasingly popular cyber cafés in China makes increasing sense. China is educating a strong base of scientists and engineers who can help build the country's computer infrastructure.

Students enrolled in science, math, and engineering courses in China represented 53% of all tertiary students in 1994–1997, as compared with 18% in Norway and 29% in the UK (*Human Development Report 2001: Making New Technologies Work for Human Development*, 2001, pp. 174–177). China also has a relatively high rate of scientists and engineers involved in research and development projects (454/100,000 compared with 3676/100,000 in the US) (*Human Development Report 2001: Making New Technologies Work for Human Development*, 2001, pp. 52–55); spends a healthy proportion of its gross domestic product (2.3%) and government expenditures (12.2%) on public education; and allocates 15.6% of its national educational funding to tertiary schooling — as compared with 25.2% in the US (*Human Development Report 2001: Making New Technologies Work for Human Development*, 2001, pp. 170–174). Further, although neither the United Nations nor any other agency provides a specific index for a nation's "digital literacy" achievement, China's "dynamic adaptor" designation suggests the nation's increasing ability to provide citizens with adequate environments for digital literacy practices and a national environment that values digital literacy as a cultural construct (see Drori & Jang, 2003).

This relationship between education, skills, and computer infrastructure also helps explain the slower progress Nigeria is making in terms of technology achievement and building an environment for digital literacy. Although Nigeria desperately needs to educate "about one (1) million cutting-edge computer scientists and engineers annually (and perhaps 5 million IT users annually)" in order to compete with the rest of the world (Uwalje, 2000), only 0.61% of the country's population own computers, only 41% of all tertiary students are enrolled in science, math, and engineering classes (*Human Development Report 2001: Making New Technologies Work for Human Development*, 2001, p. 176) and only 15 scientists and engineers per 100,000 people are involved in research and development projects (p. 55). Further, Nigeria spends only 0.7% of its gross domestic product and 11.5% of total government expenditures on public education (*Human Development Report 2001: Making New Technologies Work for Human Development*, 2001, p. 171). A recent report on the status of African Internet Connectivity (2003) explained the challenges of building a strong technology infrastructure under such conditions:

> An even greater problem is that the brain drain and generally low levels of education and literacy amongst the population has created a great scarcity of skills and expertise (at all levels, from policy making down to end user). Rural areas in particular suffer with even more limited human resources. Along with the very low pay scales in the African civil service, this is a chronic problem for governments and NGOs who are continually losing their best and brightest to the private sector. This is simply exacerbating the situation in Africa, because experienced technicians ... are able to find much higher paying jobs in Europe and North America." (*African Internet Connectivity — A Status Report*, 2002, "General Factors")

Without an adequate technology infrastructure, of course, the opportunities for the acquisition and development of digital literacies within a citizenry are dramatically reduced, albeit, as Dipo's case indicates, not eliminated entirely.

Observation #5: *Within a given cultural ecology, people exert their own powerful agency in, around, and through digital literacy — and on many levels — even though unintended consequences always accompany their actions.*

The cases of Pengfei and Dipo also illustrate how people exert their own very real and potent agency in, around, and through digital literacies, and how they shape the environment for their literacy through actions that have effects at the micro-, medial-, and macrolevels of social operations. This understanding is supported by the work of sociologists like Giddens (1979), who notes that people both shape, and are shaped by, the social systems within which they live in a complex duality of structuration, that "every competent member of every society" not only "knows a great deal about the institutions of that society," but also draws on this understanding of "structure, rules and resources" (Giddens, 1979, p. 71) to make changes in the surrounding environment. Feenberg (1999, pp. 75–99), as well, notes that technological systems are "underdetermined" spaces that can be productively shaped and influenced by individuals — in both their design and their use — even as these systems shape and influence the lives of the people associated with them.

In the two cases we have presented, it is also clear that this two-way structuration (Giddens, 1979, p. 69), takes place at a variety of levels and through a range of effects. For instance, Dipo's and Pengfei's digital literacy values and practices (e.g., the applications they used to communicate within computer environments; the ways in which they shaped their access to digital communication environments at school, at home, or in Internet cafes; their decision to play computer games or work with digital photography) occur at a micropolitical level (i.e., within a family, a peer group, or the life of an individual). However, the effects of Dipo's and Pengfei's actions also extend beyond these environments, and they gain tangential force when they are multiplied by the similar practices of friends, peers, and family members. Thus, their actions can also play out at medial- and macrolevels as well.

Dipo's and Pengfei's digital literacy practices, for example, have affected the literacy practices and values of their parents and other family members at a micropolitical level. Not only do both Dipo and Pengfei now write to their parents via e-mail, but their parents respond and write back, using personal computers that they have purchased as investments in their own and their children's future. According to Pengfei, his father specifically bought a computer so that he could correspond with his son and might not have done so without this motivation. In turn, the literacy practices and values of these two families — especially when they are multiplied by similar practices in other families — can affect medial-level patterns of technology use and spending, as well as the demands placed on local, regional, and national educational institutions. They can also contribute to a changing context for, definition of, and expectation for literacy — in China and Nigeria, and around the world. If digital literacy practices achieve a critical mass, they may also affect technology policy, spending, and infrastructure at a regional, national, or global level.

This understanding of individual agency, also helps explain how people are often able to resist the effects of micro-, medial-, or macrolevel formations depending on their talents, goals, interests, and insights, among many other factors. Pengfei, for instance, despite having no exposure to computers before he reached college, committed himself to making maximum use of computer environments he could identify — primarily Internet cafes in China, and university-based networks in the US — to further develop his digital literacies and to achieve his goal of finishing a PhD in biochemistry. Similarly Dipo's parents, even within the context of the many constraints characterizing the politics, economy, and technological infrastructure of Nigeria, found ways to prepare themselves and their family to communicate successfully in digital contexts and to face an increasingly technological age.

Of course, as these cases also suggest, the hard-won successes that these two families have experienced also depend on a range of factors: among them, people's innate or learned abilities to pursue both unexpected and predictable goals; family values and literacy histories; social, economic, and personal circumstances; commitment, confidence, and faith — in sum, whatever factors enable humans to pursue both unexpected and unpredictable goals.

As mentioned, we do not want to suggest with this discussion that people can always accomplish anything they want within social structures or that the actions they take are always effective. Clearly, people are constrained in their actions by any number of influential factors: age, class, race, handicap, experience, opportunity, belief systems are among only a few such factors. And, as we noted, certain of these factors — geographical location, wealth, and education, for instance — may exert particularly strong shaping influences on people's opportunities to develop digital literacy. Further, we should add that the actions people do undertake — because they take place within complex cultural ecologies — *always* have what Giddens calls "unintended consequences" that escape the bounds of individuals' intentions. Thus, for instance, although Dipo's and Pengfei's efforts to acquire certain kinds of technological literacy succeeded in many ways, they also resulted in their separation from family and friends — an effect that they perhaps neither foresaw nor desired.

Observation #6: *The digital divide and its effects on digital literacy will not be successfully addressed until these larger phenomena are understood as a complex related constellation of elements shaped by (and shaping) a global cultural ecology.*

Given both the complexity and the overdetermined nature of the related micro-, medial-, and macrolevel technologies that serve as contexts for digital literacy, it seems most reasonable to conclude that no one action or set of solutions is going to address the entire range of literacy issues associated with the global digital divide. Certainly, it is clear that simple physical access to computer technology is only one small part of the global digital divide — albeit a fundamentally important part.

When it comes to addressing the digital divide, providing access to technology is critical. However, too often, "access" is defined only in terms of physical access to a computer or network connection. As Ransdell et al., point out in another chapter in this volume, computers and connections are not sufficient if the technology is not used effectively because it is not affordable to use, people do not understand how to put it to use, or they are discouraged from using it. Access must be considered in a much broader context to ensure technology is integrated into people's lives. Specifically, true access is affected by the following factors: computers and connections, capacity, trust, appropriate technology, content, affordability, local economics, legal and policy framework, demographics, and political empowerment (*Spanning the Digital Divide: Understanding and Tackling the Issues*, 2001, p. 73).

Exacerbating access problems on a global scale are patterns of technology diffusion based on wealth and privilege. As a recent report issued by the U.S. Internet Council notes:

> [L]ike any new technology, this rapid global dissemination [of the Internet] has been far from uniform. A map of Internet users and innovators quickly reveals a stark global North–South divide. The Internet has planted deep roots in the regions that encouraged and fostered its early growth. Not surprisingly, these regions are also the world's wealthiest. (*State of the Internet*, 2000, p. 1)

These patterns of inequity are magnified not only by wealth, however, but by all the social formations that align themselves along the axis of wealth and create a "confluence of factors" (*Spanning the Digital Divide: Understanding and Tackling the Issues*, 2001, p. 86): power, education, and global reach, among only a few of them:

> The stark reality is that ICT usually benefits privileged communities first — those that have the education and resources to afford technology and the skills o use it. Since ICT skills can lead to higher paying job and opportunities, ICT is exacerbating existing inequalities. Likewise companies with the resources to take advantage of ICT are often larger companies or branches of foreign multinationals. These companies are increasingly able to reduce internal costs and coordinate dispersed offices and operations, and thus beat or buy their smaller, domestic competitors. (*Spanning the Digital Divide: Understanding and Tackling the Issues*, 2001, p. 86)

Importantly, wealth also has a dramatic impact on issues of national technology policy and infrastructure (e.g., how technology is identified as a national priority) and how much a nation can devote to creating and maintaining a technological infrastructure, national educational efforts (e.g., how much schools can spend on instructional technology and which schools will have technological resources).

No system is totalizing, however — not even seriously overdetermined systems like the complex relationship between technology, wealth, and literacy that forms part of the digital divide. Within the complex global ecology shaped by these factors and others, individuals such as Dipo and Pengfei make their own way, exert their own personal and, in combination with others, collective agency to acquire and develop digital literacy. Even more importantly, perhaps, they tell us their stories so that others can do the same.

6   Final Comments

We conclude our observations here by focusing briefly on the complex role that language and education assume in facilitating and supporting the acquisition of digital literacy, and how all of these factors function in relation to the global digital divide. As is

obvious from these case studies and from our own everyday use of information technologies, one must have knowledge of English to negotiate a basically Anglophone
Internet and to learn the many software programs that contribute to this negotiation.
Dipo, Pengfei, and other international students whom we have interviewed pride themselves on their facility with English, and certainly this facility enabled them to study
abroad and to succeed in their studies. Coming of age in the late 20th and early 21st centuries when the Internet remains largely English-centric underscores the necessity for
English as we know it.

Michael Cronin (2003), in his important book, *Translation and Globalization*, for
example, complicates stories of technology and globalization by emphasizing the enormous role that language and translation must play in networked conversations. In other
words, the learning of other languages and the ability to speak across cultures in languages
not one's own constitute arduous, difficult tasks that tend to become the responsibility of
those who do not speak English as a first language. Such tasks are, moreover, representative of the kinds of challenges that often must be assumed by international students seeking academic success not only abroad but also in their homelands. Accompanying these
challenges is the added responsibility of acquiring digital literacies, which also demand
English and, more and more frequently, the ability to go back and forth between English
and one's home language(s). That 91% of secure web sites in the world are in English
argues for the crucial role that English, and hence translation, continues to play in online
venues (Cronin, 2003, p. 14).

We wonder, however, if the current situation is not changing and that those of us with
English as a first language are less likely to detect the dramatic changes taking place.
While Dipo and Pengfei were attending school in the United States, for example, Stefan
Jarvis (2001) was writing that

> [t]he distinction between the global and the local is always a negotiated one
> ... . The fact that three quarters of the content on the Internet is in English has
> led many Asian governments and leaders to voice concern that the openness
> of the Internet could be detrimental to the moral fabric and cultural identity
> of some communities. However, it is possible that this position could be
> somewhat overstated. While English dominates in pure numbers, when an
> eye is cast toward what information people actually consume on the Internet,
> the validity of the "English Imperialism" argument becomes suspect. To take
> the case of Japan, over 95% of all web pages are written in Japanese in 2000,
> and there is a relatively low level of access to non-Japanese sites (5).

Daniel Pimienta (2002) – an author associated with Funredes, a nongovernmental
organization active in defending cultural and linguistic diversity on the Web — also questions the changing role of English:

- The relative presence of English on the Web has declined from 75% in 1998 to 50%
  today (in terms of the web pages in English).
- The presence of each language on the Web appears to be proportional to the number of
  web users who speak that language ... .

- The growth of English-speaking users has slowed and is close to saturation, whereas numbers in other linguistic areas are often growing very strong (with the Chinese in the lead).

Thus, the days of an English-centric Internet may be numbered or at least shifting so that many who tap into the resources of the Web will be required to work less, or at least differently, with the English language than those who came before them.

As we bring this chapter to a close, we recognize the importance of future research that extends the work we have begun here — especially important is research that focuses on the global digital divide but that also examines more substantively the role that language and education, among other factors, play in shoring up or detracting from people's acquisition and development of digital literacies. For example, can a technology-rich education at the primary or secondary, or collegiate level help remediate a lack of access to computers at home? How are different languages currently being used in digital spaces and for what purposes? What are the complex relationships between language use in digital environments and personal/cultural/national identity? Between language use in digital environments and prosperity? How can countries/individuals/groups address the global digital divide? What roles do language, education, and literacy play in these efforts? Certainly, research will need to examine these questions (and others) at many levels — in the lives of individuals, groups, cultures, and nations; within a global context; and from many different perspectives. As Castells (1996) points out, such work is essential because the cultural codes that will characterize our world in the coming decades are being forged within digital environments — articulated and shared by people like Dipo and Pengfei. Thus, if we fail to pay attention to the literacy values and practices in digital spaces *today* — and the ways in which language use and education inform literacies — we risk losing an invaluable glimpse of the future of writing and digital media and place in jeopardy our ability to prepare effectively for tomorrow's world.

Chapter 18

Proposal for a Monument to Lost Data

Barry Mauer

As our society transfers its archives from print to digital media, an unintended conse-
quence results; we lose a great amount of data. The effects of data loss can be profound;
without access to vital data, our access to history may be severely diminished. Data loss
threaten to undermine individual lives and major institutions.
This essay discusses the phenomenon of data loss in the age of digital media. I identify
the National Archives and Records Administration (NARA) in Washington, DC as a site
of data loss at a national level, and suggest mourning as a means of coping with data
loss. To facilitate the mourning of data loss at a national level, I propose a monument
to lost data that will be located at the NARA. This monument is to have an on-site com-
ponent and an online component: a network of memorial entries created by individuals
who have suffered data loss.

Our media is your memory. (Sony slogan).

> Attached to every person like a tiny galaxy will be the whole of his past —
> or what he takes to be the whole of his past. His attachment to it will con-
> stitute the whole of his present — or of what he takes to be the present. The
> neat, almost soundless instrument will contain all of each man's hope, his
> innocence, his garden. Then one by one, but with growing frequency, men
> will begin to lose their machines. (Merwin, 1969, pp. 130–131)

1 Introduction

As our society transfers its archives from print and analog media to digital media, an unintended consequence results; we lose a great deal of data. The effects of this data loss are profound; without access to our data, we lose our history, and thus our ability to function in the
present is diminished. Data loss threatens to undermine not only individual lives but major
institutions as well.

Mauer, B., (2005). Proposal for a monument to lost data. In L. Van Waes, M. Leijten & C. Neuwirth
(Vol. Eds.) & G. Rijlaarsdam (Series Ed.), Studies in Writing: Vol. 17. Writing and Digital Media
(pp. 287–309). Oxford: Elsevier.

This essay aims to generate more discussion about the issues related to data loss. It examines the ways in which data loss have worsened in the age of digital media, and it discusses the types of data that are being lost. To provide a case study for discussion, I identify the National Archives and Records Administration (NARA) in Washington, DC as a site of data loss at a national level. Though this essay does not suggest ways of reducing data loss, it does suggest a method for coping with data loss; that method is mourning. To explain how mourning functions, the essay offers a discussion of monumentality — understood as the writing of collective memory — and also proposes a monument to lost data to be located at the NARA. In addition to this on-site monument, there will be an online component: a network of memorial entries on the Internet created by individuals who have suffered data loss. These entries will be composed of traces and "phantoms" of lost data — the phantom data being analogous to the phantom limbs experienced by amputees. The various entries of the monument will be conjoined into a structure analogous to the mycelium, the branching network of root-like fibers common to mushrooms and other fungi. The monument is designed to produce new ways of thinking about data loss and will reveal to people the collective dimensions of their personal data loss.

2   The Growing Threat of Data Loss

Numerous critics blame electronic media for overtaking and undermining the public sphere, that space for the free exchange of ideas which provides sustenance for a democratic society (see the work of Noble, Postman, & Mander). These critics decry the commodification of electronic communications, the invasion of private electronic media enable, and the disinformation electronic media spread routinely (see Rheingold, 1993). Less well known is another critique; electronic communications technologies hasten the destruction of data, which in turn impedes citizens from making informed decisions. This argument is counterintuitive; does not electronic media store and transmit more data than ever? Yet the flood of data in electronic societies may be the primary cause of data loss within them.

Substantial publicity about the growing quantity of stored data may be obscuring the problem of data loss. For example, a report by researchers Lyman and Varian (2003) points to dramatic increases in data and data-storage capacity:

> Print, film, magnetic, and optical storage media produced about 5 exabytes of new information in 2002. Ninety-two percent of the new information was stored on magnetic media, mostly in hard disks. How big is five exabytes? If digitized with full formatting, the seventeen million books in the Library of Congress contain about 136 terabytes of information; five exabytes of information is equivalent in size to the information contained in 37,000 new libraries the size of the Library of Congress book collections (Lyman & Varian, 2003).[1]

---

[1] Also see New. His study finds explosive growth of world's information is only beginning (2000). "It's taken 300,000 years for humans to accumulate 12 exabytes of information. It will take just 2.5 more years to create the next 12 exabytes, according to a new study produced by a team of faculty and students at the School of Information Management and Systems at the University of California at Berkeley."

Less public attention is paid to the phenomenon of data loss. It seems to be exceptional; disasters, such as the massive data loss that resulted from the destruction of the World Trade Center, appear to be anomalies rather than regular occurrences (Joyce, 2001). Because the quantity of stored data and data-storage capacity is growing rapidly, the public might assume that data loss is becoming a thing of the past. Not so. Major institutions have been grappling for some time with the problems posed by data loss. A 1999 study conservatively estimated corporate data loss had cost the U.S. economy $11.8 billion in 1998, and the study suggested these costs were likely to increase (Lost data cost U.S. economy $11.8 billion in 1998 and 1999).

Though we have some cause to celebrate the enormous data-storage capacity of digital media, our society has not come to terms with the enormous data loss that accompanies our shift from textual and analog archives to digital archives. This project aims to draw our attention to data loss as a profound problem affecting modern life.

We should distinguish the loss of memes — which are the primary elements of collective memory — and the loss of personal data. Loss of mathematics would be catastrophic for the society, but the loss of your checkbook, while bad for you, is unlikely to affect the society as a whole. Personal data is in greater danger of loss because it exists in fewer copies. Nonetheless, personal losses can affect individual people profoundly and can affect groups when large numbers of people lose their personal data.

All societies must pass vital knowledge to succeeding generations; therefore all societies face the vexing problem of information storage. Living memory — the memory stored in the human mind — is extremely limited; it is often unreliable and cannot survive beyond the grave; thus human societies have designed memory machines — data-storage systems — and institutions, such as pedagogy, charged with the preservation and dissemination of data. Gregory Ulmer reminds us that "Writing as a technology is a memory machine, with each apparatus finding different ways to collect, store, and receive information outside of any one individual mind (in rituals, habits, libraries, or databases)" (Ulmer, 1994, p. 16).

Units of data essential to an apparatus — any institution charged with the preservation and dissemination of specialized knowledge — are called memes. Ancient rhetoricians recognized the importance of memes (though they did not use that word) by making the first and most important of the five parts of rhetoric the inventio — an imaginary storage place for "true things" (Cicero). The inventio was a kind of archive for commonplaces, the accepted units of wisdom possessed by the society.

According to Csikszentmihalyi (1996), memes are bits of information that a society passes on to the next generation in order to replicate itself. All social institutions — such as family, entertainment, and the sciences — have specialized memes that allow them to survive and maintain continuity from one generation to the next. During the early development of a social institution, new bits of knowledge appear at a rapid rate. Those deemed essential get taught to future generations, while those deemed non-essential become dormant. The selection process governing novelty in our information world is similar to the selection processes governing novelty in the natural world.

The analogy to genes in the evolution of culture are memes, or units of information that we must learn if information is to continue. Language, numbers, theories, songs, recipes, laws, and values are all memes that we pass on to our children so that they will be remembered. It is these memes that a creative person changes, and if enough of the right people see the change as an improvement, it will become part of the culture (Csikszentmihalyi, 1996, p. 7).

Memes must be learned or they will not survive. Computers, unlike humans, can replicate and store memes with little difficulty, but they do not understand these memes. Until they do, human memory and its institutional ally, pedagogy, will bear primary responsibility for storing and transmitting memes.

How fragile are memes? A historical view reveals that the fragility of memes changes over time. The memes stored during antiquity were fragile in some ways and durable in others. The libraries at Alexandria in ancient Egypt — there were actually three libraries in the system — had a mandate to collect all the knowledge in the world. At its peak, these libraries had roughly 500,000 scrolls before they were destroyed. Texts at that time were rare items; they had to be copied by hand, a very laborious process, and many existed as single copies. When the libraries were destroyed, so went the vast majority of knowledge stored until that point. Yet the memes of antiquity were durable; the fragments of ancient culture that survived have had an enduring impact on Western culture for 2500 years. "While modern scholars often lament the amount of information lost through the centuries since the Museum's fall, an amazing number of Alexandrian discoveries and theories, especially in mathematics and geometry, still provide the groundwork for modern research in these fields" (Brundige, 1995). The ancients produced a holistic way of storing essential data; small fragments (individual texts) reflected the greater whole (the society's knowledge). Much of what survived from antiquity is intertextual and thus we can find references in surviving texts to missing texts and we can make inferences about those missing texts. Additionally, we can infer from other ancient records, such as property records, gravestones, and inscriptions on buildings, about the principles governing ancient societies.

While the memes of antiquity were fragile because of the rarity of texts, the memes of modernity are fragile because of the abundance of texts in our archives. There are two defining characteristics of the modern data loss crisis. First, there are far more memes — or units

Figure 1: The National Archives and Records Administration (NARA).

of essential data — to manage because we have more institutions, and more complex institutions that require additional memes to sustain themselves. Also, because of the volume and complexity of our stored data, essential data has become increasingly harder to identify from within a larger ocean of data that may be largely non-essential. The genre of detective fiction, which arose in the 1800s as data archives grew at explosive rates, points to problems arising from our data explosion; the detective struggles to grasp the significance of seemingly insignificant data — clues — within an undifferentiated mass of facts.

The NARA in Washington, DC is emblematic of the modern data crisis. According to Stille, author of The Future of the Past, this federal agency, which is charged with storing and making available government records, "may have lost more information in the information age than ever before."

The NARA (Figure 1) was created during the 1930s on the optimistic premise that the government could keep all of its most vital records indefinitely, acting as our nation's collective memory. Now, as it drowns in data and chokes on paper, the agency is facing the stark realization that it may not be able to preserve what it already has, let alone keep up with the seemingly limitless flow of information coming its way (Stille, 2002, p. 303).

Among the massive problems facing the NARA, according to Stille (2002), are the following:

1. A huge backlog of data waiting to be transferred from decaying obsolete media to new media.
2. The need to replace "archival" digital media every few years.
3. "Decisions about what to keep ... made by default" as large portions of the archives deteriorate.
4. The speed at which "each new generation of equipment supplants the last" is leading to early obsolescence, raising the need to transfer databases, yet again, to a newer media.
5. "The newer the technology, the greater its fragility."
6. Competition for budget resources leading to tough choices between storage and dissemination.
7. Lack of physical space.
8. An increase in the amount of paper as government agencies print their computer files.
9. An increase in the amount of electronic data to be archived.
10. "Different kinds of computers, software programs, and formats."
11. Many files, such as email, existing in formats "not designed with long-term storage in mind."
12. The downsizing of federal agencies leading to the massive transfer of those agencies' records to the NARA.
13. Budget cuts at the NARA.
14. Refusal on the part of government agencies to be selective about what they add to the archive.

Stille cites a 1996 study of the NARA concluding "that, at current staff levels, it would take approximately 120 years to transfer the backlog of nontextual material (photographs, videos, film, audiotapes, and microfilm) to a more stable format" (Stille, 2002, p. 300). The 1996 study examined only non-textual materials already in the archives' collection; it does not account for new materials to be added to the collection. The collection of textual materials at the NARA is growing more rapidly as a result of a 1989 case in which "a public interest group trying to get information about the Iran-contra scandal successfully sued the White House to prevent it from destroying any electronic records. The result is that all federal agencies must now preserve all their computer files and electronic mail" (Stille, 2002, p. 304). However, Stille points out, "Because government offices use different kinds of computer files, software programs, and formats, just recovering this material has proved to be a logistical nightmare" (Stille, 2002, p. 304). If the NARA has difficulty preserving the documents from one of the most famous scandals in U.S. history, how can we be certain that other kinds of data, which may be vital to our future well being, has been preserved?

Stille concludes his chapter about the NARA with the following:

> There is not likely to be a modern Sophocles in the databases of the Department of Agriculture or the Census Bureau. The greater risk, instead, is of such a vast accumulation of records that the job of distinguishing the essential from the ephemeral becomes more and more difficult. The Archives of the future may resemble the "Library of Babel" that Jorge Luis Borges imagined nearly sixty years ago, an infinite library that contained every conceivable book in the universe. There were books that consisted purely of a repetition of a single letter of the alphabet and others in which all the pages but one were blank. The discovery of an intelligible sentence was cause for jubilation. Eventually, after many centuries, the librarians of Babel were driven to despair in their unfulfilled quest for a coherent, complete book. (Stille, 2002, p. 309)

Borges' "Library of Babel" suggests that archived data is effectively "lost" if we are unable to access it. There are enormous problems related to making searchable the data in electronic archives, not least of which is the problem of "tagging" (with SGML, XML, and other forms of searchable coding) the images stored in electronic databases. Suppose a researcher were to try generating a list of movies that contain images of apple blossoms; should the researcher assume that someone has tagged all such images in a searchable database? It would be impossible to generate all possible search tags for even a relatively limited number of images.

The Internet also draws criticism as a vast wasteland of disorganized and unsearchable data:

> The Internet has been described as a library where at the moment there is no catalogue, books on the shelves keep moving, and an extra truckload of books is dumped in the entrance hall every hour. Unless it is properly structured and constantly monitored, the positive feature of radical decentralization of knowledge will degenerate into a medieval fragmentation of the body of knowledge, which in turn means a virtual loss of information. Already it is no longer possible to rely on the speed of our networked tools to browse the whole space of knowledge and collect our information in a reasonably short time. If global plans are disregarded or postponed and financial commitments delayed, the risk is that information may well become no easier to find on the network than the proverbial needle in a haystack. (Floridi, 1995)

Though Floridi might hope for a global effort to structure and monitor the Internet, that dream seems increasingly unrealizable. Optimists will argue that science and commerce will eventually solve the problems of data management by building bigger and better hard drives, improving software for archiving and searching, and training users to back up their data. Pessimists will argue that even the best science will not save the world's disappearing languages, that advances in technology so far have exacerbated some problems of data loss, and that there will always be human error as long as there are humans.

Are modern societies in danger of losing memes? Certainly more data is stored today than has ever been stored. Oceans of data fill our libraries and computers. In general, we no longer face the problem of data "scarcity" that the ancients faced. A television show or a photograph or a written text can exist on a million computers and discs. Some of the essential texts of our culture, such as the "Declaration of Independence," "Huckleberry Finn," and "Star Wars," exist in so many copies and in so many forms that there is little danger of a catastrophic loss that would wipe them all out. There is sufficient backup to ensure the survival of this data for generations to come. Yet even this familiar data may be corrupted: the original parchment document of the "Declaration of Independence" is faded to the point of indecipherability; the manuscript for "Huckleberry Finn" was lost for over a 100 years while popular versions with hundreds of variances (errors?) from the manuscript were widely circulated; and George Lucas has released "Star Wars" after making many changes to the images and the editing. People will debate the significance of these changes to major texts in our culture for years to come.

Even though some memes are widely available, that does not guarantee their survival. Only if people understand how to access and use them will memes survive. The knowledge required to access and use any data is itself composed of memes that could disappear under certain conditions. For instance, the way we search databases has changed dramatically, and with potentially dire consequences; "For the last few years, librarians have increasingly seen people use online search sites not to supplement research libraries but to replace them" (Hafner, 2004).

> "Google searches an index at the first layers of any Web site it goes to, and as you delve beneath the surface, it starts to miss stuff," said Mr. Duguid, co-author of "The Social Life of Information." "When you go deeper, the number of pages just becomes absolutely mind-boggling." (Hafner, 2004)

In some ways, we have overcome the problem of information scarcity, but the ability to navigate and interpret the oceans of data we store poses as a significant problem for us as information scarcity once posed to earlier generations. Our colleges and universities struggle to train the next generation of researchers, in part because research methods keep changing so quickly.

Sometimes the loss of personal data does have major consequences for collectives. During the Serbian ethnic cleansing campaign in Kosovo, the Serb militias stripped the Kosovars of all identifying papers and photographs so that they could not prove who they were and where they had lived (Rueb, 2004). There was a systematic effort to deprive Kosovars of their history, their identity, and their claim to their property (see Figure 2). As such, the individual losses, taken together, were a catastrophe for the entire society, not just for each Kosovar.

Figure 2: A British KFOR officer sifts through a pile of Kosovar Albanian passports and ID cards, which had been confiscated by Serb forces and were found on June 13. The lack of ID papers is complicating the OSCE's task of registering voters (Reuters photo. Image and text from Rueb, 1999).

Increasingly, data loss threaten institutions as hackers and viruses cripple government and corporate sites and block public access to essential data. Hard drive data losses also result from power outages, storm damage, fire or explosion, hardware/software error, flood and water damage, earthquake, network outage, and human error.

A data protection industry, composed of scientists, engineers, trainers, and archivists, has arisen to address these problems. The data protection industry tries to reduce data loss through improved training, security, archival systems, and recovery techniques. Despite refinements in these techniques, the problem of data loss remains and seems unlikely to diminish. "Eventually every hard disk or backup will fail" (DataMechanix, 2004).

The data recovery industry[2] is able to rescue data from most of the crashed hard drives they receive (see Figure 3). But professional data recovery is relatively expensive — typically the cost of data recovery greatly exceeds the cost of the hardware — and the data

---

[2] See Lost in space: Data recovery (2001).

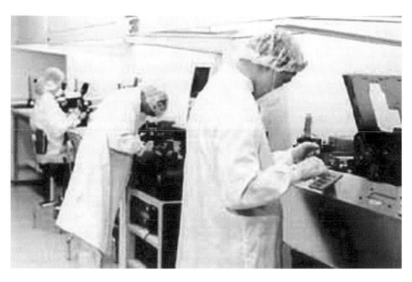

Figure 3: Life or death: a hard drive surgery (http://www.datamechanix.com/dm_clnrm.jpg).

recovery process can be extremely anxiety producing for clients. At least one data recovery company has hired counselors to help its clients deal with data-loss anxiety (see Mieszkowski, 1997).

The project described here — the monument to lost data — is relevant to those cases in which data cannot be recovered and must be considered lost. In these cases, it is appropriate and healthy to embrace a strategy for coping with loss: mourning. Mourning is the process whereby one achieves a measure of detachment from a lost person or object. (Ulmer, 1994). Mourning follows grief, which is the immediate reaction people have to a profound loss such as the loss of a loved one, but also social and symbolic losses (divorce, loss of a job, etc.).

The process of mourning, in addition to its healing effects, creates identity in powerful ways. Children learn to adopt the values of their parents and grandparents through the introjection of their elders' ego ideals. When elders die, children learn to cope with the loss by retaining the values of those who are gone. Mourning functions as a species of memory, creating continuity out of contingency; it puts loss into perspective and allows the young to adopt the values of the dying generation.

The process of introjection, however, is usually uncritical; most of us do not choose our ego ideals. But mourning can have a critical component. The monument to lost data foregrounds critical reflection in the mourning process; I explain this critical component, which includes reflections about our choices of values, in greater detail at the end of this chapter.

I support the mourning of data loss as a way of dealing with the special conditions of our information age. The most effective way to deal with data loss, I believe, is to recognize it as a collective experience and not just a personal one. A collective approach to mourning lost data provides greater perspective on the problem and will enable social networks to function as support groups for individuals who have suffered data loss.

In the previous chapter of this volume, Selfe and Hawisher examine the wide variations in digital literacy and access to digital technologies throughout the world. One result of political, economic, and technical inequities, is that collective entities — cultures, nations, and institutions — are losing essential data; some of the world's languages, dialects, rituals, oral histories, neighborhoods, and buildings are disappearing. Although components of this data can be recorded by ethnographers and historians, it is in danger of being lost as "lived memory" and thus as memory essential to a culture. According to linguist Michael Krauss, approximately 3000 languages will become extinct in the 21st century (Shorris, 2000). Reservoirs of traditional knowledge — the "data" stored in dances, songs, rituals, and myths — are disappearing from the planet, in part because the cultures and institutions in which they reside are not integrated into the global information network. Krauss implies that these losses cannot be calculated fully: "Each language is a unique repository of facts and knowledge about the world that we can ill afford to lose, or, at the least, facts and knowledge about some history and people that have their place in the understanding of mankind. Every language is a treasury of human experience" (Kolbert, 2005). When traditional cultures transfer their wisdom to electronic media, as many do, they trade one set of problems for another as they lose ritual practices that provided continuity over generations; they also face the same problems of data loss that other electronic cultures face.

Not only are our data archives unstable; the terms we use to discuss data are unstable as well. The definition of "data" itself has changed considerably in 30 years, becoming associated less with humans and more with machines. The 1971 edition of the OED defines datum, the singular of data as, "A thing given or granted; something known or assumed as fact and made the basis of reasoning or calculation; an assumption or premise from which inferences are drawn" (Datum, 1971, p. 648). This 1971 definition refers to data in human terms. Later, by contrast, connotations of automatism take over the definition. A recent entry, found in WorldCom's Communications Library, defines data as, "Any coded information that can be processed or output by a computer or other machine" (*Data*, 2001). Only machines use data, according to WorldCom, not humans — unless WorldCom was slyly admitting that we have become post-human. In this definition, machines process or output data; they neither "know" it, nor "assume" it, nor do they draw inferences from it. Ironically, since the collapse of WorldCom into bankruptcy, the website with WorldCom's definition of data is no longer available. Prior to WorldCom's definition, a government website had defined data as having human and non-human attributes; "Representation of facts, concepts, or instructions in a formalized manner suitable for communication, interpretation, or processing by humans or by automatic means. Any representations such as characters or analog quantities to which meaning is or might be assigned" (*Data*, 1996). My use of the term data is intended to be as broad as possible, encompassing both the human and non-human connotations raised by the term. Thus data loss, for my purposes, means the loss of a hard drive, the loss of a spoken language, and the loss from Alzheimer's of a person's living memory.

3   Artists Address the Shift in Data-Storage Practices

Many of the emerging issues related to data storage and data loss have been addressed in the arts. Andy Warhol and Merwin, both active in the 1960s, were among the first people to grapple with the implications of our changing data-management practices, specifically the practices involved in "passive diary keeping" (Johnson, 2005).

Warhol recorded all his encounters, no matter how mundane, using photographs, audio-tape, videotape, and film.

> The year 1969 began with a flurry of ideas. What about a television show, Andy suggested, called "Nothing Special," consisting of six hours of people walking past a hidden camera? (He had recently installed one in the Factory to improve security.) ... At Brigid Polk's suggestion, he had started taking Polaroids of penises — of any Factory visitor he could persuade to drop his trousers. He later estimated that he had taken thousands of such pictures ... Indeed, Andy's desire to record everything around him had become a mania. As John Perrault, the art critic, wrote in a profile of Warhol in Vogue: "His portable tape recorder, housed in a black briefcase, is his latest self-protection device. The microphone is pointed at anyone who approaches, turning the situation into a theater work. He records hours of tape every day but just files the reels away and never listens to them." (Bockris, 1989, pp. 246–247)

Also in 1969, Merwin, in "The Remembering Machines of Tomorrow," foretold a future of ubiquitous memory machines that would feature limitless data-storage capacity.

> Attached to every person like a tiny galaxy will be the whole of his past — or what he takes to be the whole of his past. His attachment to it will constitute the whole of his present — or of what he takes to be the present. The neat, almost soundless instrument will contain all of each man's hope, his innocence, his garden. Then one by one, but with growing frequency, men will begin to lose their machines. (Merwin, 1994, pp. 130–131)

Merwin offered two critiques of the memory machines: that the machine's archives of the past and present are composed of misperceptions, and that the loss of data stored in the machines will be crippling. Merwin painted a picture of the future that resembles our present: ubiquitous media, limitless information storage, and total surveillance. His model for the person of this future may have been Andy Warhol, ca. 1969, with one key difference; Warhol never accessed the data he had recorded. He filed it away and no one accessed his collection until after his death.

Warhol's media collection includes more than 4000 audiotapes, consisting for the most part of everyday conversations. Warhol made himself the hub of a recording apparatus, though the recordings he produced could have been made, in theory, by anybody; Warhol was part of a machine, a "factory," that produced citation. What Warhol recorded was nothing in particular and what he collected was never accessed. Warhol refused to distinguish between essential and ephemeral data. Merwin's futuristic people, however, selectively record their memories, creating inaccurate impressions that substitute for actual experience. Their memories result from a type of wish fulfilment.

Passive diary keeping, as imagined by Warhol and Merwin, is now a part of daily life for ordinary people.

> The cell phone manufacturer Nokia recently introduced a new software package for camera phones and Windows PCs called Lifeblog, which combines e-mail and the passive diary mode of the photoblog in one artful package. In essence, Lifeblog records a timeline of all the events that flow through your cell phone's memory. Schedule an appointment, and Lifeblog will put it on the timeline; take a picture, and Lifeblog will archive it; get an instant message from a friend, send an e-mail, or retrieve a voice-mail message — Lifeblog will store it away in its running account of your digital life. When you sync your phone with your PC, you can launch the Lifeblog program and see a rendered account of your time — a long thread of information, woven together with images you've captured along the way. The premise behind Lifeblog is not a new one: A number of computer visionaries, including Gordon Bell of Microsoft, have proposed software interfaces organized fundamentally around time, as a way of augmenting memory. Bell's experimental project, called MyLifeBits, chronicles the entire flow of information through his life — everything from articles and books to phone calls and home movies. That kind of data storage might seem overly ambitious if you prefer to spend your time living your life and not archiving it. But the beauty of Lifeblog's orientation around the cell phone and the camera is that it lets you record life away from the PC screen, without actively thinking about the archival process. (Johnson, 2005)

These new technologies make the worlds of Warhol and Merwin real for ordinary people. But Warhol, and Merwin's futuristic people, pose problems for us; if we choose to store everything without making distinctions, as Warhol did, the very quantity of our stored data renders it unusable. If we selectively record data, we may, to our peril, miss something vital. If, like Warhol, we never access our data, then we may not need to worry much about the consequences of losing it. If, like Merwin's futuristic people, we become utterly dependent on our memory machines in order to function, then we should worry very much about losing them.

4   The Genesis of an Idea: Mourning Data Loss

For several years before I conceived of this project, I had been interested in mourning and its relationship to electronic media (Mauer, 1996). I had intended to construct a monument that would demonstrate that the electronic realm could support mourning, but I had not identified a problem — a sacrifice to memorialize — worth the effort. Then one day, when I walked into the English Department at the University of Central Florida, I found a worthy problem; the department secretary's computer had crashed. The hard drive was lost and with it was the institutional history of the department. Many department files existed in backup copies on paper, but some data had not been backed up. The archival structure of the data, the nested folders that stored the documents, had disappeared along with the data.

The secretary was distraught; she did not know how profoundly the loss of her hard drive would affect her and would affect the department. When we lose data, I realized, we suddenly confront the fact that we are dependent on having access to it and may be crippled without it. I asked the secretary whether she would mourn the loss of her data. The idea intrigued her and we set up a time to discuss it. During the discussion, she made the following remarks:

1. Her natural memory was useless for replacing the data on the computer. There was no way she could recall the contents of all of the documents that had been stored on it and it would be impossible for her to reproduce the documents from natural memory.
2. Before her computer crashed, she had known of others who had lost data on their computers. Still she had neglected to back up her work.
3. She retained the archival structure of the data in her natural memory. If called upon to retrieve a document, she could remember the structure of nested folders and the pathways she took through the structure in order to retrieve the document. Her picture of the archive remained intact even though the archive itself no longer existed.

The secretary, as the person in charge of storing and retrieving the department's data, had a relationship to this data that was both personal and institutional. I wondered whether there was a deeper connection between the two types of data loss — personal and institutional — and whether the loss of personal data was part of a larger pattern, something with a collective dimension. I also wondered whether the experience of data loss in the modern world differs significantly from the experiences of data loss that had come before. These topics are too broad to be addressed adequately in this single chapter (a book by the author is planned). The monument I propose below seeks to create new connections between personal and collective forms of data loss.

5 Monumentality

Monumentalists — those who seek to guide collective mourning through the production of monuments — face a critical process. They must ask themselves which losses ought to be considered as sacrifices. They must ask themselves which ideals these sacrifices honor. The design of a monument reflects the monumentalist's consideration of these questions. The proposal for this monument recognizes lost data not as an accident, an avoidable mistake, but as an unavoidable loss that we may choose, if we so desire, to designate as a sacrifice. My hope is that we will recognize data loss as a sacrifice and that we will see this sacrifice as a price we pay for our collective values and behaviors. We might then choose to reconsider the wisdom of our collective values and behaviors in relation to the storage of memes. The monument to lost data will have three main functions:

1. To explore the relationship among our values, our behaviors, and our losses pertaining to data.
2. To reveal the links between personal data losses and collective identity.
3. To forge new identities around shared data losses.

The monument will support the work of mourning lost data, specifically the data loss at the NARA, but also the data loss experienced by ordinary people in their daily lives. The monument will allow for a wide variety of personal relationships to the monument because it will be constructed mostly from personal contributions, much like the Names Project — or "AIDS Quilt" — which is a gigantic monument made entirely from individual squares made and contributed by those mourning the loss of a loved one to AIDS.

Monumentality does not seek ways to avoid loss, though it has no quarrel with rationalist efforts to reduce or eliminate data loss. Monumentality aims to represent the values for which the losses occurred. Values are determined by the price we are willing to pay to sustain our behaviors. What values might be honored by data loss? A provisional answer: thousands of people suffer data loss because our society demands progress, which it defines as increased efficiency and storage capacity. Efficiency and capacity are values we are willing to pay for and pay for dearly.

Can data loss be considered sacrifice if its victims do not voluntarily destroy their data? Yes. Human beings voluntarily invest their labors in data-storage systems that produce data loss "victims"; thus we should acknowledge our willingness to sacrifice. To better understand this formulation, let us consider the loss of soldiers to war; soldiers do not volunteer to die on the battlefield, yet we recognize battlefield deaths as sacrifices because the battlefield is an environment in which death is more likely and our society willingly sends soldiers to battlefields to die. Auto deaths are a related example; people do not voluntarily die in auto accidents, yet in the United States we willingly accept the inevitable deaths of roughly 35,000 people per year for our right to own cars and drive them whenever we like.

Any monument to lost data will be "abject," meaning that data losses are not, as yet, part of the recognized category of national loss; they do not yet constitute our sense of national identity as do the deaths of soldiers during war. Because an abject loss is degraded and debased, the work of mourning abject losses is more difficult; there is little acceptance of it and support for it. Gregory Ulmer, who invented the concept of abject monuments in his essay "Abject Monumentality," proposes two abject monuments, one for auto deaths and one for pet deaths. His monuments called for recognition of sacrifices on behalf of our right to drive cars and own pets. Unlike traditional monuments, which mark the sites of the officially sacred, abject monuments mark the sites of sacrifices not yet accepted as sacred; in particular, abject monuments, according to Ulmer, mark the sites of degraded losses, such as auto deaths. How do we know auto deaths are degraded? Ulmer refers to a piece in The National Review criticizing the design of the Vietnam Veteran's Memorial Wall, claiming that the list of dead soldier's names degraded their sacrifice for the nation: "THEY MIGHT AS WELL HAVE BEEN TRAFFIC ACCIDENTS" (Ulmer, 1993, p. 8).

An abject monument claims a degraded loss as a sacred expenditure made on behalf of the collective. For example, auto deaths are necessary for the nation because those who died in auto accidents were exercising the right to drive their cars anytime, a right for which the nation is willing to sacrifice thousands. The proposed monument to lost data, also an abject monument, will recognize data loss as a sacrifice made on behalf of the nation's desire for progress, understood as our desire to augment our memories with machines.

Bataille (1988–1991) described sacrifice as "the antithesis of production, which is accomplished with a view to the future; it is consumption that is concerned only with the moment" (p. 49). Through sacrifice, according to Bataille, we transform the object from the realm of the profane — characterized by "use value" — to the realm of the sacred — characterized by "uselessness." At once destructive and creative, sacrifice unites the community, usually through ritual, by removing its objects and its members from the world of profane things and bringing them into collective, intimate contact with the sacred.

Modern people typically provide no place for sacrifice in their daily lives. As a result, Bataille argues, they do not acknowledge their expenditures as anything other than losses within the restricted economy of wealth accumulation. By neglecting sacrifice, modern people suffer a loss of intimacy and community. The goal of making a monument to lost data is to turn the destructive character of data loss into a creative one by uniting the community in its sacrifice and helping it to understand and maybe re-evaluate its core values.

In "Abject Monumentality," Ulmer (1993) argues that the electronic sphere needs its own practice of monumentality to supplement the monumental practices of literature and architecture. He proposes electronic monumentality as an answer to the claims "made by modernists" (especially in architecture) that electronic technology was largely responsible for the decline of the public field.

> The monumental function of architecture included mourning, understood as the collective version of the psychology of identification — the formation of the superego in an individual through the internalization (introjection) of ego — ideals. Monumentality was responsible for maintaining a sense of national identity from one generation to the next (hence the mourning by one generation for the loss of the previous generation, back to the Founding Fathers). (Ulmer, 1993)

Monuments, by Ulmer's definition, are places and objects that remind people of sacrifices they make to maintain their behaviors and values. They have the following features:

1. Monuments designate a set of deaths or losses as significant and ascribe to them a great value. A classic example: the historians of the French Revolution, Michelet and Renan, represented the dead of the anti-Huguenot pogrom of 1572 as fratricidal sacrifices necessary to the development of the French nation, though at the time of the pogrom the "nation" would not exist for hundreds of years, and the killers and their victims would never have understood themselves as "Frenchmen" or "brothers" belonging to the same nation. Yet these ancient slaughters became "family history" for the French historians of the 18th century. Michelet and Renan demonstrate that monumentalists put words in the mouths of the dead, claiming to reveal their "true" desires. Victims of wars become sacrifices for "the Nation ... even when these sacrifices were not understood as such by the victims" (Anderson, 1991, p. 41).
2. Monuments identify specific deaths or losses within a large narrative framework as sacrifices on behalf of shared collective values. For example, during wartime, nations honor soldiers who have died so that the nation might live. Monuments ensure their eternal life in citizens' memories, even if it is only as an anonymous victim represented by a Tomb of the Unknown Soldier.

3. The living members of a society become indebted to those who have sacrificed themselves on their behalf. At the least, that debt is to mourn them and to retain their memory. Beyond that, members of the next generation are obligated to sacrifice themselves to honor those who sacrificed themselves in the past.
4. Mourning and sacrifice enable societies to transform the contingencies of life into continuity and to transmit preferred social values to the next generation.
5. Because monuments shape memories, values, and behaviors for succeeding generations, people can take more active roles in social transformation by learning how to create monuments of their own.

In his "Abject Monumentality" essay, Ulmer (1993) does not make explicit the poetics of abject monuments, other than to note that they should be attached as "asterisks" to existing monuments. Thus the design features I offer below are intended to be specific to this monument, though they may be applicable to other monuments.

6   Phantom Data

It may come across as paradoxical and even perverse to propose a monument to lost data since what should we put in it but data? However, the data stored in the monument will be of special types — it will be the traces and the phantoms of lost data. Traces include fragments of lost texts, while phantoms include recollections of texts for which no traces survive. Traces of data might be broken hard drives whose data had been destroyed, texts in archaic languages, and found photographs. Found photographs are mysterious because they have been detached from their original context and there may be no "Rosetta Stone" — which provided researchers with translations of ancient Egyptian text into Greek — that enables us to understand their significance. For example, people may possess ancient family photographs yet have no knowledge about the people in them.

Phantom data differ from trace data. In the discussion I had with the secretary whose hard drive crashed, she explained that she had retained the archival structure of the hard drive data in her natural memory. When called upon to retrieve a document, she could remember the structure of nested folders and the pathways she took through that structure in order to retrieve the document. Her mental picture of the archive remained intact even though the archive itself no longer existed; she was haunted by the data she had lost and this haunting caused her emotional pain. I coined a neologism to describe the secretary's condition — "phantom data pain" — which can be explained by an analogy to phantom limb pain.

> "Phantom limb" pain has been recorded almost as long as people have been losing limbs and surviving. As we can see on the motor cortex, specific areas function to map out specific parts of the body. Losing a part of the body doesn't necessarily stop the cortex from continuing to "map" the missing part, adding a slight twist to Korzybski's, "the map is not the territory" (Austin, s.d.).

A common treatment for phantom limb pain is the Ramachandran Method. The practitioner uses a mirror and a box to treat the patient (see Figure 4). With the healthy arm through the hole corresponding with the reflective side of the mirror, he maneuvers his phantom arm through the other hole (be imaginative with this one to help the client do this). Thus now, the client has a reflection of his real arm that, with some maneuvering, will correspond exactly with the missing limbs' location. This enables the brain of the person to achieve feedback to the motor area of the brain corresponding with the phantom:

> Philip rotated his body, shifting his shoulder, to "insert" his lifeless phantom into the box. Then he put his right hand on the other side of the mirror and attempted to make synchronous movements. As he gazed into the mirror, he gasped and then cried out, "Oh, my God! Oh, my God, doctor! This is unbelievable. It's mind boggling!" He was jumping up and down like a kid. "My left arm is plugged in again. It's as if I'm in the past. All these memories from so many years ago are flooding back into my mind. I can move my arm again. I can feel my elbow moving, my wrist moving. It's all moving again" (Austin, s.d.).

Ramachandran asked Philip to close his eyes and Philip's phantom arm once again became lifeless until he once again opened his eyes.

Figure 4. The Ramachandran Mirror Box. Austin, A.

Curiously, despite the historical referential experiences that flooded into consciousness, 4 weeks later following 10 min a day with the box and mirror, Philip reported that the limb had gone, "all I have now is my phantom fingers and palm dangling from my shoulder." The pains had significantly reduced (only the fingers still hurt — the rest had gone) and Philip now possessed an altered but more realistic body "image" mapped onto his sensory cortex:

> "It's not clear why his fingers didn't disappear, but one reason might be that they are over-represented — like the huge lips on the Penfield map — in the somatosensory cortex and may be more difficult to deny" (Austin, s.d.) (see Figure 5).

Ramachandran's research into phantom limbs provides the following insight; although a limb may be missing, it is still represented in the mind. In both cases, phantom limbs and phantom data, we continue to receive feedback about something that is no longer there. The monument to lost data is a variation on the Ramachandran Method, designed to help us put the loss of our data in perspective and to achieve a more realistic picture of our situation in relation to augmented memory. In the Ramachandran Method, the patient uses the reflected image of a healthy limb to gain mastery over the feedback that the mind senses from the missing limb; the amputee learns to accept a new body image, and this new cognitive map of the body reduces suffering and increases adaptability.

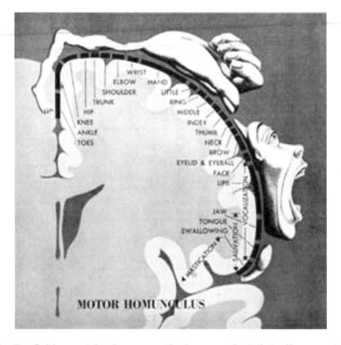

Figure 5: The Penfield map (also known as the homunculus) (http://www.eatonhand.com/hw/homunc.gif).

To help the mourner gain mastery over lost data, the monument to lost data uses a process analogous to the Ramachandran Method. In this variation, the mourner recollects and reflects upon the lost data by reference to stored data, in other words, to data that has not been lost. For example, a missing family photo album may be mourned by reflecting upon a different family photo album, perhaps an album from a different family. The loss of a hard drive may be mourned by reflecting upon the contents of another hard drive. In each case, the mourner looks for patterns, highlighting details in the stored data that resemble details in the lost data. In this way, the mourner regains some control of the feedback that the mind senses from the missing data.

7   Designing the Monument to Lost Data

Although I have put together some of my ideas, outlined below, about the location and design of a monument to lost data, there should be community deliberation over these issues. Such deliberation would raise debate about the values embodied by various options, as well as the community's investments in the monument itself. My design ideas are meant as contributions to a discussion that I hope will take place at a national level.

In my proposed design of the monument to lost data, there would be two components: one physical and one virtual. The physical part would consist of a corporeal monument at a public location, while the virtual part would consist of an electronic database accessible anywhere in the world by anyone with an Internet connection. I propose a corporeal monument in the shape of mushrooms to be located at the NARA, along with a worldwide virtual monument, accessible via the Internet, to be modeled upon the mycelium (see Figures 6 and 7). The mycelium, the branching organ of mushrooms and other fungi, is a rhizomatic structure of networked passages that gives rise to new species of fungus — in this case, new forms of memory for diverse data losses.

I chose the mushroom/mycelium as the structuring metaphor for the monument because "Fungi play vital roles in all ecosystems, as decomposers, symbionts of animals and plants and as parasites" (Dix & Webster, 1995, preface). By analogy, the monument to lost data will feed on the decaying matter of our information age, transforming it into something that might be more beneficial to the society. "Mycelium" is also attractive for its homophonic suggestiveness, namely its resemblance to the words "mausoleum" and "museum," which are also repositories for valuable things. The mycelium works well as the poetic structure for the monument to lost data because mycelia permit novel hybrids (see Figure 7). In the monument I envision, there will be novel combinations of data loss entries that will lead to new insights about the costs of our collective values and behaviors.

I envision the various data loss entries in the monument being linked using the principles of "hyphal fusion," a principle of linkage that fungi employ to share resources. Hyphal fusion permits diverse species of fungi to bond their mycelia together and share resources, and it also leads to the development of new species of fungi (Dix & Webster, 1995, pp. 15–16). By analogy, I use the principle of hyphal fusion as a poetics for structuring the virtual part of the monument to lost data; diverse data loss entries will be joined and thus will produce, I hope, new insights and possibly new memes for understanding our personal and

Figure 6: Proof of the concept — a monument to lost data, in the form of mushrooms, at the NARA in Washington, DC. As the NARA loses more data, more mushrooms will grow inside the building to represent the data loss (NARA image with mushrooms added by the author).

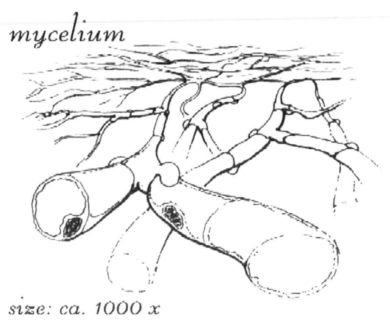

Figure 7: Branching network structure of the mycelium (http://home.wanadoo.nl/abie-mans/pict/mycelium.jpg).

collective relationships to data. Such linkages do not impede users from exploring the monument's database by using a search engine.

By placing data loss entries into new relationships with other data loss entries, we draw each one into a new context and transform personal losses into sacrifices that can be recognized as parts of collective losses. We make a similar cognitive move when we see each soldier's death not merely as a personal loss, but as part of a larger context — a collective loss. If we were to juxtapose soldiers' deaths to other kinds of losses, such as the growing loss of the earth's ozone layer, we could search for meaning in the linkage. We might conclude, for instance, that the loss of soldiers in Iraq and the loss of the ozone layer are both connected to our consumption of fossil fuels. If that is our conclusion, then we might reconsider whether our consumption of fossil fuels is worth the costs.

The principle of hyphal fusion in fungi can be carried over to the design principles of the monument to lost data. The rhizome model put forth by post-structuralist theorists such as Deleuze and Guatari explains how the principle of linking diverse texts may serve as not only an archival structure in electronic databases but also as a means of conducting further research. Ulmer puts these post-structuralist insights into practice in his development of the puncept.

Ulmer imagines teaching a "new mimesis ... based on homophonic resemblance" in which the "puncept" would coincide with the "concept." Such a pedagogy, derived from "the fully developed homonymic program at work in Derrida's style" and amply evident in the present critical writing, would seize on the puns or homophones as precisely the device which, at the level of language, is "capable of relating elements with the least motivation, hence with the greatest economy of speed" and "generating the greatest 'information' (i.e., negentropy)." Such synthetic terms may offer an instance of the "higher-order bootstraps" students will need to think a massive cultural inventory soon accessible by the terabyte, in hypertext: as the neurologist Gerald Edelman observes, "[t]hinking occurs in terms of synthesized patterns, not logic, and for this reason, it may always exceed in its reach syntactical, or mechanical relationships" (Hilton, 1995).

The puncept will be the textual version of "hyphal fusion," or linkage, in the virtual part of the monument to lost data. It permits patterns to form based on shared terms and can be used in addition to the hierarchical groupings, like the Dewey Decimal System, found in most data archives. The monument to lost data will take terms "out of context" the way a Google search does, without regard for the topics of the texts being searched; thus the word "trace" may appear both in scientific works and in art criticism, and can be used to link texts from both discourses. The monument will treat terms that cross discourse boundaries as points of linkage among diverse entries and will present juxtapositions of such entries in order to help people produce new inferences about their data losses.

The first step to employing the puncept for hyphal fusion is to find an aesthetic pattern (the sharing of a common term or attribute) then move to find other patterns (of correlation, cause/effect, etc.). For example: years ago I assigned a monument project to my class at the University of Florida. One student produced a monument to losses caused by sickle-cell anemia. I made a monument about prisons. The connection was that discourses around both topics employed the word "cell," although the term meant something different in each discourse: blood cell in one and prison cell in another. Beyond that signifier linkage, we discovered that African–Americans found themselves in prison cells and with sickle cells disproportionately more than whites. Another result of the "probing" that we did of the sickle-cell anemia/prison cell link was our discovery that social expenditures on these issues were disproportionate. In the case of prisons, disproportionately more money was spent sending black men to prison as was spent sending them to college. In the case of sickle-cell anemia, a lesser portion was spent on researching this disease compared to what had been spent on other diseases that affected whites in greater numbers. Such inferences gave us impetus to conduct additional research into race as a vital component linking both problems.

The idea of using the mycelium as a metaphor for the crossing of discourse boundaries is not new. In fact, Freud used this same metaphor over a hundred years ago to explain the way that discourses in dreams formed networks around a discursive "navel." As Weber pointed out, Freud's use of the mycelium metaphor, rather than the more common "branching roots" metaphor, created interesting problems for Freud precisely because, unlike the branching roots structure, the mycelium is a decentered structure.

> The "navel of the dream" is read through "dem Unerkannten aufsitzt" by Weber as "an untenable alternative" which Freud "straddles" (81): what I call, following Derrida, undecidability. The reference to botany leads Weber to focus on the last line of the passage — "Out of one of the denser places in this meshwork, the dream-wish rises [erhebt sich] like a mushroom out of its mycelium" — and his next piece of evidence that Freud ... is interested in the dream as dislocation, "ent-stellt" (81). Referring ... to the O.E.D., Weber finds the following for "mycelium": "Mycelium. (f. Gr. mykes mushroom, after epithelium) Bot. The vegetative part of the thallus of fungi, consisting of white filamentous tubes (hyphae); the spawn of mushrooms" (qtd. in Weber, 81). And for "thallus": "(Gr. thallos, green shoot, f. thállein to bloom) Bot. A vegetable structure without vascular tissue, in which there is no differentiation into stem and leaves, and from which true roots are absent" (ibid.) ...
>
> Interpretation's straddling of the dream-navel, and the thallus (non-roots) at the root or origin of the dream (the dream-wish), both suggest the undecidability of an unknowable rather than an unknown. This movement and undecidability, for Weber, suggest the unknowable, a différance and not a specific absence of meaning: a non-original mobile textuality rather than an original immobile text. (Anders, 2000)

The monument to lost data, like the meshwork of the dream, ought to be decentered, supporting an organic process of cultural invention. The individual participants — the mourners who add their traces and phantoms to the monument — will see their contributions linked to others. As they visit the monument and see the links to and from their entries, they may come to understand the collective dimension of their personal data loss. Thus the loss of a parent's living memory to Alzheimer's might be understood in relation to the loss of a hard drive. Similarly, the collective dimensions of data loss might be re-imagined as part of a global shift in data-storage practices. The loss of native languages might be understood in relation to the loss of Kosovars' identities, following the link between the

Kosovars' stolen passports and the minimal amount of porting (a computer networking term) of native languages onto the Internet.

Could the design I propose here lead to relationships that trivialize great losses (as might be the case if there were to be a link between the loss of a language and the loss of an iPod collection of pop songs)? To some extent, there is a risk of trivializing great losses by linking them to lesser ones. But there are also advantages to making all kinds of juxtapositions and relationships without first considering relative degrees of loss. To some extent, we can distinguish between the loss of memes and personal losses, but that line may blur; what if thousands of people were to lose their iPod collections? Would those losses be trivial? A hyphal node juxtaposing the relationship between the loss of a language and the loss of an iPod collection might prompt the iPod owner to reconsider the value of her loss. The monument to lost data itself may appear to trivialize other monuments, such as war monuments. Such appearances might give us cause for reflection, but should not deter us; the potential benefits of the monument to lost data are too great.

The monument to lost data should not be a fixed entity; its components should be linked in a process that continually renews the monument. In the execution of the monument to lost data, numerous problems will undoubtedly arise. For instance, who will make decisions about filtering content in the monument? What criteria will be used to make such decisions? Which entries in the monument will receive prominent placement, or will all placement be equal? These questions have been raised in relation to a number of public and semi-public projects, including the Names Project and Wikipedia. Large-scale public and semi-public databases are vulnerable to submissions that might be perceived as offensive, controversial, or trivial. I would argue, however, that the monument to lost data should take as broad and egalitarian a view as possible toward possible submissions. Consider a hypothetical problem that could arise; one group memorializes the loss of Indian sacred lands while another group memorializes the disappearance of statues of Columbus. Without judging the relative merits of these submissions, the monument's managers — a group that may be entrusted to guide participants' behaviors the way that web moderators do — might provide a setting and guidelines for the participants to engage in dialogue with each other. The best practices for such moderation will emerge from experience and good judgment as the project comes to fruition.

References

A Timeline of China (n.d.). Retrieved July 24, 2005, from http://www.scaruffi.com/politics/chinese.html

Adamzik, K., Antos, G., & Jakobs, E.-M. (1997). Domänen- und kulturspezifisches Schreiben. Einleitung und Überblick [Domain- and culture-specific writing. Introduction and overview]. In E.-M. Jakobs, & D. Knorr (Series Eds.) & K. Adamzik, G. Antos, & E.-M. Jakobs (Vol. Eds.), *Textproduktion und Medium; Vol. 3. Domänen- und kulturspezifisches Schreiben* (pp. 1–6). Frankfurt am Main: Lang.

African Internet Connectivity — A Status report. (2002). *African internet connectivity website.* Accessed 12 March 2003 at http://www3.sn.apc.org/africa/

African Internet Connectivity — A Status report. (2002). *African internet connectivity website.* Retrieved July 15, 2005, from http://www3.sn.apc.org/africa/

Alabi, G. A. (1996). *Case study: Empowering socio-economic development in Africa utilizing information technology, a critical examination of the social, economic, technical, and policy issues in Nigeria.* A Report of the African Information Society. Retrieved July 15, 2005, from http://www.uneca.org/aisi/studies.htm

Alamargot, D., & Chanquoy, L. (2001). *Through the models of writing.* Dordrecht: Kluwer Academic Publishers.

Amdahl, M. (1992). Aspects 1.0. *Computers and Composition, 9*(1), 89–91. Retrieved July 26, 2004, from http://www.hu.mtu.edu/~candc/archives/v10/10_1_html/10_1_10_Amdahl.html

Anders, E. (2000). Chapter 3: (Un)easily contained elements. *Disturbing psychoanalytic origins: A Derridean reading of Freudian theory.* Unpublished doctoral dissertation, University of Florida, Gainesville. Retrieved on July 8, 2004, from http://www.eric.anders.net/dissertation/weber.html

Anderson, B. (1991). *Imagined communities: Reflections on the origin and spread of nationalism.* London, NY: Verso.

Anderson, J. R. (1990). *The adaptive control of thought.* Hillsdale, NJ: Lawrence Erlbaum Associates.

Andriessen, J., Erkens, G., Overeem, E., & Jaspers, J. (1996, September). *Using complex information in argumentation for collaborative text production.* Paper presented at the UCIS '96 conference, Poitiers, France.

Anthony, L., & Lashkia, G. V. (2003). Mover: A matching learning tool to assist in the reading and writing of technical papers. *IEEE Transactions on Professional Communication, 46,* 185–192.

Appelt, W., & Busbach, U. (1996). The BSCW system: A www-based application to support cooperation of distributed groups. In IEEE (Ed.), *Proceedings of the 5th workshops on enabling technologies: Infrastructure for collaborative enterprises* (pp. 304–309). Stanford, CA: IEEE Computer Society Press.

Arecco, M. R., & Ransdell, S. (2002). Early exposure to an L2 predicts good L1 as well as good L2 writing. In S. Ransdell, & M. Barbier (Eds.), *New directions for research in L2 writing* (pp. 123–132). The Netherlands: Kluwer Academic Publishers.

Arnold, D. H., & Doctoroff, G. L. (2003). The early education of socioeconomically disadvantaged children. *Annual Review of Psychology, 54,* 517–545.

Arppe, A. (2000). Developing a grammar checker for Swedish. In *12th Nordic conference of computational linguistics, Proceedings of the NODALIDA, Trondheim: Norwegian University of Science and Technology, Department of Linguistics* (pp. 13–27).

Austin, A. (n.d.). The Ramachandran method and the NLP practitioner. *Brain, Mind and Language.* Retrieved on July 8, 2004, from http://www.23nlpeople.com/Phantom.htm

Austin, J. L. (1962). *How to do things with words.* Cambridge, MA: Harvard University Press.

Babaian, T., Grosz, B. J., & Shieber, S. M. (2002). A writer's collaborative assistant. In Gil, Y. & Leaks, D. (Eds.) *Proceedings of the 7th international conference on intelligent user interfaces* (pp. 7–14). San Francisco, CA: Association for Computing Machinery.

Bacheldor, B. (1999). Push for performance. *Information Week, 20,* 18–20.

Baecker, R. M., Waston, D. Posner, I. R., & Mawby, K. L. (1993). The user-centred iterative design of collaborative writing software. In S. Ashlund, A. Henderson, E. Hollnagel, K. Mullet, & T. White (Eds.), *Proceedings of the INTERCHI '93 conference on human factors in computing systems* (pp. 399–405). New York: Association for Computing Machinery.

Bakhtin, M. (1986). *Speech genres and other late essays.* Austin, TX: University of Texas Press.

Bangert-Downs, R. (1993). The word processor as an instructional tool: A meta-analysis of word processing in writing instruction. *Review of Educational Research, 63,* 69–93.

Barton, D. (1994). *Literacy: An introduction to the ecology of written language.* Oxford, UK: Blackwell.

Bataille, G. (1988–1991). *The accursed share: An essay on general economy* (R. Hurley, Trans.). New York: Zone Books (original work published 1947).

Baym, N. (1995). The performance of humor in computer-mediated communication. *Journal of Computer-Mediated Communication, 1*(2). Retrieved April 12, 2004, from http://www.ascusc.org/jcmc/vol1/issue2/baym.html

Bechar-Israeli, H. (1995). From <Bonehead> to <cLoNehEAd>: Nicknames, play and identity on Internet relay chat. *Journal of Computer-Mediated Communication, 1*(2). Retrieved April 12, 2004, from http://www.ascusc.org/jcmc/vol1/issue2/

Beers, S., & Quinlan, T. (2000, April). *Reading while writing: Student writers' use of the developing text.* Paper presented at the American Educational Research Association, New Orleans, LA.

Beers, S., & Quinlan, T. (2006). *Reading-during-writing and children's writing competence.* Manuscript submitted for publication.

Bereiter, C. (2002). Emergent versus presentational hypertext. In R. Bromme, & E. Stahl (Eds.), *Writing hypertext and learning. Conceptual and empirical approaches. Advances in learning and instruction series* (pp. 73–78). Amsterdam: Pergamon.

Bereiter, C., & Scardamalia, M. (1982). From conversation to composition: The role of instruction in a developmental process. In Robert, G. (Ed.), *Advances in instructional psychology* (Vol. 2, pp. 132–165). Hillsdale, NJ: Lawrence Erlbaum Associates.

Bereiter, C., & Scardamalia, M. (1987). *The psychology of written composition.* Hillsdale, NJ: Lawrence Erlbaum Associates.

Berlin, J. A. (1987). *Rhetoric and reality: Writing instruction in American colleges, 1900–1985.* Carbondale: Southern Illinois University Press.

Berlin, J. A. (1996). *Rhetorics, poetics, and cultures: Refiguring English studies.* Urbana, IL: National Council of Teachers of English.

Berners-Lee, T., & Fischetti, M. (1999). *Weaving the web: The original design and ultimate destiny of the World Wide Web by its inventor.* San Francisco: Harper.

Bernheim Brush, A. J., Bargeron, D., Grudin, J., Borning, A. & Gupta, A. (2002). Supporting interaction outside of class: Anchored discussions vs. discussion boards. In *Proceedings of computer-supported collaborative learning 2002* (pp. 425–434). Hillsdale, NJ: Lawrence Erlbaum Associates.

Berninger, V. W., & Swanson, H. L. (1994). Modifying Hayes and Flower's model of skilled writing to explain beginning and developing writing. *Advances in Cognition and Educational Practice, 2*, 57–81.

Berninger, V. W., Vaughan, K. B., Abbott, R. D., Abbott, S. P., Rogan, L. W., Brooks, A., Reed, E., & Graham, S. (1997). Treatment of handwriting problems in beginning writers: Transfer from handwriting to composition. *Journal of Educational Psychology, 89*, 652–666.

Bialystok, E. (1988). Levels of bilingualism and levels of linguistic awareness. *Developmental Psychology, 24*, 560–567.

Birn, J. (2000). Detecting grammar errors with Lingsoft's Swedish grammar checker. In *12th Nordic conference of computational linguistics, Proceedings of the NODALIDA, Trondheim: Norwegian University of Science and Technology, Department of Linguistics* (pp.28–40).

Bisaillon, J., Clerc, I., & Ladouceur, J. (1999). A computer writing environment for professional writers and students learning to write. *Journal of Technical Writing and Communication, 29*, 185–202.

Bizzell, P. (1982). Cognition, convention, and certainty: What we need to know about writing. *Pre/Text, 3*, 213–243.

Blackmon, M. H., Polson, P. G., Kitajima, M., & Lewis, C. H. (2002). Cognitive walkthrough for the web. In Terveen, L. (ed.) *Proceedings of ACMCHI 2002 conference on human factors in computing systems conference* (pp. 463–470). Minneapolis: Minnesota.

Bockris, V. (1989). *The life and death of Andy Warhol*. New York: Bantam Books. Retrieved on July 8, 2004, from coverweb/bridge.html

Bonin, P. & Méot, A. (2002). Writing to dictation in real time in adults: What are the determinants of written latencies? In J.P. Shohov (Ed.), *Advances in psychology research (Vol 16)* (pp. 139–165). NY: Nova Sciences Publishers.

Bonin, P., Peereman, R., & Fayol, M. (2001). Do phonological codes constrain the selection of orthographic codes in writing picture naming? *Journal of Memory and Language, 45*, 688–720.

Borgh, K., & Dickson, W. P. (1992). The effects on children's writing of adding speech synthesis to a word processor. *Journal of Research on Computing in Education, 24*, 533–544.

Borin, L. (2002, August). *What have you done for me lately? The fickle alignment of NLP and CALL*. Paper presented at the 'NLP in CALL' EuroCall 2002 preconference workshop, Jyväskylä, Finland.

Boschung, D., & Gnach A. (2003). *Navigation und Werkzeuggebrauch als Indikatoren für die Phasierung von wissenschaftlichen Schreibprozessen am Computer [Navigation and tool use as indicators of the phases of academic writing processes on the computer]*. Unpublished thesis University of Bern, Bern, Switzerland.

Bourdin, B., & Fayol, M. (1994). Is written language production more difficult than oral language production? A working memory approach. *International Journal of Psychology, 29*, 591–620.

Bourdin, B., & Fayol, M. (2000). Is graphic activity cognitively costly? A developmental approach. *Reading and Writing, 13*, 183–196.

Brandt, D. (2001). *Literacy in American lives*. New York: Cambridge University Press.

Breetvelt, I., Van den Bergh, H., & Rijlaarsdam, G. (1996). Rereading and generating and their relation to text quality. An application of multilevel analysis on writing process data. In G. Rijlaarsdam, H. van den Bergh, & M. Couzijn (Eds.), *Theories, models, and methodology in writing research* (pp. 10–20). Amsterdam: Amsterdam University Press.

Bridwell, L., Sirc, G., & Brooke, R. (1985). Revising and computing: Case studies of student writers. In S. Freedam (Ed.), The acquisition of written language: response and revision (pp. 172–194). Norwood, NJ: Ablex.

Bridwell-Bowles, L., Johnson, P., & Brehe, S. (1987). Composing and computers: Case studies of experienced writers. In A. Matsuhashi (Ed.), Writing in real time: Modeling production processes (pp. 81–107). London: Longman.

Bromme, R., & Stahl, E. (2002). Learning by producing hypertext from reader perspectives: Cognitive flexibiliy theory reconsidered. In R. Bromme, & E. Stahl (Eds.), *Writing hypertext and learning. Conceptual and empirical approaches* (pp. 39–61). Amsterdam: Pergamon.

Bromme, R., & Stahl, E. (2005). Is a hypertext a book or a space? The impact of different introductory metaphors on hypertext construction. *Computers & Education, 44*(2), 115–133.

Brown, J. (1999). Hotline to the underground. Salon 21st. Retrieved April 12, 2004, from http://archive.salon.com/21st/feature/1999/02/24feature.html

Bruffee, K. A. (1984). Collaborative learning and the conversation of mankind. *College English, 46*, 635–652.

Bruffee, K. A. (1986). Social construction, language, and the authority of knowledge: A bibliographical essay. *College English, 48*, 773–790.

Brundige, E. (1995). The legend of the library. http://www.perseus.tufts.edu/GreekScience/Students/Ellen/Museum.html. Retrieved on July, 8, 2004.

Buchanan, E. (2000). *SyllaBase Internet learning system grows from a USU basement to a worldwide network of students.* Hard News Café, Utah State University. Retrieved August 13, 2005, from http://www.hardnewscafe.usu.edu/archive/april2000/0421_hightech-syllabase.html

Burns, H. L. (1980, October). *A writer's tool: Computing as a mode of inventing.* Paper presented at the New York College English Association conference at Sarasota Springs, NY.

Burns, H. L. (1984). Recollections of first-generation computer-assisted prewriting. In W. Wresch (Ed.), *The computer in composition instruction: A writer's tool* (pp. 15–33). Urbana, IL: National Council of Teachers of English.

Burns, H. L., & Culp, G. H. (1980). Stimulating rhetorical revision in English composition through computer-assisted instruction. *Educational Technology, 20*(8), 5–10.

Burstein, J., & Marcu, D. (2003). Automated evaluation of discourse structure in student essays. In M. D. Shermis, & J. C. Burstein (Eds.), *Automated essay scoring* (pp. 209–229). Mahwah, NJ: Lawrence Erlbaum Associates.

Bush, V. (1945). As we may think. *The Atlantic Monthly, 176*, 101–108.

Bush, V. (1967). Memex revisited. In V. Bush, *Science is not enough* (pp. 75–101). New York: William Morrow.

Butler, W., Carter, L., Kemp, F O., & Taylor, P. (1988). *Daedalus instructional system [Computer software]*. Austin, TX: The Daedalus Group.

Card, S. K., Hong, L., Mackinlay, J. D., & Chi, E. H. (2004). 3Book: A 3D electronic smart book. In *Proceedings of the advanced visual interfaces* (pp. 303–307). NY: ACM Press.

Card, S. K., Pirolli, P., Wege, M. V. D., Morrison, J. B., Reeder, R. W., Schraedley, P. K., & Boshart, J. (2001). Information scent as a driver of web behavior graphs: Results of a protocol analysis method for web usability. In *Proceedings of the SIGCHI conference on human factors in computing systems* (pp. 498–505). NY: ACM Press.

Carlson, P. A. (1990). Artificial neural networks as cognitive tools for professional writing. In *Proceedings of the 8th annual international conference on systems documentation* (pp. 95–110). Little Rock: Association for Computing Machinery.

Carver, S. M., Lehrer, R., Connell, T., & Erickson, J. (1992). Learning by hypermedia design: Issues of assessment and implementation. *Educational Psychologist, 27*, 385–404.

Castells, M. (1996). *The Information age: Economy, society, and culture: Vol. 1. Rise of the network society*. Malden, MA: Blackwell.

Castells, M. (1998). *The information age: Economy, society, and culture: Vol. 3. End of the millennium*. Malden, MA: Blackwell.

Catlin, T., Bush, P., & Yankelovich, N. (1989). InterNote: Extending a hypermedia framework to support annotative collaboration. In *Proceedings of Hypertext '89* (pp. 365–378). New York: Association for Computing Machinery.

Cederlund, J., & Severinson Eklundh, K. (n.d). *JEdit: The logging text editor for Macintosh.* Stockholm: IPLab, Department of Numerical Analysis and Computing Science, Royal Institute of Technology (KTH).

Cerratto Pargman, T. (2003). Collaborating with writing tools: An instrumental perspective on the problem of computer-supported collaborative activities. *Interacting with Computers, 15,* 737–757.

Chafe, W. L. (1994). *Discourse, consciousness, and time: The flow and displacement of conscious experience in speaking and writing.* Chicago: University of Chicago Press.

Channel, J. (2000). Corpus-based analysis of evaluative lexis. In S. Hunston, & G. Thompson (Eds.), *Evaluation in text: Authorial stance and the construction of discourse.* New York: Oxford University Press.

Chanquoy, L., Foulin, J. N., & Fayol, M. (1990). Temporal management of short text writing by children and adults. *European Bulletin of Cognitive Psychology/C.P.C., 10,* 513–540.

Chapelle, C. A. (2001). *Computer applications in second language acquisition.* Cambridge: Cambridge University Press.

Chenault, B. G. (1998, May). Developing personal and emotional relationships via computer mediated communication. *CMC Magazine.* Retrieved April 12, 2004, from http://www.december.com/cmc/mag/1998/may/chenault.html

Cherny, L. (1999). *Conversation and community: Chat in a virtual world.* Stanford, CA: CSLI Publications.

Chesnet, D., Guillabert, F., & Espéret, E. (1994). G-Studio: un logiciel pour l'étude en temps réel des paramètres temporels de la production écrite. *L'Année Psychologique, 94,* 283–294.

Chi, E. H. (2002). Improving web usability through visualization. *IEEE Internet Computing, 6,* 64–71.

Chi, E. H., Hong, L., Gumbrecht, M., & Card, S. K. (2005). ScentHighlights: Highlighting conceptually-related sentences during reading. In *Proceedings of the 10th international conference on intelligent user interfaces* (pp. 272–274). San Diego, CA: ACM Press.

Chi, E. H., Pirolli, P., Chen, K., & Pitkow, J. (2001). Using information scent to model user information needs and actions on the Web. In *Proceedings of the SIGCHI conference on human factors in computing systems* (pp. 490–497). New York: ACM Press.

Chi, E. H., Pirolli, P., & Pitkow, J. (2000). The scent of a site: A system for analyzing and predicting information scent, usage, and usability of a web site. In *Proceedings of the SIGCHI conference on human factors in computing systems* (pp. 161–168). New York: ACM Press.

Chi, E. H., Rosien, A. S., & Heer, J. (2002). LumberJack: Intelligent discovery and analysis of Web user traffic composition. In *Proceedings ACM-SIGKDD workshop on Web mining for usage patterns and user profiles (WebKDD 2002)* (pp. 1–16). Edmonton, Canada: ACM Press.

Chi, E. H., Rosien, A. S., Suppattanasiri, G., Williams, A., Royer, C., Chow, C., Robles, E., Dalal, B., Chen, J., & Cousins, S. (2003). The Bloodhound Project: Automating discovery of Web usability issues using the infoScent(tm) simulator. In *Proceedings of ACM conference on human factors in computing systems (CHI 2003)* (pp. 505–512). Fort Lauderdale, FL: ACM Press.

Chronology of the Struggle for Stability and Democracy: AllAfrica.com. (2000). *World history archives web site.* Retrieved July 15, 2005, from http://www.hartford-hwp.com/archives/34a/index-a.html

Churchill, E., & Bly, S. (2000). Culture vultures: Considering culture and communication in virtual environments. *SIGGroup Bulletin, 21*(1), 6–11.

Clarke, H. H., & Brennan, S. E. (1991). Grounding in communication. In L. M. Resnick, J. M. Levine, & S. D. Teasley (Eds.), *Perspectives on socially shared cognition* (pp. 129–149). Washington, DC: American Psychological Association.

Cochran-Smith, M. (1991). Word processing and writing in elementary classrooms: A critical review of related literature. *Review of Educational Research, 61*(1), 107–155.

Colley, A. M., & Beech, J. R. (1989). *Acquisition and performance of cognitive skills.* Chichester: Wiley.

Collins, J. (2003). *Variation in written English.* Pittsburgh: Carnegie Mellon.

Coyne, K. P., & Nielsen, J. (2001). *Beyond alt text: Making the Web easy to use for users with disabilities.* Unpublished manuscript.

Cronin, M. (2003). *Translation and Globalization* (pp. 224). New York and London: Routledge.

Crump, E. (2000). How many technoprovocateurs does it take to create interversity? In J. A. Inman, & D. N. Sewell (Eds.), *Taking flight with OWLs: Examining electronic writing center work* (pp. 223–233). Mahwah, NJ: Lawrence Erlbaum Associates.

Crystal, D. (1998). *Language play.* London: Penguin.

Crystal, D. (2001). *Language and the Internet.* Cambridge: Cambridge University Press.

Csikszentmihalyi, M. (1996). *Creativity: Flow and the psychology of discovery and invention.* New York: Harpercollins.

Cugini, J., & Scholtz, J. (1999, September). *Visvip: 3d visualization of paths through web sites.* Paper presented at the international workshop on web-based information visualization, Florence, Italy.

Dabiri, G., & Helten, D. (1998). *Psychologische Grundlagenstudie zum Phänomen Internet Relay Chat: Qualitative Analyse der Bedeutungsschwerpunkte für die Anwender,* Diplomarbeit, FU Berlin/Fachbereich Erziehungswissenschaft FU Berlin/Fachbereich. Retrieved April 12, 2004, from http://userpage.fu-berlin.de/~chlor/

Daiute, C. (1985). *Writing and computers.* New York: Addison-Wesley.

Danet, B. (2001). *Cyberpl@y: Communicating online.* Oxford: Berg. Retrieved (Part of the text) April 12, 2004, from http://atar.mscc.huji.ac.il/~msdanet/cyberpl@y/

Danet, B., Ruedenberg-Wright, L., & Tamari-Rosenbaum, Y. (1997). *Hmmm... where's that smoke coming from? - Writing, play and performance on Internet relay chat.* Retrieved April 12, 2004, from http://www.ascusc.org/jcmc/vol2/issue4/danet.html

Danet, B., Wachenhauser, T., Cividalli, A., Bechar-Israeli, H., & Rosenbaum-Tamari, Y. (1995). Curtain time 20:00 GMT: Experiments in virtual theater on Internet relay chat. *Journal of Computer-Mediated Communication, 1*(2). Retrieved April 12, 2004, from http://www.ascusc.org/jcmc/vol1/issue2/contents.html

Data. (1996). *Telecommunications: Glossary of telecommunication terms.* Retrieved on July 8, 2004, from http://www.its.bldrdoc.gov/fs-1037/dir-010/_1401.htm

Data. (2001). *WorldCom communications library.* (No longer archived).

DataMechanix. (2004). From http://www.datamechanix.com/dm_recv.htm

Datum. (1971). *The compact edition of the Oxford English dictionary* (Vol. 1, p. 648). Glasgow: Oxford University Press. Retrieved on July 8, 2004, from dissertation/weber.html

De La Paz, S., & Graham, S. (1997). Effects of dictation and advanced planning instruction on the composing of students with writing and learning problems. *Journal of Educational Psychology, 89,* 203–222.

Denley, I., Whitefield, A., & May, J. (1993). A case-study in task analysis for the design of a collaborative document production system. In M. Sharples (Ed.), *Computer supported collaborative writing* (pp. 161–184). London: Springer.

Dillon, A. (1996). Myths, misconceptions, and an alternative perspective on information usage and the electronic medium. In J.-F. Rouet, J. J. Levonen, A. Dillon, & R. J. Spiro (Eds.), *Hypertext and cognition* (pp. 25–42). Mahwah, NJ: Lawrence Erlbaum Associates.

Dillon, A. (2002). Writing as design: Hypermedia and the shape of information space. In R. Bromme, & E. Stahl (Eds.), *Writing hypertext and learning. Conceptual and empirical approaches. Advances in learning and instruction series* (pp. 63–72). Amsterdam: Pergamon.

Dix, N., & Webster, J. (1995). *Fungal ecology.* London: Chapman & Hall.

Domeij, R. (2003). *Datorstödd språkgranskning under skrivprocessen — Svensk språkkontroll ur användarperspektiv* [*Computer supported language checking during the writing process - Swedish Language checking from a user perspective*]. Doktorsavhandling i lingvistik: Stockholms universitet.

Dourish, P., & Bellotti, V. (1992). Awareness and coordination in shared workspaces. In *Proceedings of CSCW'92* (pp. 107–114). New York: ACM Press.

Dragon naturally speaking, version 7 [Computer Software] (2004). Scansoft.

Dreyfus, H. (1992). *What computers still can't do* (3rd ed.). Cambridge, MA: MIT Press.

Drori, G. S., & Jang, Y. S. (2003). The global digital divide: A sociological assessment of trends and causes. *Social Science Computer Review, 21*(2), 144–161.

Drott, M. C. (1998, September). *Using Web server logs to improve site design.* Paper presented at the 16th international conference on systems documentation, Quebec, Canada.

Dutoit, T. (1997). High-quality text-to-speech synthesis: An overview. *Journal of Electrical & Electronics Engineering, Australia: Special Issue on Speech Recognition and Synthesis, 17*(1), 25–37.

Egan, D. E., Remde, J. R., Gomez, L. M., Landauer, T. K., Eberhardt, J., & Lochbaum, C. C. (1989). Formative design evaluation of SuperBook. *ACM Transactions on Information Systems, 7*, 30–57.

Elbow, P. (1973). *Writing without teachers.* London, NY: Oxford University Press.

Ellis, L., Gibbs, S.J., & Rein, G.L. (1991). Groupware: Some issues and experiences. *Communications of the ACM, 34*, 38–58.

Engelbart, D.C., & English, W.K. (1968). A research center for augmenting human intellect. In *Proceedings of the fall joint computer conference* (pp. 395–410). Reston, VA: AFIPS.

Englert, C.S., Raphael, T.E., Anderson, L.M., Gregg, S. L., & Anthony, H.M. (1989). Exposition: Reading, writing, and the metacognitive knowledge of learning disabled students. *Learning Disabilities Research, 5*, 5–24.

Erickson, T., Smith, D. N., Kellogg, W. A., Laff, M., Richards, J. T., & Bradner, E. (1999). Socially translucent systems: Social proxies, persistent conversation, and the design of "Babble". In *Proceedings of the ACM conference on human factors in computing systems* (pp. 72–76). New York: ACM Press.

Ericsson, K. A., & Smith, J. (1991). *Toward a general theory of expertise: Prospects and limits.* Cambridge: Cambridge University Press.

Erkens, G., Kanselaar, G., Prangsma, M., & Jaspers, J. (2003). Computer support for collaborative and argumentative writing. In E. De Corte, L. Verschaffel, N. Entwistle, & J. van Merrienboër (Eds.), *Powerful learning environments: Unravelling basic components and dimensions* (pp. 159–177). Amsterdam: Pergamon.

Evans, G.W., & E. Kantrowitz. (2002). Annual Review of Public Health. *Economic status and health: The potential role of environmental risk exposure, 23*, 303–331 (doi: 10.1146/annurev.publhealth.23.112001.112349).

Facts and Figures 2000. (2000). *UNESCO Institute for Statistics.* Retrieved July 24, 2005, from www.uis.unesco.org/

Faigley, L. (1986). Competing theories of process: A critique and a proposal. *College English, 48*, 527–542.

Faigley, L. (1992). *Fragments of rationality: Postmodernity and the subject of composition.* Pittsburgh: University of Pittsburgh Press.

Faigley, L., & Witte, S. (1981). Analyzing revision. *College Composition and Communication, 32*, 400–414.

Fairclough, N. (1992). *Discourse and social change.* Cambridge, UK: Polity.

Fayol, M. (1999). From online management problems to strategies in written production. In M. Torrance, & G.C. Jeffery (Eds.), *The cognitive demands of writing: Processing capacity and working memory effects in text production* (pp. 13–23). Amsterdam: Amsterdam University Press.

Feenberg, A. (1999). *Questioning technology.* New York: Routledge.

Feng, J., Karat, C.-M., & Sears, A. (2005). How productivity improves in hands-free continuous dictation tasks: Lessons learned from a longitudinal study. *Interacting with computers, 17*, 265–289.

Feyt, L., & Edelmuller, H. (2000, June). *Telecommunication policies and practises in South Africa and Nigeria*. Retrieved July 24, 2005, from http://nml.ru.ac.za/

Finke, M. (2000). *Ein interaktives Videosystem für Broadcasting und Internet. [An interactive video system for broadcasting and Internet]*. Retrieved July 9, 2003, from http://www.zgdv.de/zgdv/departments/z3/Z3Veroeffentlichungen/Interaktives_Videosystem

Fischer, S. R. (2003). *A history of reading*. London: Reaktion Book.

Fish, R., Kraut, R., & Leland, M. (1988). Quilt: A collaborative tool for cooperative writing. In *Conference sponsored by ACM SIGOIS and IEEECS TC-OA on Office information systems* (pp. 30–37). New York: ACM Press.

Flaherty, L., Pearce, K., & Rubin, R. (1998). Internet and face-to-face communication: Not functionally alternatives. *Communication Quarterly, 46*, 250–268.

Floridi, L. (1995). The Internet & the future of organized knowledge. *Canadian Review of Materials 1*(7). Retrieved from http://www.umanitoba.ca/

Flower, L., & Hayes, J. (1980). The cognition of discovery: Defining a rhetorical problem. *College Composition and Communication, 31*(1), 21–32.

Flower, L., & Hayes, J. (1981). A cognitive process theory of writing. *College Composition and Communication, 32*, 365–387.

Flower, L., Hayes, J. R., Carey, L., Schriver, J., & Stratman, J. (1986). Detection, diagnosis, and the strategies of revision. *College Composition and Communication, 37*, 16–55.

Fogelson, M. (2002, May). *Autonomous and recursive learning: Teaching informative writing on the Web*. Paper presented at the 18th computers and writing conference, Normal, IL.

Fogelson, M. (2002). *The informative writing room at Colorado state university*. Unpublished Master's project. Department of English, Colorado State University.

Foster, S., & Borkowski, A. (n.d.). Who Coined the Term? Origin of 'Digital Divide' Escapes Even the Experts. From the *Access Denied*: *Exploring the Digital Divide* web site. Accessed 5 March 2003 at http://www1.soc.american.edu/students/ij/co_3/digitaldivide/history.htm

Foulin, J. N. (1995). Pauses et débits : les indicateurs temporels de la production écrite. *L'Année Psychologique, 95*, 483–504.

Frase, L. (1987). Creating intelligent environments for computer use in writing. *Contemporary Educational Psychology, 12*, 212–221.

Frederiksen, C. H., Donin-Frederiksen, J., & Bracewell, R. J. (1986). Discourse analysis of children's text production. In A. Matsuhashi (Ed.), *Writing in real time* (pp. 255–290). Norwood: Ablex.

Friedman, M., Von Blum, R., Cohen, M., Gerrard, L., & Rand, E. (1982). *WANDAH [Computer software]*. San Diego, CA: Harcourt Brace Jovanovich.

Frith, U. (Ed.) (1980). *Cognitive Processes in Spelling*. London: Academic Press.

Fuller, R., & Graaff, J. J. de (1996, October). *Measuring user motivation from server log files*. Paper presented at the Proceedings of the 2nd conference on human factors & the Web, Redmond, WA.

Gale, X. L. (1996). *Teachers, discourses, and authority in the postmodern composition classroom*. Albany: State University of New York Press.

Garrett, L. N., Smith, K. E., & Meyrowitz, N. (1986). Intermedia: Issues, strategies, and tactics in the design of a hypermedia document system. In *Proceedings of the 1986 ACM conference on computer-supported cooperative work* (pp. 163–174). New York: Association for Computing Machinery.

Gee, J. P. (1990). *Social linguistics and literacies: Ideology in discourses*. Brighton, GB: Falmer Press.

Geisler, C. (2003). *Analyzing streams of language: Twelve steps to the systematic coding of text, talk, and other verbal data*. Longman.

Geisler, C. (2004). *Analyzing steams of language: Twelve steps to the systematic coding of text, talk and other verbal data.* New York: Pearson/Longman.

Gerber, P. J., Schnieders, C. A., Paradise, L. A., Reiff, H. B., Ginsberg, R. J., & Popp, P. A. (1990). Persisting problems of adults with learning disabilities: Self-reported comparisons from their school-age and adult years. *Journal of Learning Disabilities*, *23*(9), 570–573.

Gerdes, H. (1997). *Lernen mit Text und Hypertext* [*Learning with text and hypertext*]. Berlin: Pabst.

Giddens, A. (1979). *Central problems in social theory: Action, structure and contradiction in social analysis.* Berkeley and Los Angeles: University of California Press.

Glover, P.J., & Brown, G.D.A. (1994). Measuring spelling production times: Methodology and tests of a model. In G. D. A. Brown, & N. C. Ellis (Eds.), *Handbook of spelling: Theory, process and intervention* (pp. 180–190). New York: Wiley.

Goffman, E. (1981). *Forms of talk.* Philadelphia: University of Pennsylvania.

Goldberg, A., Russell, M., & Cook, A. (2003). The effect of computers on student writing: A meta-analysis of studies from 1992 to 2002. *The Journal of Technology, Learning, and Assessment*, *2*, 4–51. Retrieved September 20, 2005, from http://www.bc.edu/research/intasc/jtla/journal/pdf/ v2n1_jtla.pdf

Golovchinsky, G., Marshall, C., & Schilit, B. (1999). Designing electronic books. In *conference companion of the ACM CHI99 conference* (p. 167). Pittsburgh, PA: ACM Press.

Gore, A., Jr. (1994). *Bringing information to the world: The global information infrastructure.* Retrieved July 24, 2005, from http://www.analitica.com/bitblioteca/al_gore/superhighway.asp

Gould, J. D. (1980). Experiments on composing letters: Some facts, some myths, and some observations. In L. Gregg, & E. R. Steinberg (Eds.), *Cognitive processes in writing* (pp. 98–127). Hillsdale, NJ: Lawrence Erlbaum Associates.

Graff, H. J. (1987). *The legacies of literacy: Continuities and contradictions in western culture and society.* Bloomington: Indiana University Press.

Graham, S. (1990). The role of production factors in learning disabled students' compositions. *Journal of Educational Psychology*, *82*, 781–791.

Graham, S., Berninger, V. W., Abbott, R. D., Abbott, S. P., & Whitaker, D. (1997). Role of mechanics in composing of elementary school students: A new methodological approach. *Journal of Educational Psychology*, *89*, 170–182.

Graham, S., & Harris, K. R. (1989). Components analysis of cognitive strategy instruction: Effects on learning disabled students' compositions and self-efficacy. *Journal of Educational Psychology*, *81*(3), 353–361.

Graham, S., Harris, K., MacArthur, C. A., & Schwartz, S. S. (1991). Writing and writing instruction with students with learning disabilities: A review of a program of research. *Learning Disability Quarterly*, *14*, 89–114.

Graham, S., & MacArthur, C. (1988). Improving learning disabled students' skills at revising essays produced on a word processor: Self-instructional strategy training. *The Journal of Special Education*, *22*, 133–152.

Graham, S., & Weintraub, N. (1996). A review of handwriting research: Progress and prospects from 1980 to 1994. *Educational Psychology Review*, *8*, 7–87.

Gray, S.H. (1995). Linear coherence and relevance: Logic in computer-human `conversations´. *Journal of Pragmatics*, *23*, 627–647.

Greene, L.S., Boyko, M., Susnowitz, S., Butcher, K., Kintsch, E., & Kintsch, W. (1998). Introducing science writing and revision interactive technology environment (science WRITE). In A. S. Bruckman, M. Guzdial, J. L. Kolodner, & A. Ram (Eds.), *International conference of the learning sciences 1998: Proceedings of ICLS 98* (pp. 313–315). Charlottesville, VA: Association for the Advancement of Computing in Education.

Grego, R., & Thompson, N. (1996). Repositioning remediation: Renegotiating composition's work in the academy. *College Composition and Communication*, *47*, 62–84.

Grice, H. P. (1975) Logic and conversation. In P. Cole, & J. L. Morgan (Eds.), *Syntax and semantics* (pp. 41–58). New York: Academic Press.

Gumperz, J. J., & Levinson, S. C. (1996). *Rethinking linguistic relativity.* Cambridge: Cambridge University Press.

Gutowitz, H. (2003, April). *Barriers to adoption of dictionary-based text-entry methods: A field study.* Paper presented at the 10th conference of the European chapter of the association for computational linguistics, Budapest, Hungary.

Haake, J. M., & Wilson, B. (1992). Supporting collaborative writing of hyperdocuments in SEPIA. *Proceedings of ACM CSCW'92* (pp. 138–146). New York: ACM Press.

Haas, C. (1989). 'Seeing it on the screen isn't really seeing it': Computer writers' reading problems. In G. E. Hawisher, & C. L Selfe (Eds.), *Critical perspectives on computers* (pp. 16–29). New York: Teachers College Press.

Haas, C. (1996). *Writing technology: Studies on the materiality of literacy.* Mahwah, NJ: Lawrence Erlbaum Associates.

Hafner, K. (2004, June 21). Old search engine, the library, tries to fit into a Google world, *New York Times.* Retrieved from http://www.nytimes.com/2004/06/21/technology/21LIBR.html?hp

Håkansson, G. (1998). *Språkinlärning hos barn* [Children's language acquisition]. Lund: Studentlitteratur.

Hancock, J. T. (2004). Verbal irony use in face-to-face and computer-mediated conversations. *Journal of Language and Social Psychology, 2,* 447–463.

Handley-More, D., Deitz, J., Billingsley, F.F., & Coggins, T.E. (2003). Facilitating written work using computer word processing and word prediction. *American Journal of Occupational Therapy, 57,* 139–151.

Hård af Segerstad, Y. (2002) *Use and adaptation of written language to the conditions of compute-mediated communication.* Unpublished Doctoral dissertation, Department of Linguistics, Göteborg University, Sweden.

Harris, M., & Pemberton, M. (1995). Online writing labs (OWLs): A taxonomy of options and issues. *Computers and Composition, 12,* 145–159.

Hart, R. P. (2001). Redeveloping diction: Theoretical considerations. In M. D. West (Ed.), *Theory, method, and practice in computer content analysis* (pp. 43–60). Westport, CT: Ablex Publishing.

Häusermann, J. (2001). Der Text als Ort der öffentlichen Kommunikation. Zur sprachlichen Aus- und Fortbildung im Journalismus [The text as a place of public communication. Linguistic education and training in journalism]. In J. Korhonen, & I. Hyvärinen (Series Eds.) & U. Breuer, & J. Korhonen (Vol. Eds.), *Finnische Beiträge zur Germanistik: Vol. 4. Mediensprache, Medienkritik* (pp. 45–54). Frankfurt am Main: Lang.

Hawisher, G. E. (1988). Research update: Writing and word processing. *Computers and Composition, 5,* 7–28.

Hawisher, G. E. (1989). Computers and Writing: Where's the Research? *English Journal, 78,* 89–91

Hawisher, G. E., & Selfe, C. L. (2004). Becoming literate in the information age: Cultural ecologies and the literacies of technology. *College Composition and Communication, 55,* 642–692.

Hawisher, G. E., & Selfe, C. L. (in press-a). Globalization, agency, and counter hegemony: Designing and redesigning the literacies of cyberspace in the 21st century. *College English.*

Hawisher, G. E., & Selfe, C. L. (in press-b). Women and the global ecology of digital literacies. In B. Daniells, & P. Mortensen (Eds.), *Women and literacy: Inquiries for a new century.* Mahwah, NJ: Lawrence Erlbaum Associates.

Hayes, J. R. (1996). A new framework for understanding cognition and affect in writing. In C. M. Levy, & S. Ransdell (Eds.), *The science of writing: Theories, methods, individual differences, and applications* (pp. 1–27). Mahwah, NJ: Lawrence Erlbaum Associate.

Hayes, J. R., & Flower, L. S. (1980). Identifying the organisation of the writing process. In L.W. Gregg, & E.R. Steinberg (Eds.), *Cognitive processes in writing* (pp. 3–30). Hillsdale, NJ: Lawrence Erlbaum Associates.

Hayes, J. R., & Flower, L. S. (1986). Writing research and the writer. *American Psychologist, 41*(10), 1106–1113.

Hearst, M. A. (2000). The debate on automated essay grading. *IEEE Intelligent Systems & Their Applications, 15*(5), 22–27.

Hecht, S. A., Burgess, S. R., Torgesen, J. K., Wagner, R. K., & Rashotte, C. A. (2000). Explaining social class differences in growth of reading skills from beginning kindergarten through fourth-grade: The role of phonological awareness, rate of access, and print knowledge. *Reading and Writing: An Interdisciplinary Journal, 12*, 99–127.

Hecht, S. A., & Greenfield, D. B. (2001). Comparing the predictive validity of first grade teachers ratings and reading related tests on third grade levels of reading skills in young children exposed to poverty. *School Psychology Review, 30*, 50–69.

Heer, J., & Chi, E. H. (2002). Separating the swarm: Categorization methods for user access sessions on the Web. In *Proceedings of ACM conference on human factors in computing systems (CHI 2002)* (pp. 243–250). Minneapolis, MN: ACM Press.

Helfrich, B., & Landay, J. A. (1999). *QUIP: Quantitative user interface profiling.* Unpublished manuscript.

Herring, S. (1999). Interactional coherence in CMC. *Journal of Computer-Mediated Communication, 4*(4), Retrieved April 12, 2004, from http://www.ascusc.org/jcmc/

Herring, S. C. (2001). Computer-mediated discourse. In D. Schiffrin, D. Tannen, & H. Hamilton (Eds.), *The handbook of discourse analysis* (pp. 612–634). Oxford: Blackwell Publishers.

Hidi, S. E., & Hildyard, A. (1983). The comparison of oral and written productions in two discourse types. *Discourse Processes, 6*, 91–105.

Higgins, E. L., & Raskind, M. H. (1995). Compensatory effectiveness of speech recognition on the written composition performance of postsecondary students with learning disabilities. *Learning Disability Quarterly, 18*(2), 159–174.

Hilton, N. (1995). Lexis complexes and intentions in tension. In *Lexis complexes: Literary interventions.* University of Georgia Press. Retrieved from http://www.english.uga.edu/

Hinner, E. (2000). *Chatten.* Retrieved April 12, 2004, from http://www.netzwissenschaft.de/sem/hinn.htm

Hobson, E. H. (1998). *Wiring the writing center.* Logan, UT: Utah State University Press.

Hochheiser, H., & Shneiderman, B. (2001). Using interactive visualizations of WWW log data to characterize access patterns and inform site design. *Journal of the American Society for Information Science and Technology, 52*(4), 331–343.

Hogan, T. P. (1972). Prediction of within-school system variance in test scores from within-community variance in socioeconomic status. *Journal of Educational Measurement, 9*, 155–158.

Holdstein, D. H. (1983). The WRITEWELL series. *Computers and Composition, 1*(1), 7.

Holdstein, D. H. (1984). Computerized instruction in writing at the Illinois Institute of Technology: Practice, editing, and motivation for the engineering student. *Writing Lab Newsletter, 8*(7), 8–6.

Holkeri, H. (2000). Remarks by General Assembly President to UN World TV Forum: 'The General Assembly and the Digital Divide'. *Press Release GA/SM/216.* United Nations Web-site. Retrieved July 24, 2005, from http://www.un.org/News/Press/docs/2000/20001116.gasm 216.doc.html

Holland, V. M., & Kaplan J. D. (1995). Natural language processing techniques in computer-assisted language learning: Status and instructional issues. *Instructional Science, 23*, 351–380.

Holmes, V. M., & Carruthers, J. (1998). The relation between reading and spelling in skilled adult readers. *Journal of Memory and Language, 39*, 264–289.

Holmqvist, K., Johansson, V., Strömqvist, S., & Wengelin, Å. (2002). Studying reading and writing on-line. In S. Strömqvist (Ed.), *The diversity of languages and language learning* (pp. 103–123). Sweden: Lund University, Centre for Languages and Literature.

Holsanova, J. (2001). *Picture viewing and picture description: Two windows on the mind.* Doctoral dissertation, Lund University Cognitive Studies 83.

Honey, P., & Mumford, A. (1992). *The manual of learning styles.* Maidenhead, Berkshire: Peter Honey.

Honeycutt, L. (2003). Researching the use of voice recognition writing software. *Computers and Composition, 20,* 77–95.

Honeycutt, L. (2004). Literacy and the writing voice: The intersection of culture and technology in dictation. *Journal of Business and Technical Communication, 18*(3), 294–327.

Horsman, L. (1983). Disabled individuals can talk to their computers. *Technology and Disability, 44*(3–4), 71–74.

http://www.emc.com/news/press_releases/10242000_berkeley.jsp. Retrieved July 8, 2004.

http://www.wcom.com/cgibin/search?placetosearch=term&searchfilter=contains&search string=data&pagenum=0&page=1.

Human development report 2001: Making new technologies work for human development. (2001). United Nations Development Programme. New York: Oxford University Press. Individual Indicators. Retrieved July 24, 2005, from http;//www.undp.org/hdr2001/indicator/indic_267_1_1.html

Hutchby, I. (2001). *Conversation and technology: From the telephone to the Internet.* Cambridge: Polity Press.

International Students 2002 — Data Tables. (2002). *Open doors website of the institute of international education.* Retrieved July 24, 2005, from http://opendoors.iienetwork.org/

Internet in Iraq: Limited, Appreciated. (2001, December 16). *Digital divide network.* Retrieved July 24, 2005, from http://www.digitaldividenetwork.org/content/news/index.cfm?key=508

Internet/profile-eight.asp. Retrieved on July 8, 2004.

Is_1803_301/ai_63842598. Retrieved on July 8, 2004.

Ivory, M. Y. (2003). Automated web site evaluation: Researchers' and practitioners' perspectives. In J. Karat, & J. Vanderdonckt (Eds.), *Human-computer interaction series* (Vol. 4). Dordrecht, The Netherlands: Kluwer Academic Publishers.

Ivory, M. Y. (2003, June). *Characteristics of web site designs: Reality vs. recommendations.* Paper presented at the Proceedings of the 10th international conference on human-computer interaction, Crete, Greece.

Ivory, M.Y., & Chevalier, A. (2002). *A study of automated web site evaluation tools* (Technical Report No. 02-10-01). University of Washington, Department of Computer Science and Engineering.

Ivory, M. Y., & Hearst, M. A. (2002). Improving web site design. *IEEE Internet Computing, 6,* 56–63.

Ivory, M. Y., & Hearst, M. A. (2002, April). *Statistical profiles of highly-rated web site interfaces.* Paper presented at the Proceedings of the conference on human factors in computing systems, Minneapolis, MN.

Ivory, M.Y., Mankoff, J., & Le, A. (2003). Using automated tools to improve web site usage by users with diverse abilities. *IT&Society, 1*(3), 195–236.

Jacobs, G., Opdenacker L., & Van Waes, L. (2005). A multilanguage online writing center for professional communication: Development and testing. *Business Communication Quarterly, 68,* 8–22.

Jacobson, D. (1999). Impression formation in cyberspace: Online expectations and offline experiences in text-based virtual communities. *Journal of Computer Mediated Communication, 5*(1). Retrieved April 12, 2004, from http://www.ascusc.org/jcmc/vol5/issue1/jacobson.html

Jaffe, M. J., Lee, Y.-E., Huang, L., & Oshagan, H. (1995). *Gender, pseudonyms, and CMC: Masking identities and baring souls.* Retrieved April 12, 2004, from http://members.kr.inter.net/yesunny/genderps.html

Jagboro, K. O. (2003, February). A case study of Internet usage in Nigerian universities: A case study of Obafemi Awolowo university, IIe-Ife, Nigeria. *First Monday, 8*(2). Retrieved July 24, 2005, from http://firstmonday.org/issues/issue8_2/jagboro/index.html

Jakobsen, A. L. (1999). Logging target text production with translog. In G. Hansen (Ed.), *Probing the process in translation. Methods and results* (pp. 9–20). Copenhagen: Samfundslitteratur.

Janssen, D., Van Waes, L., & Van den Bergh, H. (1996). Effects of thinking aloud on writing processes. In C. M. Levy, & S. Ransdell (Eds.), *The science of writing: Theories, methods, individual differences and applications* (pp. 233–250). Mahwah, NJ: Lawrence Erlbaum Associates.

Jarvis, S. Asia's Internet Experience. *Asian/Pacific Book Development, 32*(2), 3–5.

Jedeskog, G. (1993). *Datorn som pedagogiskt hjälpmedel [The computer as a pedagogical tool].* Studentlitteratur AB.

Johnson, J.P. (1996). Writing spaces: Technoprovocateurs and OWLs in the late age of print. *Kairos, 1*(1). Retrieved July 28, 2004, from http://english.ttu.edu/kairos/1.1/index.html

Johnson, S. (2005). Total recall: How to develop a photographic memory without even trying. *Discover, 26*(8), 23–24.

Jones, S. (1993). MILO: A computer-based tool for (Co-) authoring structured documents. In M. Sharples, (Ed.), *Computer supported collaborative writing* (pp. 185–202). London: Springer.

Joyce, E. (2001, October). WTC paper losses spark thinking on more than data. *ATNewYork*. Retrieved on July 8, 2004, from http://www.atnewyork.com/news/article.php/898711

Jurafsky, D., & Martin, J. H. (Eds.) (2000). *Speech and Language Processing: An Introduction to Natural Language Processing, Computational Linguistics and Speech Recognition.* Upper Saddle River, NJ: Prentice Hall.

Kaplan, N., Davis, S., & Martin, J. (1987). PROSE (Prompted revision of student essays) [Computer Software]. New York: McGraw-Hill.

Karat, C., Halverson, C., Horn, D., & Karat, J. (1999). Patterns of entry and correction in large vocabulary continuous speech recognition systems. In *Proceedings of the SIGCHI conference on human computer factors in computing systems: the CHI is the limit* (pp. 568–575). New York: ACM Press (TR).

Kasesniemi, E.-L. (2003). *Mobile messages. Young people and a new communication culture.* Tampere: Tampere University Press.

Kattz, J. E., & Aspen, P. (1998). Internet Dropouts in the USA. *Telecommunications Policy, 22*(4/5), 327–339.

Kaufer, D., & Butler, B. (1996). *Rhetoric and the arts of design.* Mahwah, NJ: Lawrence Erlbaum Associates.

Kaufer, D., & Butler, B. (2000). *Designing interactive worlds with words: Principles of writing as representational composition.* Mahwah, NJ: Lawrence Erlbaum Associates.

Kaufer, D. S., Hayes, J. R., & Flower, L. S. (1986). Composing written sentences. *Research in the Teaching of English, 20*, 121–140.

Kaufer, D., Ishizaki, S., Butler, B., & Collins, J. (2004). *The power of words: Unveiling the writer and speakers' hidden craft.* Mahwah, NJ: Lawrence Erlbaum Associates.

Kaur, I. (2004). *To search or to find?* Retrieved September 6, 2004, from http://www.cs.uoregon.edu/research/cm-hci/Semantic_Search/

Kaur, I., & Hornof, A. J. (2005). A comparison of LSA, WordNet and PMI-IR for predicting user click behavior. In W. Kellogg, S. Zhai (Eds.), *Proceedings of the conference on human factors in computing (CHI 2005)* (pp. 51–60). New York: ACM Press.

Kellogg, R. T. (1994). *The psychology of writing.* New York: Oxford University Press.

Kellogg, R. T. (1996). A model of working memory in writing. In C. M. Levy, & S. Ransdell (Eds.), *The science of writing: Theories, methods, individual differences, and applications* (pp. 57–71). Mahwah, NJ: Lawrence Erlbaum Associates.

Kellogg, R. T. (2001). Competition for working memory among writing processes. *American Journal of Psychology*, *114*(2), 175–191.

Kemp, F. (1992). Who programmed this? Examining the instructional attitudes of writing support software. *Computers and Composition*, *10*(1), 9–24. Retrieved July 26, 2004, from http://www.hu.mtu.edu/~candc/archives/v10/10_1_html/10_1_1_Kemp.html

Kemp, F. (1999, March). *The computer classroom ceiling.* Paper presented at the conference on college composition and communication, Atlanta, GA. Retrieved March 6, 2003, from http://english.ttu.edu/ kemp/personal/works/cccc99.html

Kenniston, K. http://web.mit.edu/~kken/Public/papers1/Language%20Power%20Software.htm

Keniston, K. (2004). Introduction: The four digital divides. In K. Keniston, & D. Kumar (Eds.), *IT experience in India*. Delhi: Sage.

Kent, T. (Ed.). (1999). *Post-process theory: Beyond the writing-process paradigm.* Carbondale, IL: Southern Illinois University Press.

Kerbrat-Orecchioni, C. (2004). Introducing polylogue. *Journal of Pragmatics*, *37*, 1–24.

Kiefer, K., & Barnes, L. (2002, March). *This isn't where we thought we were going: Revisiting our visions of computer-support writing.* Paper presented at the conference on college composition and communication, Chicago.

Kiefer, K., & Palmquist, M. (1996a). How does access to a computer network shape writing students' interactions with peers and teachers? In G. Rijlaarsdam, & M. Couzijn (Eds.), *Current trends in writing research: Effective learning and teaching of writing* (pp. 358–371). Amsterdam: University of Amsterdam Press.

Kiefer, K., & Palmquist, M. (1996b). Adapting to the classroom setting: Research on teachers moving between traditional and computer classrooms. In G. Rijlaarsdam, & M. Couzijn (Eds.), *Current trends in writing research: Effective learning and teaching of writing* (pp. 358–371). Amsterdam: University of Amsterdam Press.

Kiefer, K., Reid, S., & Smith, C. R. (1989). Style-analysis programs: Teachers using the tools. In C. L. Selfe, D. Rodrigues, & W. R. Oates (Eds.), *Computers in English and the language arts: The challenge of teacher education* (pp. 213–225). Urbana, IL: National Council of Teachers of English.

Kiefer, K. E., & Smith, C. R. (1983). Textual analysis with computers: Tests of bell laboratories' computer software. *Research in the Teaching of English*, *17*, 201–214.

Kiefer, K. E., & Smith, C. R. (1984). Improving students' revising and editing: The writer's workbench system. In W. Wresch (Ed.), *The computer in composition instruction: A writer's tool* (pp. 65–82). Urbana, IL: National Council of Teachers of English.

King, M. L., & Rentel, V. M. (1981). Research update: Conveying meaning in written texts. *Language Arts*, *58*, 721–728.

Kintsch, W. (1998). *Comprehension: A paradigm for cognition.* New York: Cambridge University Press.

Kintsch, W., & Van Dijk, T. A. (1978). Toward a model of text comprehension and production. *Psychological Review*, *85*(5), 363–394.

Kintsch, W., & Yarbrough, J. C. (1982). Role of rhetorical structure in text comprehension. *Journal of Educational Psychology*, *74*, 828–834.

Kitajima, M., Blackmon, M. H., & Polson, P. G. (2000). A comprehension-based model of web navigation and its application to web usability analysis. In *People and computers XIV — usability or else! (Proceedings of HCI, 2000)* (pp. 357–373). London, UK: Springer-Verlag.

Klein, H. (2002–2005). *Category systems.* Retrieved on August 14, 2005, from *Text Analysis Info Page Web site*: http://www.textanalysis.info/

Kling, R. (1998). *Technological and social access to computing, information, and communication technologies.* White paper. Retrieved January 6, 2006 from http://rkcsi.indiana.edu/archive/kling/pubs/NGI.htm

Knuth D. E., Morris J. H. Jr, & Pratt V. R. (1977). Fast pattern matching in strings. *SIAM Journal on Computing*, 6(1), 323–350.

Knutsson, O. (2001). *Automatisk språkgranskning av svensk text* [*Atomatic language checking of Swedish text*]. Licentiatavhandling, KTH, NADA.

Knutsson, O., Cerratto Pargman, T., Severinson Eklundh, K., & Westlund, S. (2006, forthcoming). Designing and developing a language environment for second language writers. *Computers and Education International Journal.*

Kolb, D. A. (1984). *Experiential learning.* Englewood Cliffs, NJ: Prentice-Hall.

Kolbert, E. (2005, June 6). Last words. *New Yorker, 81*(16), 45–59.

Kollberg, P. (1998). *S-notation — a computer based method for studying and representing text composition.* Unpublished Licentiate thesis, Department of Numerical Analysis and Computing Science, Royal Institute of Technology (KTH), Stockholm.

Kollberg, P., & Severinson Eklundh, K. (2001). Studying writers' revising patterns with S-notation analysis. In G. Rijlaarsdam (Series Ed.) & T. Olive, & C. M. Levy (Vol. Eds.), *Studies in writing: Vol. 10. Contemporary tools and techniques for studying writing* (pp. 89–104). Dordrecht: Kluwer Academic.

Kommers, P. A. M., & De Vries, S. J. (1992). TextVision and the visualisation of knowledge: School-based evaluation of its acceptance at two levels of schooling. In P. A. M. Kommers, D. H. Jonassen, & J. T. Mayes (Eds.), *Cognitive tools for learning* (pp. 33–62). Berlin: Springer.

Kostouli, T. (Ed.). (2005). *Studies in writing: Vol 15. Writing in context(s): Textual practices and learning processes in sociocultural settings.* New York: Springer.

Kozma, R. B. (1987). The implications of cognitive psychology for computer-based learning tools. *Educational Technology, 28*(11), 20–25.

Kozma, R.B. (1991a). Computer-based writing tools and the cognitive needs of novice writers. *Computers and Composition, 8*(2), 31–45.

Kozma, R. B. (1991b). The impact of computer-based tools and rhetorical prompts on writing processes and products. *Cognition and Instruction, 8*, 1–27.

Kozma, R. B., & Van Roekel, J. (1986). *Learning tool.* Santa Barbara, CA: Intellimation.

Krashen, S. (1985). *The input hypothesis: Issues and implications.* Boston: Longman Publisher.

Kreiner, D. S. (1992). Reaction time measures of spelling: Testing a two-strategy model of skilled spelling. *Journal of Experimental Psychology: Learning, Memory and Cognition, 18*, 765–776.

Kreiner, D. S. (1996). Effects of word familiarity and phoneme-grapheme polygraphy on oral spelling time and accuracy. *The Psychological Record, 46*, 49–70.

Kriewald, G. (1980). Computer-programmed instruction in elements of grammar for students with remedial problems in writing. *Writing Lab Newsletter, 4*(6), 4–5.

Krolokke, C. (2003). Impossible speech? Playful chat and feminist linguistic theory. *Women and Language, 26*(2), 15–21.

Krug, S. (2000). *Don't make me think: A common sense approach to Web usability.* Indianapolis, IN: New Riders.

Landauer, T. K., & Dumais, S. T. (1997). A solution to Plato's problem: The latent semantic analysis theory of the acquisition, induction, and representation of knowledge. *Psychological Review, 104*, 211–240.

Lansman, M., Smith, J. B., & Weber, I. (1993). Using the writing environment to study writers' strategies. *Computers and Composition, 10*(2), 71–92.

Lasarenko, J. (1996). PR(OWL)ING AROUND: An OWL by any other name. *Kairos, 1*(1). Retrieved July 28, 2004, from http://english.ttu.edu/kairos/1.1/index.html

Lea, M., & Spears, R. (1992). Paralanguage and social perception in computer-mediated communication. *Journal of Organizational Computing, 2–4*, 321–341.

Leander, K., & Prior P. (2004). Speaking and writing. How talk and text interact. In C. Bazerman, & P. Prior (Eds.), *What writing does and how it does it: An introduction to analysis of text and textual practice* (pp. 201–238). Mahwah, NJ: Lawrence Erlbaum Associates.

Lee, J., & Bean, F. D. (2004). American's changing color lines: Immigration, race/ethnicity, and multiracial identification. *Annual Review of Sociology, 30*, 221–242.

Lehnen, K., & Schindler K. (2003). Repertoires erweitern. Für andere Domänen trainieren [Expanding repertoires. Training for other domains]. In D. Perrin, I. Böttcher, O. Kruse, & A. Wrobel (Eds.), *Schreiben. Von intuitiven zu professionellen Schreibstrategien* (pp. 153–169). Wiesbaden: Westdeutscher Verlag.

Leijten, M. (in press). How do writers adapt to speech recognition? The influence of learning style on the writing process in speech technology environments. In M. Torrance, L. Van Waes, & D. Galbraith (Eds.), *Writing and cognition. Studies in writing*. Amsterdam: Elsevier.

Leijten, M., Ransdell, S., & Van Waes, L. (2006). *Working memory and error detection in writing: A task analysis of error size, lexicality, and mode of writing*. Manuscript submitted for publication.

Leijten, M., & Van Waes, L. (2003). *The writing process and learning strategies of initial users of speech recognition*. A case study on the adaption process of two professional writers. Antwerp: University of Antwerp, Faculty of Applied Economics UFSIA-RUCA, Research paper 2003-022.

Leijten, M., & Van Waes, L. (2005a). *Inputlog: A logging tool for the research of writing processes*. Research paper 2005-011, Department of Management, University of Antwerp, Belgium. Retrieved September 28, 2005, from http://econpapers.repec.org/paper/antwpaper/

Leijten, M., & Van Waes, L. (2005b). Writing with speech recognition: The adaptation process of professional writers with and without dictating experience. *Interacting with Computers, 17*, 736–772.

Leijten, M., & Van Waes, L. (in press). Inputlog: New perspectives on the logging of on-line writing processes in a windows environment. In G. Rijlaarsdam (Series Ed.) & K. P. H. Sullivan, & E. Lindgren (Vol. Eds.), *Studies in writing. Computer keystroke logging and writing: Methods and applications*. Amsterdam: Elsevier.

Lété, B., Sprenger-Charolles, L., & Colé, P. (2004). Manulex: A grade-level lexical data base from French elementary school readers. *Behavior Research Methods, Instruments, & Computers, 36*, 156–166.

Levine, R. (1996). *Guide to web style*. Retrieved September 5, 2004, from http://www.sun.com/styleguide/

Levy, M. (1997). *Computer assisted language learning: Context and conceptualization*. New York: Oxford University Press.

Levy, S. (1984). *Hackers: Heroes of the computer revolution*. New York: Anchor Press/Doubleday.

Levy, C. M., Marek, P., & Lea, J. (1996). Concurrent and retrospective protocols in writing research. In G. Rijlaarsdam, H. Van den Bergh, & M. Couzijn (Eds.), *Current research in writing: Theories, models and methodology* (pp. 542–556). Amsterdam: Amsterdam University Press.

Levy, C. M., & Olive, T. (2002). Real time studies in writing research: Progress and prospects. In G. Rijlaarsdam (Series Ed.) & C. M. Levy, & T. Olive (Vol. Eds.), *Studies in writing: Vol 10. Contemporary tools and techniques for studying writing*. Dordrecht: Kluwer Academic Publishers.

Levy, C. M., & Ransdell, S. (1996). Writing signatures. In S. Ransdell, & C. M. Levy (Eds.), *The science of writing: Theories, methods, individual differences, and applications*. Mahwah, NJ: Lawrence Erlbaum Associates.

Lewis, R. B. (1998). *Enhancing the writing skills of students with learning disabilities through technology: An investigation of the effects of text entry tools, editing tools, and speech synthesis*. Final Report. San Diego, CA: Department of Special Education, San Diego State University.

Liberg, C. (1990). *Learning to read and write*. (RUUL 20). Sweden: Uppsala University, Department of Linguistics.

Lindgren, E. (2004). The uptake of peer-based intervention in the writing classroom. In G. Rijlaarsdam (Series Ed.) & G. Rijlaarsdam, H. Van den Bergh, & M. Couzijn (Vol. Eds.), *Studies in writing: Volume 14. Effective learning and teaching of writing,* (2nd ed., pp. 259–274). Dordrecht: Kluwer Academic Publishers.

Lindgren, E. (2005). *Writing and revising: Didactic and methodological implications of keystroke logging. (Skrifter från moderna språk 18).* Doctoral Dissertation, Sweden: Umeå, Department of Modern Languages.

Lindgren, E., & Sullivan, K. P. H. (2002). The LS graph: A methodology for visualising writing revision. *Language Learning, 52*, 565–595.

Lindgren, E., & Sullivan, K. P. H. (2003). Stimulated recall as a trigger for increasing noticing and language awareness in the L2 writing classroom: A case study of two young female writers. *Language Awareness, 12*, 172–186.

Lindgren, E., Sullivan, K. P. H., Lindgren, U., & Spelman Miller, K. (2006, forthcoming). GIS for writing: Applying geographic information systems techniques to data mine writing's cognitive processes. In G. Rijlaarsdam (Series Ed.) & M. Torrance, L. Van Waes, & D. Galbraith (Eds.), *Studies in writing: Writing and cognition.* Oxford: Elsevier.

Linell, P. (1982). *The written language bias in linguistics.* Linköping: Universitetet.

Liu, M. (2003). Enhancing learners cognitive skills through multimedia design. *Interactive Learning Environments, 11*, 23–39.

Lockard, J. (1996, February). Resisting cyber-English. *Bad Subjects web site.* Retrieved July 24, 2005, from http://eserver.org/bs/24/lockard.html

Long, M. H. (1991). Focus on form: A design feature in language teaching methodology. In K. deBot, C. Kramsch, & R. B. Ginsberg (Eds.), *Foreign language research in cross-cultural perspective* (pp. 39–53). Amsterdam: John Benjamins.

Long, M. H., & Robinson, P. (1998). Focus on form: Theory, research, and practice. In C. Doughty, & J. Williams (Eds.), *Focus on form in classroom second language acquisition* (pp. 15–41). Cambridge: Cambridge University Press.

Lost data cost U.S. economy $11.8 billion in 1998. (1999). *Source corporate editorials.* Retrieved July 8, 2004, from http://www.source.be/corporate/press/legato0111.htm

Lost in space: Data recovery. (2001). *Business town.* Retrieved from http://www.businesstown.com/.

Lowgren, J., & Nordqvist, T. (1992, May). *Knowledge-based evaluation as design support for graphical user interfaces.* Paper presented at the Proceedings of the conference on human factors in computing systems, Monterey, CA.

Lowry, P. B., Curtis, A., & Lowry, M. R. (2004). Building a taxonomy and nomenclature of collaborative writing to improve interdisciplinary research and practice. *Journal of Business Communication, 41*(1), 66–99.

Luginbühl, M., Baumberger, T., Schwab, K., & Burger, H. (2002). *Medientexte zwischen Autor und Publikum. Intertextualität in Presse, Radio und Fernsehen [Media texts between author and readers. Intertextuality in the press, radio, and television].* Zürich: Seismo.

Lundberg, I. (1989). *Språkutveckling och läsinlärning [Language development and reading acquisition].* In C. Sandqvist, & U. Teleman (Eds.), *Språkutveckling under skoltiden*[Language development during the school years]. Lund: Studentlitteratur.

Lyman, P., & Varian, H. (2003). *How much information?* Retrieved July 8, 2004, from http://www.sims. berkeley.edu/research/projects/how-much-info-2003/

Lynch, G., Palmiter, S., & Tilt, C. (1999, June). *The max model: A standard web site user model.* Paper presented at the Proceedings of the 5th conference on human factors & the Web, Gaithersburg, MD.

Lynch, P. J., & Horton, S. (1999). *Web style guide: Basic design principles for creating web sites.* Princeton, NJ: Yale University Press.

MacArthur, C. A. (1998). Word processing with speech synthesis and word prediction: Effects on the dialogue journal writing of students with learning disabilities. *Learning Disability Quarterly, 21*, 151–166.

MacArthur, C. A. (1999). Word prediction for students with severe spelling problems. *Learning Disability Quarterly, 22*, 158–172.

MacArthur, C. A. (2000). New tools for writing: Assistive technology for students with writing difficulties. *Topics in Language Disorders, 20*, 85–100.

MacArthur, C. A., & Cavalier, A. (2004). Dictation and speech recognition technology as accommodations in large-scale assessments for students with learning disabilities. *Exceptional Children, 71, 43–58.*

MacArthur, C. A., Ferretti, R. P., Okolo, C. M., & Cavalier, A. R. (2001). Technology applications for students with literacy problems: A critical review. *Elementary School Journal, 101*, 273–301.

MacArthur, C. A., & Graham, S. (1987). Learning disabled students' composing under three methods of text production: Handwriting, word processing, and dictation. *Journal of Special Education, 21*, 22–42.

MacArthur, C. A., Graham, S., Haynes, J. A., & De La Paz, S. (1996). Spelling checkers and students with learning disabilities: Performance comparisons and impact on spelling. *Journal of Special Education, 30*, 35–57.

MacArthur, C. A., Graham, S., & Schwartz, S. (1991). Knowledge of revision and revising behavior among learning disabled students. *Learning Disability Quarterly, 14*, 61–73.

MacArthur, C. A., Graham, S., Schwartz, S., & Shafer, W. (1995). Evaluation of a writing instruction model that integrated a process approach, strategy instruction, and word processing. *Learning Disabilities Quarterly, 18*, 278–291.

MacArthur, C. A., Schwartz, S. S., & Graham, S. (1991). Effects of a reciprocal peer revision strategy in special education classrooms. *Learning Disabilities Research and Practice, 6*, 201–210.

MacCrorie, K. (1970). *Uptaught*. New York: Hayden Book Company.

MacKenzie, I. S., & Soukoreff, R. W. (2002). Text entry for mobile computing: Models and methods, theory and practice. *Human-Computer Interaction, 17*, 147–198.

Malinowski, B. (1923). The problem of meaning in primitive languages. Supplement to C. Ogden & I. Richards, *The meaning of meaning* (pp. 146–152). London: Routledge and Kegan Paul.

Mander, J. (1992). In the absence of the sacred: The failure of technology and the survival of the Indian Nations (Paperback). San Francisco: Sierra Club Books; Reprint edition.

Malvern, D. D., & Richards, B. J. (1997). A new measure of lexical diversity. In A. Ryan, & A. Wray (Eds.), *Evolving models of language* (pp. 58–71). Clevedon: Multilingual matters.

Marshall, C. C., & Rogers, R. A. (1992). Two years before the mist: Experiences with Aquanet. In *Proceedings of the ACM conference on hypertext* (pp. 53–62). Milan: Association for Computing Machinery.

Martlew, M. (1992). Handwriting and spelling: Dyslexic children's abilities compared with children of the same chronological age and younger children of the same spelling level. *British Journal of Educational Psychology, 62*, 375–390.

Matsuhashi, A. (1981). Pausing and planning: The tempo of written discourse production. *Research in the teaching of English, 15*, 113–134.

Mauer, B. (1996). Electronic monumentality. *Kairos: A Journal of Rhetoric, Technology, and Pedagogy, 1*(3). From http://english.ttu.edu/kairos/1.3/

Mayer, R. E., & Moreno, R. (2002). Animation as an aid to multimedia learning. *Educational Psychology Review, 14*(1), 87–99.

McCutchen, D. (1987). Children's discourse skill: Form and modality requirements of schooled writing. *Discourse Processes, 10*(3), 267–286.

McCutchen, D. (1996). A capacity theory of writing: Working memory in composition. *Educational Psychology Review, 8*(3), 299–325.

McCutchen, D., Francis, M., & Kerr, S. (1997). Revising for meaning: Effects of knowledge and strategy. *Journal of Educational Psychology, 89*, 667–676.

McDaniel, E. (1986). A comparative study of the first-generation invention software. *Computers and Composition, 3*(3). Retrieved July 15, 2004, from http://www.hu.mtu.edu/~candc/archives/v3/3_3_html/3_3_1_Mcdaniel.html

McGovern, G., Norton, R., & O'Dowd, C. (2002*). The web content style guide: The essential reference for online writers, editors and managers.* London: Financial Times Prentice-Hall.

McLuhan, M. (1964). *Understanding media: The extensions of man.* New York: McGraw-Hill.

McNaughton, D., Hughes, C., & Clark, K. (1997). The effect of five proofreading conditions on the spelling performance of college students with learning disabilities. *Journal of Learning Disabilities, 30*, 643–651.

McNaughton, D., Hughes, C., & Ofiesh, N. (1997). Proofreading for students with learning disabilities: Integrating computer use and strategy use. *Learning Disabilities Research and Practice, 12*, 16–28.

Mehrabian, A., & Ferris, S. R. (1967). Inference of attitudes from nonverbal communication in two channels. *Journal of Consulting Psychology, 31*, 248–252.

Mehrabian, A., & Wiener M. (1967). Decoding of inconsistent communications. *Journal of Personality and Social Psychology, 6*, 109–114.

Merwin, W. S. (1994). The remembering machines of tomorrow. *The Miner's Pale Children* (pp. 127–131). New York: Henry Holt and Company.

Messaris, P. (1994). *Visual literacy. Image, mind, & reality.* Boulder: Westview Press.

Mieszkowski, K. (1997). What a disaster! Don't panic. *Fast Company, 11*, 74. Retrieved on July 8, 2004, from http://www.fastcompany.com/online/11/disaster.html

Miles, V. C., McCarthy, J. C., Dix, A. J., Harison, M. D., & Monk, A. F. (1993). Reviewing designs for a synchronous-asynchronous group editing environment. In M Sharples (Ed.), *Computer supported collaborative writing* (pp. 137–160). London: Springer.

Miller, C. R. (1984). Genre as a social act. *Quarterly Journal of Speech, 70*, 151–167.

Miller, C. S., & Remington, R. W. (2000, June). *A computational model of web navigation: Exploring interactions between hierarchical depth and link ambiguity.* Paper presented at the Proceedings of the 6th conference on human factors & the Web, Austin, TX.

Moran, M. R. (1981). *A comparison of formal features of written language of learning disabled, low-achieving and achieving secondary students.* Lawrence, KN: Kansas University.

Morkes, J., Kernal, H. K., & Nass, C. (1998). Humor in task-oriented computer-mediated communication and human-computer interaction. In *CHI 98, conference summary on human factors in computing systems* (pp. 215–216). New York: ACM Press.

Moxley, J. (2003). *College writing online.* Boston: Longman Publishers. Retrieved August 13, 2005, from http://www.ablongman.com/cwo

Mullis, I. V. S., Martin, M. O., Gonzalez, E. J., & Kennedy, A. M. (2003). *PIRLS 2001 international report: IEA's study of reading literacy achievement in primary schools in 35 countries.* Boston.

Munro, A. J., Höök, K., & Benyon, D. R. (1999). *Social navigation of information space.* London: Springer.

Murray, D. M. (1972). Teaching writing as a process not product. *The Leaflet*, 11–14.

National Council of Education (2002). *The nation's report card [Website]. U.S. department of education.* Retrieved January 15, 2005, from http://nces.ed.gov/nationsreportcard/

Nelson, T. H. (1965). The hypertext. In *Proceedings of the congress of the international federation for documentation*, Washington, DC.

Nelson, T. H. (1974). *Computer lib/dream machines: New freedoms through computer screens — a minority report.* Chicago: Hugo's Book Service.

NetIQ. (2002). *Webtrends reporting center*. Retrieved September 6, 2004, from http://www.netiq.com/products/wrc/default.asp

Neuendorf, K. A. (2002). *The content analysis guidebook*. Thousand Oaks, CA: Sage.

Neuwirth, C. M. (1984). Toward the design of a flexible, computer-based writing environment. In W. Wresch (Ed.), *The computer in composition instruction: A writer's tool* (pp. 191–205). Urbana, IL: National Council of Teachers of English.

Neuwirth, C. M. (1989, May). *Extending the dialogue: Using the network to initiate collaborative learning and writing*. Paper presented at the 5th conference on computers and writing, University of Minnesota, Minneapolis, MN.

Neuwirth, C. M., & Kaufer, D. S. (1989). The role of external representation in the writing process: Implications for the design of hypertext-based writing tools. In *Hypertext89 Proceedings* (pp. 319–341). Baltimore, MD: Association for Computing Machinery.

Neuwirth, C. M., Kaufer, D. S., Chandook, R., & Morris, J. H. (1990). Issues in the design of computer support for co-authoring and commenting. In *Proceedings of the 3rd conference on computer-supported cooperative work* (pp. 183–95). Los Angeles, MD: Association for Computing Machinery.

Neuwirth, C. M., Kaufer, D. S., Chandook, R., & Morris, J. H. (1994). Computer support for distributed collaborative writing: Defining parameters of interaction. In *Proceedings of the conference on computer-supported cooperative work (CSCW '94)* (pp. 145–152). New York: Association for Computing Machinery.

Neuwirth, C. M., Kaufer, D., Keim, G., & Gillespie, T. (1988). *The comments program: Computer support for response to writing* (Technical Report CECE-TR-3). Pittsburgh, PA: Carnegie Mellon University.

Neuwirth, C. M., Kaufer, D. S., Chimera, R., & Gillespie, T. (1987). The notes program: A hypertext application for writing from source texts. In *Hypertext '87 proceedings* (pp. 345–365). New York: Association for Computing Machinery.

New study finds explosive growth of world's information is only beginning. (2000). *EMC corporation webpage*. Retrieved on July 8, 2004, from nhilton/lexis_complexes/title.html

Newell, A. F., Arnott, J., Booth, L., Beattie, W., Brophy, B., & Ricketts, I. W. (1992). Effect of "PAL" word prediction system on the quality and quantity of text generation. *Augmentative and Alternative Communication, 8*, 304–311.

Newman, M. W., & Landay, J. A. (2000, August). *Sitemaps, storyboards, and specifications: A sketch of web site design practice*. Paper presented at the Proceedings of designing interactive systems: DIS 2000, New York, NY.

Nielsen, J. (1997, October). *Writing for the Web*. Retrieved September 5, 2004, from http://www.useit.com/papers/webwriting

Nielsen, J. (2001). *Jakob Nielsen's alertbox*. Retrieved August 19, 2001, from http://www.useit.com/alertbox/ 20010819.html

Niesten, R. (2005). *Communication and acculturation in an advanced CMC environment*. Doctoral dissertation, The University of Queensland, Austrialia, Manuscript in preparation.

Noble, D. Progress without people: In defense of Luddism (Paperback). Toronto: Between the Lines (April 1995)

Noël, S., & Robert, J.-M. (2004). Empirical study on collaborative writing: What do co-authors do, use, and like? *Computer Supported Cooperative Work: The Journal of Collaborative Computing, 13*(1), 63–89.

Nordqvist, Å., Leiwo, M., & Lyytinen, H. (2003, July). *From nonsense words to space adventure: Developing a test battery to study and diagnose writing*. Paper presented at the 13th European conference on reading, Tallinn, Estonia.

Nordqvist, Å., Nieminen, L., Turunen, P., Kanala, S., Leiwo, M., & Strömqvist, S. (2002, July). *Studying on-line processes of writing in 9-year-olds*. Paper presented at the joint congress of the IASCL/SRCLD, Madison, WI, USA.

Norrick, N. (1993). *Conversational joking: Humor in everyday talk.* Indianapolis: Indiana University Press.

Norris, P. (2001). *Digital divide: Civic engagement, information poverty, and the Internet worldwide.* Cambridge: Harvard University Press.

Nunberg, G. (1996). *The future of the book.* Berkeley, CA: University of California Press.

Olive, T., & Kellogg, R. T. (2002). Concurrent activation of high- and low-level production processes in written composition. *Memory and Cognition, 30,* 594–600.

Olson, J., Olson, G., Mack, L., & Wellner, P. (1990). Concurrent editing: The group's interface. In D. Diaper, D. Gilmore, G. Cockton, & B. Shackel (Eds.), *Proceedings of INTERACT 1990* (pp. 835–840). Amsterdam: Elsevier.

Olston, C., & Chi, E. H. (2003). ScentTrails: Integrating browsing and searching on the Web. *ACM Transactions on Computer-Human Interaction, 10,* 177–197.

O'Neill, J., & Martin, D. (2003). Text chat in action. In *Proceedings of the 2003 international ACM SIGGROUP conference on supporting group work* (pp. 40–49). New York: ACM Press.

Open Doors 2001—Data Tables. (2001). *Open doors website of the institute of international education.* Retrieved July 24, 2005, from <http://opendoors.iienetwork.org/

Orliaguet, J. P., & Boë, L.-J. (1993). The role of linguistics in the speed of handwriting movements: Effects of spelling uncertainty. *Acta Psychologica, 82,* 103–113.

Orth, J. (2000). *Actions that aren't: Features of speech events in textual conversation. Language, culture, and society.* Retrieved April 12, 2004, from http://julieclipse.org/language/actions

OWL Fact Sheet. (2004). Purdue University. Retrieved July 23, 2005, from http://owl.english.purdue.edu/ lab/owl/factsheet.html

Paganelli, L., & Paterno, F. (2002*).* Intelligent analysis of user interactions with web applications. In *Proceedings of the 7th international conference on intelligent user interfaces* (pp. 111–118). New York: ACM Press.

Paivio, A. (1986). *Mental representation: A dual coding approach.* Oxford, England: Oxford University Press.

Palmquist, M. (2002, March). *In search of a new destination: Re-envisioning technological support for teaching and learning writing.* Paper presented at the conference on college composition and communication, Chicago.

Palmquist, M. (2002, May). *Where should we go from here? OR where should we have been going in the first place?* Paper presented at the 18th computers and writing conference, Normal, IL.

Palmquist, M. (2003). A brief history of computer support for writing centers and writing across the curriculum programs. *Computers and Composition, 20,* 395–413.

Palmquist, M. (2006). Tracing the development of digital tools for writers and writing teachers. In O. Oviedo, J. Walker, & B. Hawk (Eds.), *Digital tools in composition studies: Critical dimensions and implications.* Cresskill, NJ: Hampton Press.

Palmquist, M., Kiefer, K., Hartvigsen, J., & Godlew, B. (1998). *Transitions: Teaching writing in computer-supported and traditional classrooms.* Greenwich, CT: Ablex Publishing.

Paolillo, J. C. (2001). Language variation on Internet relay chat: A social network approach. *Journal of Sociolinguistics, 5*(2), 180–213.

Pennsylvania's Initiative on Assistive Technology. (2001). *WAVE 3.0 — web accessibility versatile evaluator.* Retrieved September 6, 2004, from http://www.wave.webaim.org/wave/index.jsp

Perfetti, C. A., Rieben, L., & Fayol, M. (Eds.). (1997). *Learning to spell.* Hillsdale, N.J.: Lawrence Erlbaum.

Perrin, D. (1999). Woher die Textbrüche kommen. Der Einfluß des Schreibprozesses auf die Sprache im Gebrauchstext [Where the breaks in the text come from. The influence of the writing process on the language in the utility text]. *Zeitschrift für Deutsche Sprache, 2,* 134–155.

Perrin, D. (2001). Wie Journalisten schreiben. Ergebnisse angewandter Schreibprozessforschung [How journalists write. Results from applied writing process research]. In C. Mast, & S. Ruß-Mohl (Vol. Eds.), *Journalismus* (Vol. 40). Konstanz: UVK.

Perrin, D. (2003). Progression analysis (PA): Investigating writing strategies at the workplace. In D. Perrin (Ed.), *The pragmatics of writing [Special Issue]. Journal of Pragmatics, 35,* 907–921.

Perrin, D. (2005a). Zwischen Vermittlung und Instrumentalisierung: Die Rekontextualisierung im Mediendiskurs [Between conveying and instrumentalization. Recontextualization in media discourse]. In E.-M. Jakobs, & K. Schindler (Eds.), *Schreiben im Beruf* (pp. 153–178). Wiesbaden: Verlag für Sozialwissenschaften.

Perrin, D. (2005b). Den Leuten die Sachen verdichten — Kreativ schreiben unter Druck ["Compress things for people"— creative writing under pressure]. In K. Ermert, & O. Kutzmutz (Eds.), *Wie aufs Blatt kommt, was im Kopf steckt. Beiträge zum Kreativen Schreiben* (pp. 34–54). Wolfenbüttel: Bundesakademie für kulturelle Bildung.

Perrin, D. (2006). *"... weil ich dachte, es sei lustig". Strategien des Inszenierens von Vergnügen im journalistischen Schreibprozess ["... because I thought it would be funny". Strategies for incorporating amusement into the journalistic writing process]*. Manuscript in preparation.

Phelps, L. W. (1992). When 'basic skills' are really basic and really skills: The studio curriculum at Syracuse. In D. Charney (Ed.), *Constructing rhetorical education*. Carbondale, IL: Southern Illinois University Press.

Pimienta, D. (2002). *Put Out Your Tongue and Say, 'Aaah'. Is the Internet Suffering from Acute 'Englishitis'?* From the WebWorld web site. Accessed 8 January 2006 at http://www.unesco.org/webworld/points_of_views/300102_pimienta.htm.

Piolat, A., Roussey, J.-Y., Olive, T., & Farioli, F. (1996). Charge mentale et mobilisation des processus rédactionnels: Examen de la procédure de Kellogg. *Psychologie Française, 41,* 339–354.

Pirolli, P., & Card, S. (1999). Information foraging. *Psychology Review, 106,* 643–675.

Pirolli, P., Card, S., &. Wege, van Der M. M. (2001). Visual information foraging in a focus+context visualization. In *Proceedings of ACM conference on human factors in computing systems (CHI 2001)* (pp. 506–513). Seattle, Washington: ACM Press.

Platt, H. (1991). Creating a writing studio. *Writing Notebook: Creative Word Processing in the Classroom, 9*(2), 7–9.

Pontecorvo, C. (1997). Studying writing and writing acquisition today: A multidisciplinary view. In C. Pontecorvo (Ed.), *Writing development: An interdisciplinary view* (pp. xv–xxxi). Amsterdam: John Benjamins.

Popping, R. (2000). *Computer-assisted text Analysis*. Thousand Oaks, CA: Sage.

Posner, I. R., & Baecker, R. M. (1993). How people write together. In R. M. Baecker (Ed.), *Readings in groupware and computer-supported cooperative work: Assisting human-human collaboration* (pp. 239–250). San Mateo, CA: Morgan Kaufmann.

Postman, N. Technopoly: The Surrender of Culture to Technology (Vintage) (Paperback). Vintage; Reprint edition (March 31, 1993).

Poteet, J. A. (1979). Characteristics of written expression of learning disabled and non-learning disabled elementary school students. *Diagnostique, 4*(1), 60–74.

Price, J., & Price, L. (2002). *Hot text: Web writing that works*. Indianapolis, IN: New Riders.

Prior, P. (2004). Tracing process: How texts come into being. In C. Bazerman, & P. Prior (Eds.), *What writing does and how it does it: An introduction to analyzing texts and textual practice* (pp. 167–200). Mahwah, NJ: Lawrence Erlbaum Associates.

Quinlan, T. (2004). Speech recognition technology and students with writing difficulties: Improving fluency. *Journal of Educational Psychology, 96*(2), 337–346.

Rafaeli, S., & Sudweeks, F. (1997). Networked interactivity. *Journal of Computer-Mediated Communication, 2*(4). Retrieved January 9, 2006, from http://jcmc.indiana.edu/vol2/issue4/rafaeli.sudweeks.html

Ransdell, S. E., & Arecco, M. R. (2001). Bilingual long-term working memory: The effects of working memory loads on writing quality and fluency. *Applied Psycholinguistics, 22,* 117–132.

Ransdell, S., Brown, B., & Baker, N. (2005). Poverty, bilingualism, ethnicity, teacher and school resources, and child risk behaviors as school-level predictors of reading, math, and writing performance. Manuscript submitted for publication.

Ransdell, S., & Nadel, K. (2005). Sociolinguistic framing in L1 and L2 writing. Manuscript submitted for publication.

Ransdell, S., & Wengelin, Å (2003). Socioeconomic and sociolinguistic predictors of children's L2 and L1 writing quality. *Arob@se, 1–2,* 22–29. Available from http://www.arobase.to/somm.html.

Ransdell, S., Baker, N., Sealy, G., & Moore, C. (2006). Bilingual literacy and a modern digital divide. In C. M. Neuwirth, L. Van Waes, & M. Leijten (Eds.), *Studies in Writing* (p. 241).

Raskind, M. H., & Higgins, E. (1995). Effects of speech synthesis on the proofreading efficiency of postsecondary students with learning disabilities. *Learning Disability Quarterly, 18,* 141–158.

Raskind, M. H., & Higgins, E. (1999). Speaking to read: The effects of speech recognition technology on the reading and spelling performance of children with learning disabilities. *Annals of Dyslexia, 47,* 1–31.

Reason, P., & Bradbury, H. (2001). Introduction: Inquiry and participation in search of a world worthy of human aspiration. In P. Reason (Ed.), *Handbook of action research: Participative inquiry and practice* (pp. 1–14). London: Sage.

Reece, J. E., & Cummings, G. (1996). Evaluating speech-based composition methods: Planning, dictation, and the listening word processor. In C. M. Levy, & S. Ransdell (Eds.), *The science of writing: Theories, methods, individual differences, and applications* (pp. 361–380). Mahwah, NJ: Lawrence Erlbaum Associates.

Reid, E. M. (1991). *Electropolis: Communication and community on Internet relay chat.* Unpublished Honours Thesis, University of Melbourne, Victoria, Australia. Retrieved April 12, 2004, from http://www.irchelp.org/irchelp/communication-research/academic/academic-reid-e-electropolis-1991.html

Reimann, P., & Zumbach, J. (2001). Design, Diskurs und Reflexion als zentrale Elemente virtueller Seminare [Design, discourse and reflection as central elements of virtual seminars]. In F. W. Hesse, & H. F. Friedrich (Eds.), *Partizipation und Interaktion im virtuellen Seminar. Medien in der Wissenschaft. Band 13* (pp. 135–163). Münster: Waxmann.

Rheingold, H. (1993). Disinformocracy. *The virtual community.* Boulder, CO: Perseus Books. Retrieved July 8, 2004, from http://www.rheingold.com/vc/book/

Rheingold, H. (1993). Ch. 10: Disinformocracy. *The virtual community.* Boulder, CO: Perseus Books. http://www.rheingold.com/vc/book/. Retrieved on July 8, 2004.

Riffel, C. (2003). Information recovery in text-only discourse: The effect of an integrated recovery device on conversation structure. *Stanford Undergraduate Research Journal, 2,* 43–47.

Rijlaarsdam, G., Couzijn, M., & van den Bergh, H. (2004). The study of revision as a writing process and as a learning-to-write process: Two prospective research agendas. In L. Allal, L. Chanquoy & P. Largy (Eds.), *Revision: Cognitive and instructional processes* (Vol. 13, pp. 189–208). Norwell, MA: Kluwer.

Rittle-Johnson, B., & Siegler, R. S. (1999). Learning to spell: Variability, choice, and change in children strategy use. *Child Development, 70,* 332–348.

Rodrigues, D., & Kiefer, K. (1993). Moving toward an electronic writing center at Colorado State University. In J. A. Kinkead, & J. G. Harris (Eds.), *Writing centers in context: Twelve case studies* (pp. 216–226). Urbana, IL: National Council of Teachers of English.

Rodrigues, D., & Rodrigues, R. J. (1984). Computer-based creative problem solving. In W. Wresch (Ed.), *The computer in composition instruction: A writer's tool* (pp. 34–46). Urbana, IL: National Council of Teachers of English.

Rodriguez, H. (2003). *Designing, evaluating and exploring Web-based tools for collaborative annotation of documents.* Unpublished Doctoral dissertation, Royal Institute of Technology, Stockholm, Sweden.

Rodriguez, H., & Severinson Eklundh, K., (2005, July). *Giving the main role to Web documents in a distributed text based persistent conversation. HCI International 2005,* Paper presented at Las Vegas, NV, USA.

Rosaschi, G. (1978). Computer assisted instruction. *Writing Lab Newsletter, 2*(7), 4.

Rueb, M. (1999). Reconstructing Kosovo: On the right track – but where does it lead? *NATO Review, 47*(3), 20–23. Retrieved July 8, 2004, from http://www.nato.int/docu/review/1999/9903 06.html

Russell, M. (1999). Testing writing on computers: A follow-up study comparing performance on computer and on paper. *Educational Policy Analysis Archives, 7*(20). Retrieved January 9, 2006, from http://epaa.asu.edu/epaa/v7n20/

Russell, S., & Norvig P. (2003). *Artifical intelligence: A modern approach* (2nd ed.). Englewood Cliffs, NJ: Prentice-Hall.

Sacks, H. (1992). *Lectures on conversation* (Vol. 2). Oxford: Blackwell.

Sågvall Hein, A. (1999) *A grammar checking module for Swedish. Reports from the Scarrie-project: DEL 6.6.3.* Sweden, Uppsala University, Department of Linguistics.

Salaberry, R. (1999). Call in the year 2000: Still developing the research agenda. *Language Learning & Technology, 3*(1), 104–107.

Säljö, R. (1996). Mental and physical artifacts in cognitive practices. In P. Reimann, & H. Spada, (Eds.), *Learning in humans and machines. Towards an interdisciplinary learning science* (pp. 83–96). Amsterdam: Pergamon.

Sands, P. (1997). Writing software comparisons: Aspects, commonspace, Daedalus, and Norton Connect. *Kairos, 2*(2). Retrieved July 26, 2004, from http://english.ttu.edu/kairos/2.2/binder. html?reviews/sands/comparison.html

Sawyer, R. J., Graham, S., & Harris, K. R. (1992). Direct teaching, strategy instruction, and strategy instruction with explicit self-regulation: Effects on the composition skills and self-efficacy of students with learning disabilities. *Journal of Educational Psychology, 84,* 340–352.

Scardamalia, M. (2002). Collective cognitive responsibility fort the advancement of knowledge. In B. Smith (Ed.), *Liberal education in a knowledge society* (pp. 67–98). Chicago: Open Court.

Scardamalia, M., Bereiter, C., & Goelman, H. (1982). The role of production factors in writing ability. In M. Nystrand (Ed.), *What writers know: The language, process, and structure of written discourse* (pp. 173–210). New York: Academic Press.

Schegloff, E. A. (1972). Sequencing in conversational openings. In J. Gumperz, & D. Hymes (Eds.), *Directions in sociolinguistics. The ethnography of communication* (pp. 346–380). New York: Holt Rinehart.

Schegloff, E., Jefferson, G., & Sacks, H. (1977). The preference for self-correction in the organization of repair in conversation. *Language, 53,* 361–382.

Schilb, J. (1991). Cultural studies, postmodernism, and composition. In P. Harkin, & J. Schilb (Eds.), *Contending with words* (pp. 173–188). New York: MLA.

Schilperoord, J. (1996). *It's about time: Temporal aspects of cognitive processes in text production.* Atlanta: Rodopi.

Schilperoord, J. (2001). On the cognitive status of pauses in discourse production. In G. Rijlaarsdam (Series Ed.), & T. Olive, & C. M. Levy (Vol. Eds.), *Studies in writing: Vol. 10. Contemporary tools and techniques for studying writing* (pp. 61–90). Dordrecht: Kluwer Academic Publishers.

Schmitt, R. (2003). The interaction between research method and subjective competence in systematic metaphor analysis. *Forum Qualitative Sozialforschung/Forum: Qualitative Social Research* [*On-line-Journal*], *4*(2). Retrieved August 22, 2004, from http://www.qualitative-research.net/fqs-texte/2-03/2-03schmitt-e.htm

Schoffner, C. (2000). *Introduction: Globalisation, communication, translation*. Retrieved July 24, 2005, from http://literatureark.nease.net/eclass/complit/globletrans.htm

Schuetze, H., & Manning, C. (1999). *Foundations of statistical natural language processing*. Cambridge, MA: MIT Press.

Schwartz, H. (1982). Monsters and mentors: Computer applications for humanistic education. *College English, 44*(2), 141–152.

Schwartz, H. (1984). SEEN: A tutorial and user network for hypothesis testing. In W. Wresch (Ed.), *The computer in composition instruction: A writer's tool* (pp. 47–62). Urbana, IL: National Council of Teachers of English.

Searle, J (1980). Minds, brains, and programs. *Behavioral and Brain Sciences, 3*, 417–424.

Selfe, C. (1984). Wordsworth II: Process-based CAI for college composition teachers. In W. Wresch (Ed.), *The computer in composition instruction: A writer's tool* (pp. 174–190). Urbana, IL: National Council of Teachers of English.

Selfe, C. L., & Hawisher, G. E. (2004). *Literate lives in the information age: Narratives of literacy from the United States*. Mahwah, NJ: Lawrence Erlbaum Associates.

Selfe, C. L., & Wahlstrom, B. J. (1979). *Beyond bandaids and bactine: Computer-assisted instruction and revision*. (ERIC Document) no. 232182 Reproduction Science.

Selfe, C. L., & Wahlstrom, B. J. (1983). The benevolent beast: Computer-assisted instruction for the teacher of writing. *The Writing Instructor, 2*(4), 193–192.

Sellen, A. J., & Harper, R. H. R. (2001). *The myth of the paperless office*. Cambridge, MA: The MIT Press.

Selwyn, N. (2003). Apart from technology: Understanding people's non-use of information and communication technologies in everyday life. *Technology in Society, 25*(1), 99–116.

Severinson Eklundh, K. (1994). Linear and non-linear strategies in computer-based writing. *Computers and Composition, 11*, 203–216.

Severinson Eklundh, K., Fatton, A., & Romberger, S. (1996). The paper model for computer-based writing. In H. van Oostendorp, & S. de Mul (Eds.), *Cognitive aspects of electronic text processing* (pp. 137–159). Norwood, NJ: Ablex.

Severinson Eklundh, K., Groth, K., Hedman, A., Lantz, A., Rodriguez, H., & Sallnäs, E-L. (2002). The World Wide Web as a social infrastructure for knowledge-oriented work. In H. van Oostendorp (Ed.), *Cognition in a digital world* (pp. 97–126). Mahwah, NJ: Lawrence Erlbaum Associates.

Severinson Eklundh, K., & Kollberg, P. (1996). Computer tools for tracing the writing process: From keystroke records to S-notation. In G. Rijlaarsdam, H. Van den Bergh, & M. Couzijn, (Eds.), *Current research in writing: Theories, models and methodology* (pp. 526–541). Amsterdam: Amsterdam University Press.

Severinson Eklundh, K., & Kollberg, P. (2003). Emerging discourse structure: Computer-assisted episode analysis as a window to global revision in university students' writing. *Journal of Pragmatics, 35*(4), 869–891.

Severinson Eklundh, K., & Rodriguez, H. (2004). Coherence and interactivity in text-based group discussions around Web documents. In *Proceedings of the 37th annual Hawaii international conference on system sciences (HICSS'04)* (p. 40108.3) Washington, DC: IEEE Computer Press.

Sharples, M. (Ed.). (1993). *Computer-supported collaborative writing*. London: Springer.

Sharples, M., Goodlet, J. S., Beck, E. E., Wood, C. C., Easterbrook, S. M., & Plowman, L. (1993). Research issues in the study of computer supported collaborative writing. In M. Sharples (Ed.), *Computer supported collaborative writing* (pp. 9–28). London: Springer.

Shorris, E. (2000, August). The last word: Can the world's small languages be saved? *Harper's Magazine*, *301*(s1803). From http://www.findarticles.com/p/articles/mi_m1111/

Sidler, M., & Morris, R. (1998). Writing in a post-Berlinian landscape: Cultural composition in the classroom. *JAC: A Journal of Composition Theory*, *18*, 275–291.

Simon, H. A. (1957). *Models of man*. New York, NY: John Wiley.

Sinha, R., Hearst, M., & Ivory, M. (2001, June). *Content or graphics? An empirical analysis of criteria for award-winning websites*. Paper presented at the Proceedings of the 7th conference on human factors & the Web, Madison, WI.

Skehan, P. (2003). Focus on form, tasks, and technology. *Computer Assisted Language Learning* *16*(5), 391–411.

Sleurs, K., Jacobs, G., & Van Waes, L. (2003). Constructing press releases, constructing quotations: A case study. *Journal of Sociolinguistics*, *7*(2), 192–212.

Slobin, D. (1996). From "thought and language" to "thinking for speaking". In J. Gumperz, & S. Levinson (Eds.), *Rethinking linguistic relativity: Studies in the social and cultural foundations of language* (Vol. 17, pp. 70–96). Cambridge: Cambridge University Press.

Smagorinsky, P. (Ed.). (1994). *Speaking about writing* (Vol. 8). London: Thousand Oaks.

Smith, J. (1987) A hypertext writing environment and its cognitive basis. In *Proceedings of HyperTEXT '87* (pp. 195–214). New York: Association for Computing Machinery.

Smith, J. B. (1994). *Collective intelligence in computer-based collaboration*. Hillsdale, NJ: Lawrence Erlbaum Associates.

Smith, J. B., & Lansman, M. (1989). A cognitive basis for a computer writing environment. In B. K. Britton, & S. M. Glynn (Eds.), *Computer writing environments: Theory, research, and design* (pp. 17–56). Hillsdale, NJ: Lawrence Erlbaum Associates.

Smith, J. B., & Lansman, M. (1992). Designing theory-based systems: A case study. In *Proceedings of CHI '92* (pp. 479–488). New York: Association for Computing Machinery.

Smith, J. B., Weiss, S. F., Ferguson, G. J., Bolter, J. D., Lansman, M., & Beard, D. V. (1987). WE: A WRITING ENVIRONMENT for professionals. In *Proceedings of the national computer conference '87* (pp. 725–736). Reston, VA: AFIPS Press.

Sofkova Hashemi, S. (2003) *Automatic detection of grammar errors in primary school children's texts. A finite state approach*. Unpublished Doctoral dissertation, Department of Linguistics, Göteborg University.

Solomon, G., Allen, N., & Resta, P. (Eds.). (2003). *Toward digital equity: Bridging the divide in education*. Boston, MA: Allyn & Bacon/Longman.

Souza, F. d., & Bevan, N. (1990, August). *The use of guidelines in menu interface design: Evaluation of a draft standard*. Paper presented at the Proceedings of the 3rd IFIP TC13 conference on human-computer interaction, Cambridge, UK.

Spanning the Digital Divide: Understanding and Tackling the Issues (2001). Retrieved July 24, 2005, from http://www.bridges.org/spanning

Spelman Miller, K., & Sullivan, K. P. H. (2006, forthcoming). Keystroke logging — an introduction. In G. Rijlaarsdam (Series Ed.), & K. P. H. Sullivan, & E. Lindgren (Vol. Eds.), *Studies in writing. Computer keystroke logging and writing: Methods and applications*. Amsterdam: Elsevier.

Sperber, D., & Wilson, D. (1995). *Relevance: Communication and cognition* (2nd ed.). Oxford: Blackwell.

Spiliopoulou, M. (2000). Web usage mining for web site evaluation. *Communications of the ACM*, *43*(8), 127–134.

Spool, J. M., Scanlon, T., Schroeder, W., Snyder, C., & DeAngelo, T. (1999). *Web site usability*. San Francisco, CA: Morgan Kaufman.

Sprenger-Charolles, L., Siegel, L. S., Béchennec, D., & Serniclaes, W. (2003). Development of phonological and orthographic processing in reading aloud, in silent reading, and in spelling: A four-year longitudinal study. *Journal of Experimental Child Psychology*, *84*, 194–217.

Stahl, E. (2001). *Hyper — text — schreiben. Die Auswirkungen verschiedener Instruktionen auf Lernprozesse beim Schreiben von Hypertext* [*Hyper-text-writing. Effects of different instructions on learning processes during writing hypertexts*]. Münster: Waxmann.

Stahl, E., & Bromme, R. (2005). Learning by writing hypertext: A research based design of university courses in writing hypertext. In G. Rijlaarsdam (Series Ed.), G. Rijlaarsdam, H. Van den Bergh, & M. Couzijn, (Vol. Eds.), *Studies in writing, Vol. 14. Effective learning and teaching of writing*, (2nd ed., pp 547–560). Dordrecht: Kluwer Academic Publishers.

State of the Internet 2000. (2000). A report of the United States Internet council and the associates. Washington, DC: International technology and trade associates.

Steffler, D. J., Varnhagen, C. K., Friesen, C. K., & Treiman, R. (1998). There's more to children's spelling than the errors they make: Strategic and automatic processes for one-syllable words. *Journal of Educational Psychology*, *90*, 492–505.

Stein, L. D. (1997). *The rating game.* Retrieved September 6, 2004, from http://stein.cshl.org/~lstein/rater/

Stevenson, J. (2000). *Language data investigation: The language of Internet chat rooms.* Retrieved April 12, 2004, from http://www.netting-it.com/Units/IRC.htm

Stille, A. (2002). Are we losing our memory? Or: The museum of obsolete technology. In *The future of the past* (pp. 299–309). New York: Farrar, Strauss, and Geroux.

Stoddard, B., & MacArthur, C. A. (1993). A peer editor strategy: Guiding learning disabled students in response and revision. *Research in the Teaching of English*, *27*, 76–103.

Stone, P. J., Dunphy, D. C., Smith, M. S., & Ogilvie, D. M. (1966). *The general inquirer: A computer approach to content analysis.* Cambridge: MIT Press.

Storrer, A. (2001). Getippte Gespräche oder dialogische Texte? Zur kommunikations theoretischen Einordnung der Chat-Kommunikation. In A. Lehr, M. Kammerer, K-P. Konerding, A. Storrer, C. Thimm & W. Wolski (Hg.) *Sprache im Alltag. Beiträge zu neuen Perspektiven in der Linguistik* (pp. 439–465). Berlin: De Gruyter. Retrieved April 12, 2004, from http://www.hrz.uni-dortmund.de/~hytex/storrer/papers/chat.pdf

Street, Brian V. (1995). *Social literacies: Critical approaches to literacy in development, ethnography, and education.* London: Longman.

Streitz, N. A., Hannemann, J., Lemke, A., Schuler, W., Schtitt, H., & Thuring, M. (1992). SEPIA: A cooperative hypermedia authoring environment. In *Proceedings of the ACM European conference on hypertext (ECHT'92)* (pp. 11-22). Milan: Association for Computing Machinery.

Streitz, N. A., Hannemann, J., & Thuring, M. (1989). From ideas, and arguments to hyperdocuments: Traveling through activity spaces. In *Proceedings of the 2nd ACM conference on hypertext (Hypertext'89)* (pp. 343-364). Pittsburgh, PA. New York: Association for Computing Machinery.

Strömqvist, S., Holmqvist, K., Johansson, V., Karlsson, H., & Wengelin, Å. (with Ahlsén, E., Alves, R., Andersson, B., Bertram, R. Erskine, J. Grönqvist, L., Hagman, J., Hellstrand, Å., Hellum, I., Holsanova, J., Leiwo, M., Lyytinen, H., Malmsten, L., Nordqvist, Å., Solheim, O., Tufvesson, S., Henning Uppstad, P., Wagner, Å-K., & Wiktorsson, M.) (forthcoming, 2006). What keystroke logging can reveal about writing. In G. Rijlaarsdam (Series Ed.) & K.P.H. Sullivan & E. Lindgren (Vol. Eds.), Studies in Writing. Computer Keystroke Logging and Writing: Methods and Applications. Amsterdam: Elsevier.

Strömqvist, S., & Karlsson, H. (2002). *ScriptLog for windows: User's manual.* Sweden: University of Lund, Department of Linguistics, and Norway: University of Stravanger, Center for Reading Research.

Strömqvist, S., & Malmsten, L. (1997). *ScriptLog Pro User's Manual.* Sweden: Göteborg University, Department of Linguistics.

Strömqvist, S., Nordqvist, Å., & Wengelin, Å. (2004). Writing the frog-story: Developmental and cross-modal perspectives. In S. Strömqvist, & L. Verhoeven (Eds.), *Relating events in narrative — typologiocal and contextual perspectives* (pp. 359–394). Mahwah, NJ: Lawrence Erlbaum Associates.

Sullivan, K. P. H., & Lindgren, E. (2002). Self-assessment in autonomous computer-aided second language writing. *ELT Journal, 56*(3), 258–265.

Sullivan, K. P. H. & Lindgren, E. (Eds.) (forthcoming, 2006) Computer Keystroke Logging and Writing: Methods and Applications. Amsterdsm: Elsevier.

Suoranta, J., & Lehtimaki, H. (2004) *Children in the information society: The case of finland.* USA: Peter Lang Pub Inc.

Sussex, R. (2004). Abstand, ausbau, creativity and ludicity in Australian English. *Australian Journal of Linguistics, 24*(1), 3–19.

Swales, J. (1990). *Genre analysis: English in academic and research settings.* New York: Cambridge.

Tainturier, M.-J., & Rapp, B. (2000). The spelling process. In B. Rapp (Ed.), *The handbook of cognitive neurophysology: What deficits reveal about the human mind* (pp. 263–289). Philadelphia, PA: Psychology Press.

Teleman, U. (1991). Vad kan man när man kan skriva? [What do you know when you know how to write]. In G. Malmgren, & C. Sandqvist (Eds.), *Skrivpedagogik* [The didactics of writings] (pp. 11–26). Lund: Student litteratur.

Ten Have, P. (1999). *Doing conversation analysis.* London: Sage.

The Brave New World of Data Center Management. Retrieved on July 8, 2004, from http://compaq24- 7.com/nl4.asp?uid=00000340612

Theng, Y. L., & Marsden, G. (1998, June). *Authoring tools: Towards continuous usability testing of web documents.* Paper presented at the Proceedings of the 1st international workshop on hypermedia development, Pittsburg, PA.

Thorson, H. (2000). Using the computer to compare foreign and native language writing processes: A statistical and case study approach. *Modern Language Journal, 84*, 155–170.

Tønnessen, F. E. (1999a). Awareness and automaticity in reading. In I. Lundberg, F. E. Tønnessen, & I. Austad (Eds.), *Dyslexia: Advances in theory and practice* (pp. 91–99). Dordrecht: Kluwer Academic Publishers.

Tønnessen, F. E. (1999b). Options and limitations of the cognitive psychological approach to the treatment of dyslexia. *Journal of Learning Disabilities, 32*, pp. 386–393.

Torrance, M. (1996). Is writing expertise like other kinds of expertise? In G. Rijlaarsdam, H. van den Bergh, & M. Couzijn (Eds.), *Theories, models and methodology in writing research* (pp. 3–9). Amsterdam: Amsterdam University Press.

Trigg, R. H., & Irish, P. M. (1988). Hypertext habitats: Experiences of writers in notecards. In *Proceedings of hypertext '87* (pp. 89–108). University of North Carolina, Baltimore, MD: Association for Computing Machinery.

Trimbur, J. (1994). Taking the social turn: Teaching writing post-process. *College Composition and Communication, 45*, 108–118.

Troia, G. (2006). Writing instruction for students with learning disabilities and other poor writers. In C. A. MacArthur, S. Graham, & J. Fitzgerald (Eds.), *Handbook of writing research* (pp. 324–326). New York: Guilford.

Tucker, N. (1996). CommonSpace: A review. *Kairos, 1*(3). Retrieved July 26, 2004, from http://english.ttu.edu/kairos/1.3/binder.html?reviews/commonspace/openpage.html

Turkle, S. (1995). *Life on the screen.* New York: Phoenix.

Ulmer, G. (1993). Abject monumentality. *Lusitania, 1*(4): 9–15. New York: Lusitania Press.

Ulmer, G. (1994). *Heuretics: The logic of invention.* Baltimore: Johns Hopkins University Press.

Uppstad, P. H. (2006). Written language skills and the notion of "lexicon". *L1 Educational Studies in Language and Literature, 6*(1).

US Department of Commerce. (2002). www.commerce.gov

US Census Bureau Current Population Survey. (2001). www.census.gov

UsableNet. (2000). *Usablenet — website testing systems.* Retrieved September 6, 2004, from http://www. usablenet.com

UsableNet. (2002). *Lift — Nielsen Norman group edition.* Retrieved September 6, 2004, from http://www.usablenet.com/products_services/lfd_nng/lfd_nng.html

Uwaje, C. (2000). *Don't Kill Computer Training Centers, Upgrade Them.* From the allAfrica.com web site. Accessed 8 January 2005 at http://allafrica.com

Vacc, N. N. (1987). Word processor versus handwriting: A comparative study of writing samples produced by mildly mentally handicapped students. *Exceptional Children, 54,* 156–165.

Van Craaikamp, E. (2005). *Navigation, a matter of style? Study on the relation between users' cognitive styles, mental models and navigation behaviors in a hypermedia environment.* Unpublished master's thesis. University of Twente, The Netherlands.

Van den Bergh, H., & Rijlaarsdam, G. (1996). The dynamics of composing: Modelling writing process data. In C. M. Levy, & S. Ransdell (Eds.), *The science of writing: Theories, methods, individual differences, and applications* (pp. 207–232). Mahwah, NJ: Lawrence Erlbaum Associates.

Van Waes, L. (1991). *De computer en het schrijfproces: De invloed van de tekstverwerker op het pauze- en revisiegedrag van schrijvers. [The computer and the writing process: The influence of the word processor on the pausing and revision behavior of writers].* Enschede: University of Twente.

Van Waes, L., & Schellens, P. J. (2003). Writing profiles: The effect of the word processor on pausing and revision patterns of experienced writers. *Journal of Pragmatics, 35*(4), 829–853.

Van Waes, L., & Van Herreweghe, L. (1995). Computerprotokolle in der Schreibprozeßforschung: der Gebrauch von Keytrap als Beobachtungsinstrument [Computer protocols in writing process research]. In E.-M. Jakobs (Ed.), *Wissenschaftliche Textproduktion: mit und ohne Computer* [Scientific Text Production] (pp. 35–51). Frankfurt am Main: Lang.

Via voice, version 10 [Computer Software] (2004). International business machine.

Von Blum, R., & Cohen, M. E. (1984). WANDAH: Writing-aid AND author's helper. In W. Wresch (Ed.), *The computer in composition instruction: A writer's tool* (pp. 154–173). Urbana, IL: National Council of Teachers of English.

Vora, P. R. (1998). Design/methods & tools: Designing for the Web: A survey. *Interactions, 5*(3), 13–30.

Vygotsky, L. S., & Cole, M. (1978). *Mind in society: The development of higher psychological processes.* Cambridge, MA: Harvard University Press.

Vygotsky, L. S., & Kozulin, A. (1986). *Thought and language.* Cambridge, MA: MIT Press.

W3C. (1999). *Web content accessibility guidelines 1.0.* Retrieved September 5, 2004, from http://www.w3.org/TR/WAI-WEBCONTENT/

W3C. (2001). *The W3C markup validation service.* Retrieved September 5, 2004, from http://validator.w3.org/

W3C. (2002). *Evaluation, repair, and transformation tools for web content accessibility.* Retrieved September 6, 2004, from http://www.w3.org/WAI/ER/existingtools.html

Wagner, Å. K. H., & Uppstad, P. H. (2005). Bilingual literacy: Narrative performance in bilingual students. In J. Cohen, K. McAlister, K. Rolstad, & J. MacSwan (Eds.), *ISB4: Proceedings of the 4th international symposium on bilingualism.* Phoenix: Cascadilla Press.

Wallace, D. L., Hayes, J. R., Hatch, J. A., & Miller, W. (1996). Better revision in eight minutes? Prompting first-year college writers to revise globally. *Journal of Educational Psychology, 88,* 682–688.

Warschauer, M. (2003a). Demystifying the digital divide. *Scientific American, 283*(2), 42–47.

Warschauer, M. (2003b). *Technology and social inclusion: Rethinking the digital divide.* Cambridge, MA: MIT Press.

Warschauer, M., & Kern, R. (Eds.). (2000). *Network-based language teaching: Concepts and practice*. Cambridge: Cambridge University Press.

WatchFire. (2002). *Welcome to bobby worldwide*. Retrieved September 6, 2004, from http://bobby.watchfire.com/bobby/html/en/index.jsp

Wengelin, Å. (2002). *Text production in adults with reading and writing difficulties* (Gothenburg Monographs in Linguistics Vol. 20). Sweden, Göteborg University, Department of Linguistics.

Wengelin, Å., Johansson, V., & Strömqvist, S. (2006, forthcoming). Examining pauses in writing. In G. Rijlaarsdam (Series Ed.), & K. P. H. Sullivan, & E. Lindgren (Vol. Eds.), *Studies in writing. Computer keystroke logging and writing: Methods and applications*. Amsterdam: Elsevier.

Wengelin, Å., & Strömqvist, S. (2005). Text-writing development viewed through on-line pausing in Swedish. In R. Berman (Ed.), *Language development across childhood and adolescence, trends in language acquisition research (TILAR series)* (Vol.3, pp.177–190.). Amsterdam: John Benjamins.

Wertsch, J. V. (1998). *Mind as action*. London: Oxford University Press.

Whalley, P. (1993). An alternative rhetoric for hypertext. In C. McKnight, A. Dillon, & J. Richardson (Eds.), *Hypertext: A psychological perspective* (pp. 7–17). New York: Ellis Horwood.

Wildstrom, S. H. (2003). WI-FI handhelds? Not for the footloose. *Business Week*, 24. Retrieved January 9, 2006, from http://www.businessweek.com/magazine/content/03-24/b3837025.htm

Wilkins, H. (1991). Computer talk: Long-distance conversations by computer. *Written Communication*, 8, 56–78.

Williamson, M. M., & Pence, P. (1989). Word processing and student writers. In B. K. Britton, & S. M. Glynn (Eds.), *Computer writing environments: Theory, research and design* (pp. 93–127). Hillsdale, NJ: Lawrence Erlbaum Associates.

Wilson, T. (1999, July 30). The cost of downtime. *InternetWeek.com*

Wittgenstein, L. (1958). *Philosophical investigations*. Englewood Cliffs, NJ: Prentice-Hall.

Wojahn, P. G., Neuwirth, C., & Bullock, B. (1998). Effects of interfaces for annotation on communication in a collaborative task. In *Proceedings of CHI 1998* (pp. 456–463). New York: Association for Computing Machinery.

Wood, E., Willoughby, T. Specht, J., & Porter, L. (2002). An examination of how a cross-section of academics use computer technology when writing academic papers. *Computers & Education, 38*, 287–301.

Woodlief, A. (1997). Norton's CONNECT: A review. *Kairos*, 2(2). Retrieved July 26, 2004, from http://english.ttu.edu/kairos/2.2/binder.html?reviews/woodlief/conrev.htm

World Development Indicators 2002 database (2002). Data and statistics >data by topic >information technology on the world bank web site. London: Oxford University Press. From http://www.worldbank.org/

World Development Report. (2002). *Building Institutions for Markets* (pp. 228). New York, NY: Oxford University Press.

World Development Report. 2003: Sustainable Development in a Dynamic World, Transforming Institutions, Growth, and Quality of Life (2003). London: Oxford University Press. Retrieved July 24, 2005, from http://www.worldbank.org

Wresch, W. (1982). Computers in English class: Finally beyond grammar and drills. *College English, 44*, 483–490.

Wresch, W. (1984). Questions, answers, and automated writing. In W. Wresch (Ed.), *The computer in composition instruction: A writer's tool* (pp. 143–153). Urbana, IL: National Council of Teachers of English.

Wright, P. (1993). To jump or not to jump: Strategy selection while reading electronic texts. In C. McKnight, A. Dillon, & J. Richardson (Eds.), *Hypertext: A psychological perspective* (pp. 137–152). New York: Ellis Horwood.

Young, R. E. (1978). Paradigms and problems: Needed research in rhetorical invention. In C. Cooper, & L. Odell (Eds.), *Research in composing* (pp. 29–47). Urbana, IL: National Council of Teachers of English.

Young, R. E., & Neuwirth, C. M. (1987). *Writing in the disciplines: Computer support for collaborative learning*. Manuscript submitted for publication.

Zahn, C. (2003). *Wissenskommunikation mit Hypervideos — Untersuchungen zum Design nichtlinearer Informationsstrukturen für audiovisuelle Medien* [*Knowledge communication with hypervideo — investigating the design of nonlinear information structures in audiovisual media*]. Muenster: Waxmann.

Zahn, C., Schwan, S., & Barquero, B. (2002). Authoring hypervideos: Design for learning and learning by design. In R. Bromme, & E. Stahl (Eds.), *Writing hypertext and learning: Conceptual and empirical approaches* (pp. 153–176). Amsterdam: Pergamon/Elsevier Science.

Zaiane, O. R., Xin, M., & Han, J. (1998). Discovering web access patterns and trends by applying OLAP and data mining technology on web logs. In *Proceeding of the advances in digital libraries conference* (April 22–24, pp. 19–29). New York: ACM Press.

Zuboff, S. (1988). *In the age of the smart machine: The future of work and power*. Washington, DC: ADL, IEEE Computer Society.

Author Index

Subject Index

3Book, 101
academic, 120, 128, 179, 209, 218,
    241–243, 251, 252, 284
  skill, 241, 252
  writing, 179
ACCESS, 201
accessibility, 105, 106, 108, 109, 113, 132,
    136, 239
  problem, 105
acquisition, 2, 5, 7, 50, 51, 53, 60, 62, 77,
    78, 84, 88, 146, 147, 190, 227, 245,
    248, 253, 256, 257, 280, 283, 285
action research, 180, 185
ActiveMovie, 183
activity theory, 2
adaptation, 32, 40, 225
  process, 34
affection, 83
analysis
  automatic, 2, 106, 110, 112, 113, 155,
      222, 223, 226–228, 230, 233–235
  conversation, 65, 75
  data, 6, 50, 154, 155, 159, 169–171,
      180, 185
  log, 94, 109
  pause, 6, 154, 160
  performance, 107, 108
  progression, 6, 164, 165, 173–180
  repair, 35, 45
  revision, 154, 155, 159, 160, 164, 165
  rhetorical, 115
  script, 154
  statistical, 94, 109, 117, 124, 126, 160,
      185
  task, 109
  temporal, 146, 147

  text, 108, 110, 111, 114, 117, 118, 120,
      160, 163, 164
  tool, 6, 110, 117, 167, 169, 171
  web, 5, 91, 92, 94, 109
  writing, 5
annotation, 6, 99, 120, 134, 204, 205,
    207
  interface, 207
  modality, 207
  tool, 204
AQUANET, 205
archive, 121, 127, 243, 249, 289, 291, 298,
    299, 302
ARPANET, 200
Artificial Intelligence (AI), 120, 193,
    195–197, 217
ASPECTS, 203, 208
assessment, 20, 113, 226, 234, 246
  of content, 105
assistive technology, 11–13, 19, 106, 109,
    243
audio file, 81, 82, 149, 183
audio-visual information, 78, 79, 82, 87
Author's Helper, 201
auto text, 51, 60, 61, 63
automatic analysis, 2, 106, 110, 112, 113,
    155, 222, 223, 226–228, 230,
    233–235
awareness, 6, 8, 134, 136, 157, 177, 222,
    223, 226–228, 230, 233–235, 242,
    248, 250, 251

BAKOM, 173, 179
BANK STREET WRITER, 201
Bayesian Inference, 95
behaviourism, 225, 226